A Comprehensive guide to the fundamentals & details of Project Management Methodologies

A Professional Guide to
PROJECT MANAGEMENT

SRIDHAR RAGOTHAMAN M.S., PMP

ISBN   978-93-5196-961-7   (13 digit)

ISBN   93-5196-961-4   (10 digit)

Ordering Information

Quantity sales, trade bookstores and wholesalers. Special discounts are available on quantity purchases by corporations, associations, and others. For details, please write to the E-Mail address given above.

Author's Note

Thanks for purchasing your copy of 'A Professional Guide to Project Management'.

When I began preparing for one of my seminar on project management, this question came to me whether I have any books or references for the audience to substantiate the speech and colorful presentations.

It was indeed in my mind to author my own book and share the rich experience that I gained over the past twenty years of my professional career. This is my first venture into authoring a book and probably, won't be the last. But, having written the book now, I seem to have gained a significant experience in authoring a book and the flow of activities involved in bringing a book to a proper shape. The book that is in your hands is the result of a hard and tireless effort of several people, besides significant amount of inputs from your author. The book may not exactly narrate the situation that you have faced nor a solution for your past problem. But, you cannot rule out that every piece of knowledge gained from others' experience help us shape yourself up.

Having exposed to multiple domains, projects, geographies and situations, it was not an easy task even to begin working towards writing a book. The writing of the book itself became a project, having to plan, co-ordinate, design, execute, get it reviewed and bring the entire book to a definite and an acceptable shape. I am sure this book will help you understand some of the better practices in the life of a project manager.

Being my first venture into authoring, I am sure that this book will meet the expectations of the readers. I always welcome constructive feedback and healthy criticism, that helps in improving the product and enhance one's standing and knowledge.

Thank you

– Sridhar Ragothaman PMP

Contents at a Glance

Introduction to Project Management

Chapter 1 : Project Management Framework

CHAPTER 2 : Project Management Processes

CHAPTER 3 : Project Integration Management

CHAPTER 4 : Project Scope Management

CHAPTER 5 : Project Procurement Management

CHAPTER 6 : Project Time Management

CHAPTER 7 : Project Cost Management

CHAPTER 8 : Project Quality Management

CHAPTER 9 : Project Human Resource Management

CHAPTER 10 : Project Communication Management

CHAPTER 11 : Project Risk Management

CHAPTER 12 : Professional Responsibility and Ethical Conduct

Glossary

Index

Contents

Introduction to Project Management ix

1. PROJECT MANAGEMENT FRAMEWORK 1

- Learning Project Management 2
- What is a Project? 2
- Why a Project 3
- Operational Work 4
- What is Project Management? 5
- Why is a Project Management so Important? 6
- What Makes the Difference? 7
- Project Management Office (PMO) 7
- What is a Program? 9
- Where Does a Program Fit in a Portfolio? 10
- Triple Constraint Diagram 11
- Who are Stakeholders? 13
- Who is a Sponsor? 14
- Who Executes a Project? 14
- The Critical Role of a Project Manager 15
- Who are the Beneficiaries? 16
- What Organization are You Working In? 16
- Project Management Methodology in Different Industries 23

2. PROJECT MANAGEMENT PROCESSES 35

- How a Project is Managed 36
- What are Processes? 37
- How Process groups, Processes and
  Knowledge Areas are Related 40
- How a Process Group and Processes are Related to Each Other? 42
- Initiation Process Group 42
- Project Planning 45
- Organization Process Assets 49
- Enterprise Environmental Factors 50
- More on Planning 52

3. INTEGRATION MANAGEMENT 67

- What is an Integration Management? 68
- What does a Project Manager Do in Integration Management? 69
- Boundaries of a Project Manager 70
- What Gets Integrated? 70
- Project Charter 71
- Preliminary Scope Statement 77
- Project Planning 80
- Project Execution 81
- Project Monitoring & Control 84
- Change Management? 86
- Project Closure 90

4. SCOPE MANAGEMENT 111

- What is a Scope? 112
- Significance of Scope? 112
- Processes Related to Scope Management Planning 115
- Preparing the Preliminary Scope Statement 116
- Prepare the Scope Management Plan 117
- Scope Definition Process 122
- What is Scope Baseline? 128
- Create Work Breakdown Structure Process 129
- WBS Dictionary 135
- Scope Control Process 136
- Significance of Change Management in Scope 138
- Scope Validation 139
- Project Scope vs. Organization Objective 142

5. PROCUREMENT MANAGEMENT 163

- Why Procure? 164
- Where Does Procurement management Processes
  Happen in a Project? 165
- Plan Procurement Process 166
- Conduct Procurement Process 178
- Control Procurements 186
- Control ProcurementsProcess 188
- Contract Closure Process 190
- Key Points to Remember in
  Procurement Management Process 193

6. TIME MANAGEMENT 211

- What is Time Management? 212
- Significance of Time Management in a Project 213
- Time Management Planning - An Overview 213
- Activity Definition 214
- Activity Sequencing 221
- Activity Resource Estimation 227
- Activity Duration Estimation 231
- Schedule Development 235
- Schedule Control 245

7. COST MANAGEMENT 267

- Cost Management Process 268
- What are Classified as Costs? 268
- Types of Cost 269
- Cost Estimation 272
- Cost Budgeting Process 278
- Cost Control Process 282
- How to Control Overshooting Costs of Project? 292
- Impact of Cost on Quality 293

8. QUALITY MANAGEMENT 311

- What is a Quality? 312
- The Significance of Quality 312
- The Quality Processes 315
- Quality Management Planning 316
- Project Quality Control Process 320
- Differentiate Quality Control Vs. Quality Assurance 328
- Quality Assurance Process 329

9. HUMAN RESOURCES MANAGEMENT 351

- Significance of Human Resource Management 352
- Different Types of Human Resources in a Project 353
- Human Resource Planning 354
- Acquire Project Team 362
- Develop Project Team 367
- Manage Project Team 373

10. COMMUNICATION MANAGEMENT 397

- The Power of Communication 398
- How Important is Communication to a Project? 399
- Where Does Communication Happen in a Project 401
- Components of Communication Process 402
- Communication Management Process 403
- Communication Management Planning 406
- Information Distribution Process 410
- Manage Stakeholders Process 418
- Important Communication Documents 423

11. RISK MANAGEMENT PLANNING 449

- What is a Risk? 450
- Significance of Risk Management 450
- Categories of Risks 451
- Components of Risks Planning 455
- Risk Management Planning 456
- Risk Breakdown Structure 458
- Risk Identification 459
- Qualitative Analysis 464
- Quantitative Risk Analysis 466
- Why Risks are very Critical for the
  Success or Failure of a Project 469
- Risk Response Planning 474
- Risk Monitoring Process 476

12. PROFESSIONAL RESPONSIBILITY & ETHICS 497

- What it Means to be Ethical? 498
- More on Professional Responsibility 498
- The Significance of being Professional 499
- Goal of Professionalism, Ethics and Values
  in the Business Environment 500
- Common Ethical Issues 501
- Some of the commonly found Unprofessional Practices 504
- A Test of Knowledge and Understanding 509

Glossary 527

Index 533

This page is intentionally left blank

This page is intentionally left blank

Introduction to Project Management

Thank you for purchasing your copy of 'A professional Guide to Project Management'. I strongly believe that this book will help you validate your existing knowledge on Project Management methodologies and help you understand the globally accepted professional practices on managing projects.

As the economies are opened, the business world has shrunk with expanded horizons and increased opportunities, the businesses around the world have one lesson to learn, which is 'only the fittest can survive the fierce competition and to sustain their growth'.

I still remember the business environment that prevailed in the olden days. if someone wanted to buy a motorcycle and approached a dealership that sell a particular brand of motorcycles, one would have had a very different experience than what it is now. Actually, they do not 'sell' but take orders for the machines. When the order details are collected, the dealership forwards the specification to the company that manufactures the equipment. At this point of time, remember that the buyer is not aware of the color of the motorcycle, that they are going to get. The color choice were not given to the buyers in the olden days. The buyer will not know the color of the machine till it was delivered by the dealer.

That was the scenario of the business environment in many parts of the world, decades ago. However, the world has traveled far away from this age old practices. As the business climate began changing, companies felt the need for innovation, efficiency, quality, customer satisfaction and market leadership that will guarantee them growth. Of late, the businesses around the world have realized that such innovations, quality and customer satisfaction is guaranteed by superior processes, management practices and excellent planning. All these require excellent amount of resources, knowledge and skills to drive the organization forward.

Project Management is one step forward taken by the professional world, adopting itself to a more disciplined approach rather than the age old practices of casual planning and managing. Such disciplined approached resulted in having more processes and methodologies to adopt and practice. Having such innovative processes and practices resulted in better outcome for every project. Successful projects boosted the profitability of the performing organizations and their customers. In many cases, successful projects gave the organization technical advantage and market leadership over their competitors in the respective segments.

If you observe all these factors closely, you can understand the fundamental requirement to achieve great result is the efficiency and expertise of the project management skills. Every profession offers learning experience for the professionals and chance for applying the learnt practices. The practice of project management and leadership helps everyone in personal life, in terms of professional approach, better communication skills, handling issues and what not? The businesses world around has realized the advantages of having better management skills and always lookout for people with superior skills to manage their projects, large or small. Managing projects offer large amount of opportunities, challenges and experiences of different kind to everyone involved in it. These include ownership of tasks, responsibilities, monetary benefits, better career prospects and future growth.

My attempt, in this book, is to help understand the project management methodologies, their use and how they help in shaping the growth of the projects, organizations and that of project managers involved in executing them. This is my first attempt to put in my experience and thoughts on any subject and I am confident that the book is of significant help to you.

Remember that the intention of the book is not to teach every basic stuff about the project management. While writing this book, I assumed that the buyers have some or good amount of knowledge on what project management is all about and what is done while managing the projects. I have given as much explanations and input on the methodologies, inputs, outputs and tools that are listed throughout this book. There cannot be any definite and fixed components (such as inputs, outputs and tools) that satisfies the needs of every project in the business world. There are bound to be some additions and omissions to suit the organizational and project needs. So, I would recommend you to apply your own wisdom to understand and analyze the project needs.

If you keep your mind open to learning new methodologies and ideas, you would find plenty of inputs to your appetite for knowledge and growth. As a career is best nurtured by learning more and exploring new methodologies, I suggest you keep your profession as a learning exercise and enjoy it more.

Wish you a very good luck.

Thank you

Sridhar Ragothaman M.S., PMP

This page is intentionally left blank

This page is intentionally left blank

Project Management Framework

Objectives

At the end of Project Management Framework chapter, you should be able to:

- understand what is a project
- understand the difference between project and operational work
- know what is a project management
- know what is a Project Management Office (PMO) and its responsibilities
- understand what is a triple constraint diagram and how it evolved over a period of time
- understand the role and responsibilities of a project manager
- distinguish different types of organization in a professional environment

Learning Project Management

It is said that the first step towards learning something is to unlearn the subject first.

In other words, when someone is attempting to learn on a specific subject, the person should come with an open mind rather than having his/her own thoughts and opinion on the subject that they are going to learn. The primary reason for this is to make sure the learners are not influenced by their own thoughts and opinion on the subject, which may be stuck in their mind. Such opinions and thoughts might prevent them from accepting new ideas and recommendations of better practices.

However, in this book I am not going to ask you to forget everything that may be in your mind about project management. The reason is because there are more likelihood of you already following many of the recommended practices of the project management methodology. So, the book is an attempt to validate your existing knowledge and help find the gaps in the knowledge and what is being practiced in the real professional life as a project manager.

The purpose of this book is not to make you memorize the 'what-is-what' of the project management methodologies. The readers get nothing by memorizing a book of this stature. Understanding the project management concepts and applying the gained knowledge in real life gets the reader towards ultimate success.

Needless to say that there are always scope for improvements in whatever we do as management professionals. All that is required is to have an open mind that is receptive to new ideas and improvements.

What is a Project?

The Project Management Institute (www.pmi.org), describes a project as a temporary endeavor that has predetermined objectives to be achieved within a planned start and end dates. Also, such a project should produce an unique result for the benefit of the performing organization.

In other words, a project is a disciplined way of performing multiple interrelated tasks, in a controlled and coordinated way that should produce an end result or product within a stipulated timeframe. A project involves people, resources, objectives, cost and schedule besides many other components.

A Project Should be Temporary

Every project should produce an unique product or service to the customers. It should be as unique in the sense that a specific model auto produced by an automaker cannot be available from any other manufacturer in this world. Once the objectives are achieved and delivered to the intended beneficiary, that marks the end of the project.

Start & End Date

Every project needs to have a predetermined start and end dates. A project cannot be performed forever. Even a large project, such as building a dam or a massive space program is expected to have a targeted closure date. Without a Start or end date, it becomes an operational activity which is an ongoing process.

Does it sound sensible?

It is important to note that not every project has its requirements completely defined before the execution begin

When you begin working on the project, you may not have all the information that you require to complete your project execution. You might even begin with very limited clarity on the objective forcing you to make significant amount of assumptions. At times, one might tend to confuse whether a project is strictly about meeting the initial scope defined, which is not true. As the project makes progress, there may be further clarity on the scope and these amendments are expected to be part of the original project boundary.

As you progress with your reading of this book, you will learn more about handling change management process, reviewing the cost, scope and schedule baselines.

Tidbits

Why a Project

Let me take an example to define a project?

Imagine the case of a movie making initiative by a well known production company. There are many actors with extraordinary talent, technicians and other artistes available to play their respective roles in a planned new venture. Are these sufficient to get a movie ready? Certainly not. A movie needs a story, funding, schedule, co-ordination, communication and many other essential stuff to get it completed. Most importantly, it needs a plan. What can possibly achieve all of these and have the movie complete and ready for release? The task of performing all these interrelated components in a disciplined way is called a Project.

At this point, you should remember that a project might be subdivided into smaller components and each may be managed as separate projects depending on the need and objectives of the project. This decision is entirely left to the Project manager or the project performing organization to decide.

Operational Work

Having learnt about a project, there might come a natural question. Does every task handled in a formal methodology qualify to be called a project?

Obviously not.

As defined by the Project Management Institute (PMI), a project is temporary and need to have a start and end dates with the objective to produce an unique end product or result, failing which it can only be an operational work.

What is an Operational work? An operation is a group of tasks, which are performed continuously and at regular intervals without a predetermined start or end date.

Let us take the case of providing Customer support task of a Bank.

Your organization has won a major banking deal to develop an online banking application. You are the project manager and had a great team of experts. You and your team has worked very hard to design the system. The developers rocked with their skills and developed an amazing application with great features. The result is, the bank has an excellent system that handles all the banking needs of the stakeholders. The customers are very impressed with the design and its features. So, your company was given a go-ahead to extend post implementation support for a specific period of time and also maintenance of the application after the mandatory support period.

Your Organization successfully delivered the application to the customer right on time, as agreed. Now, it is time to provide post-implementation support and plan for maintenance.

To achieve this objective, your senior leadership has decided to break all of the support activities into two subtasks. First task is to plan and provide post-implementation support for 90 days. The next phase is to maintain the application on a continuous basis.

Do you think providing post-implementation support fall under the classification of a project?

Certainly it is not.

As per PMI's definition of a project, such post-implementation support do not produce any predetermined outcome or product, that is unique to the overall support task. Obviously, there is no predetermined dates set to produce the results (Do not confuse the start and end dates of the 90-day post implementation support commitments since it is a support commitment by the seller as part of the contract). The whole task is mere supporting and keeping the developed application up and running besides handling any issues in the production environment.

Similarly, maintaining the application doesn't produce any unique result. There are no committed start or end dates to achieve any specific result. The purpose of maintenance is to keep the system running, to troubleshoot any issues or to handle upgrade requests and enhancements to the already developed application.

What do you call the all of the above as? Is it a project or an Operational work?

The task of developing an application is a project, whereas the post-implementation support and maintenance tasks are operational activities.

The reason is, a project development activity has a predetermined start and end dates besides having an objective to produce a desired outcome or result. The outcome of performing the tasks result in a unique product, in this case the banking application software. A project is considered to have ended after the objectives are achieved and verified by the stakeholders.

Whereas, the full scale support and maintenance is worth being called an operational activity since all of the produced code are same and scope of the code is not going to be impacted as a result of the implementation support or maintenance activity (the occasional upgrades and updates to the original code may be impacting the code. However such updates cannot be called project unless such tasks are considered a separate project by the customer or the performing organization)

Does this make sense?

I am sure, now you have fair idea of the difference between a project and operational activity.

What is Project Management?

A very natural question to come from anyone.

Is it about managing resources or monitoring their work and timesheet?

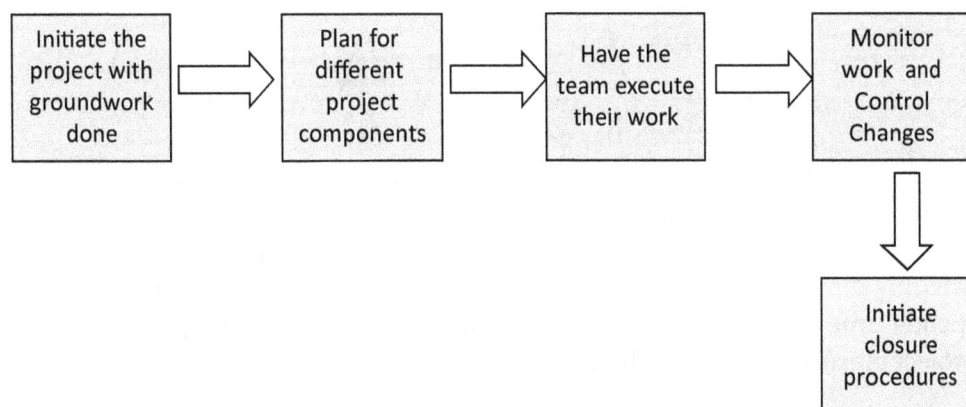

Initiate the project with groundwork done	→	Plan for different project components	→	Have the team execute their work	→	Monitor work and Control Changes

Initiate closure procedures

Certainly, not only those are the responsibilities of a Project Manager. A Project Manager is responsible to kickstart the project tasks, plan for the project, monitor the work execution and control the changes, manage the resources and each of the project activities till getting the project to a formal closure. In simple terms, a project manager accepts a high level requirement from the customer and converts it into a result, which is acceptable to the customer.

In fact, the Project Manager is responsible from picking the team till their release and to have them redeployed.

Why is Project Management So Important?

If we realize the importance of executing a project, then it automatically signifies the need of a driving force behind every project execution. A project cannot execute by itself. A project is not a robot, which can be operated by executing few computer programs. Lot of activities goes into a project till it gets implemented and the organization begin to reap the benefits of a successful project. Every successful project indicates the efficiency of a project manager.

The organization may be having a cutting edge technology, work force, organizational repositories with outstanding historical information and other artefacts. However, to co-ordinate between all these components to arrive at a project plan, kick start and to monitor a project a formal approach is essential, which is called the Project Management.

The efficiency, skills and intelligence of a Project manager can be measured only from the successful execution of the projects. Even if a manager is good in creating colorful slides and presentations with good amount of data, he will be considered inefficient if his projects haven't delivered the expected results on time or according to the cost estimation,

To put it in simple form, a project management is all about Plan, Do, Act and Check as illustrated in the below diagram. You plan for a work, get it done, monitor the progress of the work and validate the output once the work is complete.

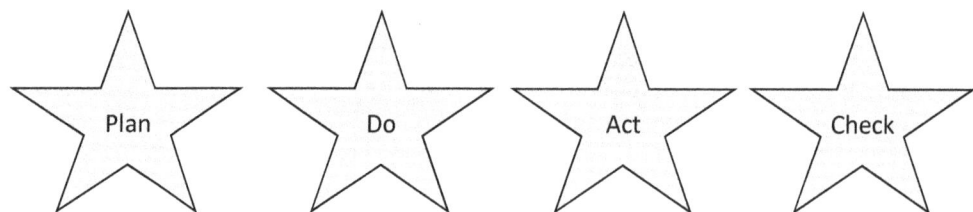

Not only the above four tasks essential for a project manager. A project manager spends time in the initial process to set the ground for planning and handles project closure processes, when all the objectives are achieved.

Where does the project managers spend most of their time in a project?

I would say, an intelligent project manager spends more of his/her time in the project planning phase. The reason is pretty simple. If a project's processes, activities and tasks are planned in a realistic and more sensible way, there should not be any troubles from the other phases of the project.

Imagine the case of identifying stakeholders. If the stakeholders are all identified during the planning phase, there may not be much changes to the scope. If the scope updates are limited, there are more possibilities of the project meetings its schedule, cost and quality objectives.

What Makes the Difference?

Since we are now focusing on understanding the project management, let us set aside the operational work.

Handling a group of tasks in an organized way makes good amount of difference when the same set of tasks is handled casually without any planning done. The rate of success of handling a project is very high against handling in an unorganized way. In any project, co-ordination and communication becomes a major challenge that determines the success and failure. It's like a production line of an auto company, having to procure all the components on time to the assembly line for producing a car on time. Any delay in procuring even a smallest of the components has a serious impact on the assembly, delivery and profitability of the organization.

Similarly, in an organization, coordinating with human resources becomes a major challenge, having to take their other engagements into consideration while planning for a project. Having the right planning and communication to the right people at the right time is achievable only by a disciplined approach. All of these tasks are the responsibilities of a project manager.

Project Management Office

A Project Management Office (PMO) is a group in an organization and consists of project management professionals, who support each of the projects with vital resources such as expertise, process documents, organization's project resources, forms, templates, historic information on project components, risks, quality guidelines and any support requirements of the project manager and the team. All of these organization assets are available in the Organization's process repository, which is usually maintained by the Project Management Office.

In a project environment, the PMO could support the project in any or all of the below tasks

- Provide assistance, whenever there is a process assistance requirement from the Organizational project repository such as quality compliance requirements
- Provide guidance through historic information of other projects
- Perform quality audits for the projects.
- Providing templates, forms and expertise on processes
- Conducting risk audits on projects
- Provide Organization's policy related information on various factors
- Provide enterprise environmental factors
- Provide guidance on change management
- Provide inputs and support during the project initiation phase
- Project closure guidance
- Troubleshoot any project management related issues

While realizing the importance and effectiveness of the presence of PMO, one should understand the fact that the presence of PMO has some challenges as well.

- In many situations, the role of PMO might directly conflict with that of Project Managers.
- Any shortcomings in the role played by PMO might weaken the performing organizations' professional capabilities, which will have serious business impact and result in loss of confidence among the stakeholders and customers.
- The roles between Project Managers and Project Management Office should be clearly defined and understood by everyone. Ideally, it is the Project Managers who run their projects and not the PMO. The PMO merely supports the Project Managers whenever there is a requirement.

To eliminate the above risks, every organization could engage strong and efficient resources as part of the PMO. It would also be a good idea to have PMI certified professionals to be part of the PMO. Defining the boundary of PMO is essential to eliminate any potential jurisdiction related issues on who is responsible for what.

At all times, both the PMO and the project managers should realize that the PMO is only a group that supports project managers and nothing more.

What is a Program?

A program is a group of projects. In other words, whenever there is a larger project being executed with interrelated tasks, it is divided into multiple projects and managed as individual tasks with separate scope, planning and execution. The individual tasks are called projects. However, all of these individual projects fall under the scope of the overall program.

As an example, imagine a project to construct a huge dam across the river flowing through the state. To make his life easier, the head of the dam building project has decided to divide the project into multiple sub-projects such as land acquisition, procurement services, civil design and engineering, construction and quality inspection. Each of these can be considered a separate project.

Another way to describe a program is it to be a collection of projects, that might share common resources such as manpower, physical resources, support services, vendors and so on.

Note that a Program might even be a combination of multiple projects and another program, depending on the overall program size and requirements.

Take a look into the diagram that helps understand the relationship between a Program and a project. It is to be noted that a program might have another program underneath, depending on the Organization and program requirements.

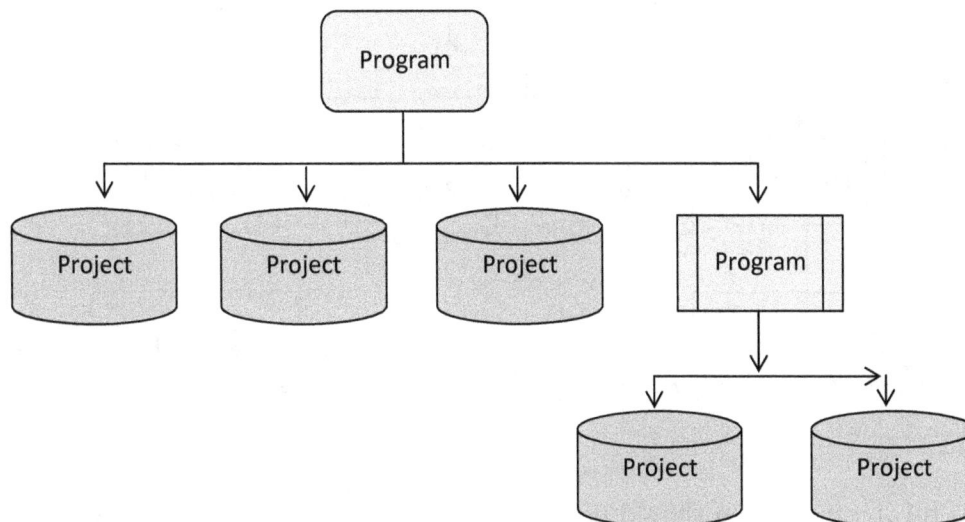

Where Does a Program Fit in a Portfolio?

A portfolio is a collection of multiple programs. The only difference between a Program and a portfolio is that all the projects and programs that come under a portfolio need not share a same set of objective and goals.

Imagine a situation, when your organization successfully negotiates with two prestigious customers to undertake building a new corporate office for Customer A and remodelling office for Customer B. Your organization decides to leverage the available hardware and manpower to help save significant amount of cost. The organization then decides to manage both these activities as a portfolio and makes you as a Portfolio Manager. Your responsibility is limited only to managing the resources that are to be deployed onto these two projects. You decide to come out with your own Portfolio Management Plan that defines the use of these resources so that both the projects get the maximum benefits of the available resources, while helping your organization save the cost of procuring different sets of resources for each of the project.

In other words, when multiple projects or programs share common resources, facilities and manpower among them, they are classified as a portfolio and managed as a single portfolio for the convenience of achieving the organizational goals.

The below diagram should help you understand, how the portfolio is organized

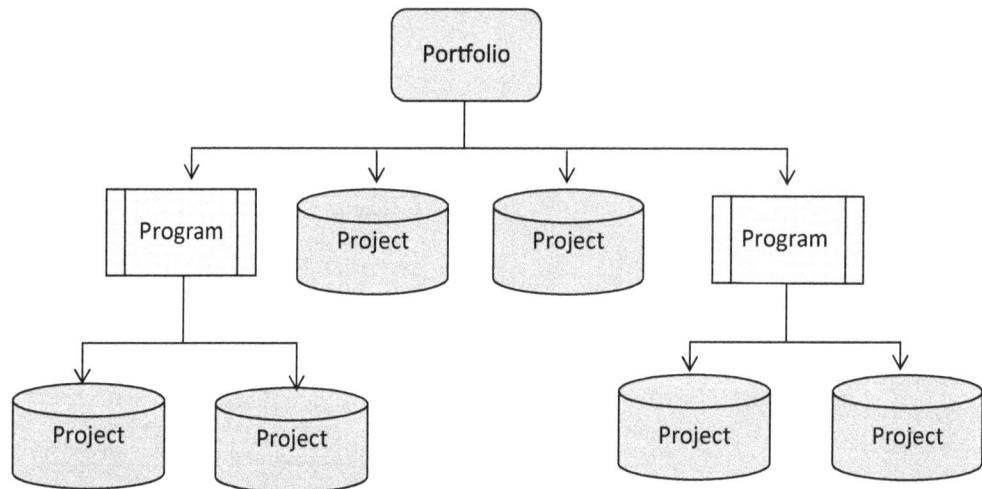

At this moment, you should be aware that all the components of a portfolio doesn't share any goals in common such as objectives or responsibilities.

Hope, the above makes sense.

Triple Constraint Diagram

Are the customer concerned about everything that is being handled or managed in a project from start to finish?

Certainly not. Then, what is the customer interested more in a project?

The project charter has given the authority to the project manager to initiate, plan and monitor the entire project work. However, the customer is specifically interested in three important aspects of the project.

The most critical aspect in a project environment is to obtain a desired output that meets the customer expectation, conformance to requirements, fitness to use, cost effective and available on time. The challenge for the project managers is to balance the Scope, Cost and Schedule of the project. The success or failure of a project is determined by how these three components are managed by the Project Manager. In turn, these three components have a direct impact on the quality of the work being done.

As we realize now, every project is built around Cost, Schedule and Scope. Any impact on any of these three factors will result in the quality of the project.

Imagine a situation, where your project is building a huge boiler for the local power plant according to specific requirements. As per the original plan, the product is to be delivered within 90 days from the start date and the total cost of the whole project is pegged at $12 Million.

When the project is completed, you find that your project delivered a great product and within 80 days. But your project cost ballooned by 22% above the estimation or else your project cost was under the budget, but the project took 3 weeks more than the estimated schedule of completion.

Does these above project delivery impress anyone in your customer's organization?

Certainly not.

Let us look at the diagram below

What does the above triangle convey?

Scope, Cost and Schedule form three walls of the above triangle. Quality output is the ultimate objective of every project.

If any one of the three factors is altered, it impacts the other two factors and the whole structure becomes imbalanced. This result in the whole structure becoming unusable. Hence, whenever there is any revision in one of the three factors the other two factors are required to be adjusted or reviewed to maintain a balance of the project objective intact.

In a real project scenario, if there is any revision in the scope of your project it involves additional effort. This additional effort results in updating the schedule, which subsequently has impact on the cost of the project. So, when there is a change in scope, the cost and schedule needs to be reviewed as well to maintain the project objective. All of these changes collectively impacts the quality of the project.

The above represent the original version of the *Triple Constraint* diagram.

Is that all About Triple Constraint?

After having reviewed the significance of Scope, Cost and Schedule, an obvious question might come into one's mind.

Is the whole project knitted only around three factors?

Obviously not. Every process group and process is more important in a project. Besides Cost, Schedule and Scope, every project has few more critical factors that decide the fate of the projects. An enhanced version of project constraints include Risk, Quality and Resources.

In addition to the Scope, Cost and Time, these three factors such as Risk, Quality and Resources are influential factors on the outcome of any project.

Risks play a very crucial and important role in every project since a risk might have serious impacts on the overall objective set for the project, thus derailing the very purpose of executing a project as a whole. Similarly, Quality is another factor that guarantees the final outcome of the project meeting the project and product objectives. The Human resources that are working on the project is key to the project's success since every activities of the projects are knitted around the project resources.

So, the amendments to the Triple Constraint resulted in a new triangle as given below

So, when you hear about Triple Constraint diagram, you should not restrict your views only to Scope, Cost and Schedule but the overall picture that includes Quality, Risks and Resources.

So, the new Triple Constraint Diagram appears as below

Who are Stakeholders?

A stakeholder is anyone, who is directly or indirectly impacted by the outcome of the project.

You might ask, as to why we should care about those, who are indirectly impacted by the outcome of the project.

An impact is an impact, whether it is major, minor or moderate. Still it would be good to keep them informed of the execution of the project and the subsequent impact within the boundary of the project scope. The purpose of having them identified as stakeholders is to make sure transparent communication is maintained with every group, who may be impacted by the project outcome. This will help them to plan for any activities in advance, rather than giving a surprise at a later stage.

Identifying stakeholders in every project is one key task that might have serious impact on the project. In fact, failure to identify all of the stakeholders ahead of the project execution might even derail the objective of the project as a whole. Here is how it could happen.

Imagine a situation, you are managing an application development project for a retail company. You have the project charter and high level requirement handed to you. Now you are about to identify the stakeholders of your project. As you begun identifying the stakeholders, you miss out one department head, whom you think is not very important.

Now you begin finalizing the detailed scope of your project by way of discussions with all the identified stakeholders. After the scope is signed off by all these stakeholders, the project team begins to develop their application. Towards the end of the project execution phase, this department head realizes about the project being executed which might very seriously impact his department's current work flow and operations. So, he raises an objection to your senior management over your failure to include him about the project execution and to notify him on the progress of the project.

Your management too feel that any impact on the department cannot be accepted since it involves financial repercussions on the organization. So, they review the overall project scope and the progress before deciding to scrap the whole project as unviable.

Now, whose fault is this?

Obviously, it is the fault of yours, the project manager, who didn't include the respective department head as a stakeholder. This ignorance was a major risk, to which no mitigation could be planned since it impacts the whole project by way of missing a key scope or dependency. Your organization is obviously not very impressed with your project management capability.

Similarly, identifying all the stakeholders at the very early stage of a project will eliminate the risks rather than identifying them at a lateral stage of the project. We will be reviewing more on the stakeholder in the Project Stakeholder Management chapter later.

Who is a Sponsor?

The person who funds the project is the sponsor. A sponsor can be an individual or a department, which is represented by one of its member. A sponsor represents the financial source for the project by way of funding.

Either the sponsor is a direct beneficiary of the project or he has been assigned the responsibility to drive the organization's objective. A sponsor naturally becomes a key stakeholder of the project and can influence the objective and changes to the scope at any given time. In many cases, a sponsor can even decide to end the project for any reasons, even before the project objectives are met.

While the sponsor doesn't monitor the project team or how the project is being executed, the manager of the project has the responsibility to keep the sponsor updated of the project status and any potential risks or issues.

Who Executes a Project?

Ideally, every member of the Project team has a predefined responsibility in the execution of a project. While the project manager manages the project and is responsible for project initiation, planning, monitoring, control and closure, the team is responsible for designing, development and testing of the product or task. The overall accountability and ownership of the project rests with the

Project Manager. A project manager takes the responsibility of what the entire team performs.

Many projects collapse or fail to deliver the desired objective due to lack of ownership during the execution phase. This is the result of poor planning and managing execution. Hence, predefined ownership of each phase and responsibilities would ensure ownership and accountability, which will result in smoother execution and implementation of the project.

The Critical Role of a Project Manager

What does a Project Manager do in a project? As a project manager, you might ask yourself.

I would equate a project manager with a director of a film. If you understand their role well, they both plan, execute and monitor multiple activities in their respective roles. A project manager and a director stay on top of things till their projects are completed. While the project manager finalize the scope, the director works on his script. They both manage their respective teams, plan cost and schedule. They both work hard to produce a quality output that is acceptable to their customers.

As narrated earlier, an intelligent project manager focuses a lot on the planning phase in order to have a smoother execution of the project. If the project has neatly planned processes, there shouldn't be any big surprises for the project manager at a later stage of the project. He may just need to make sure that the processes and plans are strictly adhered to by the team besides validating the schedule, cost and quality of the deliverable.

For example, if the project has a perfect communication plan that takes care of every possible situation, everything tend to proceed well and according to plan. It doesn't mean you can ignore the progress of the project. You still need to monitor whether the processes are being followed and for any potential gaps.

Communication is a very critical component in a project. Unless there is right amount of communication flow between right people and at appropriate time is there, there are more chances of chaotic situations prevailing in the project. Thus the project manager need to have communication plan in place and coordinate among all stakeholders effectively.

From my own project management experience, I could give a good example.

Once a senior executive of an organization approached me with an issue. One of the project being executed by his organization is having serious trouble and his customer is extremely disappointed with the way things were going. The customer is a very large player in the life sciences and healthcare market, which is highly regulated around the world. The senior executive is worried that any delay in fixing the project issues could result in losing the project and the future business flow from the customer.

When I started looking into the issues and the project's current status, I realized the issue to be the absence of project management. The team had too many tasks & stakeholders and there were plenty of communication channels and poor coordination. The team members were pulled by stakeholders from every directions. Most of the time the team was busy writing replies to the stakeholders or answering phone calls from rather than working on their tasks. Conflicting requirements and directions were flowing freely.

In such situations, a daily discussion involving the team and other stakeholders may be of great help. Discussing all open issues, raising question, getting answers, assigning responsibilities and tracking statuses help resolve most of the project issues besides smoothening the project execution activity. A project manager plays a leadership role in such situations.

Another biggest challenge for a project manager is to control the changes that might be coming his way, when the team is making good progress with their construction activities. While changes to the project scope cannot be avoided, it does have a serious influence on the overall project. We will read more on the change management process at a later chapter in this book.

I wouldn't hesitate to say, there is a very intelligent and capable project manager behind the success of every project.

Do you agree?

Who are the Beneficiaries?

A beneficiary of a project may be one or more departments of the performing organization. They are directly or indirectly being impacted by the implementation of a project. A beneficiary is always identified as one of the key stakeholder to help them stay updated on the status of the overall execution and progress of the project. The objectives of these beneficiaries are always aligned with the objectives of the performing organization.

At this point, it would be sensible to understand that a sponsor *need not always be* the direct beneficiary of the project.

What Organization are You Working in?

Before you begin learning about Project Management methodologies and techniques you should ask yourself, what sort of organization you are working in?

You might ask what an organization structure is going to matter in the project execution. Obviously, it does matter. In fact, it matters a lot more than you can think of. The way projects get executed differs between organizations.

Let us assume Mike and Sarah are friends from their college days and both are project managers in their respective organizations. Whenever they both meet, Mike feels that Sarah has more challenges, responsibilities and opportunities as a project manager while he keep collecting project status, compile them and email the report to his boss. While Sarah has several leaders and team members report to her, Mike finds none in his reporting hierarchy. While Sarah enjoys her work, Mike thinks his job suck. Mike feels that he has same amount of experience, better knowledge and expertise but his organization has been unfair to himself. Is Mike right in his judgment about his organization?

No. He is not.

The difference between Sarah and Mike in terms of responsibilities and opportunities is influenced by the type of organizations they are working with.

You will have better understanding of this, once you understand about different types of organizations.

If you are aiming to manage a project and succeed in your attempts, you should have basic knowledge of the type of your organization since the organization has an influence on the way a project is executed. To make things straight and easier, there are three types of organization we should be aware of in the work environment.
- Functional Organization
- Matrix Organization
- Projectized Organization.

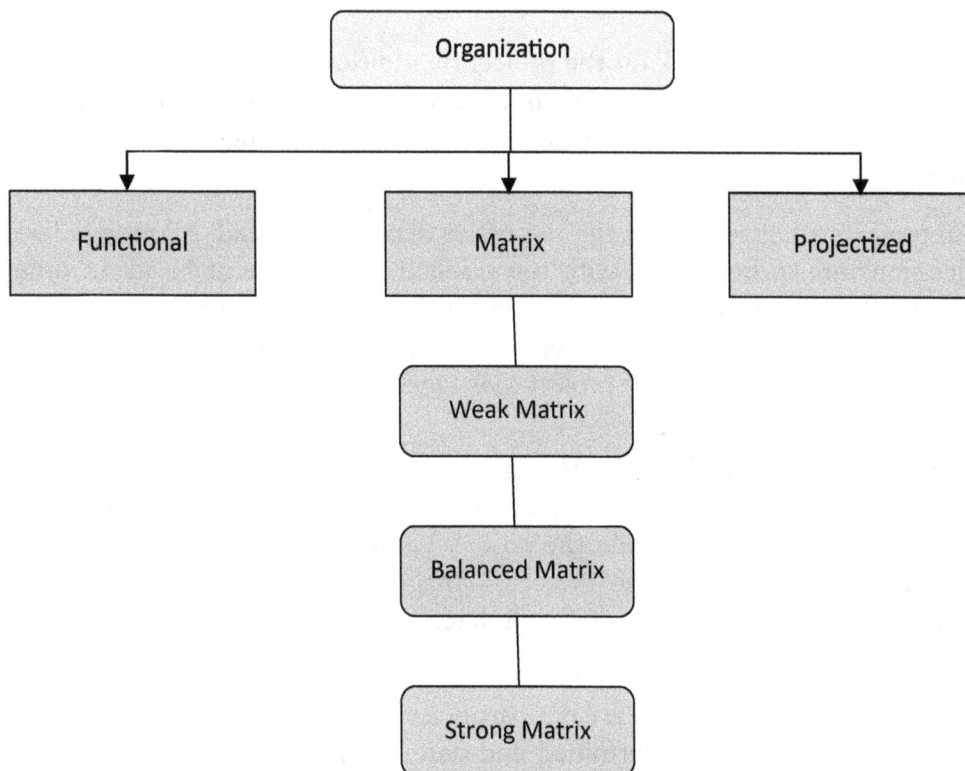

Look at the below diagram to understand how the organizations are structured Let us see each of these types of Organization in detail below.

Functional Organization

In a Functional organization, the whole team is structured around specific functions or departments of the organization. Examples of such functions are Production, Stores, Marketing and Finance. Whenever there is a project being executed in the organization, it is usually done within a specific department or function and you will be pulling resources that are part of any of such functions. You may be the manager of the project, but you will not be the owning these resources by yourself since they are primarily part of the respective departments.

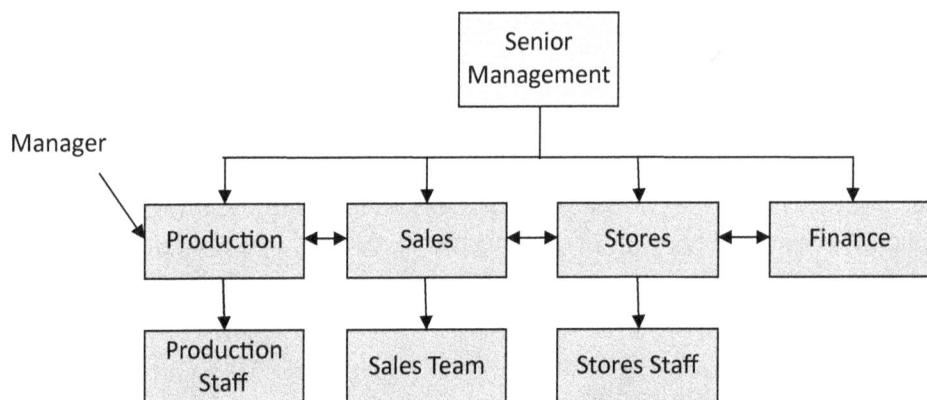

The team members work on the project in addition to their regular function responsibilities. Whenever there is a communication or requirement from another department, it goes to the rest of the team through the department head.

All projects are governed by the respective department head. All project level decisions are to be cleared with the respective Department Head. In other words, Project Managers work as assistants to the Department Heads. The primary responsibilities of the project Managers are to do administrative tasks besides working as part time project Managers.

Projectized Organization

In a Projectized organization, all projects are owned by the Project Managers. The Project Managers decide the cost, schedule, resources and everything relating to the project. The Project Manager identifies the resources and releases them when the project is complete.

The resources do not have a 'home' or a 'permanent base' in a Projectized organization, meaning they are not part of a single project permanently. Since every project has a predetermined end date, the resources get released and redeployed upon completion of their project. Once the project is completed, the project manager gets the resources released and redeployed to other projects.

In short, Project Managers own their projects from start to finish besides accepting accountability for the success and failure of their projects.

```
                    ┌──────────────┐
                    │    Senior    │
                    │  Management  │
                    └──────────────┘
```

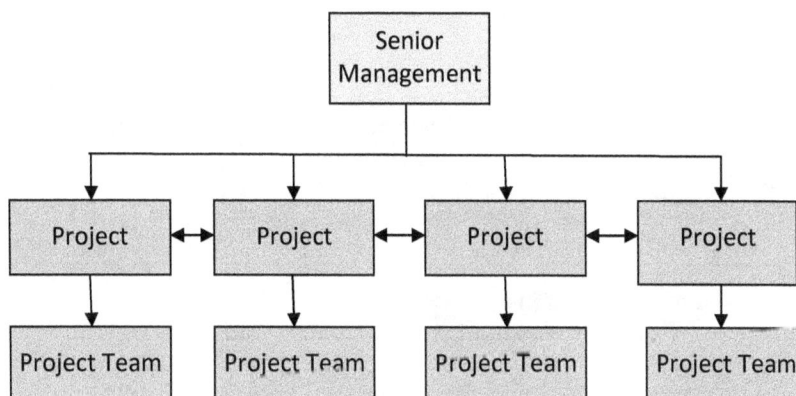

Matrix Organization

The third form of Organization is a Matrix Organization, which includes the advantages and disadvantages of Functional and Projectized Organizations.

In a Matrix organization, the resources are nested around certain hierarchy. Still, the Project Manager will not own any of his project resources. Project managers will have none to limited power to take independent decisions relating to the project. The team reports to two managers. One is you, as their Project Manager and then to the functional head, who are heading the Departments or Functions.

When we speak about Matrix organizations, we need to consider different types of matrix types.

A **Weak Matrix** organization is where a Project Manager has very limited or no authority and they do not own their project resources. The project manager doesn't do any budgeting, estimation or scheduling but work only as project expeditor. The project expeditors are considered as assistants to the department head with limited or no authority. The entire project related decisions need to be approved by the respective Departmental head.

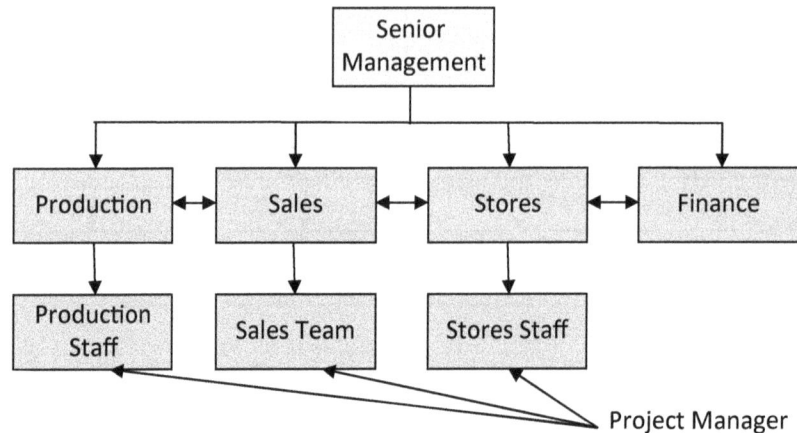

A ***Balanced Matrix*** organization is where Project Managers have limited to moderate power over their project. They act as Project coordinators, with limited decision making authority. In other words, a Departmental Head share authority with the Project Managers. The Project Managers take the Department Head into confidence while taking people management decisions. Similarly, the Department Heads get the concurrence of the Project Managers while taking project related decisions, thus making the organization more balanced.

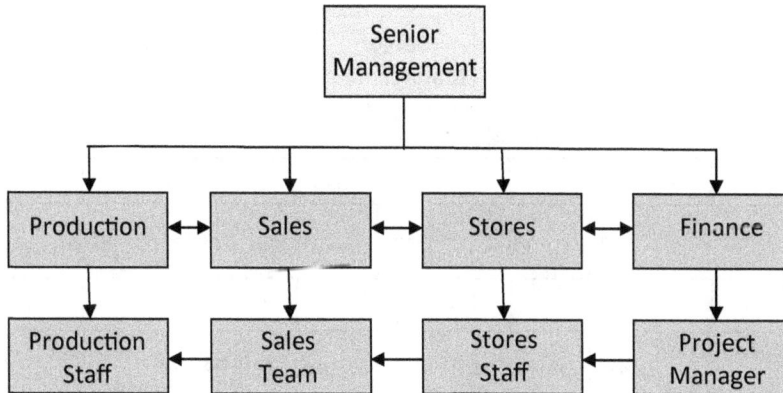

In a *Strong Matrix* organization, a Project Manager has more authority than the Functional Manager. However, the team report to both the managers. The team is nested around their project and their efficiency and performance is judged purely based on the outcome of the project. The project takes the utmost importance in a strong matrix organization.

Having understood the different types of organization, it should not be difficult for you to identify the type of organization, you are part of. That should help you plan for your project better, as we discussed earlier in this chapter.

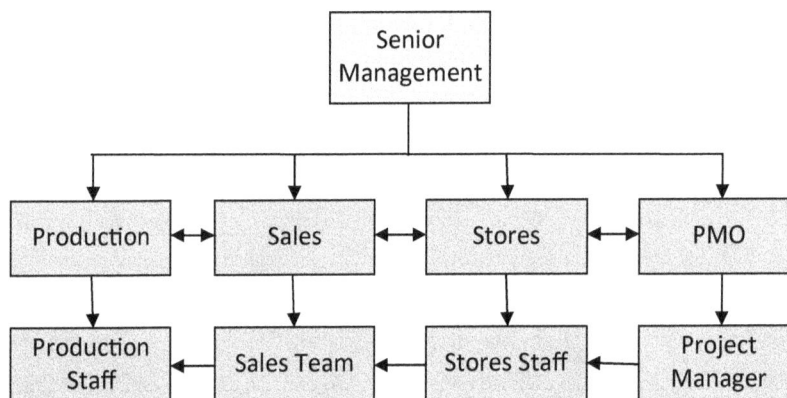

Now, as a practice exercise, could you list down the advantages and disadvantages of each of the Organization that we learnt above? Once listed, try to find out which type of organization you are working with.

Advantages

Functional	Matrix	Projectized

Disadvantages

Functional	Matrix	Projectized

Project Management Methodology in Different Industries

One might wonder, if I speak about different methodologies in managing projects for different industries. It may be appear weird but true.

Assume your organization has two divisions, Engineering and Information Technology. Both these divisions handle projects of different types. The Engineering divisions executes large civilian projects such as building stadiums and overpasses. The Information Technology division execute application related IT projects.

If you closely observe, both the divisions follow unique project lifestyles. Many of the performed tasks appear to be common but unique to the project requirements. While the IT projects commence with requirement gathering and identifying the stakeholders, the construction project involves conducting a feasibility study before designing the model. The IT projects do not have a model designed before the actual application begins.

In Construction or other non-IT projects, procurement management plays a critical role while it need not be the case with IT projects. The idea is to help the reader realize that the type of industry plays a significant role in the project management lifecycle. As we read through this book, you will realize that not all the processes are required to be performed in every project.

This book has been written keeping in mind the overall project management requirement across all business segments and make sure every project manager gets inputs and expertise in managing their projects effectively.

EXERCISES

Choose the Right Answer

1. A team of workers working on a assembly line to produce cars is
   a) Project work
   b) Maintenance activity
   c) Operational work
   d) None of the above

2. An event being managed in the local town hall is a
   a) Operational Work
   b) Project
   c) Maintenance work
   d) None of the above

3. The Systems department printing everyday reports for various departments is
   a) Maintenance work
   b) Project
   d) Operational work
   e) None of the above

4. Regular performance checking of an electric motor used to pump water is
   a) Maintenance work
   b) Project work
   c) Operational work
   d) None of the above

5. Preparing a cake for a wedding is
   a) Operational Work
   b) Project

6. Fixing a faulty electrical line is
   a) Operational Work
   b) Project

7. Providing a resolution on a problem ticket
   a) Project
   b) Operational Work

8. **Managing a musical event is**
   a) Project
   b) Operational Work

9. **Preparing an itinerary and monitoring the travel plan is**
   a) Operational Work
   b) Project

ANSWERS

1. c
2. b
3. c
4. a
5. b
6. a
7. b
8. a
9. b

Test Your Knowledge

1. Which of the following is NOT true about a project?

    a) Unique

    b) Systematic

    c) Progressively elaborated

    d) Known start and end dates

2. Bill is a project manager working on a system integration project for his high profile customer and is managing a large team of resources who work on strict timeline. One day, his supervisor Rodney calls Bill for an emergency meeting. It looks like Rodney's has run into deep trouble after his another project got implemented a month earlier. After the project was implemented, Rodney's customers found several of their other projects began reporting data related errors. Upon investigation, the customer found the root cause to be Rodney's project, which access and updates their database. They wanted Rodney to have it fixed on an emergency basis and has given a week to get this issue fixed, since it is causing them enormous amount of trouble. Rodney is asking Bill to take charge of fixing this issue. What would be Bill doing as part of his newly assigned responsibility?

    a) Problem fixing

    b) Project Management

    c) Operational Work

    d) None of the above

3. Sarah and Jack are very good friends right from their college days and are still in contact with each other. Often they meet over lunch as they are working in close proximity to each other. During a luncheon meeting, Sarah explains the difficulty she is having in managing her project since she is responsible for everything from project scope till the deliverable reaches her customer. She has the responsibility to setup project kickoff meetings, prepare schedules, cost budgeting, identify her resources, keep them occupied and motivated, collect the metrics and report the status to stakeholders. She gets exhausted on many days due to this work load. Jack feel very sorry for her and says, he do not have so much of pressure. He do not have a team reporting to him. All he does is to collect data from the project team and prepare report to send to stakeholders. He do not prepare schedules or budget. He is happy for what he is doing as he gets sufficient amount of time to spend with friends in the evenings. What type of organization Jack works in?

a) Balanced Matrix

b) Projectized Organization

c) Functional Organization

d) Weak Matrix

4. **Who has the maximum authority in an organization, that executes all its contracts as projects?**

a) Project Manager

b) Functional Head

c) Project co-coordinator

d) None of the above

5. **Robert is a project manager working on his product design for his customer. He has done with the initial draft of his design work and will be done with his design by the following Friday. He has plans to get the design reviewed next week. On Wednesday, his customer approaches him and informs of some amendments to the original requirement. After his brief discussion with the customer, Rob understands that accepting this change request wouldn't require much changes to the design. So he gives a oral consent to the customer for the change and requesting for a written request from the customer. Do you approve Rob's action in this regard?**

a) Yes

b) No

c) Can't say

d) It doesn't matter since the design is not complete yet.

6. **The company ABC Motor Corporation is an industry leader in the auto industry in Europe. Allan works as a project manager in their production department. His daily schedule includes accepting production targets from his General Manager and request for the components from the Stores department to the assembly line. He has to set the production target for his workers. His production line was unique since it produces special purpose vehicles for the army and the product design was approved by the technical team. What type of work Allan is managing?**

a) Operational work

b) Project work

c) Manufacturing

d) None of the above

7. Cindy has joined a new organization and assigned as a project manager. Upon starting to work, she finds that she is part of a Functional organization and gets nervous about her responsibilities and the type of work she expect to perform. What is mostly likely her cause for worry?

   a) Being part of a functional organization, she is worried that she will be assigned to manage the functional requirements of the organization rather than managing their project.

   b) Career growth is less likely in a non-project work environments.

   c) Being part of a functional organization, scope for ownership of the projects and the team is unlikely and she will not be able to manage a project independently

   d) None of the above

8. Deborah is conducting a workshop on project management to her team and other aspiring PMs of her organization. Which of the following statements is true about the responsibilities of a Project Manager in a Projectized environment?

   a) Project requirements are to be frozen and restricted for updates before the team can get into their construction phase

   b) Project team building activity need not be the responsibility of the project manager but might be the responsibility of the functional head.

   c) Projects exist in every organization and executed in a closed environment

   d) Stakeholder identification, kick-off meetings, managing change requests and integration of several planning phases are part of the project management

9. You are assigned as a project manager for a new project. As you begin to work on the project, you find that the project size keeps growing along with the scope of the project. At some point, you begin to worry about your ability to manage the project due to its complexity and the critical schedule. In a meeting with your project stakeholders, you hear that there was another project executed by your organization, which was very similar to yours. What should you do in this situation?

   a) Ignore the information since you are confident about your own skills and ability to drive the project successfully.

   b) Contact the Project Management Office (PMO) and ask for assistance and details about the project artifacts of the other project executed in the past

   c) Contact the Project Manager, who managed the other project and ask for help to resolve your issues

   d) None of the above

10. **The primary reason for organization to have Project Management Office (PMO) is to**

    a) Interfere and take the management control of the project, if the project manager struggle to bring the project under his control

    b) conduct reviews on the project processes and approve them

    c) conduct quality reviews and audits

    d) provide support to the project managers with process guidance, templates, forms, audits, historic information

11. **Your organization is in the manufacturing sector and supplies specific components to the customers on need basis. Whenever the company receives an order for components, the company signs a contract with the customers. The company has multiple priority preferences to its customers depending on the size of the contract signed. As part of the company's business strategy, the company has decided to treat all the contracts valued above $300,000 as projects while the rest will continue to be operational activities. The decision is taken to give the customers the best that they deserve.**

    You are working on an 'order' that is valued about half a million dollars in deliverable. As per the company, yours become a project and you are asked to manage the project. You are given 3 months to complete your 'project' and is not required to do any planning, prepare cost budget and no need to manage the stakeholders. All that is expected is to produce the product as per the given specification and get it verified before delivering to the customers.

    Is this qualify to be called a project?

    a) It does not qualify to be a project since, the objectives of the activities do not meet the definition of a project. You do not plan for anything, the activities do not have a predetermined start and end dates given and the objectives are not unique or progressively elaborated.

    b) It is obviously a project, since your organization has taken a strategic decision.

    c) It qualifies to be a project since it has a strict deadline given and has a cost associated with the order.

    d) None of the above

12. Laura has replaced Mary as a project manager in the middle of the project execution and she is monitoring her team performing the construction activities. She had few change requests coming in from the stakeholders and is working towards getting them approved. Meanwhile, the situation in the project is chaotic with absence of processes, lack of templates and unclear documentation to help drive the project. Upon investigation, Laura finds that she is not able to find any of the process planning done by Mary.

    What should she do?

    a) Trace the whereabouts of Mary and find out if she could help in getting the processes straight

    b) Since Mary has left the project, Laura should begin establishing the processes required for managing the project without impacting the current construction activities or schedules

    c) Report the issue with the PMO and make sure they coordinate with Mary and get the processes created by her

    d) None of the above

13. You are assigned as a project manager for an upcoming project. You are told that you are required to manage the cost, schedule and delivery requirement from end to end, whereas the department head will manage the resources.

    What type of organization do you belong to?

    a) Projectized

    b) Functional

    c) Matrix

    d) None of the above

14. Which of the following is NOT true about Triple constraint?

    a) Quality is impacted if there is change in scope but cost and schedule remains same.

    b) Scope, Cost and Schedule have direct impact on quality

    c) The quality of the outcome gets better with an enlarged scope of the deliverables

    d) A project manager should always be very careful while accepting change requests since changes impact one or all of the triple constraints.

ANSWERS

1.   **Answer: B**

     Justification: The definition of a project says, it is an unique endeavor with predetermined start and end dates and is progressively elaborated to produce an end result or outcome.

2.   **Answer: C**

     Justification: The issue narrated in the question do not qualify to be considered a project work, since it was a problem resulted by an implemented project. Since every project should produce an unique result within a determined start and end dates and is required to be progressively elaborated. The issue Rodney encountered is good to be considered as operational work, which includes problem fixing.

3.   **Answer: D**

     Justification: The actual role played by Jack in his organization is that of a project expediters, who work as assistants to the functional or departmental head with no authority. Most of the time the project expediters spend their time collecting details and preparing reports to be shared with the functional head. On the contrary, Sarah is part of a Projectized organization, which means she has complete responsibility, ownership and control over her project objectives and resources. She is responsible for planning the budget, schedule, resources till the project deliverables are verified and signed off by the customer.

4.   **Answer: A**

     Justification: Obviously, the project manager takes the complete command and control of the projects in an organization, where contracts are converted as projects for execution. The project manager becomes the owner of his project and takes complete responsibility from start to finish of the project. He identifies his team during the planning phase of the project and releases them once the project objectives are met.

5.   **Answer: B**

     Justification: What Rob has done is unacceptable in terms of the professional standpoint of a project. Irrespective of the magnitude of the change being request, a wise project manager thoroughly analyze the quantum of change being requested and investigates the impact of carrying out the change onto the design document. An 'initial brief' review of the change requested might appear simple, but there are more likelihood of such changes having larger impact elsewhere on the project components or objectives.

6. **Answer: A**

    Justification: Going by the narration of Allan's work, it clearly indicates that he do not do any planning or estimation of cost or schedule. He do not pick his own team members but simply work with the team that is already in place. He do not even estimate the production targets for any particular day but simply accepts the target set by his supervisor. The product that is produced may be unique vehicle model, but that uniqueness was not resulted by any of Allan's responsibilities. He do not have a target start or end dates. All these are characteristics indicate that he simply carries the production of specially built vehicles based on a military order.

7. **Answer: C**

    Justification: In a functional organization, the scope of managing project is very less as the projects are controlled by the functional head. Project managers work as assistants to the functional head and have no authority over the team or their assignments. The team do not report to the project manager.

8. **Answer: D**

    Justification: Identifying and managing stakeholders, scheduling kickoff meetings and managing change requests are some of the critical tasks to be performed by a project manager. Choice (a) appear to be true, but the project scope cannot be restricted from getting updated as there are more chances for the change requests knocking the door of the project team. Such change results in the project scope getting updated to have a new scope baseline. Choice (b) is incorrect since the scenario of this question specifically speaks about a projectized organization and not a functional one.

9. **Answer: B**

    Justification: The very purpose of most organizations having a Project Management Office (PMO) is to provide support to the project managers, whenever there is a need of process related artifacts, templates, guidance, forms and any historical information that might be of help. In this case, asking for help from the other manager may not do much good to Deborah. The best option for her is to consult the PMO and seek details of the project artifacts of the previously executed projects.

10. **Answer: D**

    Justification: The answer for this question is similar to the question 9. The primary responsibility of the PMO is to have control over all the processes, templates and historic information related to every project executed by the organization. In addition to these, the PMO can help the project managers with guidance on quality audits, work product reviews and troubleshooting requirements with respect to the project management issues.

11. **Answer: A**

    Justification: Irrespective of the volume and size of the contract signed, this do not qualify to be called a project. A project, as it is defined, has certain characteristics to be called so. Unless a project getting initiated formally with a project charter or preliminary scope given, there cannot be any planning done to arrive at a detailed scope, not to mention about the other planning components. The project resource requirement do not get planned in this case. The project simply accepts the order and produces an outcome for the customer requirement.

12. **Answer: B**

    Justification: The very purpose of Laura being brought into the project as manager is the failure of Mary from handling her own responsibilities. Having said that, approaching PMO or Mary to get the processes to establish the processes is not going to work well. The better option for Laura is to begin analyzing the important issues and bottlenecks of the project and begin working on creating the processes that will help straighten the things up. While doing so, Laura should make sure the current construction schedule is not impacted and look for urgent issues for a fix.

13. **Answer: C**

    Justification: Whenever you see statement such as "team will report to the functional or department head" it simply means you are not talking about a projectized organization. In a projectized organization, the team report to the project manager. In this case, the project manager is responsible for managing the project, its processes and owns the deliverables whereas the Functional Manager owns the project resources. This is a perfect example for a matrix organization, wherein the functional head go by the project manager for project related decisions.

14. **Answer: C**

    Justification: On the contrary, an enlarged scope of the deliverable means more areas of quality concern to the project manager. An enlarged scope means more features of the outcome of the project, each of which needs to be verified for scope compliance.

This page is intentionally left blank

Project Management Processes

Objectives

At the end of Project Management Processes chapter, you should be able to understand:

- How the project management processes are organized and interrelated
- the details of process groups, processes and knowledge areas
- what comes first and performed next
- what is an Organizational process assets and Enterprise Environmental Factors

I am pretty sure, you are aware that every project has its lifecycle and the processes are executed in a specific sequence in order to achieve the project objectives. You must have worked on Software Development Life Cycle (SDLC), if you are from the computer software industry. Assume the project lifecycle to be the equivalent of SDLC. The main difference between SDLC and Project lifecycle is SDLC is about the steps involved in developing an application beginning with understanding the requirements and end with a developed and a tested application ready for implementation on the customers' system, whereas project lifecycle is all about how the projects are planned, managed, monitored and closed.

A project is managed with the help of process groups, multiple processes, knowledge areas, tools, templates and every piece of information available with the project manager. A project manager generates huge amount of data, templates and forms as the project makes headway into various phases from start to finish. We will be reading about these in detail in the next several chapters of this book.

How a Project is Managed

When you are managing a project, one key thing you should keep in mind is how a project is executed, what processes are performed in the project and what goes in and what comes out of each of the processes. In addition to these, you should be aware of how to process the information and what tools fit best to your project. We will be using several tools to process the input information to produce a desired output of each of the process.

At this moment, remember that every process uses multiple tools to process the input. Do not get confused that every process is required to use all the tools that are listed against that particular process, which need not be true. Probably, you will understand this better and in detail, as we make further progress with the processes.

In short, a project is executed as a sequence of interrelated steps, each of which performs a specific task. These tasks takes specific data or information as input and produce a processed data or information as output, which might become input for another process and so on.

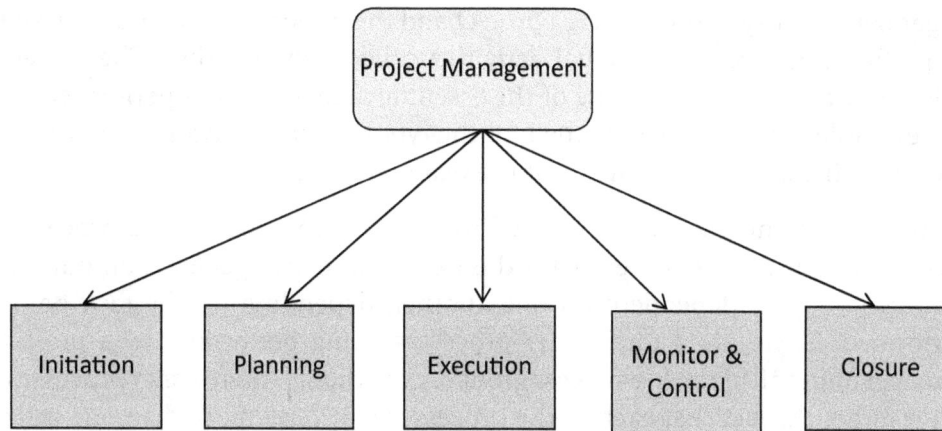

The above diagram illustrates project management process groups. The five activities shown in the above diagram (such as Initiation, Planning, Execution, Monitor & Control and Closure) are called Process Groups. Hope, you are now clear on what a process group is all about, as the names are self-explanatory.

In other words, a Process group is a collection of multiple processes. We will learn more on the process groups and processes in the next few pages.

What are Processes?

To illustrate a process in simple term, you are a project manager who successfully completed a large project and want to throw a party to your team. How do you go about organizing a party?

- You would want to plan the type of event to organize
- Decide on the invitees to be part of the celebration
- Finalize the venue
- Decide on the time of the event
- Estimate the cost for the party
- Finalize the menu and activities during the event
- Get the party on
- Have fun and don't forget to take pictures to remember the memories
- Settle the bills

If you consider each of the above bulleted points as individual activities that are required to be completed in order to get your plan into reality, then you are talking about processes.

Organizing a party to the team is a project and the project objective is achieved by performing several individual activities collectively together. The project objective wouldn't be met if one of the essential activities is not performed. In this example, if you haven't planned for the type of food in advance, you would end up with displeasures of many of the team members.

A Project is an integration of the five Processes groups. Each of the processes accept an input, process them with the help of a tool to generate an output. Processes may be dependent on one another, depending on the task being performed. There are a total of 47 processes being performed by a project manager under all of the five process groups. Even though there are 47 processes, never forget the fact that each of the processes may have more than one tasks for a project manager to execute.

As an example, if a project manager is generating a status report as part of a process, he may have to do lot of work and get all of the columns filled in the status report. Each of this effort involves one or more tasks for the project manager. We will understand this as we learn more on individual processes.

Typically, every project begins with Initiation process group followed by planning. These two tasks are primarily performed by the Manager, who are identified to manage the project and its outcome. In the Execution process group, most of the tasks are performed by the staff members of the project team under the supervision of the Project Manager. The Monitor & Control process group are to monitor and carry out amendments and changes, as required. The last of the process group, Closure process group is the primary responsibility of the manager. In the Closure process group, validating the project outcome is done against the original scope followed by administrative and financial closure activities are performed by the manager, besides collecting details of the issues, risks and lessons learnt during the various phases of the project.

Remember that every process can be part of only one process group. You cannot do the same process across process groups.

To clarify more, if you consider a sample process say, Cost budgeting. You will not be doing the cost budgeting in initiation or monitoring & control process group. The cost budgeting is done only in the planning phase.

(When there is a change request raised, which might result in a cost update, it is done through a separate change management process, which is part of the monitoring & control process group)

Process Challenge

From the initial understanding of the processes and process groups, why not try to match the processes against their respective process groups

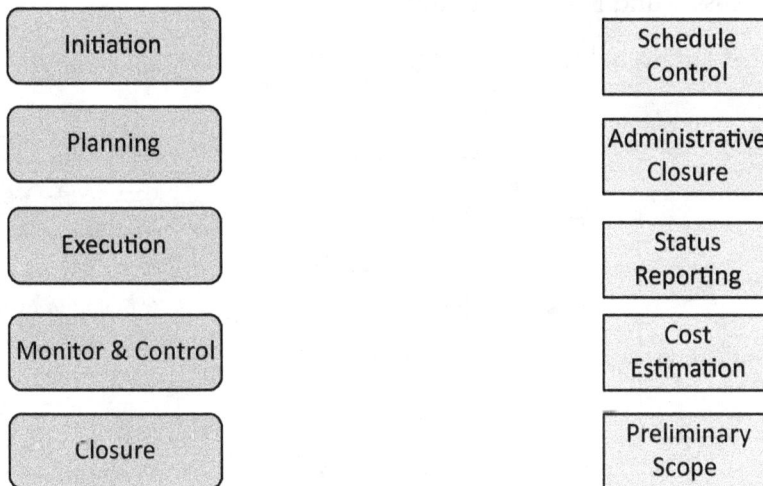

I recommend you to check the answers below and validate yours

Answers

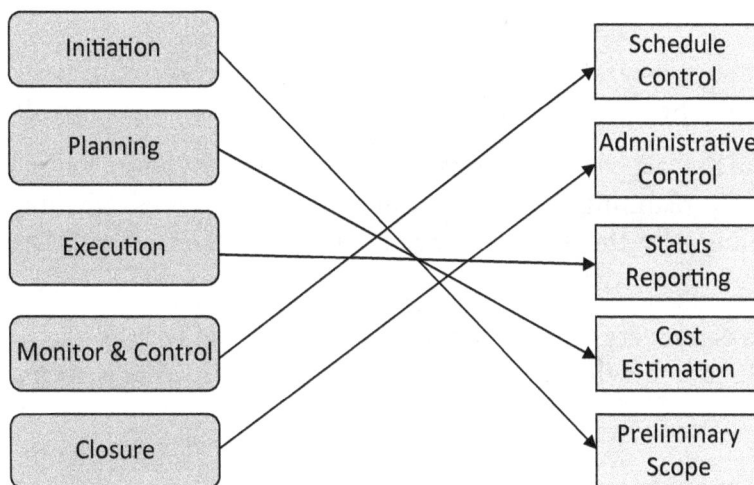

How Process Groups, Processes and Knowledge Areas are Related

Now, you might be having a question on the relationship between Process groups, Processes and Knowledge Areas.

Look at the diagram below for easier understanding

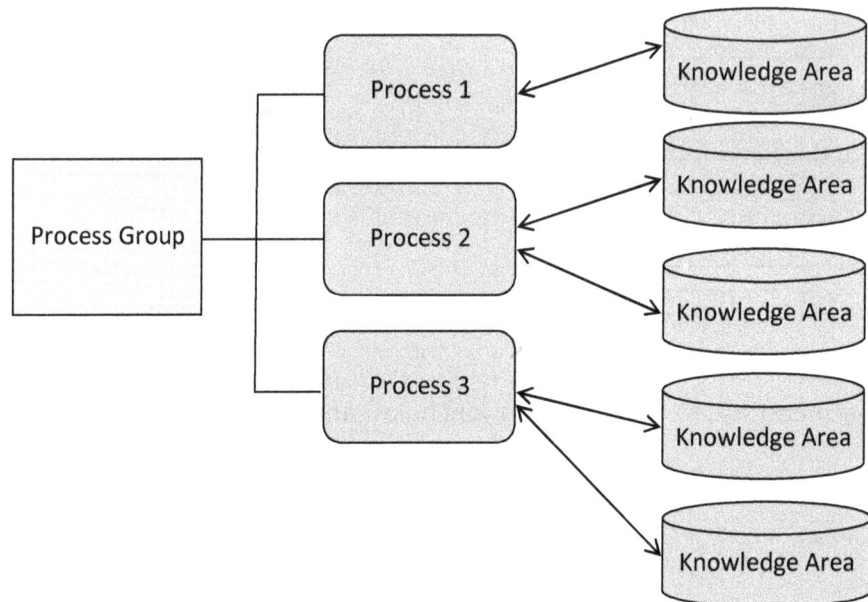

From the above diagram, you can see that every Process group has processes under it. Every process has relationship with more than one knowledge area.

To illustrate the last part of the above sentence, assume you are in the planning process group planning for your cost budgeting. You access the outputs that were generated by the Time Management process and Scope Management process.

I hope this is not very difficult to understand. Now, let us take a look into the below table to know the list of processes to be performed in a normal project execution.

Process Groups					
		Initiation	Planning	Execution	Monitor & Control	Closure
Knowledge Areas	**Integration Management**	Develop Project Charter	Develop PM Plans	Direct Project Execution	Control Project work / Perform Change Management	Perform project closure
	Scope Management		Collect Requirements / Define Scope / Create WBS		Scope Control	Validate Scope
	Time Management		Define Activities / Activity Sequencing / Activity Resource Estimation / Activity Duration Estimation / Develop Schedule		Control Schedule	
	Cost Management		Cost Estimation / Develop Budget		Control Costs	
	Quality Management		Quality Planning	Perform Quality Assurance	Perform Quality Control	
	Human Resources Management		Develop Human Resource plan	Acquire Project Team / Develop Project Team	Manage Project Team	
	Communication Management	Identify Stakeholders	Communication Planning	Information Distribution / Manage Stakeholders	Monitor Communication	
	Risk Management		Risk Management Planning / Identify Risks / Qualitative Risk Analysis / Quantitative Risk Analysis / Risk Response Planning		Monitor Risk	
	Procurement Management		Procurement Management Planning	Conduct Procurement	Monitor Procurement	Procurement Contract Closure

How a Process Group and Processes are Related to Each Other?

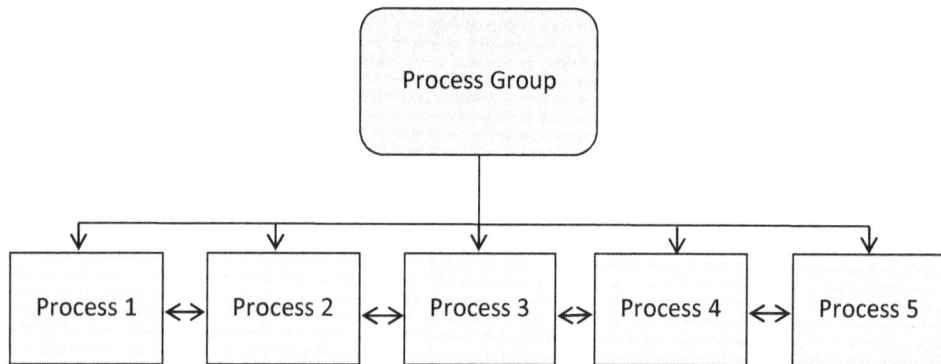

```
                    ┌─────────────────┐
                    │                 │
                    │  Process Group  │
                    │                 │
                    └────────┬────────┘
                             │
   ┌──────────┬──────────────┼──────────────┬──────────┐
   ▼          ▼              ▼              ▼          ▼
┌────────┐ ┌────────┐   ┌────────┐   ┌────────┐ ┌────────┐
│Process1│←→│Process2│←→ │Process3│←→ │Process4│←→│Process5│
└────────┘ └────────┘   └────────┘   └────────┘ └────────┘
```

Remember that each of the process in a process group may be interrelated and bidirectional as narrated in the diagram above. Similarly not all the processes need to be performed for every project. As an example, not every project involves procuring products or services from external vendors. A better way to plan for the processes is to list, what is to be performed by the project and what is not.

Let us now move onto individual process groups and discuss what forms part of these groups.

Initiation Process Group

To begin with, you will perform the groundwork for the project planning. This task is called **Initiation Process group**. In this, you will get assigned as a Project Manager and be given very high level expectations, budget and beneficiary details among few other inputs to consider. Using the project charter, you are expected to come out with preliminary scope statement, which is an extended version of the high level requirement.

The high level requirement is found in very brief as Project Objective in the Project Charter. During the initiation phase of a project, detailed expectation of the project is unknown.

Remember that, even though Project Initiation process group has two processes listed above, there are many activities to be done by the project managers.

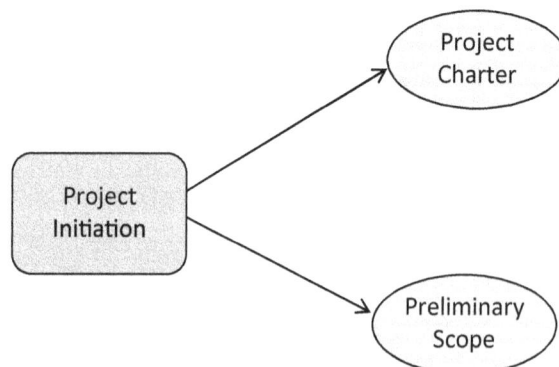

```
                                        ┌──────────┐
                                        │ Project  │
                                    ╱──→│ Charter  │
                                   ╱    └──────────┘
              ┌──────────┐        ╱
              │ Project  │───────╱
              │Initiation│───────╲
              └──────────┘        ╲
                                   ╲    ┌────────────┐
                                    ╲──→│ Preliminary│
                                        │   Scope    │
                                        └────────────┘
```

Take the example of Project Charter. A charter is the document that assigns the Project Manager to the project besides giving very high level overview of the project scope and other expectations. At times, a project manager might end up creating the project charter. In such cases, it is for the Project Manager to identify the high level cost details, objectives, expected delivery dates. Each of these activities involve sufficient amount of effort.

In short, a Project Charter doesn't mean preparing a formal document and share with someone, but involve multiple activities to be performed before arriving with this project charter.

Let us now try to list down the tasks that are performed before the initiation process group and the purpose of doing them. Remember that not all of these activities are done by every project manager but only optional. A project manager might begin working on the project from any stage.

Activity performed	Purpose of activity
Business Requirement Analysis	The need for executing a project and the possibility of achieving the required objectives without a need for a separate project is analyzed. An extensive analysis is done about intended users, benefits to performing organization, alternate options, existing setup and what if the project is not executed (gains and loss of opportunities)
Product or Service analysis	Description of the product or service being planned as part of the project, service and cost benefits of the outcome
Market Analysis	Analysis of the existing competitors, advantage of having the project outcome, impact of the outcome on company business & strategy
Skilled resources availability	The potential human resources available within the organization, their availability, requirement, expertise and benefits of engaging them in the project
Execution Strategy	Strategy on how the project may be executed, whether fully in-house development or outsourced. Analysis on the impact of both these strategies.
Customer/User Analysis	Detailed understanding of the customer/ users and analysis of working with them in the past. Any issues and points to be noted in this regard
Business Risks	Any potential business related risks in executing the project and their impact on the business prospects of the customer

The above are only sample activities being performed prior to initiation process. There may be many more activities, depending on the Organizational requirements.

Business Need and Purpose of Project Execution

Unless there is any market or strategic and cost advantage, no organization will want to spend money and resources to execute a project. This is called the Business requirement that mandated the project requirement.

Thus, it is the primary responsibility of the project manager is to identify the business case that led to this project required to be executed. This will help the project manager plan for the project and have better control over requirement, schedule and scope.

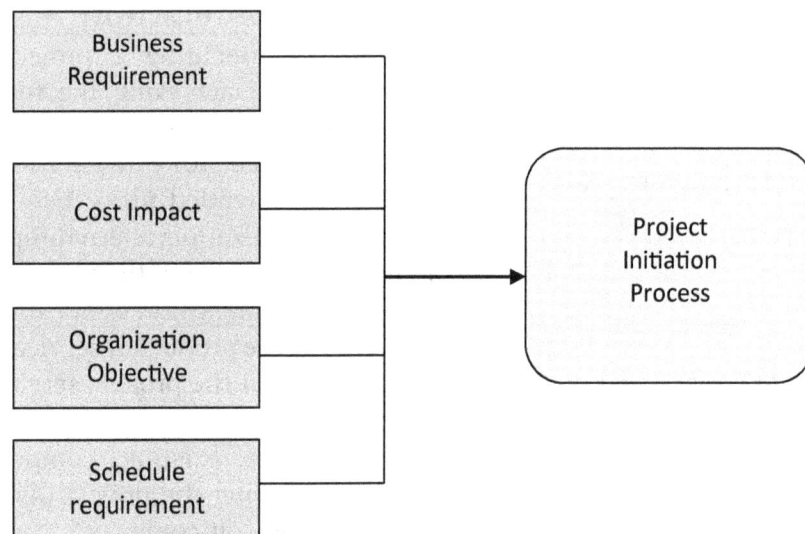

```
┌──────────────────┐
│    Business      │──────┐
│  Requirement     │      │
└──────────────────┘      │
                          │            ╭─────────────────╮
┌──────────────────┐      │            │                 │
│   Cost Impact    │──────┤            │     Project     │
│                  │      │────────►   │   Initiation    │
└──────────────────┘      │            │     Process     │
                          │            │                 │
┌──────────────────┐      │            ╰─────────────────╯
│   Organization   │      │
│    Objective     │──────┤
└──────────────────┘      │
                          │
┌──────────────────┐      │
│    Schedule      │──────┘
│  requirement     │
└──────────────────┘
```

In the above diagram, Cost impact refers to the high-level expected cost of the project, while the schedule requirement refers to the delivery expectation from the customer.

Project Planning

After Initiation phase, your actual job of detailed planning starts. This phase is called **Project planning** phase. We will be discussing lot about the ten knowledge areas and most of the 47 processes during the planning phase of the project.

Let us now take a brief look into the activities performed in each of the knowledge areas.

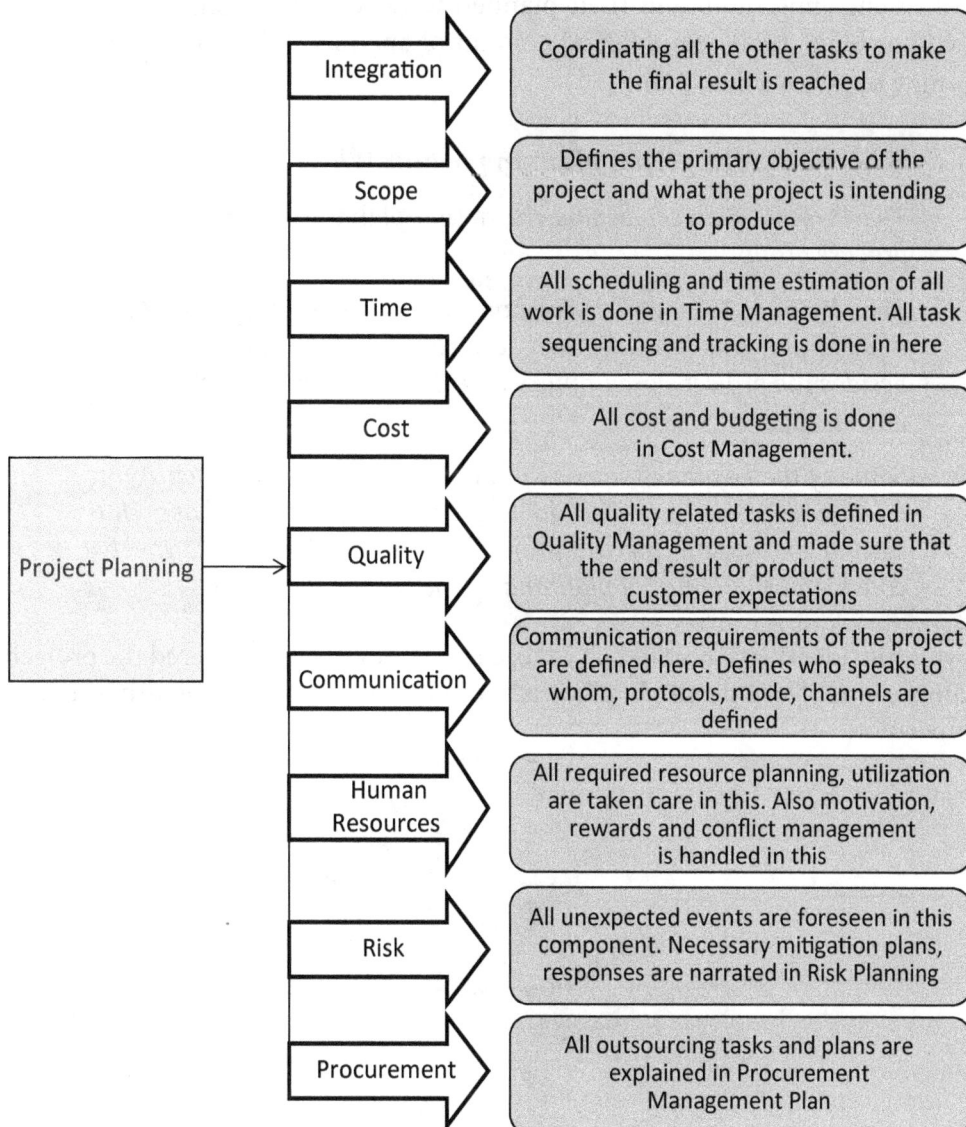

Integration	Coordinating all the other tasks to make the final result is reached
Scope	Defines the primary objective of the project and what the project is intending to produce
Time	All scheduling and time estimation of all work is done in Time Management. All task sequencing and tracking is done in here
Cost	All cost and budgeting is done in Cost Management.
Quality	All quality related tasks is defined in Quality Management and made sure that the end result or product meets customer expectations
Communication	Communication requirements of the project are defined here. Defines who speaks to whom, protocols, mode, channels are defined
Human Resources	All required resource planning, utilization are taken care in this. Also motivation, rewards and conflict management is handled in this
Risk	All unexpected events are foreseen in this component. Necessary mitigation plans, responses are narrated in Risk Planning
Procurement	All outsourcing tasks and plans are explained in Procurement Management Plan

Project Planning →

As a project manager, you plan for each of the above components, which are also called as knowledge areas. Good amount of effort is spent by the project manager to transform all of these knowledge area components into a more meaningful and realistic plan components during the project planning phase. Besides planning for each of the processes, whole lot of data and information is collected by way of multiple processes that would help plan for each of the processes under each knowledge areas.

For example, when the cost is being planned for the project, the project manager refers to the list of available resources, their current engagements, duration of their availability, duration of the task, target start and end dates of the tasks, cost of engaging them and their planned work for future. Similarly, each of the knowledge areas require good amount of analysis and workaround before coming out with a final plan.

Tidbits

Where does the actual planning begin? Why?

The Project manager begins the actual planning in the initiation process group.

The Project Manager is responsible for collecting the basic information and provide high level estimate the dates and cost besides the project's preliminary objective while the project is in the initial stages.

Some of the key tasks such as project kickoff meetings, identifying a leadership team are also done during the initiation phase, thus setting the ground for the project's start. All these tasks involve considerable amount of planning by the project manager.

If you consider the project to be a cake, each slice of it are considered the project components. Not one single piece is more important, while the other is less important.

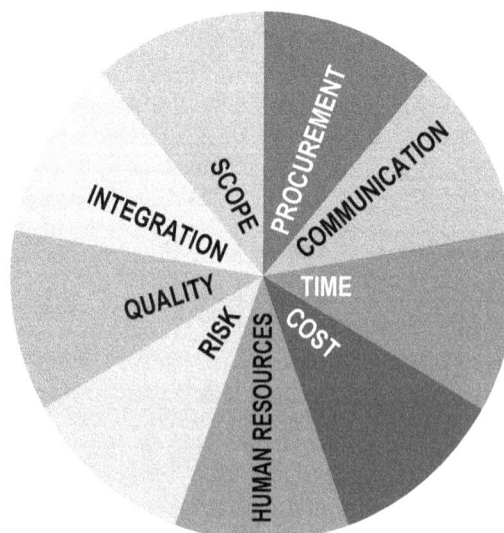

During the **Execution** phase, you really set the ball rolling with the actual work getting done. Though your team has most responsibilities of this phase, you will still hold the responsibilities such as identifying and acquiring the project team, managing the project execution by the team members, gathering work performance information, handling unexpected risks, their resolution, communication issues as your primary responsibility.

Besides the above, much more responsibilities lies with a project manager during the execution phase. Some of them include

Activity	Purpose
Ensuring clarity of the scope among team members	Project team should be made aware of the scope of their work, expectations and their boundary
Managing the stakeholder expectation	The project manager should make sure the project is progressing as per the expectations set and discuss any issues with the stakeholders
Team building activities	As part of the human resource management, hold team building activities to keep the team focused and motivated
Hold scheduled team meetings	Hold regular team meetings to understand the progress of the activities, problems and risks. Prepare meeting minutes and circulate among all the participants to confirm the understanding
Project deviations	Keep an eye on any policy or scope deviations
Troubleshooting issues	Project manager can use the technical expertise and management capabilities to troubleshoot any problems during this phase
Process improvements	Constantly work towards improving the processes with the help of real time project progress, issues and risks encountered

The Project Manager is expected to stay on top of his project team to track the work being executed and look for any challenges, surprises and opportunities during the execution phase. In addition to these, there are chances of more risks, conflicts and new issues coming up as the team is engaged in construction activity.

During the **Monitoring & Control** phase, you will monitor the progress being made; analyze variance in cost, schedule and their impact on quality. Also, you will be handling the most critical task of Change Management. A Change

Management is very critical in the sense that it has the potential to decide the fate of the project. The projects testing and implementation tasks are planned and monitored and executed in the Execution & Monitoring phases.

At this point, you should note that Execution and Monitoring & Controlling phases are performed repeatedly till project objectives are achieved. The reason being, as you make progress with your execution phases, there are much possibilities of the original scope requiring many updates and multiple change requests might come up.

I would equate a change management process itself with a project, but of much lesser magnitude, since it involves a good amount of effort on gathering information, planning, discussion, revising baselines of scope, cost and schedules and so on. Impact analysis can also be performed prior to getting the change management implemented.

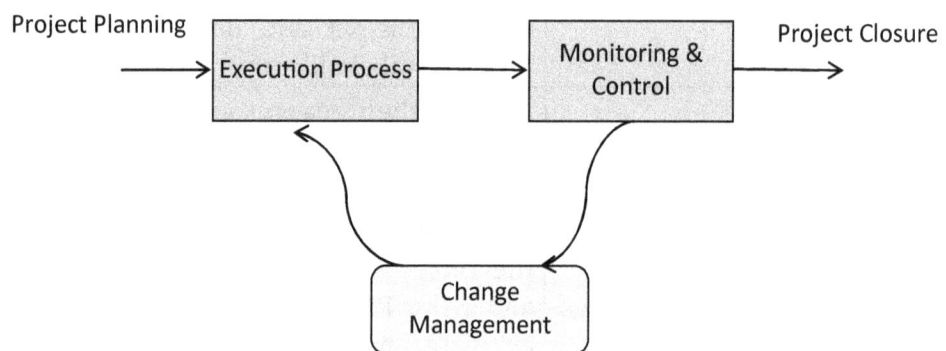

Project Planning   Project Closure

```
             ┌──────────────────┐      ┌──────────────────┐
  ──────────→│ Execution Process│─────→│   Monitoring &   │──────────→
             │                  │      │     Control      │
             └──────────────────┘      └──────────────────┘
                       ↖                         │
                        ↖                        ↓
                       ┌──────────────────┐
                       │      Change       │
                       │    Management     │
                       └──────────────────┘
```

For every updates to the original scope or objectives of the project, the scope baseline need to be revised forcing the project team take care of the changes requested.

Finally, the wrapping up formalities of your project is performed in the **Close Project** phase. This phase is to be performed after the objectives of the project are achieved. The project team should be complete with their development of the product or outcome, verified their conformance to client requirement by way of testing, prepared to implement the product or outcome.

In the Closure process, the project manager will perform the project's administrative and financial closure.

Administrative Closure : In the administrative closure phase, the scope verification is done by the project manager involving the other stakeholders. The purpose of this is to make sure the developed product or outcome is in conformance to the customer expectation and requirements. A formal signoff is obtained from the stakeholders after the verification of the scope is completed.

In addition to this, all the project related artifacts such as risk, cost, resource, quality, schedule and other important information are gathered and uploaded

into the respective organization's process repository as historical information of the executed project. Such uploaded information provide a vital resource for future projects as reference information.

Financial Closure *: All cost related data are collected and settled to the last dollar and cost statement is reconciled and verified against the cost estimation and the actual spending. All financial settlements are done to the vendors, who provided the required components or services to the project.*

Did you ever come across a situation, when your customer or your organization decide to scrap the entire project when your team is in the middle of their construction phase?

In such situations, what would you do?

Irrespective of the project completion or termination process initiated, the project manager is expected to follow all the project closure process such as administrative closure, financial closure, collecting all the lessons learnt, project assets and artifacts and storing them in the organization's process repository for future reference by other project managers.

Similarly, if the project is shelved for any reason, the Project manager releases his team and gets them redeployed into other assignments before the project is formally closed.

Key Components of Project Management

There are a couple of subjects you will be coming across too often in this book.

•   Organization Process Assets

•   Enterprise Environment Factor

Organization Process Assets

Every organization of this professional world maintains a repository of historic data, lessons learnt, list of risks and how they were handled, assumptions made, issues encountered and their subsequent resolution, quality related information, schedule and cost related details in their repository. In short, the entire project relation information and data goes to the organization's repository as historical information.

Historical information is one very critical component that helps in the planning and execution of every project. It is a trove of project related information and experience of other project managers, which were executed successfully or unsuccessfully by your organization. Usually, all these historic information are controlled by the Project Management Office (PMO) of every organization. Whenever you kick start your project, it would be wise to have a representative of the PMO to be part of your project so as to collect all historic information and to coordinate with your project tasks and audit requirements.

This repository and the information provide very vital inputs to every project that is executed by your organization. While this data is important, it is to be noted that they can be customizable to suit individual project needs. As an example, a cost budget of a similar project executed in the past might be customized by the current project to arrive at a Cost baseline.

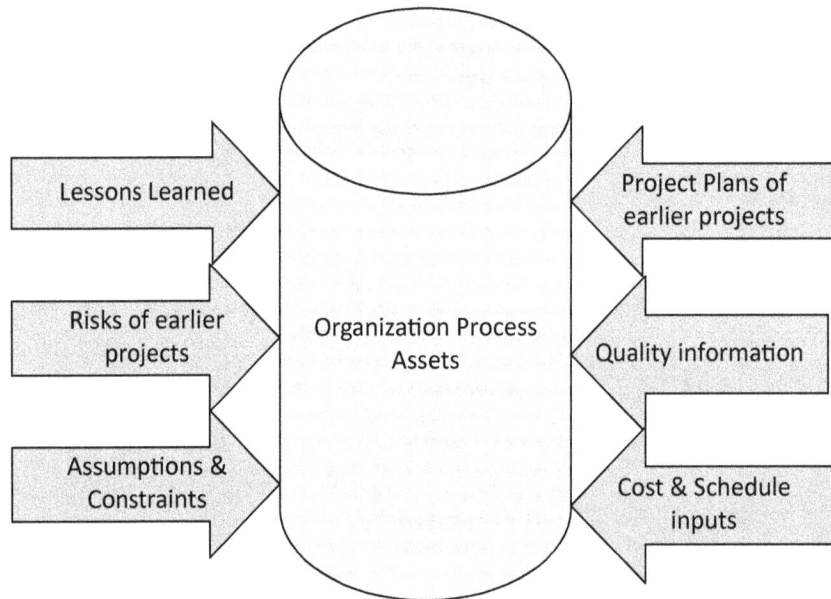

Using the below table, can you list any of the project resources that are available in your Organization's process repository.

Process Asset	Purpose of the asset

Enterprise Environmental Factors

Every Organization has its own processes, work environment, policies and project execution methodologies that are unique to it. These factors differ between one organization to another, between regions and cultures as well. Sometimes legal obligations decide certain requirements of the organization.

In short, an Enterprise Environmental factor provides guidance as to how your organization runs business and executes work.

While having these factors may not entirely alter the scope or objective of the projects, it is recommended to pay attention to understanding the business environment, model and methodologies of your organization or your customer while planning for the projects. The reason for this being, your Organization might have demonstrated its capability, project execution methodology, process compliance and tools to the customers. You wouldn't want to ignore any of these factors while you plan on your project execution.

Does it make sensible?

What Goes In & What Comes Out

How does each of the process work?

To get the work done, you require certain input and a processing done with the available input. The inputs, processes and outputs might differ between each of the process and knowledge areas. However, each of these inputs and outputs are interrelated.

The simple process that takes place in each of the processes are narrated in the below diagram. I am sure it is not difficult to understand this

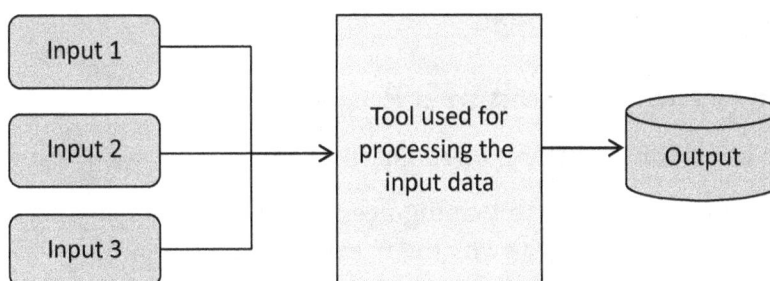

Input   :   Usually, the output of one process becomes input to another process. However, you will find that the standard input for many processes are the Organizational practices and historical information

Output   :   The processed data of one process is the Output. In most cases, such output are used by another process to carry out specific processing

Tools   :   A tool is used to process the input and to obtain a desired output. Example of a tool can be Project Management Information System or PMIS, which is a project management tool and organization's process assets that houses various organizational standards, templates and forms. Similarly when you are working on a travel services business, the online booking portal becomes a very good tool that helps you process the input from your customers.

Note that the output of one process can be input to another, whose output becomes input to another. I do not want to confuse you with an example here, since it is too early to narrate this. You will understand this better, as we make progress through the planning process group.

More on Planning

Why a Planning is Required

Let us recall the example of a movie making venture, that we discussed in the previous chapter. No project will be complete without planning its tasks in advance. This includes planning for resources, equipment required to make the film, funding, scheduling and a lot more stuff. A planning helps in better co-ordination, appropriate use of resources and having funds at the requirement time besides making the film itself. Unorganized handling of any project will result in mere chaotic situation, ballooning of cost and schedule. At the end, the entire project itself will collapse.

Am sure, this helps in understanding the criticality of the project, project leadership and the project team.

Who Does the Planning in a Project?

If you are asked this question, you might instantly reply "Project Manager."

But, it is not entirely true. A planning need not be done only by the manager. However, a project manager owns the overall project planning responsibility, on behalf of the team. He is accountable for all the work that is done by the team as well.

Then, who are all part of the planning process? The answer is anyone in the project team can be part of the planning process.

Take the case of a new product being planned. The Manager doesn't do all of the planning. If a design document is to be prepared, the respective team is assigned the task. Members of the design team takes up the task and begin to *plan* their work. Good amount of brainstorming and analysis are required to be done, that involves scheduling. Similarly, Risk planning might involve all the stakeholders and the team. It would be interesting to note that Risks are part of the agenda of every team meeting.

Setting Up Overall Goal for the Project Teams

Ideally, the overall goal of the project is similar to the high level scope defined in the project charter. The high level scope is elaborated further into detailed scope statement. However, the overall goal is broken into individual tasks, depending on various teams of the project and assigned to them. In other words, each of the teams, such as designing, development, Quality control and testing, will be assigned individual responsibilities and expectations. All these objectives are closely aligned with the overall objectives of the project itself.

As a strategy, if you are planning to subdivide your project into multiple subprojects for easier managing, make sure you set the goals for each of the sub-projects that aligns with your overall project goal. This will ensure easier tracking.

Identifying the List of Tasks and Objectives

The best approach to identify the list of tasks is to take the top-down approach. Do you have any thoughts on how to list down the planned list of tasks to be performed during difference phases of the projects?

One of the critical element that might come in handy in this is the use of historical information from the Organization repository. Every organization maintains the record of previously executed projects, tasks performed, lessons learnt, risks, issues and assumptions. This information is kept for reference purpose. Unfortunately, many PMs, even the better ones, doesn't pay much attention to the historic information. The historical information is nothing but someone else's real time experiences. May be, it might remind you of some tasks that might have gone missing from your mind while planning.

Another useful approach is to involve the team and get their inputs while listing the tasks for the project. Use of Work Breakdown Structure (WBS) chart will help schedule the overall list of tasks. We will be learning more on the Work Breakdown Structure in the Scope Management Plan chapter.

Identifying the Project Team

Identifying the team, that executes the project is one big challenge often faced by the managers. Reasons vary from availability of desired skills, their time, and location constraint to name a few. Sharing resources sounds like a good idea, however, many factors are to be considered before planning to engage shared resources into a project.

Availability of the resource at the right time is a very critical factor that might have impact on the completion of the relevant task. If a resource is shared among projects, communication between the managers becomes critical as well. If you decide to optimize any of your resources across projects, clarity on the plan is essential to eliminate potential resource utilization conflicts in future.

At this point, it is to be noted that the Project manager is not expected to possess technical knowledge on whatever project that is being managed. However, a project manager should be strong with managing skills and should have sufficient knowledge on the processes, communication skills, confidence and easily approachable to the stakeholders and anyone who are involved in the project.

An ideal project team would consist of technical and functional experts besides the workforce that is really working on the deliverables. A representative from the Project Management Office would prove to be very useful in guiding the project with their expertise. Most organizations, especially in the Information Technology sector have a dedicated Testing practice that provides testing support to the development team. This is very helpful to eliminate any defects or issues before the deliverables are delivered to the customers.

A sample project team structure could be found in the below diagram

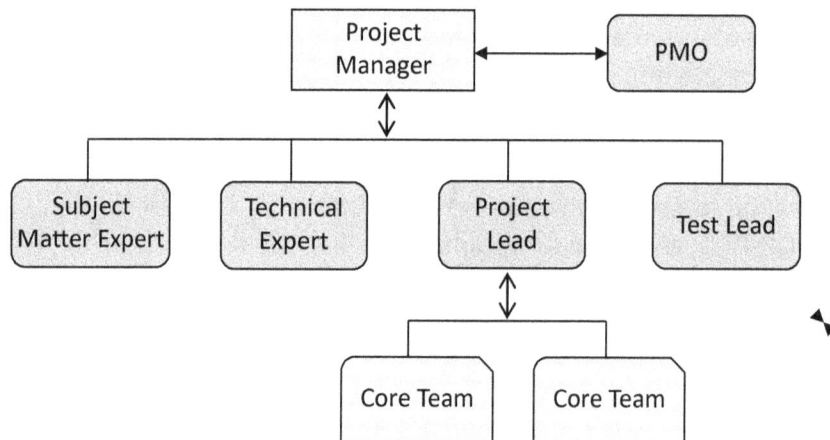

Identifying the Post-Completion Support Needs and Relevant Planning

An intelligent manager plans for everything much in advance, even if it is not critical during any of the phases of the project. One such critical task is the post-implementation support activities. This may not be a critical task or even considered out of the project scope, but paying attention to the planned support activities might even give some insight into any potential issues or risks during the project execution. In other words, imagine yourself to be an user, when you are working on a project. What would you expect from a project that you have interests in?

The issue of providing support happens to be tricky at times. You may not be the same person, who is going to handle the support responsibilities of your own project. In many cases, you might become a stakeholder of the support activities as well. The post-implementation support activities may be a continuous process with no end dates set. You might be able to understand the significance of such support activities well, if you realize that the original project objectives and the support requirements are interrelated.

Remember that Project Management is not all about preparing documents that runs into number of pages. The information relating to the project are kept in the form of easily understandable data to help the others.

Case Study

Let us assume you are given the responsibility to manage a 5 KM marathon event in your town of over 100,000 population. The theme of the event is 'Blood donation and its importance to community.' The event is organized by your town council and funded by several corporate having operations in the town.

Could you list all the activities you will require to do to get this entire event completed and successful? Use your project management skills to come with the list in the blank space below.

EXERCISES

True or False

1. In the Knowledge area planning, Risk management has the top most priority due to its criticality   (**True** / **False**)

2. A process can be part of more than one process group   (**True** / **False**)

3. Integration management means integrating each of the knowledge areas together   (**True** / **False**)

4. Execution and Monitoring process is performed repeatedly till the project objectives are achieved   (**True** / **False**)

5. Planning task is done only by the Project Manager   (**True** / **False**)

Fill in the Blanks

1. You can find all company policy related information in the _____ _____ .

2. _____ is the document that 'nominates' a project manager to a project and sanctions authority to manage the project and make decisions.

3. _____ and _____ process groups are performed repeatedly till the project deliverables are ready for verification.

4. The primary input to the scope statement process is _____ .

5. The last scope process is performed in the _____ process group.

ANSWERS

True or False

1. False
2. False
3. True
4. True
5. False

Fill in the Blanks

1. Enterprise Environmental Factor
2. Project Charter
3. Monitor and Control
4. Preliminary Scope Statement
5. Closure

Test Your Knowledge

1. You are managing a project that will create a new application software for a large banking customer of your organization. You are already done with your project planning and have the baselines approved by the stakeholders. Your team is currently working on the development phase. You are expecting them to complete their construction activity in another 6 weeks.

   Which process group is your project currently in?

   a) Monitoring & Control
   b) Initiation
   c) Execution
   d) Pre-closure

2. You are the project manager of a construction project that is aiming to build a massive oil pipeline between an oil refinery and a nearby city. Your team of construction workers are busy with their work and you are engaging quality supervisors to inspect the work being done and its worthiness. During one such inspection, your quality supervisor notice an underground rail line intercepting the proposed pipeline. He raises serious concern since such an interchange means dangerous condition for both the train network and the oil pipeline. Your management is not impressed with this lapse in planning and want you to immediately look at the option of rerouting the oil pipeline away from the existing railway line. You consider this as a change request over the existing scope of the project. You have prepared a change request with the details of the issue and alternative options to submit to the Change Control Board.

   Which process group you are in now?

   a) Planning
   b) Monitoring & Control
   c) Change Process
   d) Execution

3. Which of the following is NOT a stakeholder of a project

   a) A buyer who buys the company's products from the market
   b) The project team that has just completed construction of the project and is testing it
   c) The testing team that has been assigned the task of validating the project deliverables
   d) The department head, whose request resulted in this project execution and is funding the project.

4. In which of the listed project group, the WBS Dictionary gets created
    a) Initiation
    b) Execution
    c) Monitoring and Control
    d) None of the above

5. You have completed with the Work Breakdown Structure and WBS Dictionary for your project. Your key project personnel are being identified. One of your stakeholder from the customer organization approaches you with a request to include a dedicated quality person be included in the project The stakeholder informs you that you can charge for this quality resource as the customer is worried over increasing issues being reported by the user group at their end over the quality of the product in the past. You realize that the quality of the project outcome was largely impacted due to indiscriminate changes to the original scope. Nevertheless, you decided to consider the stakeholder's request to add a quality control resource into the team.

    Which of the process group, you are currently in?
    a) Initiation
    b) Execution
    c) Monitoring & Control
    d) Planning

6. The project team has completed its construction and testing phase of the project deliverables. They are busy with collecting all the lessons learned and other historic information of the project to consolidate and upload into the organization repository. You are having a discussion with the stakeholders over validating the project deliverables against the scope. During the discussion, one of the stakeholder from the customer end claims there are some defects identified by the testing team which might have serious impact on the implementation of the solution. It appears that a key change requested by the stakeholder is missing from the scope of the deliverable and he cannot approve the results unless this functionality is taken care as soon as possible. You agree to get the fix in place as soon as possible.

    Which of the process group are you in?
    a) Closure
    b) Monitoring and Control
    c) Execution
    d) Initiation

7. Your project team is done with their construction phase of the project and the testing team has done their job. You have notified your stakeholders about the completion of the development and testing phase of the project and requested the testing team at the customer end to verify the deliverables against the scope agreed earlier in the planning phase. After a week, you are notified that the customer has done the verification and identified some issues in the deliverables. It appears that certain functionality of the deliverable is impacting another business unit of the company, who wanted this discrepancy be fixed immediately to maintain the market leadership through innovation of new ideas and technology. Upon investigation, you realize that this was not your fault, since your scope of project was decided by the customer, who gave the initial requirement.

   The customer has agreed to fund the requested change and wanted you to begin working on the change to the project scope. In this scenario, which project phase you would be working on?

   a) Begin with the project initiation phase, since the change requested is totally new and deserve to be considered a project.

   b) Start with planning phase, since you have the project charter on hand already and you will work with the same stakeholders and the application

   c) Immediately begin the closure process and seek a signoff from the customer on the completed scope before you could consider the new change as a separate project.

   d) Work on the monitoring & control process group, since the requested change needs to be analyzed and documented.

8. The project planning process group is the primary responsibility of the

   a) Sponsor

   b) Project team

   c) Project Manager

   d) Project Management Office

9. The overall responsibility of Triple constraint rests with

   a) The scope is the responsibility of the customer, while the project manager takes care of the quality and cost

   b) Project manager is responsible for all the components of the triple constraint

   c) The PMO owns the project schedule and cost, while the project scope is owned by the project sponsor and the project team is responsible for the quality of the deliverables

   d) None of the above

10. You are assigned as a project manager and given a project charter. Based on the high level expectation and your meeting with your customer you could collect more inputs on the project requirements. The customer reviews the preliminary scope document and gives his consent to proceed further. The customer makes it a point to stress the urgency of the project completion and do not want you to waste time and committed all their support from their end. So, it becomes important for you to start working on the project as quick as possible.

    What is the next task that you are expected to do?

    a) Begin working on planning for the project and work on creating subsidiary plan components.

    b) Prepare a risk register and include the urgency of the customer as a risk and include the customer's expectation as a risk and begin working on mitigating it

    c) Tell the customer that the project can be completed only according to the resource availability and urgent delivery may not be possible.

    d) Start working on identifying the team members and assign tasks to them, since the customer do not want any time to be wasted due to the urgent requirement.

11. Where can the details about the risks of the previously executed projects be found?

    a) Enterprise Environmental factors

    b) Identify the name of the project manager and contact the person

    c) Check with your supervisor and seek his guidance

    d) Contact the Project Management Office (PMO)

12. In which process group, a project cost is tracked by the project manager?

    a) Monitoring and Control

    b) Initiation

    c) Execution

    d) Planning

ANSWERS

1. **Answer: C**

   Justification : Whenever you hear about construction or development is in progress, it ultimately means the team is in the execution phase. The execution phase is considered complete only when the development activities are considered finished and the deliverables are ready for testing or review.

2. **Answer: B**

   Justification : In this case, the project team is busy with their core development work, which means the work is not complete. The customer finds a serious trouble in the original scope and they want it to be fixed by you to ensure safety of the community and the oil pipeline. This is a perfect example of a change management process. You have the analysis done and change request prepared, which is awaiting scrutiny by the Change Control Board. All these activities are part of the Monitor & Control process group.

3. **Answer : A**

   Justification : A stakeholder is someone, who is part of the project and scope of the deliverables and are positively or negatively impacted by the execution of the project. It may be anyone in the customer organization, yourself, your project team or anyone associated with the project. However, in this case, a buyer is someone, who is outside the scope of the project. Probably, the features of the product are attractive to the buyers, they chose to buy the product.

4. **Answer : D**

   Justification : A WBS Dictionary is created along with the Work Breakdown Structure in the project scope planning process. It consists of detailed information about every work packet or task that is planned to be performed in the project. This means, WBS dictionary is created in the Planning process group.

5. **Answer : D**

   Justification : Based on the narration of activities given in the question, it appears the project team is not yet identified which means the execution phase has not commenced yet. You are working on identifying the team, which can happen in the project planning process group.

6. **Answer : A**

   Justification : The question is little tricky. As per the narration given in the question, the project is in the closure phase and the stakeholders are reviewing the deliverables to verify its conformance to the agreed scope.

During the discussion, it seems there was a concern raised by one of the stakeholder about a discrepancy in the deliverables in the form of a missing requirement. You haven't began your analysis of the nature of the issue or the quantum of fix that may be required. At this moment of time, you are part of the scope verification process, which is part of the Project Closure process group.

7. **Answer : D**

   Justification : The whole issue is the result of a unclear scope definition in the initial phase of the project. Without getting into discussing, who is right and who was not, the fix require a change process to be initiated. Whenever such a change request is received, it is the responsibility of the project manager to investigate the change requested and have the justification ready supporting data to take the change requested to the Change Control board for their approval.

8. **Answer : C**

   Justification : Project planning is the primary responsibility of the project manager, who decide on how he is going to run his project and monitor it. The PMO can only provide guidance and support wherever required, in terms of templates, historic information and forms. An important point to remember, when engaging the PMO is that the group do not manage the project, but only limited to supporting the project manager and his team, whenever required.

9. **Answer : B**

   Justification : All the components of the triple constraint (namely Scope, Time, Cost and Quality) are the responsibility of the project manager. The project manager is expected to plan, manage and monitor all of these subsidiary planning processes. The project manager is also responsible to exercise his control over any change requests that are raised by any of the stakeholders that might directly or indirectly impact scope, time and cost component of the project, which ultimately impacts the quality of the project and the deliverables.

10. **Answer : A**

    Justification : Irrespective of the urgency and pressure being exerted on the project manager or the team, it is the responsibility of the project manager to plan on the project's subsidiary components. There may be many situations, when the customers require the solution or deliverables reach them quickly. However, the project manager may not be aware of the possible delivery and plan unless he works on the schedule and develop it. The project's core team cannot begin working on their work packages unless the project schedule, scope and cost are approved by the sponsor.

11. **Answer : D**

    Justification : All the historic data and other information about previously executed projects are available in the organization's process assets. In most of the organizations, the Project Management Office is given the ownership of maintaining the organization's process assets. In this case, it would be appropriate to contact and engage the PMO for any information requirements.

12. **Answer : A**

    Justification : It is in the monitoring and control process group, the project managers monitor the status of each of the planned components, including the cost performance of the project.

This page is intentionally left blank

This page is intentionally left blank

Integration Management

Objectives

At the end of Integration Management chapter, the reader should be able to understand:

- what is an integration management and its significance in a project
- the role of a project in getting the processes integrated
- the seven important activities that goes into a project execution
- the importance of project charters and its use for the project manager
- what is a preliminary scope statement and how it gets prepared
- what is a project planning
- who executes and the role of the project manager in the project execution
- how the projects are monitored
- what is a change control process and how it is handled
- what forms part of the project closure process

What is an Integration Management?

Imagine a situation wherein you are planning to conduct training in your organization. Out of faith in your organizational and managing skills, the management of your organization lets you plan, organize and conduct the training by yourself. Thus it becomes your responsibility to coordinate all tasks and make sure the training program goes as per your plan.

When you begin preparing for the training session, you realize that planning and coordination are the most critical tasks of completing the training session successfully.

What Can Possibly Go Wrong?

You realize that you cannot perform all tasks by yourself but require significant amount of coordination with other groups, vendor, teams and resource groups in order to achieve your training objective. You have listed down the tasks that are essential for the successful completion of your training session. Unless you perform each of these tasks on time and in the same sequence, it will result in chaos in your training sessions.

For example, you may be ready with a projector but not the training content. Imagine your position, in front of the participants of your training program.

Similarly, you have the assessment questionnaire readily available, but you are running late to the training by 2 hours. Does having the assessment and all gadgets going to be of any help?

If you have every gadgets and materials on hand, but couldn't get the training hall booked?

What would the above misses result in?

I bet, your boss will never find such a poorly organized event in his lifetime? Your management is not going to be impressed with your organizing skills. Are they unfair in their judgment?

Certainly they are not.

When you execute a project or any major task, integration becomes the key factor that decides the acceptance and even a success or failure. It is the task of managing to get multiple processes tied together to produce a great result successfully, meeting everyone's expectations and needs.

You may be a great cook, but unless you plan and coordinate your entire tasks well, you will not be able to produce a great food. Integration can also mean effective coordination between multiple processes executed in an appropriate sequence. Unless this coordination is there, it will not result in efficient delivery but only confusion and chaotic situation among stakeholders.

Integration can be defined as a coordination of multiple tasks to achieve a unique objective. From a project management standpoint, performing multiple interrelated activities to produce an end result that meets the customer expectation and conformance to standards.

In a real time project environment, the efficiency of the Project managers is visibly seen in the successful execution and coordination of multiple teams, tasks and processes. Even if the entire team has done a great work in producing a product, the project will be considered a failure, if the end-product is not delivered to the customer on time or not meeting expectation. After all, the project team is only responsible for working on the deliverable.

However, a project is much more than construction alone.

What Does a Project Manager Do in Integration Management?

That's a very good question.

In brief, the Project Manager is responsible for the end-to-end project delivery, irrespective of the business type.

A Project Manager's responsibility begin after getting assigned as a manager of the project till the project gets closed. A project manager plans, monitors, troubleshoots, communicates, controls and closes the project. Unfortunately, in many project environments the role of Project Managers have become lesser important than the executing team. This is due to the misunderstanding that a project is all about producing an end product alone.

No wonder, many of the projects end up with failures due to poor management reasons.

However, in reality, unless a Project Manager does the job effectively, there cannot be an end result or successful execution of the project.

If you watched the movie 'Titanic' many of the lead artistes in the movie were pretty new or little known in the film industry. They might have to be taught the art of performance in front of the camera. Not all of their past movies were successful at the box office. But, the skills of the director of 'Titanic' compensated for all these and no wonder the movie leaped into the history of the film industry. A project manager can be equated with that of a movie director.

Do you agree?

Boundaries of a Project Manager

If you are asked to define the boundary of a project manager in his project, how would you define?

I would say, it depends on the organization he/she is working in. As we saw in the previous chapter, there are three types of Organization viz. Functional, Matrix and Projectized Organizations.

For practical purpose, let us assume you are working in a Projectized Organization. Keeping this in mind, a project manager's role is seen all over the project, right from the project initiation phase till the closure of the project. A Project Manager exists as long as a project exists. The Project Manager controls the Project teams, cost, scope, schedule, risks, quality and decides on the execution of the project. Depending on the requirement, he can even break the project into multiple but manageable subprojects for easier handling. A Project Manager's responsibility extends to the level of releasing the project team after the completion and redeploy them into their next assignment.

In short, the Project Managers are the owners of the project and takes responsibility for the outcome of the project and the end-result.

What Gets Integrated?

Here comes the real question. What all components that gets integrated in a project?

In reality, it is the five process groups get integrated. As seen earlier, each of these process groups has 47 processes in all. Planning process group has 9 knowledge areas, each of which have their own subsidiary plans or plan components.

The below diagram represents the overall view of the entire project management lifecycle. Remember that all of the nine knowledge areas and forty four process are hidden in this diagram.

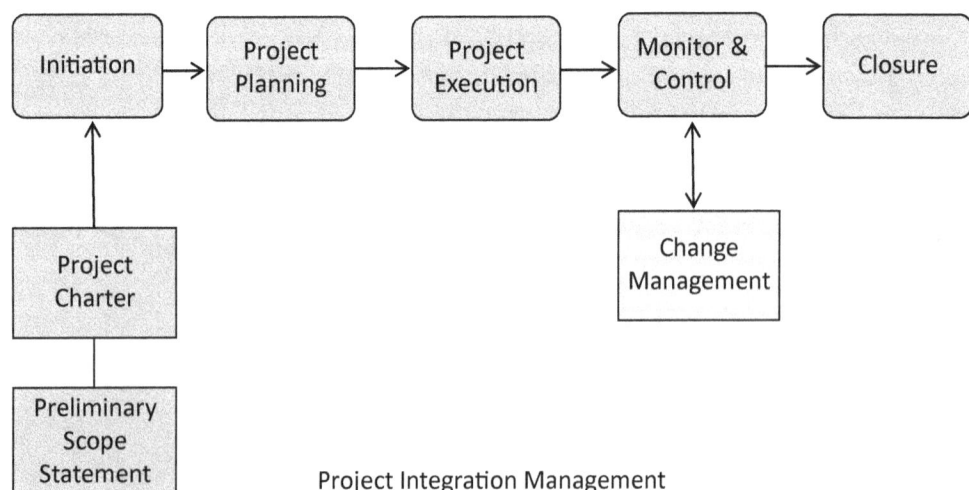

Project Integration Management

Process Groups Further Decomposed?

In all, there are seven key tasks that forms part of the Integration management that forms part of the five process groups.

- Develop project charter
- Prepare preliminary Scope statement
- Develop Project Management plans
- Execution of the project
- Monitor & Controlling of the project
- Change Management
- Project Closure

Integration of all these above seven tasks is collectively called *Integration Management*. The sequence of tasks and their critical nature should help you understand the importance of the process groups.

Each of the above tasks gets an input to produce an output. It needs to process (Here, do not confuse with the 47 processes that we discussed as part of Process groups) the input to produce an output, same as how a computer program does.

Project Charter

Being one of the preliminary documents that are prepared by either the Project Sponsor or the Project performing organization, sometimes the Project Manager is directly involved in the preparation of the Project Charter. However such charters need to get approved by the sponsor. The project charter is prepared as part of the *project initiation* process group. Since the charter is prepared at a very early stage of the project execution all the information it contains are high level in nature.

The Project Charter provides authorization to the Project Manager in performing the responsibilities through all the phases of the project from beginning till its closure. The Project charter also defines the high level requirement besides schedule, key stakeholders and proposed budget etc.

There are no prescribed or strict rules about the format for a project charter. Just make sure, it gives a overall or high level view of the objectives of the project for the senior executives, who may be more interested in the overall cost, schedule and objectives.

Prior to working on the project charter, it would be good to verify whether a charter does exist or should it be prepared by you. The below diagram illustrates the 'Develop project charter' process for your easier understanding.

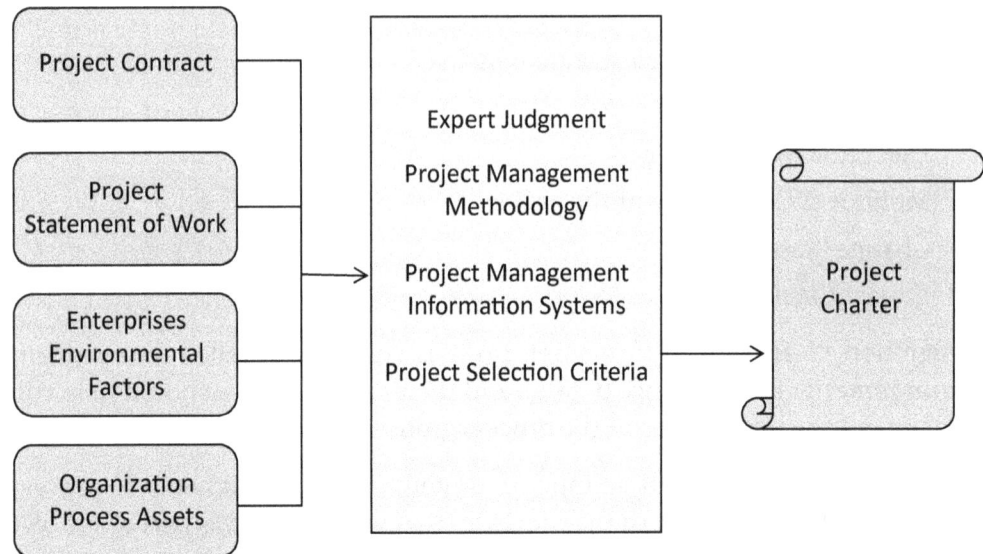

Inputs to the Project Charter Process

Irrespective of who prepares the project charter, there are some essential inputs that goes into the process of preparing a project charter.

Since the project charter is to provide a high-level objectives of the project in few lines, the information can be obtained from the *Project Contract* and *Project Statement of Work* (PSoW). Besides the objectives, the Contract and PSoW provides some very high level expectations agreed between the customer and the project performing organization. Some of the key features of these expectations can be referenced in them.

While preparing a project charter, understanding the business strategy of the performing organization is the most important aspect since every organization has its unique business strategy and policies. These details are referred as the *Enterprises Environmental Factor*.

Similar to the above, Organization's process assets provide assistance in the preparation a project charter. In fact, if a Project Manager is new and is assigned the responsibility of preparing a project charter, the first place he/she should look for a template is the *Organization's process assets*.

Tools Used in Project Charter

From the above diagram, you can notice several tools that are used in the preparation of Project Charter. To narrate each of them in detail

Expert Judgment

Every Organization has several experts and experienced resources that have in-depth knowledge of projects and project management methodology of the performing organization. They might help as a valuable tool in guiding the projects. Getting them occasionally involved and their inputs would eliminate issues that might come up in future.

A project charter is not just a document to be typed and shared with others. It should include some basic details that conveys the overall objective and expectations of the project to the senior managements of the customer and project performing organizations.

An expert's hand might be of great help in identifying the charter requirements.

Project Management Methodology

Exploring more knowledge and utilizing them to complete one's job is always exciting. Is it not?

The world has plenty of knowledge and resources available that might offer solutions to occasional challenges that one face in the project. Project Management Institute (PMI) has a great repository of Project Management methodology in the form of experiences from other Project Managers. Project Management – Book of Knowledge (PMBoK) is one such resource that will answer many of the questions of a project manager. The PMBoK has multiple process groups and all the processes defined in detail. Sometimes, reading some other project managers' experiences in a magazine might guide others in having a strategy with respect to managing their own projects.

However, every organization has a unique way of managing these processes and in a particular sequence depending on their project execution methodology. You need to consult your Organization's way of project execution for more detailed inputs on this.

Project Management Information System

The Project Management Information Systems (PMIS) are standard tool available in the market that help manage the projects.

An example of such readymade tool is Microsoft Project Planner. Such tools have several helpful options to choose to easily plan and manage the project tasks.

Project Selection Criteria

Every organization has certain policies with respect to executing projects.

Imagine a situation of two organizations, one specializing in developing Banking & Financial application solutions while the other is developing Healthcare based applications.

These organizations have their own strategies and policies with respect to choosing projects to undertake. Some of the factors such as having expertise, resources to build their products, available technology and infrastructure play a crucial role in their decisions. One company is more keen to tap the huge market for the Banking and Financial application market and decide to focus on it, while the other sees huge potential in the Healthcare domain.

Though they both operate in the same industry, they have their unique strategies in choosing projects to execute for their clients. In this case, the companies mainly focus on their line of business or respective business units.

Their individual project selection criteria fall within two primary categories. They are *Benefit Measurement Model* and *Mathematical model*.

Benefit Measurement Analysis

A *Benefit Measurement Model* is the most common way to choose between projects. Simple mathematical calculations are used to identify the benefits such as cost and risks to the organization before approving or rejecting the project proposals. In many cases, Organizations take a strategic decision while choosing projects. Such decisions might result in exploring new avenues or aimed at other larger projects in the pipeline or even community goodwill.

Also known as *murder board*, this project selection methodology means involvement of multiple key members of an organization assembled together to analyze the benefits and risks involved in execution of a project. Participants of such meetings ask too many questions to kill the project proposal for various different reasons. Such brainstorming sessions help analyze various aspects of selecting a project for execution.

Mathematical Model

The mathematical model of project selection involves analyzing plenty of data related to pros and cons of the project execution, cost benefits and various other factors. Certain complex mathematical formulae are used to arrive at the quantitative benefits of executing such projects. Hence, this is called *mathematical model*.

At this point, one should remember that there is no strict rule about the content of a project charter. It is a document that provides required and available information to the Project manager and provides an understanding of the objectives to the available stakeholder.

Now, let us take a look into a sample Project Charter prepared for an Organization.

Spectrum Aerospace Plc.
Ann Arbor, MI 17021

PROJECT CHARTER

Project Name	: **Production Management System**
Description of Project	: Spectrum is planning develop a new model helicopter named Hercules S210 that will replace the ageing Hercules S170 vehicle.
Project requirements	: The objective of the project is to design and build the Hercules S210 with most advanced features and not detected under radar. The primary focus of the Hercules S210 helicopter is to serve the military use.
Assigned Project Manager	: Bob Dylan PMP
Level of authority of PM	: The Project Manager will be given overall authority to initiate, plan, direct, control and closure of the project. He will be responsible for planning and tracking cost, schedule and will be owner of the resources that are working on the project.

Milestones	:	Initial phase	: June 01 – June 19, 2014
		Prototype Design	: June 24 - July 07, 2014
		Project Planning	: July 01 – July 31, 2014
		Product Dev.	: Aug 20 – Dec 19, 2014
		Testing & Trials	: Jan 03 – Jan 21, 2015

Stakeholders	: The project will have Jack Dawson of the Product Development as a key stakeholder besides Paul Aspin of the Marketing dept., Jack White will represent Corporate Strategy and David King will represent Technical support
Assumptions/Constraints	: Estimated project budget: $ 18 Million. Assembly & testing facility would be made available at the company's Ann Arbor production base.
Business justification	: The existing Hercules S170 is being retired from production as part of Company's business strategy. A more advanced version of the Hercules model is to be released with latest available technology and to help the company stay above the competitors.
Signed	

---------------------------   -------------------------------
Steve Cook   John Chambers
Project Director   Executive Vice-President

One of the key component in any planning phase is to work in an vacuum space with respect to requirements. In other words, not all the expectations are known in the initial stage of the projects. More often, the project manager and his team may end up with ambiguous information, which might keep them guessing. However, such ambiguity doesn't stop the project clock as well.

To overcome this scenario, the project managers can make assumptions about the unknown parts and include the effort for this assume portion in the schedule and cost estimates. This assumptions are highlighted specifically to the customer and get their concurrence before proceeding with the project planning. It is a recommended and globally accepted practice.

Similarly, constraints are any potential obstacle that might threaten the project execution at a specific point of time. These constraints are required to be highlighted to the customers and look for ways to overcome these obstacles.

We will be reading more on the Assumptions and Constraints later in the communication management planning chapter.

Project Contract

A project contract is scope of the work, the customer and the project performing organization have agreed to do as part of the project. The terms of the contract might include the project outcome, financial details, schedule and resources related undertakings from both the ends.

Usually, a project contract is prepared by the customer or by project performing organization with inputs obtained from the customer. However, the project contract is not a legally binding either the customer or the vendor until it is approved and signed by both.

Project Statement of Work

A Project Statement of Work (SOW) is a lengthy document that sets the customer's expectations for the project team to deliver. The SOW is the very initial document that originates from the customer with details of the delivery expectations, scope of the project outcome and details of the project's role in the organization's business strategy.

When the project manager begins working on the project charter, it is these details that serve as a starting point to understand the objectives.

Kickoff Meetings

One of the most important activity to take place during the initial phase of the project is the kickoff meeting involving identified stakeholders. At the initial stage of a project, it is not necessary to have the entire team or all stakeholders identified.

The purpose of the kickoff meeting is to have a handshake between the customers and project performing organization and understand the 'who's who' of both sides. Initial expectations and understandings are discussed in the meeting besides any specific expectations from either end. The project manager usually convenes the kickoff meeting.

Preliminary Scope Statement

A preliminary Scope is nothing but an expanded version of the high level requirement listed in the Project charter.

A high level requirement is nothing but a very short narration of the project requirement for easier understanding. It is further expanded to come with a preliminary scope statement. Vital inputs for preparing the preliminary scope is the contract signed with your customers and the statement of work, which is to be executed as part of the project. Besides the above two documents, you would be considering the Enterprise Environmental factors and any other organizational assets that may be available as historic information.

The preliminary Scope is mainly used for interaction with stakeholders to understand the requirement and the progress being made. Any change to the scope is carried out in the preliminary scope statement. Once all the updates and changes to the preliminary scope is collected from each of the stakeholders, the Project Manager would begin working on the detailed Scope statement, which becomes the baseline version of the overall functional requirement of the project.

At this point of time, you should understand that there is a difference between Scope statement and Scope management plan. Scope statement is the detailed and baseline objective of the project. However, scope management is how you plan to manage the scope.

We would be knowing more on the differences in the Scope Planning chapter of this book. So, stay tuned. The below diagram illustrates preparing the Preliminary scope statement

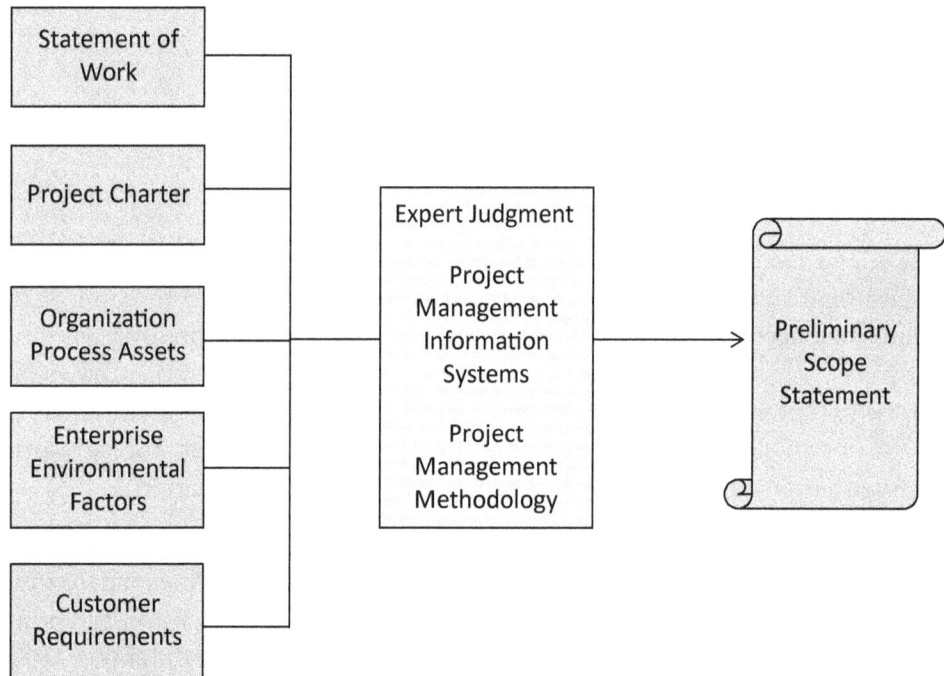

```
┌──────────────┐
│ Statement of │────┐
│    Work      │    │
└──────────────┘    │
                    │
┌──────────────┐    │      ┌───────────────────┐                    ┌─────────────┐
│Project Charter│───┤      │  Expert Judgment  │                    │ Preliminary │
└──────────────┘    │      │                   │                    │   Scope     │
                    │      │     Project       │                    │  Statement  │
┌──────────────┐    │      │   Management      │                    │             │
│ Organization │────┤      │  Information      │───────────────────▶│             │
│Process Assets│    │      │   Systems         │                    │             │
└──────────────┘    │      │                   │                    │             │
                    │      │     Project       │                    │             │
┌──────────────┐    │      │   Management      │                    │             │
│  Enterprise  │────┤      │   Methodology     │                    │             │
│Environmental │    │      └───────────────────┘                    └─────────────┘
│   Factors    │    │
└──────────────┘    │
                    │
┌──────────────┐    │
│   Customer   │────┘
│ Requirements │
└──────────────┘
```

Note from the above diagram that, we are using the same tools that were used to prepare the project charter. This means that there is no tailor-made tool available but one's expertise, project management guidelines and available resources are helpful in preparing these key initial documents during a project execution.

The primary purpose of the preliminary scope statement is to keep all the stakeholders informed of our understanding of the project objectives in an elaborated form and also to help prepare the detailed scope statement of the project.

Now, let us take a look into a sample preliminary scope statement from the below document.

Spectrum Aerospace Plc.
Ann Arbor, MI 17021

PROJECT PRELIMINARY SCOPE STATEMENT

Project Objective	:	The business objective of the Organization is required to be achieved
Expected outcome of the project	:	The end result of the project is to be narrated in this column
Project Acceptance criteria	:	Usually this is the verifiable portion of the end product or service
Project boundaries	:	This part is about limitations and constraints of the project. Also, the overall jurisdiction of the project is defined here.
Project Stakeholders	:	List the initially identified stakeholders of the project
Project Deliverables	:	List the agreed and expected deliverables to be produced by the project
Assumptions & Constraints	:	The initial assumptions and constraints, the project team working with.
Initial identified risks	:	List the risks identified by the Project Manager or the sponsor.
Scheduled Milestones	:	Agreed and expected milestones to be met by the project team along with the details of the phases.
Cost Estimation	:	The high-level and initial cost estimation is to be listed here
Approving Criteria	:	List the name of the approving authority against each of the deliverables

Project Planning

In short, the task of planning the project involves multiple processes being performed in a sequential order and according to the needs of the project. Ideally, each of the knowledge areas are focused and you plan your processes with expectations set for yourself and the team.

When I say Project planning, it means you will put in your strategy as to how you are planning to handle each of the 9 knowledge areas and associated processes. You will be setting the objective, boundary, expectations and how you plan to manage each of the plans. Subsequently, all of these plans become the driving force of your project till its closure.

It's always a good idea to define the templates that will be used to track the progress and other data in the planning phase. Don't forget to get an approval from all of the stakeholders. Why I am pointing this in particular at this moment is it might eliminate any misconception and expectations set right in the initial stages itself.

Does it make sense?

The below diagram presents the project planning process in a high level form. Note that each of the planning might involve a lot more inputs, tools and output. I recommend you to refer to each of the following chapters to understand how the planning is done for them.

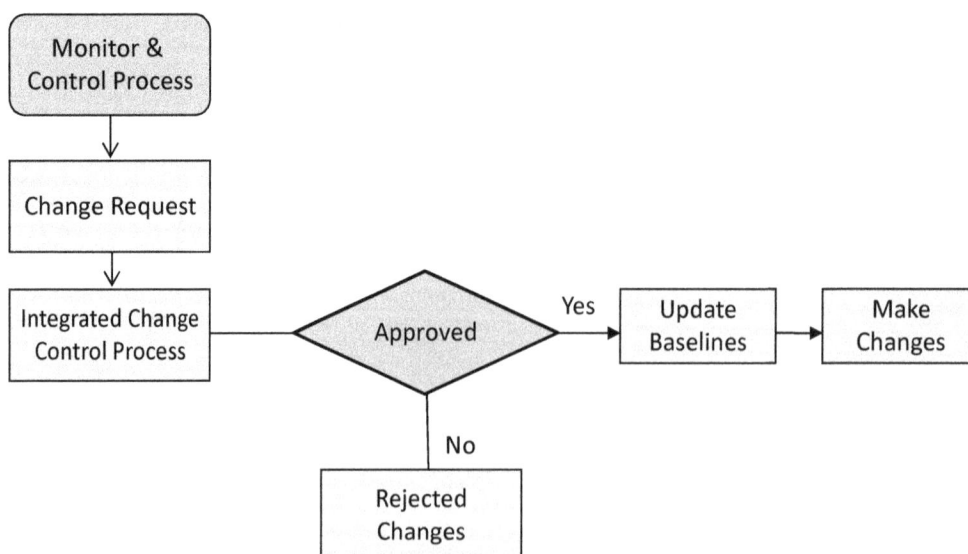

From the above diagram, Project Management Plans are prepared for each of the nine knowledge areas, depending on the project need. These Project Management Plans are also known as *subsidiary plans*. Such subsidiary plans are created for each of the knowledge areas namely

- Integration Management Plan
- Scope Management Plan
- Time Management Plan
- Cost Management Plan
- Quality Management Plan
- Human Resource Management Plan
- Communication Management Plan
- Risk Management Plan
- Procurement Management Plan

Detailed views of each of the knowledge areas, their focus and contents are explained in the subsequent chapters. For now, please remember that Project planning is one of the seven key components of project execution.

I am sure, the above inputs gives a fairly good idea on the project planning process. We will be learning the details of this planning phase throughout the book for different knowledge areas and in the form of several processes.

Project Execution

This is the phase, where the actual work of the project takes place. The team is now set with expectations, design, specifications, project plans and objectives. The outcome of the project execution phase differs between industries. It is called development phase that produces deliverables in the software industry, while the construction phase producing products in the production based projects. It is also called construction phase in different businesses. All of these refer to the same activity.

As a Project manager, you have the responsibility to track the execution phase and to resolve any issues or risks that might come along. All of your plans, prepared during the planning phase are to be strictly followed by your team during the execution phase and the Project Manager is responsible for tracking and collecting the *work performance information* of the processes.

Work performance information is the quantitative data that keeps track of the efficiency of each of the subsidiary plans applied in your project. The work performance information is important information that provides idea on the health and progress of the project, as per your plan.

Let us see more of the Project Execution phase through the below diagram

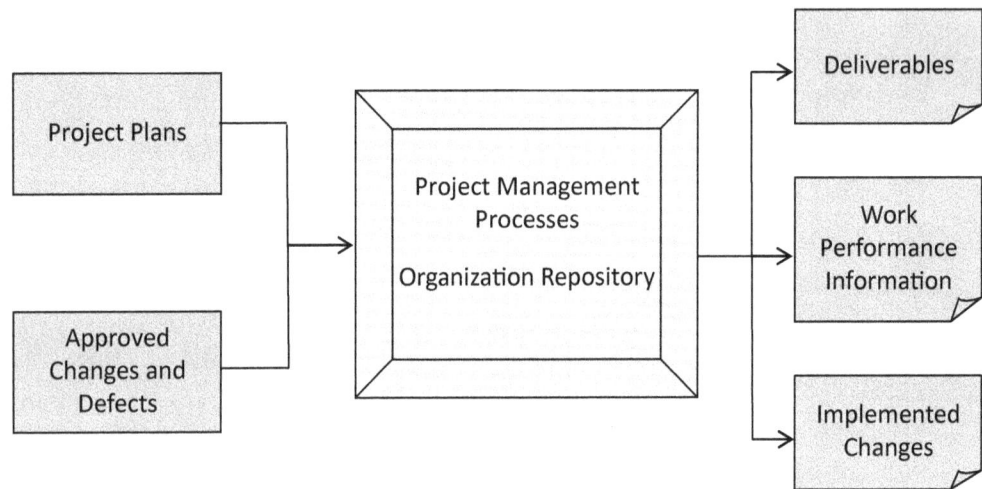

Project Execution Phase Explained

In the above diagram, we use each of the project plans (subsidiary plans) to manage the work being performed by the team. In fact, the project management plans that you prepared in the planning phase are put to use to the maximum extent in the Execution phase of the project.

As an example, let us assume the team is working on their respective product construction. A couple of team members find their products have dependency on each others. To have better clarity on the dependency both of them setup a meeting together and begin discussing. At some point, they get into difference of opinion on their approach. Unable to sort out the issues among themselves, they approach you, their project manager.

What would be your reaction to this issue?

As a project manager, you should be referring to the Human Resource Management Plan that you have prepared in the planning phase of the project. A smart manager would first listen to both the team members, keep them cool and will begin to understand the problem before attempting to resolve.

Similarly, what if one of the resource complains that she is running behind her schedule by three days due to an unexpected issue. This delay might impact her other scheduled activity and so want her other task adjusted with revised dates.

The WBS is the right place to look for schedules and dependencies between tasks. It may or may not be easy to reschedule but certainly the smart project manager has planned for such unexpected scenarios while creating the project plans.

The tools being used are primarily the Project managers' expertise and the organizational standards and repository of project management.

Now, if you have observed the above diagram, you are most likely to raise a question as to why Approved Changes and Defects are considered as inputs in the execution phase. You should remember that the Execution and Monitoring & Controlling phases of every project are performed several times repeatedly depending on the need.

Every organization has specific standards, policies and documents relating to managing their projects. These are considered best practices for the organization's business, vision and business objectives.

In other words, when the project execution phase is being performed for the first time in a project, there are unlikely to have any changes since it is just the beginning of the execution phase. However, as you make progress with the execution phase and begin monitoring the progress of the project, you might find needs for changes to the scope or encountered defects in the deliverables. This might require you to follow the change management process before you could proceed with the work. This means you need to revisit your scope, cost and schedule baselines and amend them. The Change Management Process is little more explained in the next few pages.

Once amended, you might need to carry these desired updates to your work product, which is being built in the Execution phase. To update these changes, you need to use the requested changes as input.

Does this justify the use of Approved change requests as input in the project execution phase?

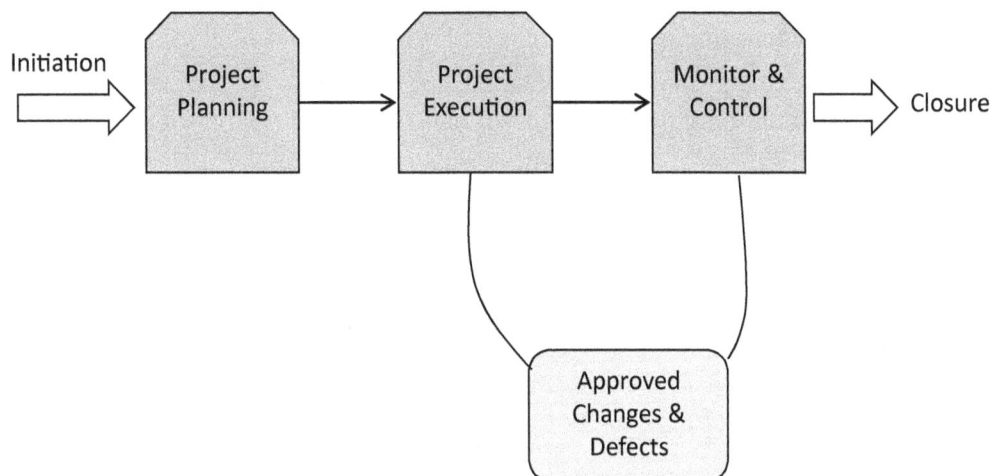

Project Monitoring & Control

During the project monitoring and control phase, the project progress is closely monitored and any deviation from the scope is tracked. During any project execution, not everything can go as planned. There are most likely chances of changes required or defects found during the project execution. These are identified during the Monitoring and Control project phase.

Any changes to the scope is recorded and taken care, subject to the approval by the Change Control Board (CCB) and other stakeholders.

If you come across any discrepancies during the monitoring & control phase, use the defect management process to have them fixed. At this point, you may have to think of a couple of defect prevention methods. They are *Preventive action* and *Corrective actions*. If you come across any specific instances of issues which occur in any systematic pattern, you might need to analyze it and fix them. This is to prevent further occurrence of similar issues. This is preventive action. Whereas, if you identify an issue and subsequently fix it as a reaction to its occurrence it means corrective actions. It is always good to keep an eye on what the team is doing and have them reviewed after completion.

At times, people get confused between defects and change management plans. Both are different in the sense that defects are resulted by erroneous design or code whereas change is an amendment to the scope.

```
┌─────────────┐   ┌─────────────┐   ┌─────────────┐
│    Work     │   │   Project   │   │  Rejected   │
│ Performance │   │ Management  │   │   Change    │
│ Information │   │    Plans    │   │    data     │
└─────────────┘   └─────────────┘   └─────────────┘
```

┌──────────────────────────────────┐
│ Expert Judgment   │
│   │
│ Organization Project   │
│   Standards   │
Monitoring & │   │
Control   │ Project Management │
│   Methodology   │
│   │
│ Earned Value calculation   │
└──────────────────────────────────┘

```
┌──────────┐ ┌──────────┐ ┌──────────┐ ┌───────────┐ ┌───────────┐
│Requested │ │ Required │ │Preventive│ │Deliverables│ │Project Plans│
│ Changes  │ │  Defect  │ │    &     │ │           │ │           │
│          │ │ details  │ │Corrective│ │           │ │           │
│          │ │          │ │  action  │ │           │ │           │
└──────────┘ └──────────┘ └──────────┘ └───────────┘ └───────────┘
```

┌──────────────────────────────────┐
│ Expert Judgment   │
│   │
Change   │ Organization Project │
Management   │   Standards   │
│   │
│ PM Methodology   │
└──────────────────────────────────┘

```
╔═══════════╗   ╔═══════════╗   ╔═══════════╗
║ Approved  ║   ║           ║   ║           ║
║Corrective ║   ║ Approved  ║   ║  Change   ║
║    and    ║   ║  Defects  ║   ║ requests  ║
║Preventive ║   ║  details  ║   ║           ║
║  actions  ║   ║           ║   ║           ║
╚═══════════╝   ╚═══════════╝   ╚═══════════╝
```

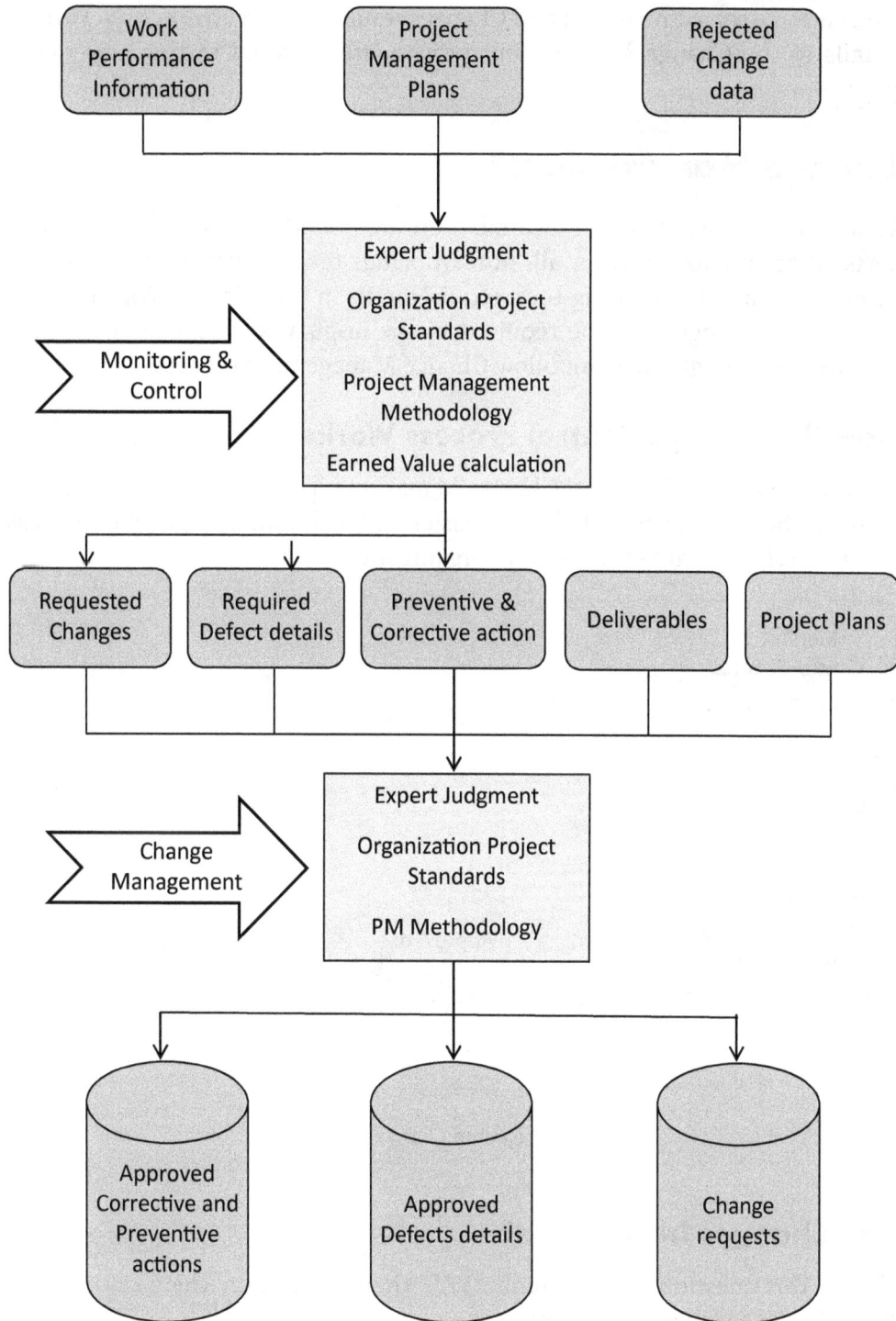

The above diagram illustrates the complete **Monitoring & Control Process group**. In the first part of the diagram, monitoring process is handled that result in obtaining requested changes, list of defects identified and approved preventive and corrective actions. In the second part of the diagram, these three reports are used as inputs along with deliverables and project plans to process the Change management.

Defects force *corrective action* and Changes results in *preventive action*. Further details of the Change Management process are narrated in the subsequent pages.

Change Management?

Whenever a large project is executed, there are bound to be some misses of all sorts going to happen. After all, human beings tend to make some mistakes or misses in accommodating their requirements in the original scope or some unexpected changes may be required to the original scope. To handle such situations you might need to follow Change Management process.

How the Change Control Process Works

To know more on how the Change Management process works, let us go through the diagram given below for easier understanding. The overall process to handle changes are same in every organization.

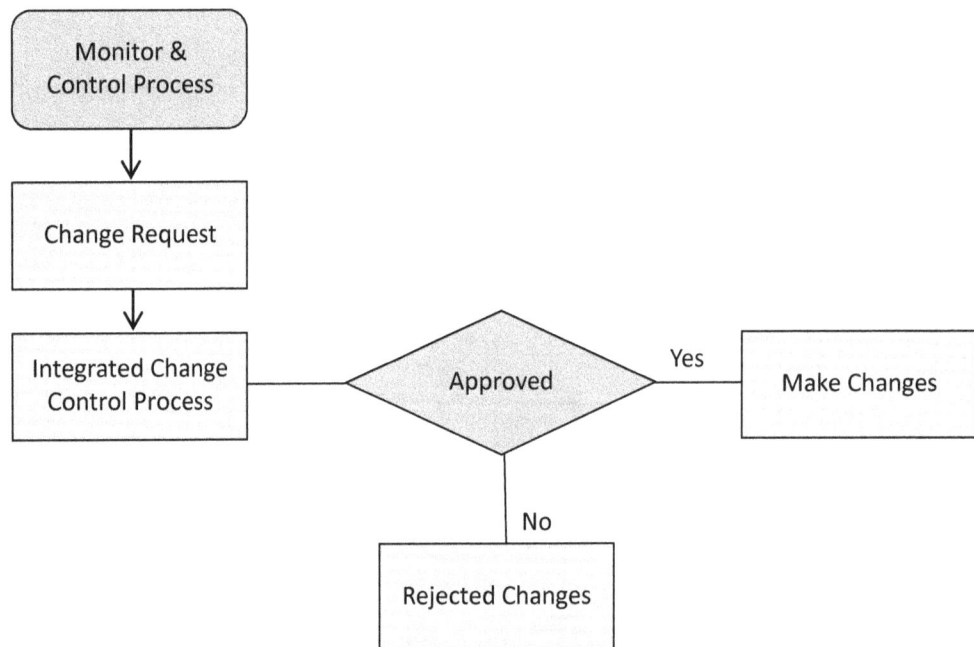

```
┌──────────────────┐
│   Monitor &      │
│ Control Process  │
└────────┬─────────┘
         │
         ▼
┌──────────────────┐
│  Change Request  │
└────────┬─────────┘
         │
         ▼
┌──────────────────┐          ◇                    ┌──────────────┐
│ Integrated Change│───────⟨ Approved ⟩───Yes──────│ Make Changes │
│ Control Process  │          ◇                    └──────────────┘
└──────────────────┘          │
                              No
                              │
                              ▼
                    ┌──────────────────┐
                    │ Rejected Changes │
                    └──────────────────┘
```

Can Changes be Avoided?

If I ask this question and you reply "YES" then I would say there cannot be a better Project Manager than you.

Besides occasional human errors of failing to capture all the requirements, there are several factors that might influence or trigger a change to the scope of any project or product. As an example, when the project makes significant progress there may be changes to the scope required to keep the project on par with the objectives of the performing organization.

Of course, none want to burden themselves with too much loads of work. However, sometime changes might be challenging and might open up more growth than the original scope of the work being performed. Imagine a situation, when a project team realizes a better way to perform the project that might offer substantial cost savings than the original budgeted cost.

Cost savings brings more smiles for all of us. Doesn't it?

Impact of Changes on Schedule

Certainly, there is most likely to have an impact of changes on the schedule baseline of the project. However, there are possibilities to eliminate the impact on schedule.

After a careful analysis, the project manager will determine the possibility of a change impacting the schedule. There may be different situations where a change occurs in a project. Imagine a situation, where you are just considering a change to the way you work on a component or rearranging the sequence of tasks from the original plan. You will not be introducing any new tasks, but just changing the sequence of the task execution for whatever reason. There are not going to be any changes to the duration of performing these tasks. It's just change in the way you execute your project.

Do you agree?

The Impact of Changes on Cost

Where there is a change in scope, there are bound to have cost impact due to the proposed change. The impact of cost might be in the form of schedule revision. Such schedule revision might result in engaging additional human & other resources. Easier and sensible approach to assess the cost impact is to analyze the schedule impact first and the plans to handle it. At times, using the same number of resources might eliminate any major schedule impact. If so, the chance of cost impact on the project can be minimal or none.

The overall revision of all of these will be felt in the cost baseline as well.

The Impact of Changes on Quality

In reality, there shouldn't be any impact of changes on quality since Quality is a predetermined objective and process driven by definite set of quality guidelines. It shouldn't change, no matter how many products or processes are produced by a project. This might sound correct.

However, if the changes result in adding a new functionality to the existing scope? This would result in adding more verification test cases and test samples to make sure the end product still produces an output according to requirements.

If you recall the triple constraint diagram, discussed earlier in this book, it would always be a good idea to analyze the impact of cost and schedule on the quality aspect of the changes. Remember, we are not talking about revisiting the quality objective but trying to eliminate the quality deviation due to the proposed changes.

Does this make sense?

The Impact of Changes on Overall Project Execution

Of course, there are going to be overall impact on project schedule and execution. So, extreme care needs to be taken to revisit the cost and schedule baseline of the projects, after the change is analyzed. The involvement of all stakeholders in the communication is critical to reduce the impact since each of the stakeholders might have to revise their own plans at their end.

The overall impact of changes is reflected in the pre-determined baseline of the cost, schedule and scope.

How Change Management is Handled

Every Change requested itself becomes as important as a project itself, since it directly impacts cost, schedule, scope and quality aspect of the project lifecycle. Whenever a Change request is received, the Project manager validates the request and, if required, gets additional input from the stakeholder who raised the change request.

Extensive analysis is carried prior to raising a formal change request with details of the scope, cost and schedule impact due to the implementation of the change. The Change request is passed on to the Change Control Board for scrutiny and approval. Once approved, the Project manager gets the scope, schedule and cost management plans revised and this revised version is considered the latest baseline.

Let us assume, you are working on building a product. After you made significant progress, there comes a change request. Upon looking at the change requirement, it appears a minor change, which might not require additional effort.

What should you do?

Irrespective of 'what' and 'how' it appears to your eyes, it is always a recommended practice to carry out a thorough analysis to assess the change request and its potential impact on the product. At times, the impact may not be visible to you.

Let us assume, you are working on developing an application program for a larger application. Your program access multiple interfaces to send processed data. Another developer approaches you with a request to make a cosmetic change to a particular field of your program, which sends data to his program.

If you accept his request and do the change, it might impact some other program, which access this field.

So, ideally every change is to be treated like a project itself with utmost care and responsibility. You might come across terms such as 'baseline' in the following few paragraphs.

What is a Change Control Board and Who Forms Part of It

Change Control Board is a group of people, who validate every change proposed to them and approve, if they consider it beneficial to implement.

Change Control Board comprises of people, who are stakeholders of the project and other experts. The Project Manager is definitely a key member of the CCB besides key stakeholders, whose operations are positively or negatively impacted by the execution of the project. The sponsor can also be a member of the Change Control Board, though not mandatory to include.

One of the traits of bad project management is not to pay attention to changes during the project execution. A Change Control Board is the best forum to validate the merit of a proposed change, since it has all key stakeholders informed of the requested changes.

Defects, Corrective and Preventive Actions

At this moment, you should familiarize with few terms that may be useful while you begin to manage your project.

A *defect* is a bug that was identified during or after the completion of your project. Ideally, defects are identified as part of the review process or while validation of your project objective during the project execution. When defects are identified in your work, a defect fix request is raised and submitted to the manager for further review and validation. Once found valid, a defect fix is carried out

A defect is different from a Change request, since a change involves reviewing the original scope whereas a defect is a bug.

A *corrective action* is a fix that may be required due to an identified defect.

A *Preventive action* means someone proactively identifying an issue that has potential to impact the project outcome or the deliverable. Usually, such preventive action might involve raising a change request and processing it as part of the Change Management process.

Does it make sense?

Project Closure

Another important task in a project lifecycle is the closure. A project cannot simply be considered closed after the delivery of the intended product or service to the customer or to the performing organization. There are several steps involved prior to declaring an end of the project.

Validation of Objective with Final Outcome

This validation process involves you, as the Project Manager and other stakeholders. The original scope is validated with the final outcome of the product or service. A better practice is to have a checklist of objectives prepared and circulated among each of the stakeholder prior to the execution of the project development lifecycle. The same checklist might come in handy during the closure to validate the objectives.

A written confirmation or acceptance from each of the stakeholder is to be obtained prior to signing-off of the project.

Financial Closure

This means all accounting tasks of expenses, billings and other financial instruments are done to the accurate dollar amount and all records are forwarded to the sponsors and other stakeholders. A formal acceptance is required to be obtained, in order to consider this task complete.

If there is a procurement done, as part of the project, then the financial settlement with the vendor is carried as part of financial closure.

Administrative Closure

An administrative closure is where all the pending and outstanding tasks are closed. This includes recording all lessons learnt, risks, issues, assumptions in your organizational repository.

Every project throws plenty of experiences, risks and issues. How we handle them becomes greatest trove of treasures for the organization that might drive future projects. Such lessons are to be collected in the organization repository for any future references.

Ideally, such historic information should be owned by the Project Management Office (PMO) of every organization, who provides support services to the project managers with vital inputs from previous projects.

Do you have the habit of collecting these lessons in your projects? Have you had a chance to browse thru historic lessons from your organizational repository?

Once all these data are collected and filed into your organizational project repository, the team is dismantled releasing all the resources that were working on the project. It becomes the Project Manager's responsibility to notify the concerned resource management teams and get the team redeployed, wherever required.

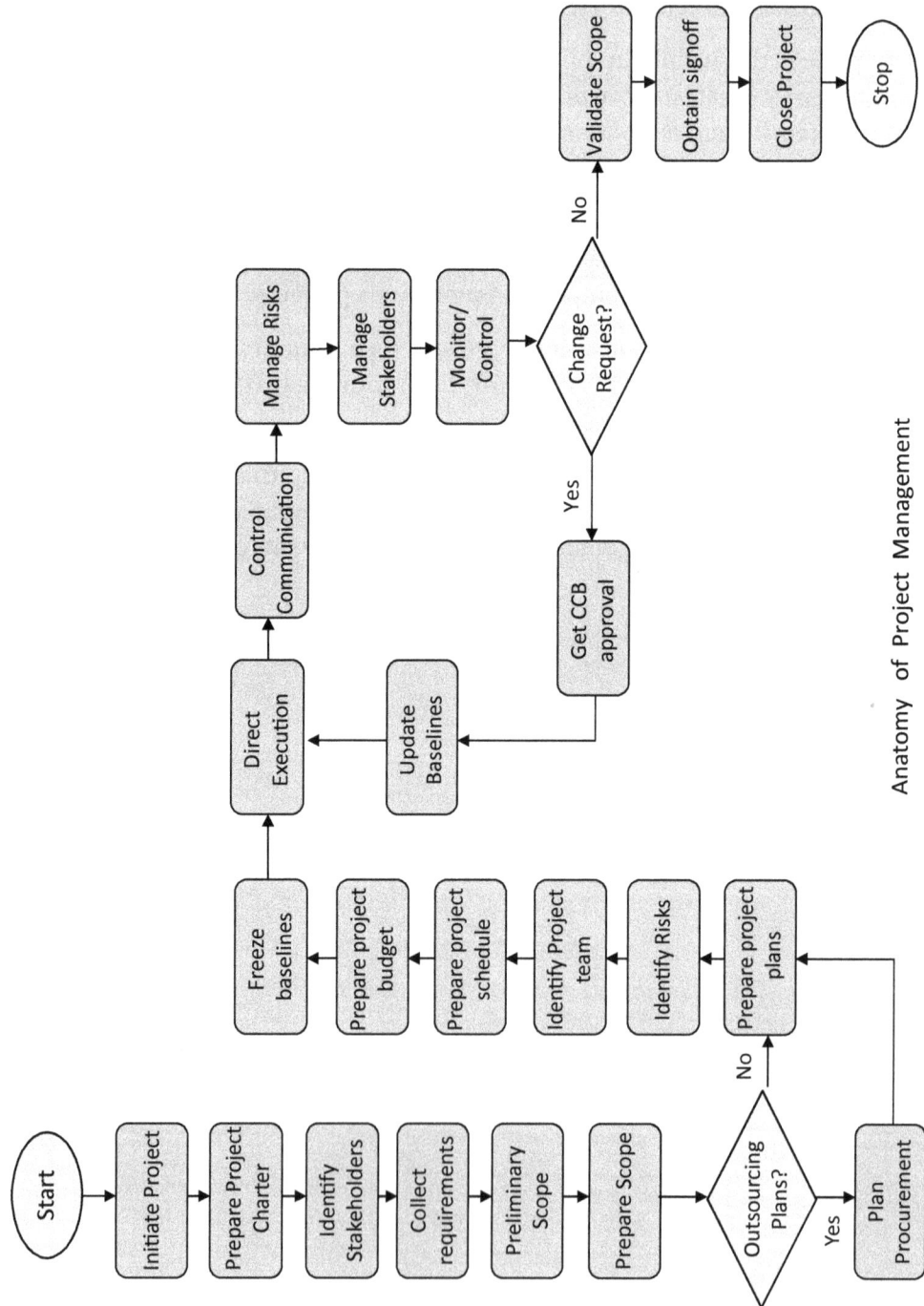

Anatomy of Project Management

EXERCISES

Robert was shifting his home to a new property over the weekend. Accidentally, his puzzle got mixed up. Help him rearrange the puzzle.

Project Charter	:	Results in revising the scope baseline
Initiation Process group	:	Lessons learnt are gathered and stored as process assets
Administrative Closure	:	A document that gives authority to a Project Manager
Corrective Action	:	Also means fixing a problem
Change Process	:	A Project Manager does high level planning here

True or False

1. Handling a change request at the end of the project will not cause any damage or impact to the overall delivery or quality (**True/False**)

2. Not every processes need to be performed in every project, as part of the project management (**True/False**)

3. Under project selection methodology, organizations market themselves desperately to get projects signed (**True/False**)

4. Referring to newspaper columns & magazine articles are acceptable forms of Expert Judgment (**True/False**)

5. Enterprise Environmental Factor is a constant information about Organization's policies and other important information (**True/False**)

Fill in the Blanks

1. When the project manager is uploading all his project related information and data into his company's process database, he is performing _____ .

2. Validation of product scope is performed in _____ process group.

3. A change cannot be performed unless it is approved by the project's _____ .

4. The other name of the project management plans is _____ .

5. In the project selection methodology, the other name of benefit measurement model is _____ .

ANSWERS

Puzzle

Project Charter	:	The document that gives authority to a Project Manager
Initiation Process group	:	A Project Manager does high level planning here
Administrative Closure	:	Lessons learnt are gathered and stored as process assets
Corrective Action	:	Also means fixing a problem
Change Process	:	Results in revising the scope baseline

True or False

1. False
2. True
3. False
4. True
5. False

Fill in the Blanks

1. Administrative Closure
2. Closure
3. Change Control Board
4. Subsidiary plans
5. Murder Board

Test Your Knowledge

1. Your organization has received a business opportunity from one of the reputed manufacturing company that is engaged in the electronic business. They wanted their procurement process be automated with a new application software and your company leadership want to look at the feasibility of executing a project for this customer, since your organization is working on similar project for another customer, who are competing in the same business. Your manager asks you to setup a meeting of select executes in the business unit to discuss this issue that will help arrive at a decision whether to go sign a contract with this company.

    In the meeting convened to discuss this issue, you notice that the audience are divided over the proposal. Over half of the participants are strongly in favor of signing the contract and execute the project since it will help the company develop expertise in the business domain, whereas another section of the participants strongly oppose the idea since the existing customer may not be accepting the decision and might even threaten to pull their project out.

    Based on the above scenario, which exactly is happening now with the project proposal?

    a) It is called War room, since neither side is accepting the other's view and there is conflict of ideas

    b) Project selection method, in which the participants assess the benefits and disadvantages of taking a decision. A section is trying to kill the project proposal for a specific reason

    c) Active and healthy work environment, where you have freedom to express your opinion

    d) None of the above

2. You are managing a project to build a bridge over a river. As your team is in the middle of their construction phase, your customer approach you with a change request to increase the height of the bridge by another meter due to larger than expected vessels to use the river over a long period of time. You consider this as an update to the scope of the work, that is already agreed to.

    You begin working on analyzing change requested.

    What phase of the project are you in?

    a) Monitoring and Control

    b) Execution

    c) Planning

    d) Initiation

3. You are approaching the Project Management Office (PMO) for some process related guidance and seeking them to share templates to begin working on your project planning. Since you are a new face in the organization and this is the first time they are being approached by you, the PMO member is not able to recognize you and they didn't have any notification from your supervisor about a formal introduction of yourself or the new project to the PMO. So, the PMO member is asking you to share the formal document that is authorizing you as the Project Manager for the new project.

   Which document would the PMO member be referring to?

   a) Project Contract

   b) Project Statement of Work

   c) Project Charter

   d) Preliminary Scope Statement prepared by you with your name printed on it

4. You are managing a project that is in the middle of execution and you are monitoring the project team and their work regularly through various means. Your customer approaches you with a change request on one of the deliverable. He feels that the specification given in the beginning may not be meeting their original expectation. But, you feel that any changes to the original scope might have an impact on the cost and schedule. Still, you think you can verify if there are any possibilities of carrying changes at this moment.

   What would you plan to do now?

   a) Tell the customer you cannot guarantee accepting their change request, but would try if time permits

   b) Refer to the project charter and find if you are authorized to assert your position and take a decision on such requests.

   c) Check with your boss and find out, if it is ok to accept the change

   d) Check the project contract and look for clauses that might provide guidance on handling such change requests during the project execution.

5. Which of the below is not part of the Project Scope Statement creation process

   a) Work Breakdown Structure

   b) Organizational Process Assets

   c) Enterprise Environmental Factors

   d) Preliminary Scope Statement

6. Which among the below are considered as one of the project selection methodology?

    a) Expert Judgment

    b) Forecasts

    c) Business scope optimization

    d) Murder Board

7. You are working on an engineering project to construct a massive turbine in a local energy manufacturing facility being built by your customer. You have worked with this customer on earlier project and have a good rapport with them and the customer have faith in your organization's capability and delivery commitments. Your organization is hopeful of this project meeting the agreed delivery commitments as well.

    During one of the project review meeting, your customer is asking for a change in the original scope and is insisting for getting the scope changed. When you review the project contract, you find that this is a fixed bid contract and this scope change is outside of the original scope agreed to earlier.

    What would your next action be?

    a) Pull out the project charter and make the customer aware that you are the Project Manager and given authority to accept or refuse changes

    b) Accept the change request since the customer is a long term business partner

    c) Carry an analysis of the change requested and document the details. With the details, speak to your boss and consult the legal department on how to handle this change request, since the contract is Fixed price and the change request is outside of the original scope

    d) Reject the change request, since it is a fixed bid and the change request is outside of the original scope.

8. Which of the following is TRUE about a project charter?

    a) A project charter is a document that signifies the beginning of a project and narrate the scope of the contract

    b) A project charter permits the project manager to begin planning for the project

    c) A project charter is a document that authorizes the project manager to plan and drive the project till its closure.

    d) A project charter is a document that is required for process compliance

9. Which of the following process groups are iterative in nature?

    a) Initiation and Planning

    b) Execution and Monitoring & Control

    c) Planning and Execution

    d) Initiation and Closure

10. The two important output of the Project Initiation process group are

    a) Project Charter & Preliminary Scope Statement

    b) Project Charter and Project Scope

    c) Contract & Project Charter

    d) Contract & Statement of Work

11. You are a project manager currently compiling lessons learned, test data, all forms and process plans to be uploaded into your organization's process repository.

    Which process group are you into?

    a) Monitoring & Control

    b) Planning

    c) Initiation

    d) Closure

12. You are a project leader in your project and is assisting your manager with all the management related help required. Your manager is always busy in meetings and working on her reporting stuff. Hence, she wanted you to help her manage certain portion of her responsibilities.

    Another intention of asking your help is to get yourself familiar with the project management processes, since you may be managing the next project in the organization. You are excited about this and want to be very careful not to make any mistakes or mess up with stuff in the project.

    One day you got a question from your customer on a proposed change to the scope. You are well aware of the change management plan, but not sure how the change process is defined for this project. You decide to check with your manager for guidance and find that she is busy in her meetings. When you buzz her to get a reply, she gives a one line reply 'check the appropriate subsidiary plan for details.'

    What would you do next?

    a) Wait for her to finish her meeting and you can get clarity on her reply later

    b) Search the whole project folder for information on change process planned for the project

c) Take your own call and inform the customer that it is difficult to include any changes at this moment of the project.

d) Check Scope Management Plan

13. **The success of a project integration is dependent on the effecting handling of**

a) Risk Management

b) All of the project management plans

c) Time Management

d) Cost Management

14. **In a project, integrating all the plan components is the responsibility of**

a) The project team

b) Stakeholders

c) Customer

d) The project manager

15. **You are managing a large development project for your banking customer. The project team is in the middle of their construction phase of the deliverables. The team comprise of 20 developers and three subject matter experts, who are well versed in the banking domain. In addition to this, you have four resources from the customer, who can help the developers with testing, review and providing test data. One of the stakeholder from the customer side approach you and inform that he want all these four resources be released from the project and redeployed within their organization to work on much more important assignments immediately. However, the customer do not mind replacing these four resources with someone from your own organization.**

This is a bad news for you, the project manager, since your project schedule was arrived after considering the testers' expertise with the bank's application and their operations environment.

You are afraid that pulling these four resources will cause serious impact on your schedule and subsequently impact the cost and quality as well.

What should you do now?

a) Refuse the customer to release the resources, since you do not have any resources to replace.

b) Escalate the issue with your management and notify the supervisor of the stakeholder, who made the release request.

c) Setup a meeting with the stakeholder and discuss with him the impact of releasing the four resources

d) Show the project charter to the stakeholder and let him know that you are the project manager authorized to identify and release resources.

16. **Which of the following is not part of a Project charter?**

a) High level risks involved in the project

b) High level business objective of the project

c) 'Nomination' of the project manager and the authority given to the manager.

d) None of the above

17. **When speaking of managing the scope of a project, Linda has messed up her list of processes that helped her understand how the scope needs to be handled in a project.**

Can you help her choose the right sequence from the list below?

a) Scope Management, Scope definition, Decompose work packages, Monitor scope & Verify scope

b) Define scope, manage scope, monitor scope, decompose work packages & verify scope

c) Define scope, Verify scope, manage scope, monitor scope & decompose work packages

d) Decompose work packages, scope management, define scope, monitor scope & verify scope

18. **You are managing a project, that is part of a larger program. For the sake of easier handling, the program was divided into multiple projects and you have been asked to name one of the project.**

The project is very critical for the overall program since it handles a portion of the critical interface requirement that does the maintenance of an important application. Your responsibility is the end-to-end planning till the verification of the project scope and performing a formal closure process for your project specific components.

What is the boundary of your responsibility in terms of the overall program?

a) You are part of the program, which means your boundary is not limited only to your project. You should make sure your project outcome is verified together with other projects.

b) Your responsibility is limited only to planning, execution and monitoring of your project.

c) Your responsibility is limited to your project till its scope verification and formal closure project. The program manager is responsibility of the overall program objectives

d) None of the above.

19. Richard is conducting a project management training for the aspiring managers of his organization. He has a nice slides prepared with a lot of details and he enjoyed presenting them in front of his colleagues. At the end of the session, one of the participant asks him to briefly explain the project management activities in the most simple terms.

    If you are asked to answer this question, how would you have explained?

    a) Project Planning- Preliminary Scope- Execution- Project charter- Change request-- Monitoring & Control - Closure

    b) Project Planning-Project Charter-Preliminary Scope Exccution- Monitoring-Change Management-Closure

    c) Preliminary Scope-Project Charter-Execution-Planning-Change Management-Monitoring-Closure

    d) Project Charter-Preliminary Scope-Planning-Execution-Monitoring-Change Management-Closure

20. You are busy planning for your project and working on creating cost planning done. You have prepared the cost estimation and converted it into cost budgeting. Once your cost budget gets approved, it becomes your cost baseline.

    What process group are you in at this point of time?

    a) Planning

    b) Execution

    c) Monitoring & Control

    d) Initiation

21. Which of the following is an output of Monitoring & Control process group?

    a) Project Cost baseline

    b) Work Performance Information

    c) Project Management Plans

    d) Recommended Corrective & Preventive actions

22. In which process group a project manager would ideally collect the lessons learned details for the project?

    a) Project Closure

    b) Monitoring & Control

    c) All through the project phases

    d) Execution

23. Sarah is a project manager working on her civil engineering project for a prestigious customer.

    The project has multimillion dollars at stake for her organization. She has the scope, cost and schedule reviewed and approved by the customer and the team is busy in executing the construction phase of the project.

    A key stakeholder of the project is now approaching her with a request to replace one of the design replaced with another. The customer says it will not have any impact on the schedule that is already approved. When Sarah took a quick review of the risk, she is convinced that the effort involved with both the designs are same and may not inflate the schedule with additional effort.

    What should be the next action of Sarah?

    a) Sarah should refuse to accept the request, since the design and scope is already finalized and approved. The team has already begun its construction activity.

    b) She should consult her supervisor and seek advice on accepting or rejecting the change requested, since there are multimillion dollar stake involved

    c) She should just ignore the request as the project execution has already begun

    d) She should check the other components of the triple constraint to verify the impact of accepting the change.

24. You recently received your new assignment that will involve managing a huge project to construct a shipyard for a prestigious customer of your organization. When you started working on the planning process, you are invited to a meeting of all stakeholders. During the conversation you hear terms such as 'bids,' 'contract,' 'sellers,' evaluation criteria,' 'bidder conferences' and so on. Since you do not understand any of these terms, you ask someone on what are they discussing about. You are being told that the other folks are planning for the project.

    What are the participants planning about?

    a) Project Management Planning

b) Procurement Planning

c) Resource Planning

d) Scope Planning

25. Risks are identified in a project at what stage?

a) Project Initiation

b) Planning

c) Anytime from start to finish

d) Monitoring & Control

ANSWERS

1. **Answer : B**

    Justification : Project selection methodology is also called murder board, where a section of the participants in meetings ask too many questions and raise several points to discourage from accepting project proposals for various reasons. Though the name murder board might convey a negative meaning, but it is an acceptable practice to have such objections raised in every organization.

2. **Answer : A**

    Justification : Change requests are part of the monitoring and control process group. While the project is still in the construction stage, the project manager is expected to have his eyes on the project construction and look for any factors that might influence a change in the original scope of the project. While change cannot be avoided in many cases, having a change request raised towards the advanced stage of the project construction brings pressure on the project manager and the team having to manage and incorporate such changes to the original scope of the project.

3. **Answer : C**

    Justification : A project charter is the first important document that is produced as part of every project. It is a document that 'nominate' a project manager to a project and defines his authority over the processes, resources and anything that is related to the project. In short, a project charter is a license to a project manager to plan, execute, monitor and close the project phases in a systematic way.

4. **Answer : D**

    Justification : It may never be a good news, if a change is requested when the project is in its advanced stage of construction. However, such changes couldn't be refused for the reason as well. When such change requests are raised by the stakeholder, it is always a good idea to carry an analysis of the nature of the change requested and document the information. Unless the project manager has a detailed information available on the scope and the impact, there cannot be any discussion over the need to include the change or not. There are multiple possibilities of handling such changes. If it doesn't impact the triple constraints of Schedule, Cost and Scope it can be considered. However, most changes requested might involve change to one or all of these three components. While changes are one key risks to projects, they also create new opportunities for the performing organization.

5. **Answer : A**

   Justification : A Project scope statement is among the few initial output of the project management plans. A Scope statement is created using the preliminary scope statement that was approved by the customer validating the understanding of the project objective. However, Work Breakdown Structure (WBS) is created by decomposing the scope of the work into smaller and easily manageable tasks for construction and testing.

6. **Answer : D**

   Justification : A murder board is nothing but a forum in an organization, where multiple people participate in discussion to take strategic calls on execution of projects. At times, participants of such meetings ask too many questions over the worth and benefits of executing a specific project and such questions might even end up killing any possibilities of project proposal.

7. **Answer : C**

   Justification : The biggest disadvantage of executing a Fixed Bid project is that the seller is responsible for any scope related risk. At times, it might become tricky for project managers to accept or reject change requests raised. In this case, it is clear that the change requested is outside of the original scope. Ideally, the price agreed on a fixed bid contract is applicable only for the approved scope. If the scope is increased, there are chances of renegotiating the price, which can be justified with data. The best strategy to adopt in this case is to analyze the change and document.

8. **Answer : C**

   Justification : A project charter assigns a project manager to the project. It further authorizes the project manager to plan, identify resources, execute, monitor and complete the project according to the objectives agreed in the contract.

9. **Answer : B**

   Justification : When the project manager is monitoring the project progress, there are chances of defects identified or changes requested. Whenever there is a change requested, the project manager is expected to follow the change management process and study the impact on the triple constraints of the project. Once the Change Control Board approves the change, the scope, schedule and cost baselines are updated. The construction team begins working on the change and make the changes as required. Thus, the Execution and Monitor & Control process groups are repeatedly performed until the project meets all the scope objectives.

10. **Answer : A**

    Justification : The project charter and preliminary scope are the two important output of the project initiation process group. The preliminary scope is considered in the planning phase to arrive at the project's detailed scope. A project contract is an agreement reached with the customer for the execution of the project.

11. **Answer : D**

    Justification : During the project closure phase, all scope verifications are performed and a formal signoff is obtained by the project from the stakeholders that signify project meeting its objectives. All the lessons learned, risks related information and every other project related information is consolidated and copied onto the organization's process library. Such process assets become a key input for future projects executed by the performing organization.

12. **Answer : D**

    Justification : A project management plan is also called Subsidiary plan. In this case, every change related plan is listed in the project's scope management plan. Every organization and project may have its unique way of managing the scope. A Scope management plan narrates how the scope will be defined, managed, monitored and verified to enable the project meet its objectives. At this moment, I suggest not to get confused between Project Scope Management Plan with that of Scope Statement.

13. **Answer : B**

    Justification : Integration Management means coordinating all the plan components effectively so as to produce an effective result, in this case the project meeting its objectives. As we will see in subsequent chapters of this book, every plan component is related with one another. An output of one process might become input for another. Unless the project manager is effective in integrating all the processes, there are possibilities of the project going out of control.

14. **Answer : D**

    Justification : It is the obvious responsibility of the project manager to plan and coordinate each of his plan components in an effective way to enable the project meet its intended objectives.

15. **Answer : C**

    Justification : From the narration of the issue in the question, it becomes clear that the project manager has completed the project schedule and have an approval on the schedule as well. When a project schedule is developed, the details of the tasks and the capability of the resources are considered as vital input to arrive at the effort requirement for completing the particular task. This effort gets converted into a start and end dates for the task. The developed schedule becomes the baseline for the project upon approval. After the schedule baseline is finalized, if the resources are pulled out it becomes a key risk for the project. One of the key risk for any project is the resource commitment for the project.

16. **Answer : A**

   Justification : A risk is identified when the project manager begin his planning phase. A project charter do not contain any reference about the risks involved in the project execution. The charter contains high level project requirements, assumptions and other brief information besides naming a project manager to manage the project and the level of authority given to help manage the project.

17. **Answer : A**

   Justification : When planning for the project scope, the project manager should first define how the scope will be managed followed by defining the scope, listing the work packages and decomposing them. During the monitoring & control phase of the project the scope is monitored and the deliverables are verified against the defined project scope.

18. **Answer : C**

   Justification : When a project manager is working as part of a larger program, the manager's responsibility is limited to the project. The project manager is expected to understand the boundaries and make sure the project scope is very clearly defined and deliverables are verified against the defined project scope. Thus, the program manager assumes the overall responsibility of the program.

19. **Answer : D**

   Justification : A project gets kick started with the nomination of a project manager by way of a project charter. The project manager puts his initial analysis of scope to prepare a preliminary scope statement followed by planning for the project. Then the project team begins construction phase while the project manager monitors and controls any changes that might be raised. Once the construction phase is completed, the deliverables are verified against the project scope and a formal project closure process in carried.

20. **Answer : A**

   Justification : The processes that are narrated in the question are part of the planning process group. The plan component that we are talking is Cost.

21. **Answer : D**

    Justification : When the project is being executed and monitored by the project manage, there are no dearth of information prepared and exchanged. When a defect is identified on any deliverable, preventive or corrective actions are required and the same are tracked in the Monitoring & Control process group.

22. **Answer : C**

    Justification : Every lesson learned in the project by the project manager or the team gets recorded right from the start of the project till the closure phase. The lessons learned collected are very vital input that helps organizations to analyze and take strategic decision and also help other project managers manage their issues effectively. All the lessons collected are consolidated in the project closure phase and uploaded into the process repository of the organization.

23. **Answer : D**

    Justification : Irrespective of impact on the project schedule, it is very important that the project manager verify the other components of the triple constraint for any potential impact of changes to project scope. There may be situations when unknown components of other deliverable or components get impacted by the change to the scope.

24. **Answer : B**

    Justification : If you strictly go by the word 'Contract' in the question, you might tend to confuse with the project contract statement of work. When you refer all of the terms together and try to find answer, it clear refers to the procurement planning process. Sellers and Buyers are referred in the procurement process besides bids and evaluation criteria that assess the bids and the sellers' capability.

25. **Answer : C**

    Justification : Risks are identified and monitored in a project from the start to finish of the project phases. A risk can be in any form and come from every possible direction. One risk can lead to another or many others.

This page is intentionally left blank

This page is intentionally left blank

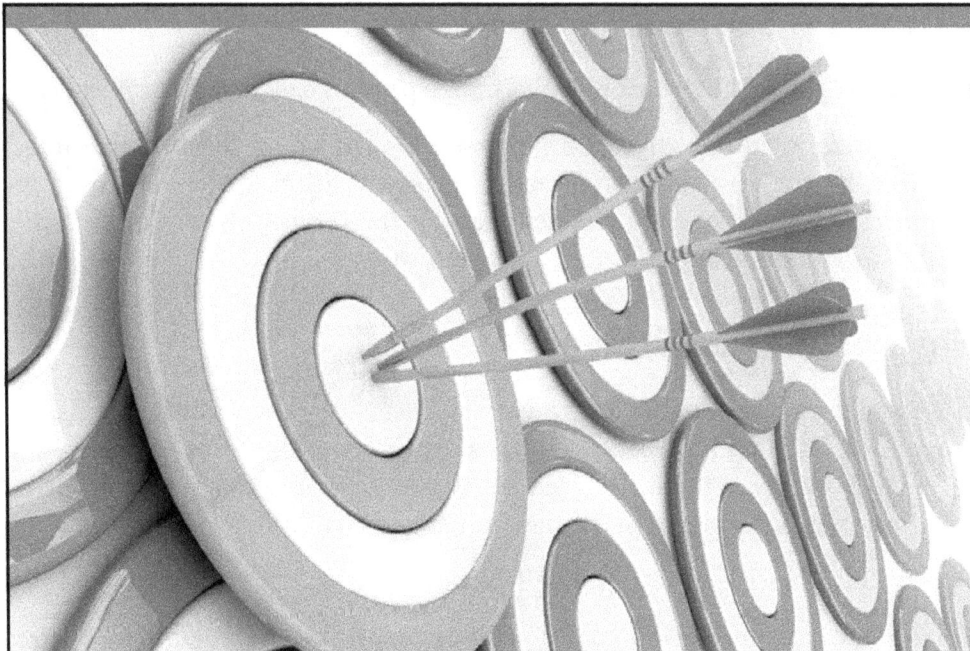

Project Scope Management

Objectives

At the end of the Project Scope Management chapter, you should be familiar with:

- what is a scope and the purpose of managing a scope
- what is a Scope Management Plan?
- understand how the project requirements are gathered from the stakeholders and different methodologies are used to gather requirements
- how preliminary scope turns into project scope during scope definition process
- the influence of stakeholders on the project scope
- differentiate project scope and product scope
- scope baseline, scope statement, Work Breakdown Structure (WBS) and WBS dictionary
- controlling scope and the impact of change requests on the scope and project schedule and cost
- how scope gets validated

What is a Scope?

I would call the scope as an 'objective' or 'purpose' of executing a project.

Unless there is an objective or a purpose, there is not going to be a project required by the customer or performing organization. Such objectives are defined in the form of a Scope document for the project. An entire project is knitted around its scope.

Significance of Scope?

Let us assume you are planning a visit to Europe for the holidays. A visit to France and Italy has always been in your dream for years. After having waited for several years, you finally decided to get things moving this year. You decide to utilize your time to gain maximum benefits of your holiday travel.

How would you make things work effectively?

Certainly, you would have had a big list of places to see, including a visit to Venice, Rome and Paris. However, due to terrific workload and time constraint, you decide to make your travel plan on the go after reaching Europe. Imagine the result of that decision.

You would end up skipping most of the places due to poor planning. The net result is spending huge amount of money for nothing. Why has this happened?

The reason is, you haven't planned for what you want to do on your travel. You wanted to do too many things but not planned for anything in advance. You ended up spending most of your time searching for a good hotel to stay and a travel agency that can take you around in Italy. When you landed in Paris, you were overwhelmed by too many choices and ideas and you had no clue on what to do first and how to move around. The solution to such a mess would have been defining the objectives in detail and plan well in advance.

In a typical business environment, definition of the objective helps eliminate most of the potential problems in the initial stage itself. As defined by the PMI, every project is working towards producing a predetermined product or service within a specific time and under the acceptable budget. A scope is the primary objective and goals, towards which the project and its team will be working. Basically, the scope of the project is aligned to the business objectives of the organization.

In other words, the Scope is your guidance document that is going to define what your project is planning to do and how you are planning to achieve the objectives of your project. The scope of the project is derived from the high level requirement proposed by the sponsor or the performing organization. This high level requirement is transformed into preliminary scope statement, which further developed to become Project Scope Statement. It is this Project

Scope Statement that is considered the baseline version. Whenever speak of Project scope, remember that we are referring to this baseline version of the scope. Any progress of work, changes or accomplishments of the project goals are directly referred to this Project Scope Statement.

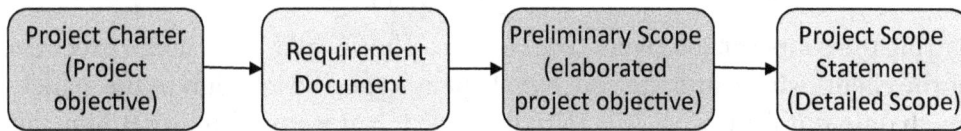

Project Charter (Project objective) → Requirement Document → Preliminary Scope (elaborated project objective) → Project Scope Statement (Detailed Scope)

Planning for your Scope

In short, scope planning is to define the objectives of your project work before you actually begin working on it. In other words, a Scope is the definition and boundary of the project objectives.

Scope doesn't automatically guarantee a desired outcome of the project. The customer can provide only the high level requirement to you. He may not be much interested in knowing how you going to get these expectations transformed into a full-fledged scope and work towards achieving the goals of your project.

There are multiple steps and processes to be performed before we achieve the objectives of the Scope. To begin with, you need to define your project goals and then define how you are planning to reach the goals. These processes collectively performed are collectively called Scope Planning.

Does it sound sensible?

Why is Scope Planning so Important?

To briefly define the importance of Scope planning ... It is doing the right thing in the right way to produce an acceptable result. A Scope management planning is a disciplined approach towards achieving the objectives of your project and satisfying the customer requirement. Unless you define your project objectives clearly, you will not have anything to validate the outcome of your project.

At times, you might be wondering what is so important about scope. It's after all, a high level requirement from your client or your sponsor, which later gets transformed to a full-fledged scope. What can go wrong with the scope?

This is a very valid question in everyone's mind. You should understand that most of the project failures are caused by trouble in defining the scope or unclear scope statement. Managing the scope of the project is equally critical as any uncontrolled scope might result in the project losing track of its objective. Managing all these challenges is really important for the project and the project manager.

Imagine a situation, you are customizing a recreational vehicle from a chassis manufactured by an automaker. The order is for a special corporate customer and for specific quantity. You begin working on the client requirement and specification. Based on the initial requirement handed over to you, you arrive at a cost and schedule, which is subsequently approved by your customer.

During the course of your work, you receive a phone call from a senior executive of the client, who wants the couch be kept at a specific location in the vehicle, much different from what was initially agreed. Not wanting to upset him, you accept the new requirement without revisiting your cost, schedule or originally agreed scope. Some other day, you receive another executive from the client, who comes to inspect the progress of your vehicle building work. He suggests the design be altered according to his choice. Over the next 2-3 weeks, you have about a dozen such changes to the original requirements coming your way and you think you can accommodate all these changes, since it might get you more money. So, you just overlook the schedule of the project. But, the client want the recreational vehicle be available ahead of the holiday season.

Now, let us consider, each of these executives are already identified as stakeholder in your project and they are kept informed of the original requirement and even the requested changes to the original design plan.

Just a week before the originally scheduled delivery date, you realize that you are heading nowhere with your project due to multiple requirement changes from the stakeholders. These changes have thrown the original design of the vehicle building project out of shape and the recreational vehicle is totally not going to impress the clients nor will you be completing the project as per the originally agreed date.

What could Potentially Happen?

After everything got messy, you decide to sit back and think of the reasons for all your trouble. Do you care to share now?

The impact of wrong decisions and incomplete scope would be anywhere from moderate to catastrophe.

Certainly, your client is not going to get their vehicle delivered on the date you committed. They are not going to be impressed with your new design. They are not going to pay you the money. Your reputation as a successful project manager is at stake and might even potentially ruin your career.

Satisfying the clients in return of goodwill and more business is perfectly alright. However, the above attempts to impress the client reflect the Project Manager's poor management skills. Your focus should be to stick to the original scope. You cannot indiscriminately accept changes as and when it comes, without realizing the project and business impact of it.

Processes Related to Project Scope

Out of the many recommended processes performed during various phases of your project, the below are the list of activities performed during the scope management planning phase. Each of these processes is self-explanatory of their functions.

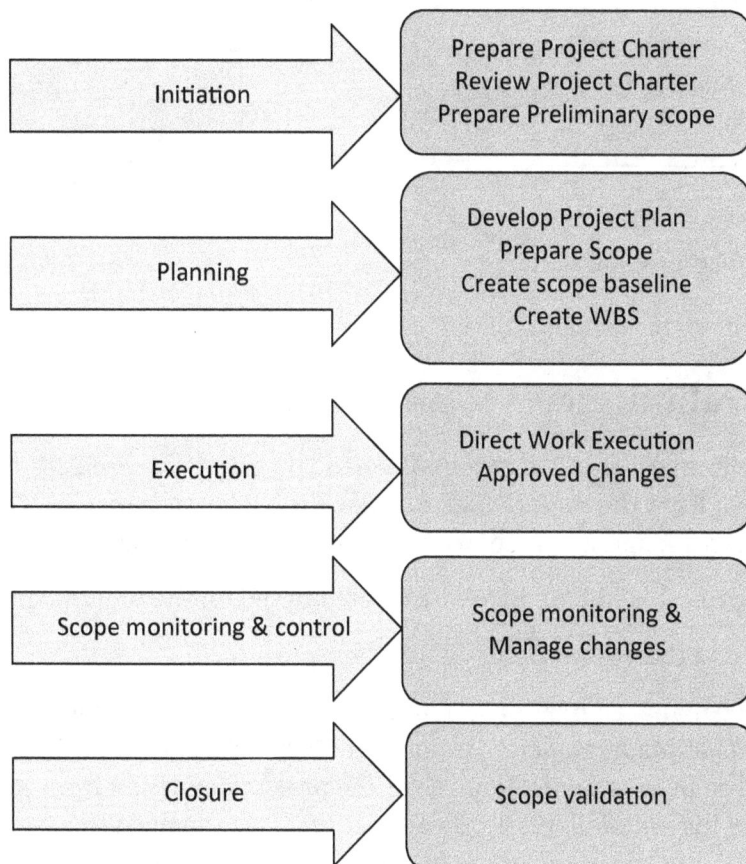

Phase	Activities
Initiation	Prepare Project Charter, Review Project Charter, Prepare Preliminary scope
Planning	Develop Project Plan, Prepare Scope, Create scope baseline, Create WBS
Execution	Direct Work Execution, Approved Changes
Scope monitoring & control	Scope monitoring & Manage changes
Closure	Scope validation

Preparing the Preliminary Scope Statement

Before we get onto the Scope Management Planning process, let us understand that the preliminary scope statement is the initial understanding of the Project Manager about the scope of the project. The project charter and contract are used as primary input in addition to initial kickoff discussions with the client to understand the expected objective of the project.

Thus, the preliminary scope statement is derived from the project charter and would contain high level objective of the project scope. It will remain preliminary until more insight and details emerge on the intended objectives of the project. The detailed requirement of the stakeholders are collected with the help of Collecting Requirement process that we will be reviewing in the next few pages. This requirements document play as a critical input to the scope definition process.

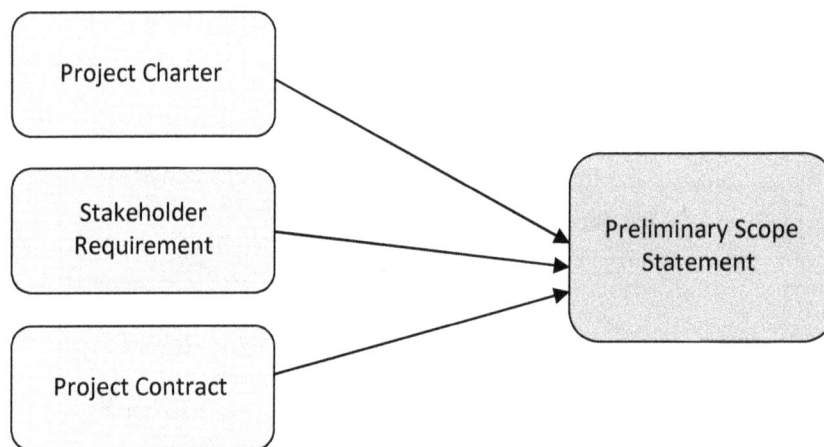

Why Preliminary Scope Required

Why a preliminary scope is required, when you know the project's high level requirement from the project charter? Can't the Project manager simply work on the project's scope statement without wasting his time on preliminary scope.

Well. The project is not going to be executed based on the preliminary scope.

It is easily said than done.

The project manager may have few lines of information about the project objective. That is not sufficient even to understand the expectations fully. He is required to put his understanding of the project objectives from the project charter and his initial discussions with people. Thus he need to have an initial draft version of the scope, which he uses to speak to the customer or anyone associated with the project.

The project manager uses this preliminary scope to validate his understanding and objectives before he begin working on the project scope statement. In other words, a preliminary scope is a step by step elaboration of the scope process before arriving at a project scope.

What are the Key Tasks Performed in the Scope Management

In all, there are six important tasks that collectively forms part of the Scope Management Process. The below diagram, the tasks listed on the left are the list of tasks performed during the Scope Planning process.

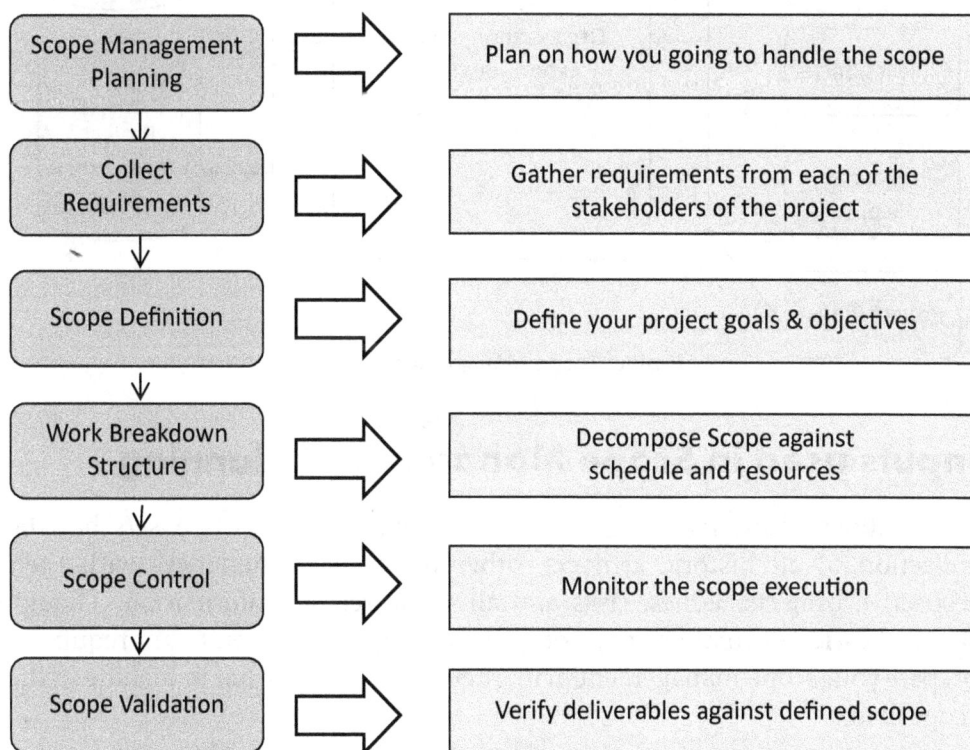

Scope Management Planning	→	Plan on how you going to handle the scope
Collect Requirements	→	Gather requirements from each of the stakeholders of the project
Scope Definition	→	Define your project goals & objectives
Work Breakdown Structure	→	Decompose Scope against schedule and resources
Scope Control	→	Monitor the scope execution
Scope Validation	→	Verify deliverables against defined scope

Prepare the Scope Management Plan

From the above diagram, it should not be difficult to identify the process which generates Scope Management Plan

Do not get confused between Scope Management Planning and Scope definition. Scope Management Plan is where you plan on how you will be managing the scope of the project. In Scope definition, you will be actually defining what your objectives and goals of the project are going to be.

Does it make sense?

Now, it's time to get into the act and find out what inputs do you require in generating Scope management plan.

As discussed earlier in this book, your Organizational repository and Enterprise Environmental factors are the standard inputs in preparing the Scope Management Plan. In addition, we will be considering the Project charter and the Contract as inputs to define the scope management plan.

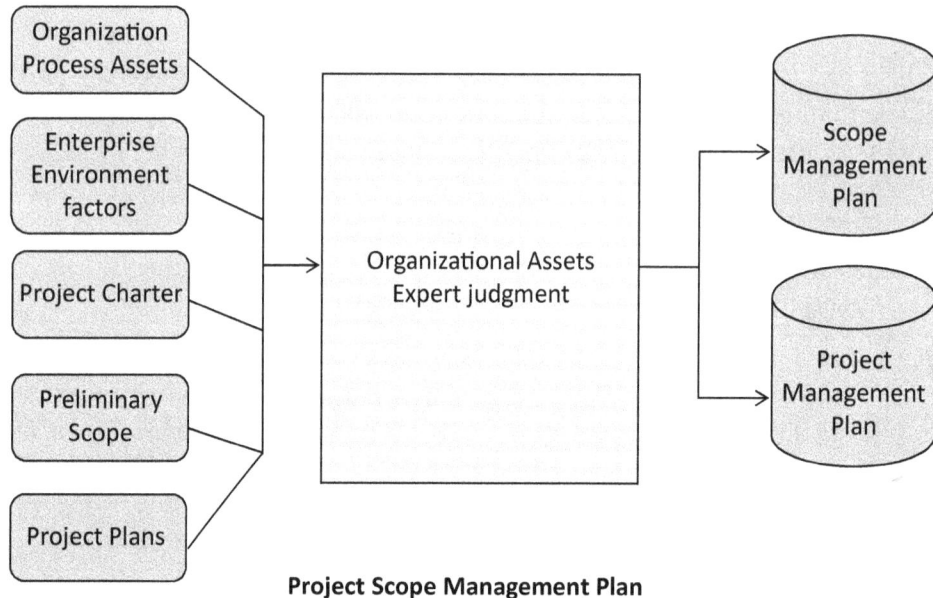

Project Scope Management Plan

Inputs used in Scope Management Planning

In the above Scope Planning diagram, *Organization Process Assets* has the collection of all historic artifacts, other managers' experiences with their respective projects, issues, risks and all scope related information. Though these historic information may not give exact inputs that you might require to prepare your scope management plan, they guide you on what to include in the scope plan.

Enterprise Environmental Factor is another Organizational repository that has all policies, procedures and the business environment & strategy related details of the performing organization.

Project Charter and *Preliminary Scope* statement are documents that has the high level expectations and intended objectives of the project. These two inputs are critical to the Scope planning phase of any project. In other words, it is what the customer and the project performing organization agreed to produce.

At this point, remember that we have only high level objective of the project known and we are still away from having a detailed project statement.

Scope Planning Tools – A Review

From the above diagram, you can notice two tools being considered for preparing the Scope Management Plan.

The *Organizational Process Assets* can be obtained from the Project Management Office (if your organization has a PMO). Usually, in most organizations, the PMO has control over their Organizational process assets, which includes all approved templates, standards and artifacts from the earlier projects executed.

If your Organization doesn't have a PMO group, you can find out the source of these process assets. In some organizations, there may be a Quality Management group in place of Project Management Office.

Expert Judgment is one important tool, wherein you will consult with some experts or other Project Managers, who have handled such Scope Management planning in the past. Such experts should have better insight into the contents of the scope planning process and the related issues associated with the scope management plan. The advantage with consulting such experts is that they might have already faced some issues related to defining the scope, which would help you to eliminate the same from occurring in your project.

You may also refer to the lessons learnt documents available in your Organizational repository for any potential issues encountered related to the scope in other similar projects executed in your organization.

A better way to prepare the Scope management plan is to include the details of the stakeholders in the form of a Stakeholders register, their role and authority level. This can be supplemented by the list of individuals who are authorized to approve any changes to the scope. A scope approval is one of the most critical activity to happen in a project since it is around the scope, the whole project is centered. Finally, it is the Project Manager who is responsible for working on any changes requested and get it scrutinized by the Change Control Board before approving the changes to the scope.

You can find a sample Scope management plan in the below diagram as reference. Note that you can customize any template to suit your project needs.

Production Management System	Project Id XXXXX
Scope Management Plan	

Table of Contents

Introduction

Provide brief intention and purpose of the scope management plan along with the scope of the product & project work and details

Scope Definition

Narrate the ways you are planning to define the scope of the project, how to get the reviews done and approval details

Terms & Acronyms

Provide details of the terms used in the document along with their definition and acronyms

Scope Monitoring & Control

List details of how you intend to monitor the scope of work

List of stakeholders to be part of Change Control Board

List the names of all the stakeholders who will analyze and approve or reject the requested changes.

Work Breakdown Structure

Provide details of how you are planning to decompose the work, classify them strategically and assign them to complete. Also, provide details of the WBS dictionary for each of the work components

Scope Validation

This section should narrate details of how you are planning to get the scope verified after the work is completed. Details such as scope verification plan, any specific strategy to be adopted and who approves the scope compliance

Roles & Responsibilities

Provide details of stakeholders who are engaged in the Scope management process along with their roles and authority level. You can include the tools and standards that you are planning to use in the scope management plan

Collecting Requirements

Before you could proceed with the scope definition, you require to have the requirement objectives from each of the stakeholders. The project charter defines the requirement in brief. However, it is the project manager, who collects detailed requirements from each of the stakeholder and put the understanding in the form of a scope statement.

Let us take a look into the below diagram to understand more on this process

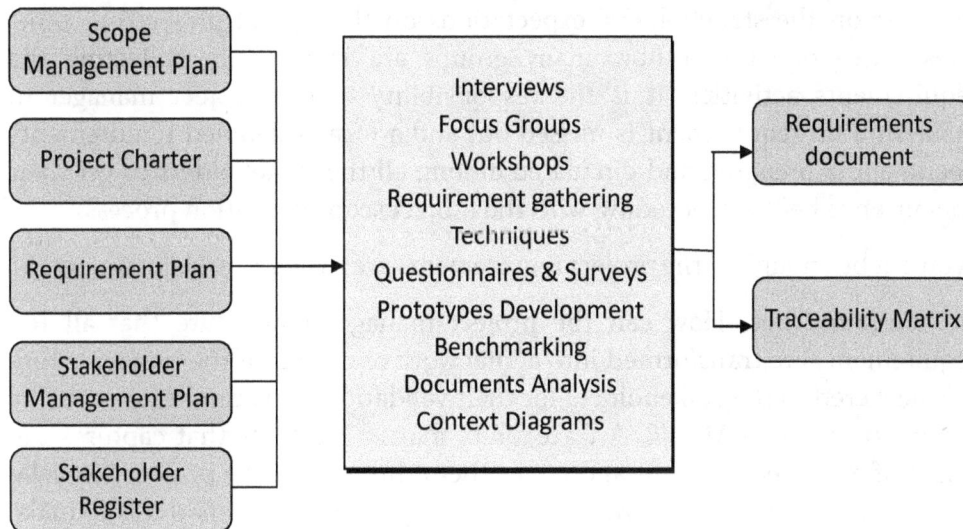

```
┌──────────────────┐
│      Scope       │
│ Management Plan   │──┐
└──────────────────┘  │     ┌─────────────────────────────┐
                      │     │         Interviews          │
┌──────────────────┐  │     │        Focus Groups         │        ┌──────────────────┐
│ Project Charter   │──┤     │         Workshops           │        │   Requirements   │
└──────────────────┘  │     │   Requirement gathering     │───────▶│     document     │
                      │     │        Techniques           │        └──────────────────┘
┌──────────────────┐  ├───▶ │  Questionnaires & Surveys   │
│ Requirement Plan  │──┤     │   Prototypes Development    │        ┌──────────────────┐
└──────────────────┘  │     │        Benchmarking         │───────▶│Traceability Matrix│
                      │     │     Documents Analysis      │        └──────────────────┘
┌──────────────────┐  │     │      Context Diagrams       │
│   Stakeholder     │──┤     └─────────────────────────────┘
│ Management Plan   │  │
└──────────────────┘  │
                      │
┌──────────────────┐  │
│   Stakeholder     │──┘
│    Register       │
└──────────────────┘
```

Inputs used in Collecting Requirement Process

Among other inputs listed in the diagram above, *Requirement Plan* contains the details of how requirements are planned to be gathered and managed. The requirement plan document is generated as part of creating project scope management plan.

Similarly, Stakeholder Register contains the list of all the stakeholders involved in the project. Extreme care should be taken to identify all the stakeholder before beginning on the scope of the project, failing which there are bound to be wide gaps in the customer expectation and what is being delivered.

Tools used in Collecting Requirement Process

Among all the tools used in the process, *Requirements gathering techniques* refers to forming a group of stakeholders in a structured way to hold discussions and understand the expectations. The group can be headed by a Chairperson, who will steer the group and the discussions, resolve issues, troubleshooting and coordinate with members of the group and those outside of the group to facilitate collecting the requirements.

Other forms of collecting requirements involve conducting interviews with individual stakeholders, conducting workshops specific to projects, reviewing documents to understand the existing systems or applications, circulating questionnaires to stakeholders with questions specific to the project requirements and conducting surveys.

Output of the Collecting Requirement Process

Requirement gathering document contains the understanding of the project manager on the stakeholders' expectations on the overall project outcome. Irrespective of who or how many groups are involved in collecting the requirements activities, it is the responsibility of the project manager to make sure no requirement is missed out and a formal detailed requirements document is prepared and circulated among all the stakeholders to get their concurrence before proceeding with the project scope definition process.

Would it be enough, if the project requirements are gathered and documented?

No. Certainly not. How can the project manager make sure that all the requirements are transformed into actual work or output of the project before it is delivered to the stakeholders for their validation. This can be achieved by having *Traceability Matrix*. A traceability matrix is a table that captures the origin of every requirement and traces them throughout the project lifecycle. The primary purpose and advantage of having a traceability matrix is to make sure every requirement is monitored and tracked. Having traceability adds business value to the customers, in terms of meeting the project objectives.

Scope Definition Process

The ownership of the Scope statement lies with the Project Manager.

The PM is responsible to transition the high level requirement into a full-fledged Scope statement. In finalizing the scope statement, the project manager needs to interact with all the stakeholders including the subject matter experts (SMEs) of the respective function to get the opinions and inputs.

Obtaining the final signoff of the scope becomes the responsibility of the Project Manager too. The PM ultimately owns the scope baseline as well. At this point, one needs to quantify the scope objective of the benefits. Quantifying the benefits will help validate the scope as well as justifying the objectives of the project to your stakeholder while seeking their approval for the scope.

It is important for the Project Manager to consider the scope validation process at the time of defining the scope since a scope statement should help validate the scope statement before closing the project.

How Scope is Defined?

As explained briefly earlier, scope of the project is nothing but step by step expansion of the high level expectation set out by the customer in the project charter and project statement of work. We have already seen how the project charter gets transformed into a preliminary scope statement in the earlier pages of this chapter.

Once the project scope statement is prepared, this detailed scope statement is discussed with the stakeholders and get their approval before proceeding with the rest of your planning. Once signed off by the stakeholders, this version of the detailed scope statement becomes the scope baseline. This baseline version becomes the key driving force of the subsequent project execution. Whenever there is a change approved, the baseline version of the scope is revalidated and revised (You will be learning more on the Change Management process in subsequent pages of this chapter)

Now, coming to the process of defining the scope, refer to the diagram below for clarity.

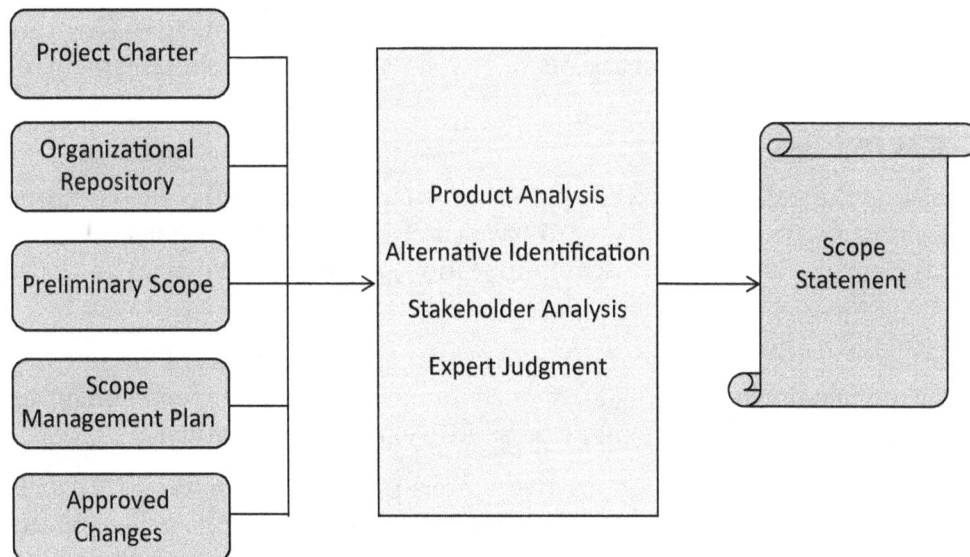

Inputs used in the Scope Definition Process

Now, you have the *preliminary scope statement* on your hand. Remember that the requirements gathered in the previous process is used to prepare the preliminary scope statement, which will further be transitioned into a detailed scope of the project.

The *scope management plan* provides input to the project manager on how the scope is planned to be defined and further managed, validating the scope, how changes are going to be handled and who is the approving authority of the scope.

The *Organizational Process Assets* help the project manager to have better insight into the scope definition process handled by the other project managers.

As the project manager progress with defining the project scope, there are possibilities of changes to be made. These changes cannot be directly implemented but through a formal change management process being followed by the performing organization.

Organization's process assets must help the project manager with samples of project scope statements of previous projects, templates and other vital guidelines in defining the project scope statement.

Now, you begin to develop the detailed scope statement. How do you achieve? There are few tools to get this done. Let us consider the tools in the above diagram.

Tools to Define the Scope of your Project

Not every task can be independently done by every project manager. There are few tools, which might offer assistance to you to define the scope statement

Stakeholder Analysis

Engaging the stakeholders while performing important activities such as scope definition is one important way to have clarity on the project objectives and goals. Besides eliminating miscommunication, this would help everyone to be aware of the scope being planned, progress of the project, risks and issues.

Since a stakeholder is going to be the direct or indirect beneficiary of the outcome of the project, it becomes their responsibility to present the expectation of the project. Ask as much questions as possible to eliminate ambiguity.

While analyzing the scope requirements, every possible information and data is to be considered for discussion. Considering alternate option for achieving the objectives, available subcontracting options, any internal resource availability will help making a more feasible decision on the scope.

Tidbits

Stakeholders and their importance

Among many other things, identifying and managing stakeholders are most crucial tasks to be performed by a project manager. Unless all the stakeholders are identified in the initial stages of the project, there is no way for a project manager to have the clarity of the scope. Missing a stakeholder is a very costly mistake to be committed by a project manager. Its impact will be felt right from beginning of the project till its closure and the project might end up as a failure.

Similarly, identifying a stakeholder at a later part of the game will force major updates to the project scope and the impact of such major updates would be far reaching on the overall scope, schedule and cost of the project.

So, a project manager should be extremely careful not to ignore any stakeholder of a project.

Product Analysis

When a team is working on producing a product, the objectives of the product should be clear, even before the team can begin working on their construction. Such clarity of expectations can be achieved, when the project manager does a detailed analysis of the product, his project is intending to produce. Such clarity is possible by way of getting inputs from each of the stakeholders.

The product scope is tied with the project scope, thus producing a great product. Remember that it is always good to have a quantifiable scope derived, since it helps in validating the scope of the product in the Project Closure process group.

Alternatives Identification

Whenever a project is being planned, it is always good to have multiple options of executing the work. This will help the project manager to choose the option that suits his organization and customers the best.

As an example, if your project is to build a new transport line across the river that is flowing through your city, two options are considered. First is to have the tunnel underneath the river and the other building a bridge overpass on the river. By having two choices, it becomes easy to identify the risks and benefits of having these options and pick the one that suit the best in terms of cost and quality of the outcome.

Expert Judgment

Expert judgment is one important tool that you might find helpful in defining the scope of your project. Similar to Project Management Office (PMO), an expert judgment is a repository of information which might provide suggestions or solution based on the available data.

To define the scope of your project, you could use any subject matter experts or a manager, who has already handled similar project for vital inputs.

Prior to involving experts, you might want to do a complete analysis of the product or outcome that you are intending to produce. This will make sure you are aware of the key differences between your product or service function and that of other Project Managers, who might have handled similar projects.

Output of Scope Definition

Having seen what are used and how the processing is done in the Scope definition process, let us move onto the output part.

The *project scope statement* is the only output of the Scope Definition process. Ideally, the scope statement defines the actual objective of executing the project and the expected outcome in detail. Remember that once the Scope Statement gets approval of the stakeholders, it becomes the final baseline version and this final Scope Statement is the driving force for the project team, when they begin the execution phase.

To reiterate again, do not get confused between the project scope and product scope. The outcome of the scope definition is the scope of the product or service that is being produced by the project.

Let us now look how a sample Scope Statement looks like

Trans-European Telecommunications Corporation
Retail Billing Applications - Alpha

Scope Statement

Project Objective:

Provide a detailed overview of the project objectives such as the application name, purpose of the project and what the intended outcome of the project

Product Objective:

Write a detailed overview of the expected outcome of the project such as what the product is intended to perform, the characteristics of the individual subcomponents and features, whether there are any dependencies of this product and interface details.

Scope Limitations:

Provide details of the requirements of the project, their boundaries with respect to operational limitations, constraints.

Expected Deliverables

What the project is intended to deliver to the stakeholders. List every deliverable such as final product outcome, designs, test components, project budgets, schedule plans, quality plan, Project Management Plans, defect reports and list of changes requested.

Project acceptance terms

The acceptable criteria for the outcome of the project such as meeting the set expectations, conformance to customer requirements, completed testing along with test results, defect resolution, completion of user acceptance testing, required documentation and user manuals.

Assumptions & Constraints

List of initial assumptions and constraints being made with respect to the scope of the project and product besides any other unknown requirements of the project. The assumptions could include using customer expertise or human resources in understanding the existing setup. Any changes to the assumptions made in this Scope document will involve a formal Change management process being initiated.

Proposed Project hierarchy

List the initial and intended human resource plans such as number of managers, project team, experts and testing professionals.

Special Notes

Any special requirements of the project such as project features requirements, required deliverable schedule and implementation requirements.

What is Scope Baseline?

In other words, a Scope baseline is nothing but a final version of the scope statement. The original requirement is now transitioned into a detailed scope statement. The Project Manager is responsible for sharing the scope statement with all the identified stakeholders.

It would be a good idea to setup a meeting of all the stakeholders to discuss the contents of the scope statement and get it reviewed. Once the final version of the scope statement is frozen, a formal and written signoff is required to be obtained from each of the stakeholders. This signed-off version of the scope statement becomes the baseline version.

Remember the fact that, at no point of time during the project phases does the scope baseline be violated. Any further scope changes are to be routed thru a formal Change request. The Change management process is narrated in detail under the Project integration chapter.

Importance of Obtaining Sign-Off on Scope

If you obtain a formal signoff on the scope, it might potentially keep the smile on your face throughout the project phases and can get you plenty of time on the weekend to have fun.

It's true.

Most of the issues in project execution surface due to ever changing scope or unclear scope of any or all of the stakeholders. The best project managers pays significant attention in creating a clear and detailed scope statement and shares with all of the stakeholders. Having obtained a signoff from each of them is your ticket to the weekend rugby game. Unclear scope results in numerous change requests, which impacts the cost, quality and schedule.

Besides obtaining a sign-off, insisting on Change management process could even guarantee a timely execution of the project itself. Ironically, this is where many project managers make the mistake of not insisting on change management process or rely on oral approvals.

Difference between Scope Management Plan and Scope Statement

When you are reviewing the Scope Planning process, one common confusion for many is, how to differentiate between Scope Management Plan and Scope Statement. The confusion is because both these sound alike. But, one should realize that they both are entirely different.

If you ask me to define them both, I would call Scope Management Plan as 'How' of the Scope Planning and Scope Statement as 'What' of the Scope Planning process. Still confused?

In other words, Scope statement defines what the project is planning to deliver, whether it is a product or a service. The features of the outcome are defined in the scope statement. Whenever there is a change in these features, the scope statement gets updated and all the stakeholders are kept informed.

The Scope management process is a pre-defined sequence of tasks that you are planning to perform in your project which facilitates an outcome.

Scope Statement	Scope Management Plan
This is what the project is planning to produce or accomplish	This is how the project is planning to accomplish the scope
Scope Statement doesn't get updated by itself	Scope Management Plan guides the process to include any changes required on the Scope Statement
Plays direct role in the creation of an end result	Do not directly generate any end result or outcome but drives the project in the right direction to creating an output
Used to get the end result verified for meeting customer expectation and conformance to requirement	Scope Management plan drives processes to get the Scope Statement meeting current requirement
Cannot exist by itself but has dependency on Scope Management Planning process	Scope Management plan process cannot exist independently but require Scope Statement to operate a project

Create Work Breakdown Structure Process

As the name suggests, a Work Breakdown Structure (WBS) is a tool which is used in decomposing the larger work packets into multiple smaller and easily manageable activities for easier development and validation. Remember that the WBS is a very critical component of a project since the entire project schedule is centered around a WBS. Obviously, the cost is derived out of the project schedule. A project schedule and cost plan are most important acceptance criteria for a project to get started.

The decomposed tasks are logically inter-related to each other. A simple example of the WBS is seen below

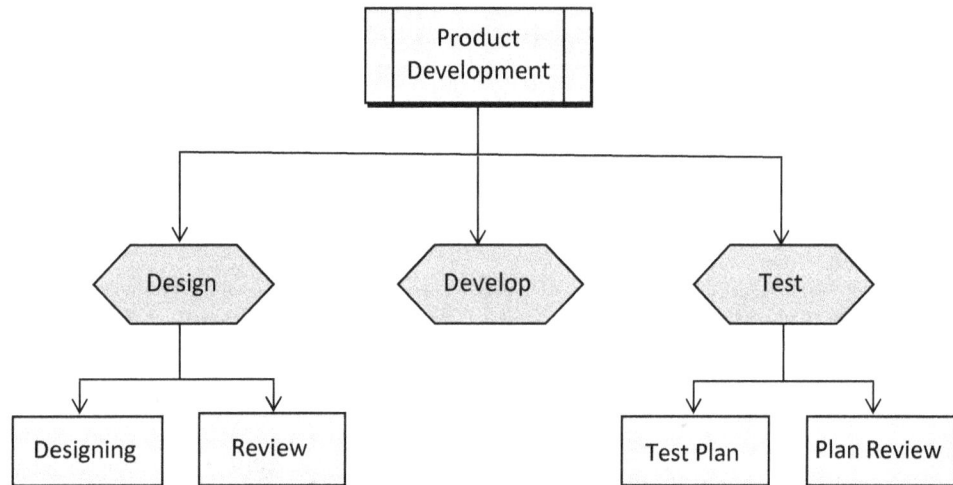

In the above diagram, the larger task Product Development is decomposed into multiple smaller tasks (which can be further decomposed depending on the need of the project). After decomposing into smaller and easily manageable tasks, resources can be assigned with start date and end dates. The duration of the tasks will be calculated if you are creating a WBS through standard project management tools. Interdependency between each of the tasks are clearly established for easier tracking and to trace any overlapping issues.

A sample WBS is given below for easier understanding.

Task Name	Duration	Start	Finish	Actual Finish	Predecessors	% Complete	Resource Names
Reuse Analysis and recommendation	22 days?	**Thu 3/13/14**	**Fri 4/11/14**	NA		32%	**Mike**
Recommend Assets for April	12 days?	**Thu 3/27/14**	**Fri 4/11/14**	NA		0%	Mike
Analysis on assets which need customization	9 days?	Thu 3/27/14	Tue 4/8/14	NA		0%	Candice
Analysis on assets added after Jan 15th - Delta dump	6 days?	Tue 4/1/14	Tue 4/8/14	NA		0%	Candice
Shortlist the Assets for April	4 days?	Tue 4/8/14	Fri 4/11/14	NA		0%	Mike
Certification	19 days?	**Mon 3/10/14**	**Thu 4/3/14**	NA		91%	**Robin**
Review of the M/F certification course content	1 day?	Thu 3/27/14	Thu 3/27/14	NA		0%	Ron
Baseline the M/F certification Course content	1 day?	Fri 3/28/14	Fri 3/28/14	NA		0%	Ron
Launch the Course and publish	1 day?	Thu 4/3/14	Thu 4/3/14	NA		0%	Robin
Training	17 days?	**Thu 3/13/14**	**Fri 4/4/14**	NA		82%	Victoria
Conduct Training	10 days?	Mon 3/24/14	Fri 4/4/14	NA		50%	Candice
Training Calendar for FY14	4 days?	Wed 3/26/14	Mon 3/31/14	NA		50%	Victoria
Course Material - validate	3 days?	Thu 3/27/14	Mon 3/31/14	NA		0%	Candice
Solution Accelerator	15 days?	**Mon 3/10/14**	**Fri 3/28/14**	NA		87%	**Bill**
Review Solution Accelerator	1 day?	Thu 3/27/14	Thu 3/27/14	NA		0%	Mike
Baseline the SA	1 day?	Fri 3/28/14	Fri 3/28/14	NA		0%	Robin
Capability Deck	10 days?	**Mon 3/17/14**	**Fri 3/28/14**	NA		75%	Victoria
Review	3 days?	Tue 3/25/14	Thu 3/27/14	NA		50%	Mike
Baseline Capability Deck	1 day?	Fri 3/28/14	Fri 3/28/14	NA		0%	Victoria

In the above sample WBS, the task names refer to the decomposed tasks that are easily manageable. The duration refers to the amount of effort involved in completing each of the task (for easy handling, the efforts are converted into business days), Start and End dates refer to the planned start and end dates.

Predecessors refer to the dependency details of each of the task. "% Complete' refers to the amount of work that has been completed for each of the listed tasks and the last field is the name of the resource that is working on each of the tasks.

The above sample WBS is for a project that is in the middle of execution. The intention of listing this sample is to make sure the readers understand each of the columns of a WBS.

Creating Work Breakdown Structures

The easiest way to schedule your work and get them assigned to the right resources is by way of the Work Breakdown Structure. It is similar to a excel sheet but with several automated features that will help you decompose your entire project tasks into smaller and easily manageable components. In real terms, the WBS doesn't decompose the tasks into simple and easily manageable smaller tasks for the project managers but to be done by them manually before listing the tasks in the WBS.

To have the WBS created, first you need to analyze all the tasks that are required to be done in your project. List down all of your tasks in sequence and assign resources, estimated start and end dates. The below diagram should help you understand the creation of WBS.

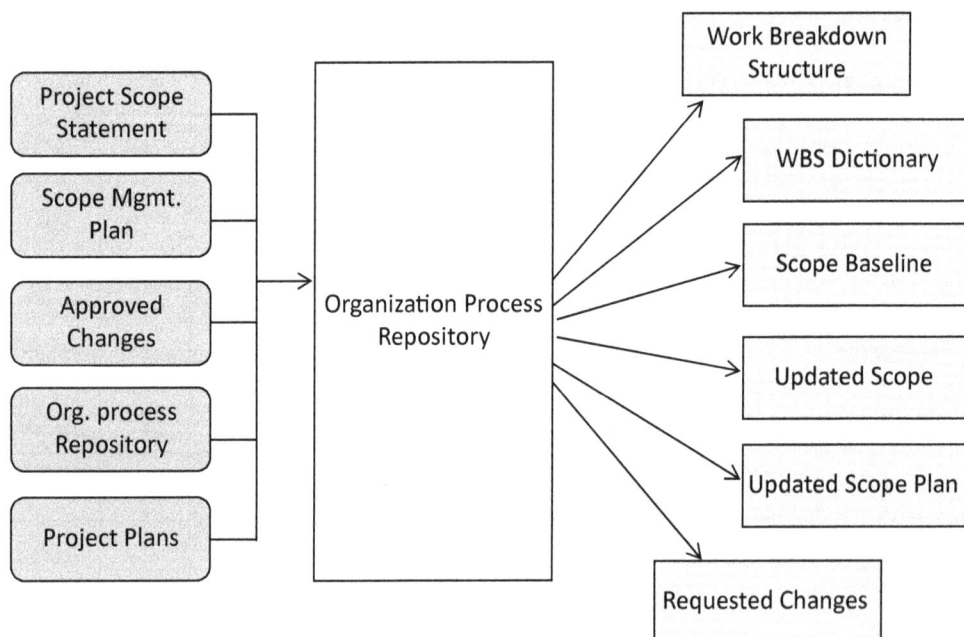

Inputs to Create Work Breakdown Structure Process

Among all other inputs, the *Project Scope Statement* is the most important input of the Create WBS process since the Project Scope provides all the required details of tasks that are essential input to the WBS creation. These tasks are further decomposed to arrive with the list of smaller and easily manageable tasks.

The project *scope management plan* details the way, the scope will be managed. While the manager is working with the project scope, any changes that comes will be recorded and updated in the project scope.

Project Management Plans are useful to ascertain if the other project plans have any impact on the scope. Since a WBS has a lot to do with schedule and human resources, there may be several references made against these project plans.

When the project manager is working on the scope planning process, there are chances for changes required to the scope management plan or scope statement. Thus, these *approved change requests*, if any, are used as input in this process.

Tools Used in the Create WBS Process

The only tool used in the Create WBS process is the use of Organization Process Repository. If the Project Manager is smarter enough he could able to list all the individual tasks and decompose them into smaller and easily manageable activities.

However, referring to the historic information available in the Organization Process repository is recommended for more inputs and better practices in defining the WBS. At times, referring to such Organization repository helps catch issues in advance.

Outputs of the Create WBS Process

The entire WBS can be generated by two different ways. First is by the Function of the project tasks and by task itself. The option to generate the WBS is dependent on the project requirements. You may refer to the sample Work Breakdown Structure given in the previous pages for better understanding.

By Phase

When I say, creating a Work Breakdown Structure by phase, I mean to have the entire list of decomposed tasks be grouped around each of the phases that are going to be performed in the project. Design, Specification, Development and Testing are all some examples of phases in any project or product development environment.

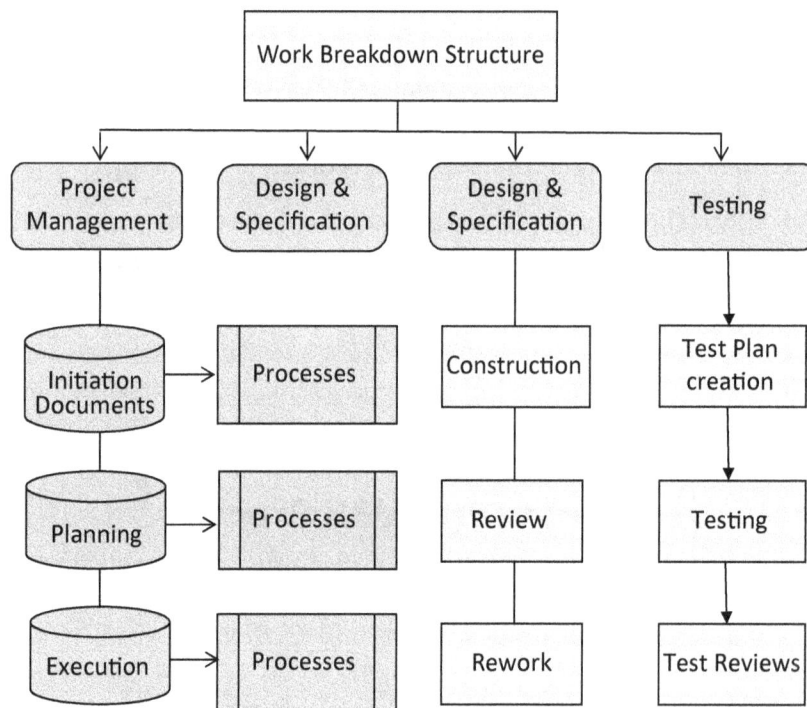

In the above diagram, the Processes refer to the respective processes to be performed as part of the Scope Management plans. These processes are listed in the beginning of this chapter.

By Deliverable

Another way to define a Work Breakdown Structure is to group the tasks by Deliverables that your project is intending to deliver.

If you are working on a project that plans to develop a multimedia based animation project, you ideally would deliver project plans, design of the final output, developed code or package, testing documents and implementation plans to the customers.

In this above example, each of these components becomes a deliverable which further has multiple tasks under them before those deliverables goes to the customers. List down each of these tasks and create a schedule with resources and planned start and end dates.

I am sure, it is not too difficult to achieve the above.

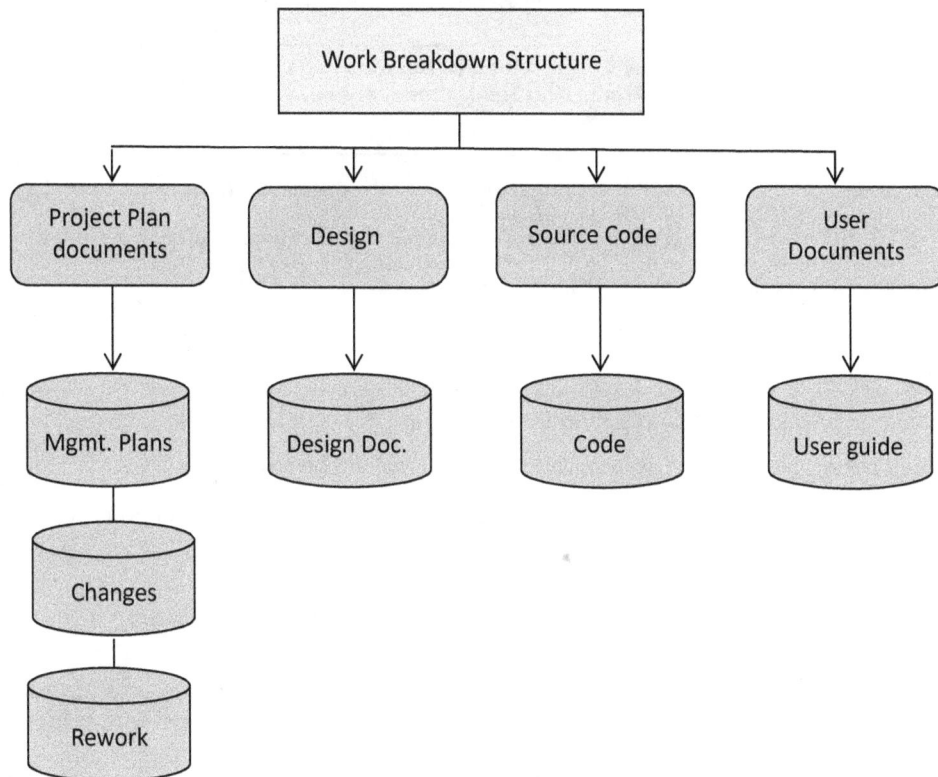

```
                    ┌─────────────────────────┐
                    │ Work Breakdown Structure │
                    └─────────────────────────┘
```

Project Plan documents	Design	Source Code	User Documents
Mgmt. Plans	Design Doc.	Code	User guide
Changes			
Rework			

Now, it should not be very difficult for you to create your Work Breakdown Structures by phases and Deliverables. You might want to refer to the sample WBS given earlier in this chapter.

As every project is dependent on multiple tasks and utilization of manpower, the Work Breakdown structure lists each of the tasks that are planned to be executed in a project and the resources are identified for each of these tasks in the WBS.

This should help you understand the significance of the Work Breakdown Structure.

WBS Dictionary

A *WBS dictionary* is an important document that is produced out of the Work Breakdown Structure. A dictionary is nothing but details of each of the Work packages that are defined and narrated in a WBS. An example is, you are decomposing the Development phase into individual components or programs in a large application such as Program A, Program B and Program C.

For each of these programs, you need to have a document that should narrate the functionality of the code in detail. Having this document should help anyone to begin construction without much assistance. As I always say, there need not be any standard template for these documents. So, you just prepare your own WBS package or dictionary that suits your project requirements.

	ABC Corporation Plc. Allentown, PA **Production Management System** **WBS Dictionary**	
WBS Code	:	List the appropriate code of the work packet that is defined in WBS
WBS Level	:	Provide the corresponding work packet level that is defined in WBS
WBS Element Name	:	Name of the Work packet
Assigned resource	:	List the name of the resource who owns this work packet
Description	:	Write a short description of the functionality of the work packet that is being worked on by the team
Target Dates	:	List the milestones for the work packet element
Assumptions	:	List any assumptions made with respect to this specific work packet
Dependencies	:	List all dependencies for this work packet
Acceptance Criteria	:	Provide details of the expected functionality of the element and any verification criteria that is agreed to by the customer
Effort required	:	Provide the amount of effort involved in completion of this work packet. Also list the number of resources required and for which activities.
Approved By Name : Authority :		Date :

In the above sample WBS Dictionary, the WBS Level, WBS Code and WBS Element name can be obtained from the Work Breakdown Structure that you have on hand. The Description of Work is a brief summary of the individual work product that is decomposed. Deliverables and Resources are self-explanatory.

Besides the Work Breakdown Structure and WBS Dictionary, any change requests raised to the Scope management plan, Scope Statement and scope baseline result in updates to these documents. These updated documents are considered as output of the Create WBS process, as it can be noted in the above diagram.

Scope Control Process

While you plan the scope of your project in the planning phase, it is during the Monitoring & Control phase that you keep track of the direction of your project against the planned scope. This Scope control is one critical task of your project that might potentially seal the fate of the project itself.

During the Scope control phase, you analyze the performance information of your scope and compare them with the scope baseline. The variance details that you collect with the analysis activity are considered to measure the health of your project. In addition, the changes requested and approved by the Change Control Board (CCB) plays a critical role in reviewing the scope baseline.

At this moment, let us understand that Scope control and Scope planning are inter-related with each other. This is because Scope control phase deals with analyzing work performance and analyzing change requests. These two important tasks results in the scope being revisited for a fresh review. In other words, based on the work performance information and approved change requests, the overall scope of the project gets reviewed and a new baseline is set.

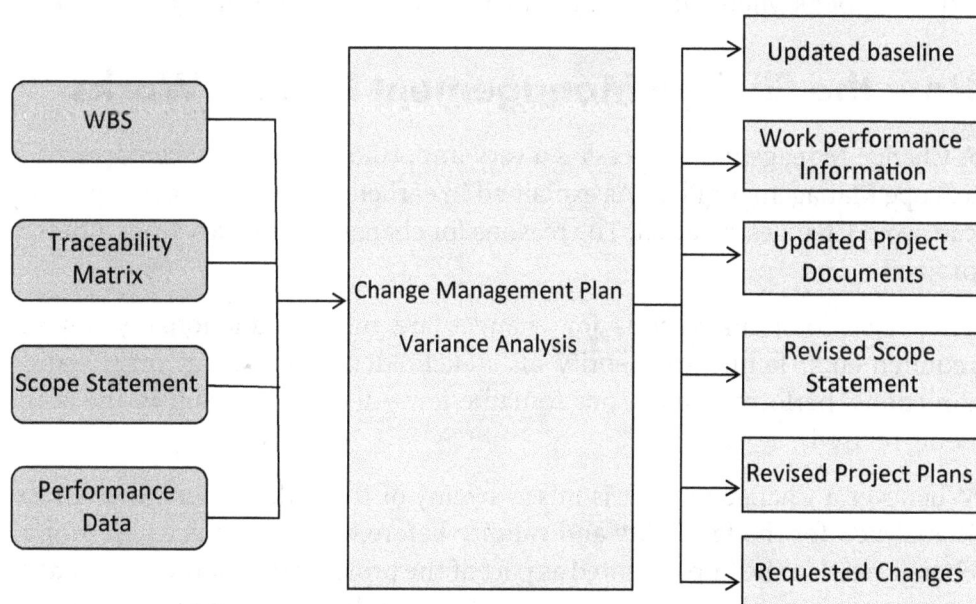

How do you control Scope?

Let us assume, your team is working on the construction phase. How would you, as their Project Manager, make sure they are constructing the scope according to the original baseline?

One way to validate the scope is to have the work reviewed with the help of a Work Product Review (WPR). The WPR takes into consideration the functional and technical aspects of the construction phase and validates against the original scope.

We will see more on the WPR in the communication management chapter.

Significance of Change Management in Scope

The biggest and most impacted component of a change is obviously the Scope. The success and failure of every project hovers around the pre-determined and agreed scope of work to be executed.

Whenever you hear the terms 'Change Management' or 'Revised requirement,' you are most likely to refer to the Scope statement of your project. Since change to the scope impacts the cost and schedule involved in the execution of the project, which subsequently might impact quality. Hence, Change Management assumes extreme amount of significance in any project, irrespective of their size.

What happens when critical requirements are missed while defining Scope?

How the Change Management Process Works

A Change Management Process is a very important and critical component in a Scope Management Plan. As explained in earlier chapters, not many projects can avoid Changes required. The reasons for changes might vary from different projects.

The most common reasons for changes are missed functionality, revised requirements, failure to identify all stakeholders, changes in organization directions, performance reasons to name few. All of these result in the scope being revised.

Whenever a Change request is raised by any of the stakeholders, the request is analyzed for the feasibility and validity before taking the next step. Not all change needs to be implemented as part of the project execution since a change involves revising the original scope, cost, schedule and subsequently impacts the quality and the delivery as well.

Tidbits

Significance of Change Management process

Ignoring to follow the formal Change Management Process is one significant reason for many of the project failures or schedule/cost overrun these days. In other words, as there are scope changes received the project managers and team do not bother much about following the change management process and begin including the updates into the scope without revising the scope baseline. This result in scope getting overblown, which in turn result in schedule and cost overrun.

So, a careful analysis is required to be carried to identify the feasibility of the change requested and the variance between the original scope and the revised scope. Such analysis should involve the impact on the scope, cost and schedule plans. All the stakeholders should be kept informed of the requested change and the outcome of the analysis that you carry. The outcome of the analysis should be documented in necessary templates and submitted to the Change Control Board (CCB). Once the CCB approves the change, the scope baseline should be revised to include this Change.

Since most of the changes impacts Schedule and Cost, those plans should also be revised. Once the revised Scope, Cost and Schedule plans are ready, the Work Breakdown Structure is revised to include the effort requirement of the requested change. This is called *Replanning* task in a project.

If the Sponsor is not part of the Stakeholder group, an approval is to be obtained from the sponsor. Now, you have a revised baseline for Scope, Cost and Schedule plans.

I am sure, you should be clearer on how the Change processes are handled in a project.

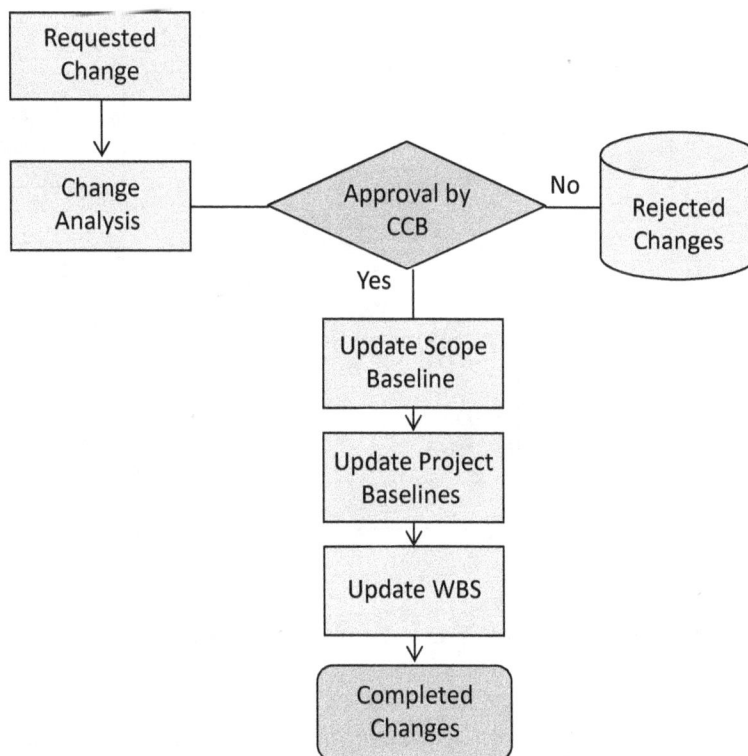

Scope Validation

Scope validation is one critical task in a project execution. It is this task that validates whether your final product is meeting the original objective of the project before the end product reaches the customer.

To be clearer, you define the project objectives and goals during the scope definition phase. You discuss the objectives with all the stakeholders and the sponsor. Once all their expectations are gathered, you would have expanded the Preliminary scope statement into a detailed Scope statement. As narrated earlier in this chapter, you quantified the objectives of your scope in the scope statement.

It is in the Scope validation task that you validate the original objectives with that of the outcome of the end-product. To get the product verified, the recommended practice is to get the final deliverable or finished product inspected. The inspection can be done by anyone, who are qualified and capable of performing the inspection. In Software Services business, there are multiple levels of reviews and testing being carried out to complete the scope validation. First level of testing is carried within the project team and this task is called peer review. In the second phase, the project manager takes a review of the deliverable before delivering the product or package to the customers. At the customer end, user acceptance testing is carried before a final signoff is given.

This is a very good practice since it eliminates any human errors during the development and testing phases. The below diagram would clearly illustrate the Scope validation process.

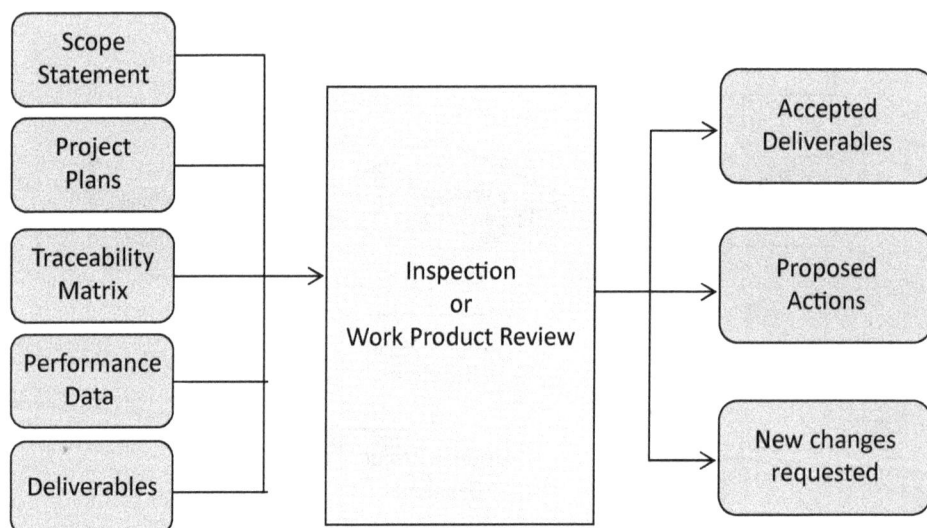

```
┌─────────────┐
│   Scope     │───────────┐
│ Statement   │           │
└─────────────┘           │
┌─────────────┐           │                              ┌──────────────┐
│  Project    │───────────┤         ┌──────────────┐     │  Accepted    │
│   Plans     │           │         │              │────▶│ Deliverables │
└─────────────┘           │         │              │     └──────────────┘
┌─────────────┐           │         │  Inspection  │     ┌──────────────┐
│ Traceability│───────────┼────────▶│     or       │────▶│  Proposed    │
│   Matrix    │           │         │Work Product  │     │  Actions     │
└─────────────┘           │         │   Review     │     └──────────────┘
┌─────────────┐           │         │              │     ┌──────────────┐
│ Performance │───────────┤         │              │────▶│ New changes  │
│    Data     │           │         │              │     │  requested   │
└─────────────┘           │         └──────────────┘     └──────────────┘
┌─────────────┐           │
│ Deliverables│───────────┘
└─────────────┘
```

Inputs to the Scope Validation Process

Since we are going to validate the constructed end product or results against the original scope, we require the *Deliverable* and *Scope Statement* as critical inputs.

The *WBS Dictionary* provides brief description of the intended functionality of each of the work product being constructed.

A *scope management plan* is required to refer and understand how the scope of the work products are to be handled.

Traceability Matrix provides details about the intended objective of the scope performance Vs. actual performance of the project scope. In other words, a Traceability Matrix reflects the actual performance of the project scope.

Tool Used in Scope Validation Process

A standard *inspection* or *work product review* are to be performed to make sure the constructed work product meets the agreed scope baseline and conforms to customer expectations. Such inspections are performed by the stakeholders or anyone designated to carry out such validation process.

An inspection means taking samples of the products produced by the project and verifying them against the agreed scope. The test results are to be captured in the form of quantifiable data for easier verification.

A work product review is same as an inspection, however the WPR is more prevalent in the software services industry. We will be knowing more on the Work product review in the Communication Management chapter.

Output of the Scope Validation Process

The deliverables that underwent the inspection process successfully is all that is expected by a project manager and his team. Of course, none would be interested to redo their work.

At times, it is possible that some of the completed work products may not pass the scope validation process for various reasons. The reviewers recommend *proposed actions* on such work products and turn them back to the project team for rework.

Any *changes* recommended as a result of the scope validation process are considered another key output.

Once the requested actions and changes are carried out by the project team, get them verified against the scope before submitting the final product for approval by the stakeholders.

> **What is the difference between Scope Control and Scope Validation. Which one should come first?**
>
> *Scope control is all about monitoring the team meeting the scope objectives and looking out for change requests, that might potentially impact the original scope of the project. Scope control process is to be performed before the Scope validation since Scope validation refers to validating the project deliverables to make sure they meet the scope objectives of the project agreed.*

Project Scope Vs. Organization Objective

Ideally, a project scope is aligned closely with the organization objective of the performing organization. In other words, the organization objective is at a much high level goal over a project. Remember that an organization's business objective is much larger than the objectives of a project.

While defining the project scope, it is always important to have an understanding as to where it fits into the organization objective and what are the benefits it carries to the performing organization. As an example, if an organization has a vision to specialize in developing its expertise in banking business by providing specialized solutions to its customers, the project objective should be in line with such objective and do its piece of work in enriching the organization's expertise and hold on the business.

Product Scope Vs. Project Scope

There are many instances when you tend to confuse between the scope of a product and that of a project.

A product scope is nothing but the specification of a product. That means, the expected performance, features and functions of a product that you are trying to develop. If you are developing a LED television, what do you expect the device to perform once it is fully developed and tested?

Obviously you expect it to beam your favorite Television sports events, music, drama and lot of other features that are expected out of a standard LED Television device. This is the expected output of the product scope.

A project scope is how you & the project team will be performing your work to achieve the objectives of the project. A project scope has well defined objectives, goals and how the progress is to be assessed. A project scope statement becomes the bible of your team till the objectives and goals are to be achieved.

More on Product Scope Vs. Project Scope

To put it in a simple statement, you are required to follow certain processes to build your desired product. Right?

So, you need a scope for the product and a scope of the work that you planning to perform to build the product.

Imagine your company has won a huge project to construct a skyscraper in your town. Your company has signed a contract with the local council and undertook to plan, design, build and deliver the skyscraper within a specific timeframe. You are assigned to manage the entire project. All resources, both human and material, are at your disposal.

As part of the project planning & execution, you begin your work. You have the responsibility to deliver couple of critical deliverables before you could begin the execution phase. First is what you want to build along with the features of the final outcome. In this case, you have to submit the plan, design and specifications of the building you undertook to build. This is product scope, which usually contains the area of the building space, parking, essential infrastructure plans, number of floors of the building, intended electrical, electronic & security installations etc.

Similarly, you have the responsibility to narrate how you intend to execute the project with your management skills. This is the project scope. By now, you should be able to tell what is contained in a project scope statement.

In this case, you are responsible and own the project scope statement since you will be driving the entire project from start to finish. However, you need not design the product scope. You can engage a specialist to design the product but you might need to own the product scope unless the task of creating the product scope falls out of your project scope.

Does it make sense?

Good Changes and Bad Changes

Change is not bad always. Many times, it helps having our end product in a better shape. Any change that cost less amount of effort and money but gives a better and desired result is called a *Good change*. As an example, you are heading on a freeway to reach another town from yours. You have your navigation device tuned to travel through route A. However, you hear that there are possibilities of delays due to road congestion caused by construction activities. You are warned of a long line of vehicles that are moving slow. So, you decide to reprogram your navigation device and take an alternate route, which will save you time and energy. This change may involve driving a mile extra, but it eliminates risk of getting stuck and spending more on fuel.

Bad Change is something, which looks colorful and attractive initially, but when the project team begin working on it, things go on the other direction and consumes good amount of effort and money to carry it through.

The better idea for the project manager is to analyze every change for their potential impact and strictly adhere to the change management process.

What is Scope Creep?

Scope creep is same as what was defined in the beginning of the chapter. It is uncontrolled changes to the scope. Remember you are jeopardizing the interests of your own project if you deviate from your original requirement without any control on it. Earlier in this chapter, we have seen an example of your company building a recreational vehicle, which fails to deliver due to uncontrolled scope changes.

To put it straight again, most of the project troubles around the world are resulted by uncontrolled scope or ignoring the change management process.

What is Gold Plating and is it Good?

Sometimes, one might tend to go extra mile as part of their contribution to the project. This means, people attempt to add additional features or functionality to the original scope. This is often called 'Gold plating.'

Though there are risks of some unknown functional impacts hidden elsewhere in the project, any such 'extra offering' should be strictly avoided unless it is formally approved by the stakeholders. Such extras are not going to do any good to the project nor get any additional revenue to the performing organization. It might add more complexity and risks to the project.

Let us imagine, you have defined a scope of the product and handed to your team. As per the scope, you were expecting your team to come up with a video game with six special features. Based on this scope, you were negotiating with some buyers about selling this video game license after its completion.

How would it be, when you find that your team has put 'more' effort and included another half dozen features by themselves without consulting you.

Remember that you already negotiated and signed a licensing agreement with your buyer for the video game and committed a date of delivery too. Certainly, you would never like this 'proactive' attitude of your team.

So, having Gold plating is not a very good idea, though it might be mistaken as being proactive. But, it is not. Of course, none likes surprises in a business environment. Do they?

What Next?

Now, we have the Project Scope on hand. So, what next?

If you strictly go by what you heard from other Project Managers, you might tend to say "It is time to plan the project schedule". Don't you feel like saying so?

I wouldn't call it totally incorrect. However, you should realize that , before you begin working on your project schedule, you should identify whether your project require any procurement done or going to be completely executed in-house. There is a reason behind this.

If your project has plans to procure any products or services from external sources, it might dramatically impact your project schedule, cost, quality, resources and every component of the project. For example, imagine your organization has decided to outsource some critical components from outside. These components are essential for the completion of your project. If your organization has decided to go for a Fixed Price contract with the vendor, it will impact your role, ownership and responsibility on the outsourced part of your project. This will alter many of the subsidiary components, that you plan to work on.

We will be reviewing more on the Procurement planning later in this book. At this point of time, it would be better to identify about the procurement requirements of your project before proceeding with further planning.

Does it make sense?

Case Study 1

Assume you are the Chief Electoral Officer of your local civic council. The term of the current council is about to end in another four months. So, as the Electoral Officer it becomes your responsibility to prepare for conducting the council election in your town, with a population of little over 100,000 voters. There are a total of 35 council seats, one for each block. The jurisdiction of the Electoral office begins at announcing the election dates till completion of vote count and subsequent declaration of elected representatives.

Write a sample Scope Management Plan and Scope Statement to have this accomplished? You can make your own assumptions wherever required.

Case Study 2

Your Organization is moving from a leased premises to its own premise, which is of great standard. You are assigned the responsibility of moving all of the project teams, their desktops, materials, stationery and all equipments that are used by them. You will also be handling their security requirements to deactivate at the current facility and at the new premises. Your management has given you ten days time to get all of these activities done without any impact on the existing project work.

Write a sample Scope Management Plan and Scope Statement to have this accomplished? You can make your own assumptions wherever required.

EXERCISES

The list got messed up. Help match rearrange it in the correct order of sequence

1.	Scope Control	:	To define how the project scope is to be managed
2.	Scope Validation	:	List all the decomposed tasks to have resources assigned
3.	Scope definition	:	Done in project closure phase
4.	WBS Creation	:	This is where Changes to the scope is created and managed
5.	Scope Management	:	Project preliminary scope gets transformed into Project Scope

True or False

1. Product Scope and Project Scope are one and the same since both of them deal with the project outcome (**True/False**)

2. Project Scope remains unchanged even if the Product scope undergoes update (**True/False**)

3. Scope Definition is a onetime activity in a project lifecycle (**True/False**)

4. Scope validation is completely the responsibility of the customer (**True/False**)

5. WBS & WBS Dictionary are created in the same process (**True/False**)

6. A Project Manager's boundary of the scope is to manage only project scope (**True / False**)

ANSWERS

Puzzle

1. Scope Control : This is where Changes to the scope is created and managed
2. Scope Validation : Done in project closure phase
3. Scope definition : Project preliminary scope gets transformed into Project Scope
4. WBS Creation : List all the decomposed tasks to have resources assigned
5. Scope Management : To define how the project scope is to be managed

True or False

1. False
2. True
3. True
4. False
5. True
6. False

Test Your Knowledge

1. You are a project manager working on a massive construction project with over 100 team members reporting you. Your project started off very well with timely scope definition, schedule and cost planning done and approved. However, when the team start working on the construction, there were numerous changes requested by the customer and the scope was redefined very often and good amount of time was lost due to this scope updates. At one stage, the project went out of control and chaos prevailed in the project.

   After the scope was verified, your customer says the scope was not handled properly that lead to all these confusions. Which of the process are they referring to as not handled well?

   a) Scope Definition

   b) Risk Management

   c) Preliminary Scope

   d) Scope Management

2. You are managing a project and the project is in the closure phase. Your customer finds the validation process has thrown lot of issues and missing requirement when compared with the contract statement of work, despite the fact that the expectation was defined clearly in the contract and subsequent discussions. Your organization is not very much impressed with such a feedback from the customers and decide to investigate the root cause of the whole fiasco.

   What would have been the potential cause of this chaotic outcome?

   a) Poor risk planning

   b) Stakeholder identification

   c) Scope Management

   d) Overall project management

3. Let us revisit the Question 1 here. If you are asked to define the reason for the whole issue in fewer words, how would you put it in project management terms?

   a) Unrealistic change requests

   b) Unclear scope identification

   c) Scope Creep

   d) None of the above

4. During a meeting with one of the senior executive of the customer, you are explaining the objectives of the project. The executive is not a stakeholder of your project but he has some business interest in the project execution, so he monitors the project's progress.

   He gets the updates on the project from one of your stakeholder. During the meeting, the senior executive has some questions on the scope and wants you to forward the relevant document that help him understand the features of the project output. He want to have the approved scope of the project.

   Which among the below is the one he is interested in?

   a) Scope Statement

   b) Project scope management plan

   c) Test Plans

   d) Project Preliminary Scope

5. One of the below listed is NOT an input to the Scope Control process.

   a) Work Breakdown Structure

   b) Project Charter

   c) Work Performance Information

   d) Project Scope Statement

6. You are managing a large project with 20 members in your project team. The project is to develop an application software for a banking customer. The stakeholders identified by you have given a detailed expectation on the scope and you got your scope statement approved by them. Your project team has done an exceptionally great work and completed their work on time. The unit testing phase of the application is over and your project is ready to be verified by the customer.

   During the scope validation phase, one of your stakeholder has raised concern about one of his program having some extra features than what was expected. When you speak to your developer, you are told that the feature was included and will not impact the functionality of the program since it generates one extra report to the customer, that he feel may be required for the customer and will please them. On the contrary, the customer is not impressed and upset about this extra feature.

   Why is the customer upset, even if he has been given an option to generate an additional report?

   a) The customer has been unfair in their criticism

   b) The customer would have been happy, if he was informed about this extra in advance

c) This particular customer do not like surprises, even though such extra features is acceptable

d) Gold plating is never a good idea in a project and it should be avoided

7. **You are a project manager working on an event management project. The event is going to host an internationally popular music group for their performance in your town. You are preparing the scope of the project to be handed over to the sponsor of the event. Which of the following is IRRELEVANT for the project scope plan?**

a) Objectives of the project

b) Detailed description of the planned accomplishments

c) Authorization for the project manager to plan and manage the event

d) None of the above

8. **When does the scope gets verified in a project?**

a) During Execution phase

b) During Monitoring & Control phase

c) During Closure phase

d) During Planning

9. **Who is responsible for defining the Scope Statement?**

a) Sponsor

b) Project Manager

c) Collectively as a team

d) Project Management Office

10. **You are the project manager for a key data warehousing project for one of your Telecom customer. The customer is a market leader in their area of operations. Due to the critical nature of the project, the customer has let you use some of their staff to work on your project. It has been helping you to get the activities moving fast. One day the customer calls you to inform that they have decided to pull three of their six resources that were assisting you with the project. However, the client do not want to pull the critical resources but only those with less work load and having their deadline approaching soon. The stakeholder is asking you to get the details of the resources and their current assignment.**

What is the stakeholder expecting from you?

a) Work Breakdown Structure

b) WBS Dictionary

c) Project Scope Statement

d) Resource list

11. In which process group, a schedule gets tracked by the project manager?

   a) Execution

   b) Monitoring & Control

   c) Closure

   d) None of the above

12. Your team is done with their development phase that has produced a specific design engine for a business partner, who is planning to execute a special order for a customer with the powerful engine. The team has done a good amount of testing on the developed product. Everything went well with the testing and you have notified the customer to verify the product and confirm its meeting their expectation.

   During the scope validation phase, the customer identifies serious problems with the functioning of the engine based on their test procedure. One of the valve that is installed wouldn't fire-up in a specific sequence. Unless this issue is fixed, the customer wouldn't give an approval. The team argues that the product was designed according to the requirements and it passed their test, which is not convincing the customer. Finally, the customer is asking you to share the requirement document that the core team used as an input for developing the engine.

   What document is the customer asking you to share?

   a) Project Management Plans

   b) Scope Management Plan

   c) Quality plan

   d) Scope Statement

13. Which among the below is the output of Scope Validation process?

   a) Project Scope statement

   b) Project Management Plans

   c) Corrective Action

   d) Approved Deliverables

14. One of your stakeholder want a change request be included in the scope since it is a critical functionality of the requirement, that cannot be ignored. After a thorough analysis of the change requested, you come with the details of the overall impact, which is significant in terms of the scope. You decide to take up this request to the Change Control Board for their scrutiny and approval.

After having the Change request approved, what gets updated?

a) Project Scope Statement

b) Scope Management Plan

c) Scope, Time & Cost baselines

d) Project Management Plans for Scope, Time & Cost

15. Your stakeholder is getting confused after seeing the list of tasks that you have created for the project. The confusion is the task name given, which do not signify any meaning to him. He is asking whether you have any narration of each of the task recorded anywhere that might help him understand the purpose and details of each of the project's tasks.

What could help him in such a situation?

a) WBS Dictionary

b) Project Scope Statement

c) Work Breakdown Structure

d) Scope Management Plan

16. Which one among the below are true about WBS Dictionary?

a) WBS Dictionary gets created as part of the WBS creation process

b) WBS Dictionary is created by decomposing project's work package.

c) WBS Dictionary is used for tracking the status of work assignments to the team

d) None of the above

17. In which process, Revised Scope statement is named as an output?

a) Scope Management Planning

b) Scope Control

c) Scope definition

d) WBS Definition

18. One of the tool used in the project's scope management process is

a) Organizational Process assets

b) Product Analysis

c) Expert Judgment

d) Variance Analysis

19. Jackie was managing her first project, which started off very well. She could define the preliminary scope and got it validated by the customer without any trouble. She could define all the plan components successfully. The team did a great job of supporting her with timely completion of their tasks. During the scope validation

phase, she had trouble answering the questions of the stakeholders. When the customer asked about one of the deliverable and its objective, she couldn't find any reference about the functionality being questioned. The customer is not able to understand as to what could be the trouble there, since the changes were formally requested, documented and explained to Jackie and she acknowledged with few questions.

From the above scenario, what could have gone wrong for Jackie? Help Jackie with a suggestion.

a) The stakeholder is asking confusing questions and should have shown the written change request to help her understand what he is talking about.

b) Jackie should immediately share the Scope statement with the stakeholder

c) Sharing Scope along with WBS & WBS Dictionary would silence the stakeholder

d) The requested change was not updated in the Scope baseline

20. Which of the following statement is TRUE about the Scope?

a) A project manager need not wait for complete requirement be known but he can begin his planning activities. It is acceptable practice, since the PMI's describes a project as progressively elaborated

b) A scope change in the earlier phase of the project is easily manageable than at a later stage

c) The project scope management is considered complete, once the team complete their construction activities and test the deliverables.

d) A scope planning process is independent of every other planning processes.

21. The significant difference between Product Scope and Project Scope is

a) Product Scope refers to the intended objective of the outcome, whereas the project scope means how the project is planned to be managed that will facilitate the successful completion of the project objective.

b) Product scope refers to product specifications while project scope is about how you define the specifications and design by way of scope statement

c) They are same

d) None of the above

22. You are engaged in a scope validation process with the stakeholder. You are accompanied by your core team member, that worked on that particular task to provide any clarification on the task. During a

discussion, your stakeholder asks you to briefly explain the objective of the particular task that was completed, since he is not finding any reference of individual tasks in the project scope statement that he has on hand.

Where would you refer to get brief description of the particular task?

a) Ask the core team member to help the stakeholder by explaining the objective of that particular task.

b) Work Breakdown Structure should help with an answer

c) Refer the WBS dictionary of the specific task

d) Pull the email that were exchanged by the core team member who sought clarifications from the customer in the past.

23. **What among the below list is a tool used to define the scope statement**

a) Expert Judgment

b) Stakeholder analysis

c) Alternative identification

d) All of the above

24. **Which of the following narrate the features of a video game software**

a) Scope Management Plan

b) Project charter

c) WBS Dictionary

d) Scope Statement

25. **You are managing a large project to construct a skyscraper in the downtown and the customer is regularly monitoring the project status. You have weekly calls scheduled with your stakeholders representing the customer to apprise them of the status of each of the project tasks.**

Which of the following scope documents are useful while attending such status meetings?

a) Scope Management Plan & Scope Statement

b) WBS, WBS Dictionary & Project Status report

c) Project Charter, Project Management Plans and Scope statement

d) All of the above

ANSWERS

1. **Answer: D**

    Justification: When it comes to scope management, the primary responsibility of a project manager is to have a detailed processes defined on managing the scope and implement the process very strictly, in order to have a control over it through the phases of the project. In this case, you could have defined the initial scope management plan and the scope statement well. As the project progress further, there are bound to be change requests coming in. Once the changes are analyzed and approved, the scope, cost and schedule baselines should be reviewed and updated to include the additional effort and cost requirement for the change. This might be the problem in this scenario to have the scope going out of control.

2. **Answer: B**

    Justification: The potential reason for this issue may be a missed stakeholder. If you read the question very carefully, the high level requirement was clearly defined by the customer and was clarified in subsequent meetings. It is the responsibility of the project manager to pick this high level requirement and transition it into a detailed scope. In the case of this issue, it seems one of the stakeholder might not have been identified, which resulted in the high level requirement was overlooked while preparing the project scope statement. As narrated repeatedly, identifying all the stakeholders is very essential, if the project manager do not like surprises at a later stage of the project.

3. **Answer: C**

    Justification: Scope creek means uncontrolled scope. When multiple changes floods a project, it might potentially create a situation where the project manager and the team losing track of the original scope. To eliminate such risks, every project should have a very clear change management protocols to have control over the change requests.

4. **Answer: A**

    Justification: Whenever someone speak about the project scope document or baseline during post-planning phase of a project, they should be referring to the project scope statement. Once the stakeholders approve the project scope statement, it becomes the project's scope baseline, which is considered as the bible of the project. Any changes or references to the scope should be made against this scope statement.

5. **Answer: B**

   Justification: The project scope is not an input to the Scope Control process. A project charter contains only a very high level initial requirement and is a document that authorizes a project manager to plan and manage the project.

6. **Answer: D**

   Justification: Once the scope is finalized for any project, it becomes the responsibility of the project team to strictly adhere to what is defined in the scope. Personal opinions or assumptions should always stay out of the project scope. Such 'extra offerings' are called Gold Plating in project management term, which is not an acceptable practice. When an expectation is set by the customer, there may be some business need and reasons behind it. Such 'extras' might derail their objectives potentially. In this particular situation, the project manager should have discouraged the team from practicing such gold plating approach.

7. **Answer: C**

   Justification: An authorization is usually not required once the project gets into the planning phase, since a project manager's authority is accepted by every stakeholders. The high level requirement, narrated in the project charter, is already converted into preliminary scope statement, which will be an input to the project scope planning phase. Among all the four possible answers listed in the question, option C sounds sensible choice of answer.

8. **Answer: C**

   Justification : The development team might have completed their construction and validation before the project enters the closure phase. But, a formal verification is required to be done by the stakeholders, who validate the deliverables against the scope statement. This stakeholder verification takes place in the project closure phase.

9. **Answer: B**

   Justification: Defining a project scope is the responsibility of the project manager as part of the project Planning process.

10. **Answer: A**

    Justification: During the project planning phase, the project manager transforms the project scope into several tasks of smaller magnitude and easily manageable ones. The Work Breakdown Structure (WBS) contains the list of every project task and the resources assigned to each of these tasks. The WBS dictionary might also be required by the customer, since the WBS Dictionary provides more inputs such as the description of the tasks, preceding and subsequent task details and the dependencies about each of the tasks. However, the WBS qualify to be a better choice of answer to the question asked.

11. **Answer: B**

   Justification: Whenever you see term such as 'tracking,' it refers to monitoring by the project manager. The most important work of a project manager during the monitoring and control phase is to keep an eye on the activities being performed by the project team.

12. **Answer: D**

   Justification: Project Scope statement contains the specifications of the intended output of the project. The scope statement is the primary input for the project teams, who execute the development activities.

   (You must also remember that, every individual tasks of the project may have individual scope and specifications. For example, if an application software is being built, the whole application might be divided into 'n' number of smaller programs and each of the programs might be having its scope defined and approved by the stakeholders. However, the concept of scope do not change, whether it is a product scope or individual tasks' scope)

13. **Answer : D**

   Justification: The purpose of the Scope validation is to validate the deliverables against the project scope statement. Once the stakeholders complete their validation, the deliverables are either approved or rejected. If any discrepancies are noticed, they are recorded and changes are requested or recommended actions are proposed over the deliverables.

14. **Answer: C**

   Justification: If you could remember the triple constraint diagram that we reviewed in the earlier chapter of this book, whenever there is a change to one of the three components, the other two components get impacted and the overall impact will be felt on the quality of the outcome. In this case, since the scope change and the impact is considered significant, there are more likelihood of its impact on cost and schedule. Once the CCB approves the change request, the project manager is expected to update the cost, scope and schedule baselines. Thus, the revised baselines become the standards for the respective components of the project.

15. **Answer : A**

   Justification: The purpose of having WBS dictionary is to provide little more details about each of the tasks that are listed in the Work Breakdown

Structure. The WBS Dictionary also contains tasks that have dependencies on one another and any brief information required to have an understanding of the particular task.

16. **Answer: A**

    Justification: The WBS Dictionary do not get created as any separate process but it is a byproduct of WBS creation process. The purpose of WBS is to list each of the decomposed project tasks. Each of the task is substantiated with a detailed description for easier understanding.

17. **Answer: B**

    Justification: Now, take a moment and tell when a scope gets revised? Is it during the project planning phase or closure phase? Obviously not. A project scope gets created in the planning phase, whereas the scope is verified in the closure phase after the team completes the construction activities. During the monitoring & control phase of the project, there are chances of change requests made by the stakeholders. Once the change is approved, the scope baseline gets updated with the change requested and the outcome is the revised scope statement for the project team to work with.

18. **Answer: C**

    Justification: When the project manager begin working on the scope management planning process, there may be possibilities of someone within the organization or other experts having expertise on creating the scope management plan. Consulting experts on certain activities might help identify issues or risks in advance and design the plan by eliminating such risks or plan for them. The Project Management Office might be of help to the project manager in identifying such experts within the organization.

19. **Answer: D**

    Justification: Though this might appear a simple issue to many, but the impact of not getting the scope baseline updated would prove catastrophe in every project. The primary input for the project's development team is the scope statement. Ideally, if there is something not documented in the scope statement means not to expect the functionality in the final output of the project. Keeping this in mind, whenever a change request is raised and subsequently approved by the stakeholders, it is mandatory to get the scope baseline. In the case of Jackie, she planned for everything well till the change request was approved. Her failure to update the scope baseline resulted in chaos during the scope validation process, since the stakeholder was expecting the functionality, which was unknown to the development team.

20. Answer: B

Justification: A change to the scope may not be avoided in most of the project scenarios due to various reasons. However, all that matters is timing of the change requested raised. If the change request is raised in the initial phase of the project, the potential impact on the scope is minimal. Any change proposed towards the later stage of the project might require extensive analysis due to an enlarged impact.

21. Answer: A

Justification: A product scope is all about the specification, features and objective requirement of the product or service that is to be produced by the project. The boundary of the product or service, expected performance requirements of the outcome is called as a product scope. A scope of the project is how the project is planned to be executed, monitored and verified from start to finish. There is a significant difference between the two, though they appear to be similar.

22. Answer: C

Justification: As seen earlier in this chapter, the WBS dictionary contains brief details about the objective of individual tasks, their dependencies, effort details and the planned dates of start and completion for quick reference.

23. Answer: D

Justification: When a scope definition process is handled, consulting experts within the organization is a good idea for easier handling of the task. As explained earlier in this chapter, stakeholder identification and managing them plays a very crucial role in ensuring clarity of the scope and to avoid any future surprises. Another important tool is alternative identification, whereby the project manager considers every other options towards achieve his project objective before going ahead with scope definition of his project.

24. Answer: D

Justification: The question refers to the feature of a product, that is planned to be produced by a project. Obviously, this refers to the product features and specifications that are narrated in the project's scope statement.

25. Answer: B

Justification: There is no definite report requirement that helps a project manager while attending such discussions to take stock of the project status. However, in this case the question clearly speaks about the status of each of the project task. The Scope Management Plan is all about how the project manager plans to manage his scope, which may not be essential while attending such status meetings. Similarly, project charter and project management plans are not very relevant to attend such meetings. So the most appropriate choice of answer is B among all the available options.

This page is intentionally left blank

This page is intentionally left blank

Procurement Management

Objectives

At the end of Procurement Management chapter you should be able to know:

- What procurement management is all about and its significance in a project
- what processes form part of procurement planning
- details of each of the procurement planning processes
- who is a seller and how the seller is related to the buyer
- what a contract is and how the contracts are defined
- how the procurement bids are invited and the successful bidder is chosen
- what are the procurement documents and their importance
- the legal background behind every procurement process
- how the sellers are assessed
- how the contracts are managed
- the impact of project management processes in a procurement contract
- contract closure procedure

Why Procure?

When working in a business environment, outsourcing some products or services is inevitable due to various reasons. Such reasons differ between organization depending on their priorities in business and focus.

A good number of companies outsource their products to save cost. There are many organizations chose to outsource services such as business processes to save cost. Few other companies want to focus on their core business rather than having their nose buried into some support activities that can be better handled by outsourcing.

In a project environment, such procurement of products, services or support may be essential to achieve the objective of the projects. Such products or services or support task may be actually performed outside the project environment but the results are made available to the project team to complete its objective.

Tidbits

Can you take a moment to think and identify one most important difference between Procurement management and all other management plans (or knowledge areas)?

Well. The major difference between them is that Procurement planning is only optional for every project, whereas all other plans are mandatory for every project.

Not every organization is expected to procure products or services to support the project's objectives. In many situations the project teams handle every requirements of the project internally.

Whereas, every other knowledge areas are required to be planned and managed by every project. No project can be executed without a scope defined, risks assessed or quality planning done.

Note that an organization can either be a buyer or seller of these products or services. At times the project performing organization might execute the whole project in order to support a customer, who may be executing a larger project.

Take an example of a construction company assigned the project to build a huge baseball stadium in the city. Since the company do not have much expertise in furniture installations they hire your organization to take responsibility to install seating arrangements in the new stadium. This means that your project will support the construction company to complete their project objective.

Without discussing the rationale behind such strategies, let us review how the procurement management process works in an organization.

Where does Procurement Management Processing Happen in a Project?

Like any other project process, the procurement management processes are spread across multiple process groups beginning with Planning phase and end at the Closure process group. In fact, the procurement planning process is unique in such a way that every procurement contract signed with the customers are required to be formally closed in the Closure process group, whereas most of other subsidiary plans are completed even before the Closure process group.

The procurement process performed during the Closure process group is more about meeting legal and administrative requirements of the contract signed. In all, there are four processes performed as part of procurement management. They are

- Plan Procurement
- Conduct Procurement
- Control Procurement
- Close Procurement

Among the above processes, Plan Procurement happens during the planning stage, while Conduct Procurement takes place during the execution phase. Controlling the planned procurement is done during the monitoring & conduct process group. Shortly before winding up the project, Closure of procurement process is conducted.

Remember that, wherever you come across procurement process, we are talking in terms of procurement contract in this chapter. Let us refer to the procurement processes in a detailed form using the below diagram.

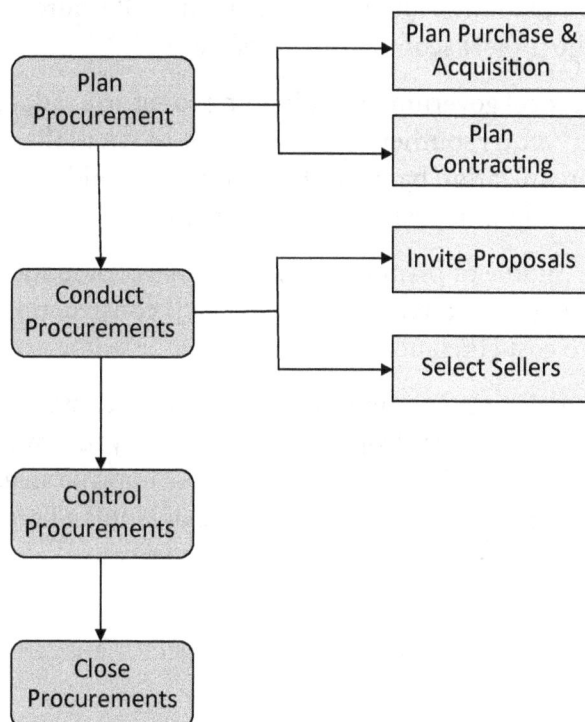

The boxes on the left refers to the actual processes that takes place in the procurement, while the boxes on the right narrates the activities or sub processes , which form part of their respective processes.

Let us now review each of these processes below.

Plan Procurement Process

As the project manager gets into the process of planning for the project components and processes, one of the important task required to be done is to pay attention to the project scope, boundaries and what will be performed by his project team. There may be more likelihood that some of the products or services required to be outsourced outside the project team or organization.

As I recommended in the Project Process chapter of this book, the Project Manager to work on the outsourcing plan even before he begins working on most other subsidiary plans. The ideal strategy is to analyze the procurement plans or needs of the project, after the project scope is finalized. If there is a plan to procure products or services, it would be a good idea to pay attention and finalize the details of the product or services before continuing with planning for further components.

Any guess as to why is this suggested?

During the planning stage of the project, every planning is done around the scope of the project requirement. This means unless the Scope Management Plan is frozen, the Project Manager cannot work on identifying risks or schedules. If the schedule is not completed, the Project Manager cannot begin working on Cost Management planning. Quality, Risks, Human Resource planning are all knitted around the project scope and boundaries.

Let us assume the local government is planning to setup a radar tracking center in a remote island off its southern coast in order to strengthen the security of its waters. Your organization has won the contract to build and setup key radar installations and other infrastructure requirement.

As you are in the middle of planning for your project components, your senior manager approaches you to tell that specific civil construction is going to be outsourced due to cost efficiency.

When you begin analyzing the impact on your planned components, you realize that this will alter your original scope significantly and you may not need 20% of the planned resources. Similarly, some of the risks may not need to be tracked by you since it becomes the responsibility of the outsourced organization. This cuts the planned cost by a sizeable proportion and so on.

Thus, the scope of the project is directly related to what the project is planning to produce and the outsourcing plans. The Project Manager will have better understanding and clarity on the scope boundary of the project once he finalizes the procurement plans, if any. Once the procurement plan and scope is finalized, the Project Manager will be in a better position to plan for every other knowledge areas of the project.

Does this justify the decision to take a look into the outsourcing strategy before working on other plan components?

To narrate the Procurement process in short, first the project manager identifies the need for procuring products or services, which will facilitate the execution of the project. This is followed by conducting the procurement. This involves identifying the sellers, negotiation, selecting the sellers. In the Monitor & Control process group, the project manager is expected to track the progress of the contract execution and look for risks, issues and expected schedule of the procurement and compare them with the planned terms of the contract. In the Closure process group, a formal closure process is followed to verify the terms of the procurement contract against the planned terms.

Now, let us take a look into how the Plan Procurement Management process works.

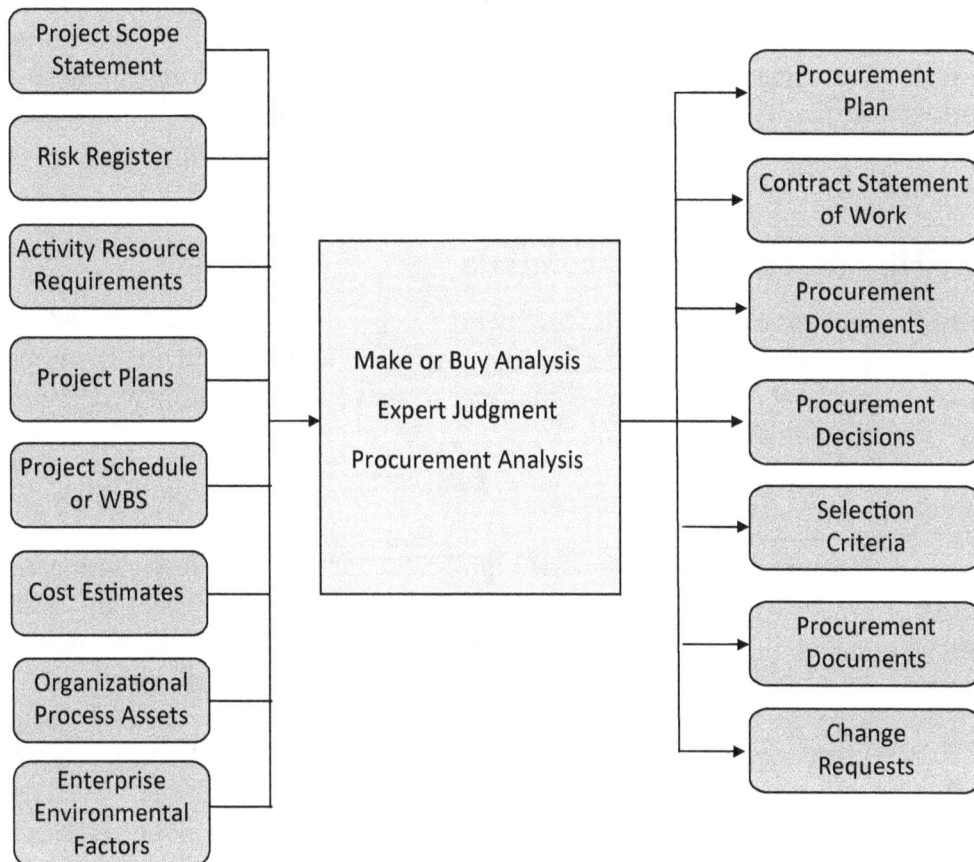

```
Project Scope
Statement
                                                    Procurement
                                                    Plan
Risk Register
                                                    Contract Statement
                                                    of Work
Activity Resource
Requirements
                                                    Procurement
                                                    Documents
Project Plans          Make or Buy Analysis
                                                    Procurement
                       Expert Judgment             Decisions
Project Schedule
or WBS                 Procurement Analysis
                                                    Selection
                                                    Criteria
Cost Estimates
                                                    Procurement
                                                    Documents
Organizational
Process Assets
                                                    Change
Enterprise                                          Requests
Environmental
Factors
```

Input to the Plan Procurement Process

Project Scope Statement

The very basis of the planning procurement process is the objective of the project. This is defined in the Project scope statement. Hence, the scope statement becomes the primary input required for the procurement planning process. When I say Project Scope Statement, it refer to the requirements that has been gathered from each of the stakeholder, which is transformed into a overall scope baseline of the project

The Project Scope statement is used as a reference by the Project Manager to analyze and to take a call whether to produce the product internally or to outsource. In addition to this, the Project Scope Statement will help the Project Manager define the contract requirements of the project.

Risk Register

While the project manager is planning for a procurement, one of the critical factor that is required to be taken into account is the risks identified with the project. A risk can be related to anything, internal or external factors.

The primary reason, several organizations adopt to procurement of products or services is to eliminate overheads and risks of cost and technical advantages. Ideally, risk register should have each of these risks identified and have a mitigation plans in place. Risks influence several organizations to procure products or services, in order to maintain their market advantage besides cost savings.

Activity Resource Requirements

Another key reason behind procurements happening is the cost involved on engaging resources by the performing organizations. An Activity Resource Requirement list help the project manager to arrive at a procurement decision for specific activities of the project.

Project Management Plans

Among all other plan components, the important factors that will be considered in the Plan Procurement process are related to Risks (Risk Register and Risk related contractual agreements), Resources information and Cost inputs. These data help the Project Manager analyze the advantages and risks related to outsource the product or services. In addition to them quality plans help finalize the quality process to be followed during the scope verification process of the procurement process and the Human Resources Planning process help understand the resource requirement. Cost and Schedule planning helps understand their impact on the overall project plan.

In addition to the above, these details help the Project Manager to define the terms of the Contract agreement.

Work Breakdown Structure (WBS)

The WBS helps the Project Manager refer to know the type of work being done by the project team. This subsequently helps in deciding as to which work can be outsourced. A WBS also refers to the proposed schedule of the project.

Cost Estimates

As illustrated above, cost is one of the key element that influence several organizations to take the procurement path. While not all organizations would want to outsource their entire project, having an estimation of cost of executing each of the project tasks would come handy, when the project manager preparing for the procurement planning of the project.

At this point, remember that besides human resource cost, there may be different types of cost involved in a project execution. Some of the examples include materials cost and administrative costs. All these costs are required to be analyzed, if the project is executed for a manufacturing company.

Enterprise Environmental Factors

The Organization environmental factors describe the amount of expertise the performing Organization possess related to the product or service being outsourced besides the organizational policies and market condition related to the contracting.

In this process, the performing organization's policies on procurement plays a critical role since nothing can progress unless the organization's policy facilitates procurement process of its products and service requirements.

Organizational Process Assets

The Organizational repository has the historic data related to the contractual work being considered or handled by the past projects. Referring to the past contractual terms will help understand the issues, assumptions and risks encountered in the past projects.

Organizational process assets come handy for many project manager when they are working on procurement planning. This is because, when they begin working on the procurement planning most of their plans and requirement might be ambiguous since they may not be sure of the boundary of the procurement process, vendor details, potential issues and risks to expect. Expertise of other project managers might help them to understand these in much details in advance.

Does it make sense?

Tools Related to Plan Procurement Process
Make or Buy Analysis

One of the most critical aspect of the Procurement process is to analyze performing Organization's capability to produce cost effective solutions, products or services indigenously. As explained in the previous pages of this chapter, a decision to make or buy has an overall impact on the project planning process spanning all subsidiary plans. Building a product internally might involve buying equipments, hiring people with special skills and so many planning to be done. If producing the products internally involves new equipments, then it becomes the responsibility of the Project Manager to assess the cost of leasing the equipment or buying it. At times, buying the equipment might appear cheaper than leasing it.

Besides the above factors, building products or establishing service desks needs time and this timing constraint should fit into the planned schedule of the project to have the products or services available on time for the project team.

Thus, it becomes the primary responsibility of the Project Manager in the Procurement process is to carry a detailed analysis to assess the realistic scenario about his project or Organization's capability before deciding to plan for outsourcing the product or services. Cost, Schedule and expertise plays a crucial role in helping the Project Manager taking a decision whether to build the product internally or to outsource. Sometime, building a product internally might give the performing organization with expertise on the specific product.

Let us assume the project is going to setup a new assembly line in a large auto plant. As part of the project plan, multiple production tracking work stations are to be installed. The options available are to approach the software division to provide an upgraded version of their production assembly software to the newly installed workstations or to procure cost effective software solutions already available in the market.

The Project Manager takes an assessment of various factors before deciding to go with one choice. His decision is mostly influenced by the cost factor and the fitment of the software to the original requirement. In addition, the impact on the schedule, quality and human resource requirement for building the software internally is also assessed.

In most organizations, procurement decisions needs to be approved by the senior management that require a justification from the Project leadership. The assessment activities done by the Project Manager should help come out with a detailed analysis and justification report to be forwarded to the senior management for their reference and approval.

Expert Judgment

An expert judgment is about meeting & consulting people with expertise in handling such contracts or procurement processes in the previous projects executed in the organization. As an example, let us assume the project performing organization has a list of preferred vendors, who might have expertise in executing specific types of work and have done business with them in the past.

However, if the project manager wants to get opinion or inputs about working with a specific vendor, he might contact one of the previous managers who had a procurement contract with the same vendor for a product or service. Such opinions might help the Project Manager to understand any potential risks or issues in working with the vendor.

Sometime, the Project Manager might need to consider certain legal aspects while entering into procurement contracts with suppliers. In such scenarios, legal advisers of the performing organization are consulted to get their opinion before finalizing the contracts.

For example, if the project involves usage of restricted and hazardous chemical substances, necessary permissions may be required to be obtained from the government agencies. The legal department of the performing organization is consulted for assistance to get such permissions.

Procurement Analysis

Name the most important tool that any project manager would consider prior to planning for procuring a product or service?

If you ask me, I would say studying the market and understanding the trend that is evolving in the business world. Though an organization need not adopt to the same strategy as their competitors, there is nothing wrong in analyzing the advantages, disadvantages, risks and issues involved in procurement process. Carrying out a market research will help the project to take a meaningful decision on procuring product or services.

Similar to Risk Management, an analysis of the market study and research would help identify the risks and issues much in advance, thus helping the project manager focus on eliminating such risks in the project.

Output of Plan Procurement Process

Procurement Management Plan

The primary output of the Plan Procurement process is the Procurement Plan containing the following factors.

- Planned scope of the procured product or service
- Planned delivery dates of the product or services
- Type of contracts to be used to honor the procurement
- Who will prepare independent estimates
- The scope of the procurement team and the boundaries of the project team
- Which standard documents shall be used
- How multiple vendors shall be managed
- How the procurement is embedded into the other project management plans
- List of constraints and assumptions
- How the time for purchasing or acquiring is integrated into the schedule plan
- How the work of make-or-buy-decision is linked to the activity list
- How mitigate procurement risks are handled
- How the contract work breakdown structure shall be maintained
- Which format shall be used for the contract statement of work
- How the contracts and sellers shall be evaluated

The overall objective of the procurement management plan is to plan and manage any type of situation that might arise during the procurement phase or subsequent execution phases till closure process.

Contract Statement of Work

This SOW is nothing but the illustrated details of the scope of the work along with the cost and schedule details.

The basic input for preparing the SOW are the Project Scope statement, Work Breakdown Structure (WBS) and WBS Dictionary. Each organization has its unique format of the SOW. The organization repository should have the SOW templates and earlier contracts signed for other projects.

At this point, the reader should not confuse between the Project Statement of Work and Contract Statement of Work. Can you identify the difference between these two SOWs?

The project SOW & Contract SOW are logically useful for similar purpose, but where they are used makes the difference.

While the Project SOW speaks about the overall expectation or objectives of the project being executed, whereas Contract SOW is specific to the outsourcing or procurement contract of products and services. The Contract SOW is the objective set for the suppliers and product or service acceptance criteria.

Another important point to note is, the Contract SOW need not or may not be referenced anywhere in the Project SOW.

Procurement Documents

Procurement documents are those that convey information about the whole procurement process, product or service related details to the potential bidders of the product or services.

Some sample procurement documents prepared and sent to potential bidders are Contract Statement of Work, Request for Proposal or Bid, Request for Quote, detailed description about the product or services being procured and so on.

Request For Bid (RFB) and *Request for Proposal (RFP)* are similar. The buyer is requesting the potential sellers to submit proposal for being considered. The criteria for choosing bidders is left to the discretion of the buyers.

Many Organizations have a list of preferred vendors, who have established their capability and efficiency to get into the preference list of such Organizations. If the Organization decided to approach any of these vendors to buy products or service, then a *Purchase Order* is prepared and shared with the seller after initial discussions on cost and procurement terms.

Procurement Decision or Make-or-Buy Decision

As illustrated earlier in this chapter, justification for every decision needs to be documented and submitted to the senior management or other stakeholders for approval. The justification is more of the rationale behind the decision to produce the product internally or to procure from external sources depending on various factors.

In this, the Project Manager explains in detail the factors that influenced his decision and the benefits of producing or procuring the products or services besides any risks, assumptions and constraints involved in this.

Requested Changes

When the Project Manager is working on procurement planning and finalizing the contracts, there are more likelihood of changes required for other plan components. These changes are documented and shared with the stakeholders.

Standard Procurement Documents

At this point, let us speak more of legal terms and look at things from the legal point of view.

This is because, whatever the documents we will be preparing and sharing with suppliers are done with two purposes in mind. First is to set an expectation and share the understanding of what is expected as part of the contract and how the contract terms will be monitored by both the buyer and sellers. Since planning a procurement contract involves many legal obligations, the Legal department of the performing organization is involved in this activity.

Some of the standard forms used to prepare the Contract include Memorandum of Understanding, Non-disclosure agreement, standard contract documents, checklist of product or service evaluation criteria, description of products and services and so on.

Another most important document used in procurement contracting is called Request For Proposals or RFP. When there is a larger procurement plan is considered by the buyer, the product and service related expectations are documented in a formal way and shared with potential sellers of such products and services. Each of these potential sellers are requested to submit a proposal containing their schedule, cost, quality and other details related to the delivery of the products and service before certain date set by the buyer.

After the buyer receives multiple proposals from different sellers, each of these proposals are closely scrutinized by their representatives to analyze the cost, schedule and product or services advantages before taking a decision on choosing one supplier. The advantage of having this arrangement is the buyer gets multiple options and cost competent solutions.

When we speak about procurement contracts of products and services, can you think of a best example of global procurement process being practiced in the world?

There are many governments, especially in the developing countries have large projects such as building nuclear reactors, dams, large scale refineries and offshore oil rigs in their countries. In order to get technological and cost advantages, they follow a procurement process called global tender or bidding process, wherein the governments or agencies invite bids from suppliers around the world. Such bidding process is similar to Request for Proposal (RFP).

Such global invitation of tenders give countries and companies ability to have projects executed with latest technical knowhow and affordable cost. Many governments or agencies use such global procurement process to improve their relationship with other governments.

Since every organization have their own templates of such contract documents, the Organization Process repository is the best place to learn about these document templates and how they are handled by your Organization.

Evaluation Criteria

A globally accepted fair procurement practice guides the buyers to share the evaluation criteria of procurement process with the potential sellers in advance.

Thus the sellers will have a chance to know how the buyer does business with vendors and their evaluation process in advance. Every Organization have their unique way of doing their business driven by their policies and processes. Unless the buyer keeps the sellers informed of their way of evaluating bids, the whole procurement process may not be effective for either.

Some of the possible evaluation criteria used to assess the ability of the sellers are

- Seller should be experienced in delivery of similar product range or services
- Seller's facility should comply with quality standards set by the buyer
- Seller's quality process should be well established and certified by global organizations like International Standards Organization (ISO)
- Seller's ability to manage the work efficiently and meet the criteria set by buyer

Updated Project Plans

While the Project Manager is analyzing and preparing the contract documents, there are possibilities of coming out with changes to the process and these changes are updated in the Project Plan components. If you could remember, a positive procurement decision taken in a project plays a significant role in altering the overall project planning, thus altering the scope of the project work significantly.

Types of Contracts

Once a decision is taken about procuring products or services, then the Project Manager need to finalize the type of procurement contract to enter into with the supplier.

There are three types of contracts namely, Fixed Price Contract, Cost Reimbursable and Time and Material contracts.

Fixed Price Contracts

In a Fixed Price contract, the buyer choose to buy a product or service for a price determined with the seller. Usually, purchase orders are raised with details of the product or service and exchanged between the contract parties. Statement of Work is involved giving larger details of the work to be carried as part of the contract.

In such Fixed Price contracts, all the equipments, manpower and material cost is factored into the price of the purchase to be acceptable to both buyer and sellers. Thus the buyer gets the desired product or service while the seller gets the price for his work.

Though Fixed Price contracts are adopted by several organizations worldwide, it has certain disadvantages as well. First is the price do not change, no matter how much time or how many resources are involved in executing the work. If the contract is signed to produce a product involving 1000 business hours of effort and 20 resources but the seller finds more time and resources to complete the work, he do not get paid for the excess effort and resources engaged.

Another disadvantage with Fixed Price contract is, it is difficult to manage scope changes. An alternate way to manage this disadvantage is to include the possibility of scope changes to the contracted work and its impact on the cost of the contract.

Cost Reimbursable Contracts

Sometime when the buyer buys products or service from the seller, cost of the product or service is reimbursed along with a fee or rate. This fee is the actual profit made by the seller.

Different mode of Cost Reimbursement are Cost Plus Percentage of Cost (CPPC) which means the cost of producing the product or service is paid along with a percentage of cost as service fee.

Other ways of reimbursing the sellers are Cost Plus Incentive and Cost Plus Fixed Fee.

Time and Material Contract

Time and Material (T & M) contracts are a mix or Fixed Price and Cost Reimbursable types of contracts. In a T & M contracts, the seller charges for the time spent by his resources in producing the product or services besides the cost of material involved. The human resources billed by the sellers get a fee as their salary or wage and the seller gets the remaining portion as their service charge.

The major disadvantage of the Time and Material contract is that the risk of meeting the targets and scope lies on the part of the buyer. Such T & M contract types are common in the Information Technology industry.

Now, take a moment to list your understanding on the three types of contracts against the listed factors. Use the box provided below.

Factors	Fixed Bid	Cost Reimbursement	Time and Material
Delivery			
Schedule			
Cost			
Resources			
Quality			
Risk			
Scope			

Once you are done listing your understanding, you can use the answer on the next page to validate the differences between each of these types of contract that I have given in the next page.

Factors	Fixed Bid	Cost Reimbursement	Time and Material
Delivery	Delivery of products and services is the responsibility of the seller	Delivery of products and services is the responsibility of the seller	Delivery of products and services is the responsibility of the buyer
Schedule	Seller owns the schedule management and control	Seller owns the schedule management and control	Buyer owns the schedule management and control
Cost	Project cost is fixed for buyer and seller	Project cost changes depending on the resource cost	Project cost is owned by buyer, who pays the seller for using the resources
Resources	Buyer do not own resources but seller does	Buyer do not own resources but seller does	Buyer do not own resources but utilizes them for a cost
Quality	Quality is the responsibility of seller, while buyer validates	Quality is the responsibility of seller	Quality is the responsibility of buyer
Risk	Project risks are owned & managed by seller but buyer is impacted by risks	Project risks are owned & managed by seller but buyer is impacted by the risks	Project risks are owned & managed by buyer
Scope	Scope is owned by seller	Scope is owned by seller	Scope is owned by buyer

Conduct Procurement Process

Having done the initial ground work on procurement planning process, the Project Manager should be now having the procurement documents and Procurement Plan available. We have established assessment criteria to evaluate the sellers based on their ability to deliver the products or services and meeting the terms of the contract. The Procurement Statement of Work illustrates the details of the intended product or service specifications.

Now it is time to invite the sellers to submit their interests in the form of Request for Proposals or Request for Bids. The Conduct procurement process monitors how the procurement process is implemented in choosing the right supplier to do the right job and according to the terms of the procurement contract. The selection process involves requesting potential suppliers to submit their proposals and assess the types of responses received from the sellers. Inviting the sellers can be done by many ways such as inviting the preferred sellers to submit their proposal, meeting their representatives and requesting for bids, through the newspapers and so on.

Let us refer to the below diagram for pictorial representation of the conduct procurement process.

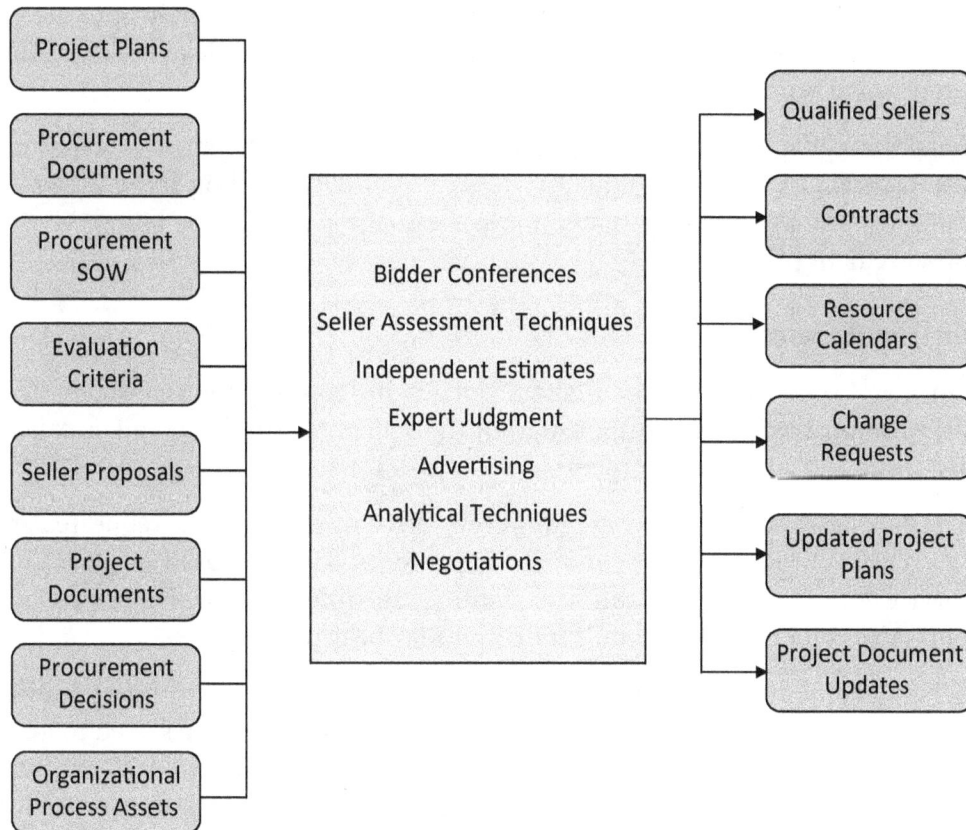

```
┌──────────────┐                                          ┌──────────────┐
│ Project Plans│──┐                                     ┌→│Qualified Sellers│
└──────────────┘  │                                     │ └──────────────┘
┌──────────────┐  │                                     │
│ Procurement  │──┤                                     ├→┌──────────────┐
│ Documents    │  │                                     │ │  Contracts   │
└──────────────┘  │                                     │ └──────────────┘
┌──────────────┐  │     ┌─────────────────────────┐     │
│ Procurement  │──┤     │   Bidder Conferences     │     ├→┌──────────────┐
│ SOW          │  │     │                          │     │ │  Resource    │
└──────────────┘  │     │Seller Assessment Techniques│   │ │  Calendars   │
┌──────────────┐  │     │                          │     │ └──────────────┘
│ Evaluation   │──┤     │  Independent Estimates   │     │
│ Criteria     │  ├────→│                          │────→├→┌──────────────┐
└──────────────┘  │     │    Expert Judgment       │     │ │  Change      │
┌──────────────┐  │     │                          │     │ │  Requests    │
│Seller Proposals│─┤     │      Advertising         │     │ └──────────────┘
└──────────────┘  │     │                          │     │
┌──────────────┐  │     │   Analytical Techniques  │     ├→┌──────────────┐
│ Project      │──┤     │                          │     │ │Updated Project│
│ Documents    │  │     │       Negotiations       │     │ │  Plans       │
└──────────────┘  │     └─────────────────────────┘     │ └──────────────┘
┌──────────────┐  │                                     │
│ Procurement  │──┤                                     └→┌──────────────┐
│ Decisions    │  │                                       │Project Document│
└──────────────┘  │                                       │  Updates     │
┌──────────────┐  │                                       └──────────────┘
│ Organizational│─┘
│ Process Assets│
└──────────────┘
```

Inputs to Conduct Procurement Process

Though we have seen all of the input documents in the previous processes, let us take a brief review of them again below

Project Management Plans

Since procurement of the product or service has significant impact on other planned components such as schedule, cost, risk, human resource management and communication, all these plans are considered as critical input to the Conduct Procurement Process.

Procurement Documents

All documents related to procurement processes, information about products or services sought. By now, I am sure you must be familiar with the standard procurement documents that are used in procurement contracts.

Procurement Plan

By now, the project manager should have a detailed plan on how the procurement process is planned to be carried in the project. The procurement plan refer to what is to be procured, responsibility, ownership, schedule and cost of the products or services that is being planned.

In addition, the project manager should have a mechanism defined on tracking the progress of the procurement process and about handling the issues and risks related to the procurement. All these components are found in the procurement plan.

Seller Proposals

Once you send out the procurement documents to the potential sellers, the next thing to expect is a response from the sellers for the bids. This is called Tender or Bid submission process.

The bids or tenders usually contain every piece of information requested by the buyers through the procurement documents. The proposed product and service details, their specifications, quantity, schedule and cost of each product or services and any other details the buyer may be expecting.

When it comes to government contracts for larger projects, the tenders or bids are submitted by the sellers in strict confidence in the form of a sealed tender. When the agencies receive all bids or tenders on a predetermined date, the bids are opened and scrutinized for their proposals. This is to make sure every seller gets a fair treatment in the bidding process.

Seller Evaluation Criteria

As illustrated in the previous pages, the project manager should have a clear understanding on how the received proposals and sellers are to be assessed before arriving at a procurement contract plan. This understanding form part of the Procurement Plan of the project.

Some of the selection criteria could be expertise of the sellers, past track record, cost, quality of the product or services, market leadership and the available infrastructure with the seller, that makes them capable or incapable of supplying the intended products or services.

Procurement Decisions

Planned by the project manager during the Plan Procurement process, a procurement decision refers to the decision on procuring products or services or to handle it internally. In other words, it is a decision as to make the product internally or to outsource.

Organizational Process Assets

Besides having a list preferred vendors, every Organization has details about each of these vendors. Such details include positive feedbacks and issues encountered with them, their quality processes, commitment to schedule, cost inputs and their delivery accuracy. These inputs comes in handy for the project managers, while they work with procurements.

The Organizational process assets have details about the Organizational policies relating to procurement of products and services.

Tools used in Conduct Procurement Process

Bidder Conferences

Every Organization has its unique and own way in handling its vendors when it comes to procuring products or services. Some Organizations go to media or internet (in their websites) to announce its procurement intention and invite proposals from prospective vendors. Some organizations issue press releases about their procurement plans and few others pick up their own preferred vendors and contact them directly.

So, there is no single correct strategy in procurement process. It is the Organization's business approach.

One of many fairer way to handle the vendors is to hold a conference for all the potential vendors under one roof and announce the details of the contract and the terms. Holding such bidder conferences will bring confidence in the bidders and have all their questions answered. Thus the buyer will eliminate any missing pieces of communication or provide more inputs to one bidder while withholding for the other. In such conferences, the buyer will explain how their procurement process works.

Proposal Evaluation Technique

There are many techniques adopted by different organizations to assess the credibility and worth of the submitted proposals. That can range from any of the above or some techniques that are very unique to the performing Organization.

For example, some Organizations might expect the sellers to supply sample products to justify their capability and efficiency. When the buyer collects multiple such samples, they compare the features between each of them before shortlisting the most impressive one. Once the choice is made, the buyer might set a product quality baseline before signing the contract with that particular seller.

Tidbits

> **Can you list identify some more evaluation techniques being practiced in different industries around the world?**
>
> *Some organizations on the Information Technology space practice developing pilot project for their customers and some engineering or products manufacturing companies practice developing prototypes or samples to justify their capability.*

Independent Estimates

Before beginning to assess each of the seller responses, every buyer carries out its own estimation of the cost involved in the purchase of the products or service but the same data is not published anywhere. When the sellers send their proposal, the cost data of each of the proposal is captured and mapped against the independent estimated cost.

Thus the buyer is in a better position to take a realistic and feasible call on which proposal appears attractive from the cost point of view. Since cost plays a very important role in selecting such proposals this independent estimation mechanism proves effective with many organizations.

Expert Judgment

The process of engaging experts of the contract negotiation process is more effectively seen in the procurement management. Since the Project Manager may not be aware of everything about the identified sellers or the procurement process in the initial stages of planning besides preparing independent estimates of the procured products or services, Project Managers or Legal team or any other experts from inside and outside of his Organization might be of greater help in making his life easier.

Engaging the experts in the procurement management and contract negotiation process reduces the risks for the Project Manager since experts can foresee issues before they might occur. For example, the legal team looks everything from the legal standpoint when supporting the Project Manager, thus the risks of something going from with the procurement is kept to the minimum.

Advertising

As explained earlier, an easiest way to reach as many sellers as possible is through the media. Publishing advertisements in newspapers with details of the product and service requirements and procurement plans. Reaching sellers through advertising is popular for government funded projects.

As explained earlier in the chapters, many of the governments use the global tender system to invite bids and to execute large projects in their countries to have an technological superiority and to save cost of procurement.

Contract Negotiations

Once the buyer has picked up his choice of seller for the procured products or services, it doesn't result into signing a contract instantly. Once the decision on the proposed seller is made, the buyer and seller reassemble for a contract negotiation to understand each of their expectations, terms and conditions related to the contract.

Once the specific points about the contracts are discussed, the contract documents are prepared and signed by both the parties.

Analytical Systems

Seller Rating Systems

The Seller rating is primarily an historic information available in every Organization's process repository. The sellers' ratings are arrived based on a standard guidelines established by the buyer. The guidelines are common for every seller irrespective of the products or services they offer.

The sellers ratings are reached based on their level of services, quality of the deliverable, schedule, cost and carries less risk for the buyer. The organization's process assets should have detailed view of the organization and its managers' experience on working with individual sellers. In several organizations, the existing rating of each seller is considered a critical input in making procurement decisions. Needless to say, several organizations prefer working with their existing vendors.

Weighing Systems

When a tender or proposal is scrutinized for assessing the efficiency and capability of the seller, it is mandatory that every seller is treated in a fair manner and such fairness can be established only if the qualitative analysis of the sellers' background is analyzed and verified by the buyer. This will ensure personal likes and dislikes do not come in the way of making selections. As a response to the bidding process, every seller sends enormous amount of information to justify their ability. Such data is pulled from their earlier engagements, expertise and delivery capability.

As the buyer begin assessing these data, a better way to compile them is to prepare a checklist of critical assessment criteria and prepare a report containing each of these criteria and rate each of the seller against them. Once the report is prepared including all the sellers, the buyer will have clarity of data to take a decision on the capability of the seller.

Screening Systems

Another important way to shortlist a seller from the list of proposals is to screen each of them to understand their capabilities, expertise, past track record of delivering similar products or services and their success rate of timely and quality delivery. This screening system is widely followed across industries around the world.

As part of the screening system, the buyer has established a criteria for minimum acceptance and each of the seller is assessed against this criteria. After the screening process, the sellers' proposals are rated from worst to best. A final call is taken by the Project Manager based on this assessment.

Output of Conduct Procurement Process

Selected Sellers

The ultimate output of the Select Seller Process is the list of selected seller or sellers for the specific products or services.

In the Selected Sellers process, the list of sellers are shortlisted based on specific evaluation criteria set by the buyer. Initial draft of Contract is prepared with each of these sellers. After the specific Seller is picked, the initial draft is finalized and awarded to that successful bidder.

Remember that every contract finalized and signed with chosen sellers are unique with differing contract terms and cost factors.

Contract

A Contract is a deal or a detailed document that is legally binding the buyer and seller together to carry a predetermined task of supplying products or service.

The terms of the Contract is mutually agreed between both the parties. Once a Contract is signed, it obligates the Seller to supply the products or services in return for a fee by the buyer.

Resource Availability List

There may be instances when the terms of your contract involves resources of the seller working on your project and form part of the team itself.

Imagine a situation, where a project hire contract staff to provide infrastructure support to a larger team. The reason for having such procurement contract may be to reduce cost or technical expertise of the contractor in the specific technology. Any resource that is included as part of a contract should be identified and included in the staff planning process.

Requested Changes

Whenever the Project Manager is working on plan components, there are larger scope for updates to the original plan and these updates are carried through a formal Change Management Process.

Updated Procurement Plan

At times, the select seller process might force review of the procurement planning to make it in line with the realistic scenario. Any updates to the Procurement Process or the terms result in the Procurement Plan updated.

Updated Project Documents

Any procurement process involves significant amount of updates to the project related documents such as Resource Plan, Schedule and Cost Plans. In addition, documents such as RASI Chart undergo changes to themselves as a result of procurement process. These updates are captured as output of the Conduct Procurement Process.

Control Procurements

What it Means to Manage a Procurement Contract

The procurement process doesn't end with selection of the sellers or signing the contract document with the seller for the supply of products or services. Unless the signed contract is managed well, things might go wrong that might derail the very basis of the procurement process.

Imagine a situation, you work as a Project Manager for an automobile company and managing a project to build limited number of special vehicles for the Army. You procure specially designed suspension systems from one of your vendor, with whom you have signed a contract with the required numbers and the required by dates. As a responsible Project Manager, you need to keep track of the supply plan of the vendor and make sure the suspension systems are delivered before you could begin assembling the vehicles at the assembly line since, without the suspension system available, you cannot proceed beyond procuring other components required for assembling the vehicles.

Thus, it becomes very critical to manage the vendors and their supply plans in order to proceed with your project towards the completion. Moreover, the Project Manager is expected to make sure that the supplies of the products or services meet the terms of the contract signed with the vendor. The quality of the supply becomes another critical factor having impact on the project progress.

Similar to the other processes of the procurement planning, the control procurement is not only important but also complex to manage. The Control Procurement process is very crucial task, as it helps in building and managing a relationship between the buyer and seller, which benefits both of them and help achieve their business objectives.

Control Procurement is the only Procurement Process that is performed in the Manage & Control Process group.

Like any other knowledge areas, any changes to the original plans of the Control Procurement will result in a change request being raised, analyzed and scrutinized by the Project Manager who will follow the standard Change Management process to get it approved by the Change Control Board before updating the Procurement Management Plans and the relevant baselines.

Just In Time (JIT)
In order to reduce the cost of storage, several companies of this world follow the practice of procuring their required products just before they begin assembling them. This means, they enter into procurement contracts with their vendors which guarantees the required procurements arriving at the assembly plants on the day of the planned assembly.
The advantage of adopting to this practice is to save money on warehouses to store the products in advance. However, this strategy requires extreme caution and excellent planning since any deviation of the contractual obligations by the vendors might derail the assembly plans, thus costing time, money and effort.

Why Should the PM Need to Focus More on the Control Procurement Process

More than any other processes, it is the Control Procurement process that requires more focus and scrutiny of the Project Manager.

Do you understand why?

In a Procurement process, the products or services are outsourced by way of a Contract executed with the seller. This means that the Project Manager have less or no visibility on the process of producing the project or service but is notified of its availability upon completion.

If there are any issues during the contract execution by the seller, the buyer may not even be aware of the trouble until it is blown out. The only mode of communication for the buyer is with the help of Performance Reports and Work Performance Information shared by the seller.

With such low level of visibility, it becomes essential for the Project Manager to stay on top of the Contract execution process by way of occasional reviews and tracking the status of the work being performed by the seller.

Now, let us see how the Control Procurement process works with the help of the below diagram.

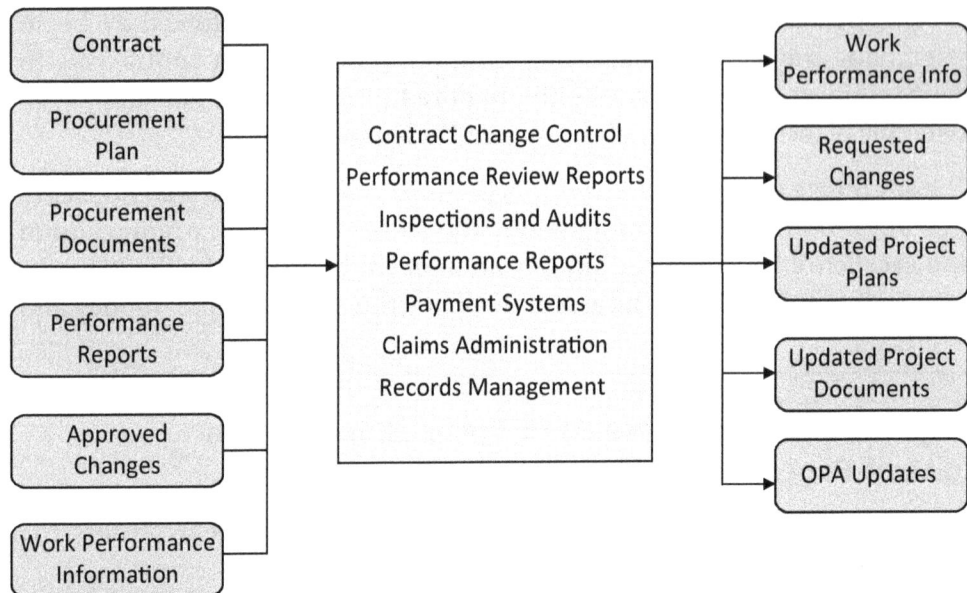

```
┌─────────────────┐                                        ┌─────────────────┐
│    Contract     │─┐                                   ┌──│      Work       │
└─────────────────┘ │                                   │  │ Performance Info│
┌─────────────────┐ │   ┌───────────────────────────┐  │  └─────────────────┘
│   Procurement   │ │   │  Contract Change Control   │  │  ┌─────────────────┐
│      Plan       │─┤   │ Performance Review Reports │  │  │    Requested    │
└─────────────────┘ │   │                            │──┤  │     Changes     │
┌─────────────────┐ │   │   Inspections and Audits   │  │  └─────────────────┘
│   Procurement   │ │   │    Performance Reports     │  │  ┌─────────────────┐
│    Documents    │─┼──→│     Payment Systems        │─→├──│ Updated Project │
└─────────────────┘ │   │    Claims Administration   │  │  │     Plans       │
┌─────────────────┐ │   │     Records Management     │  │  └─────────────────┘
│   Performance   │ │   └───────────────────────────┘  │  ┌─────────────────┐
│     Reports     │─┤                                   │  │ Updated Project │
└─────────────────┘ │                                   │  │    Documents    │
┌─────────────────┐ │                                   │  └─────────────────┘
│    Approved     │ │                                   │  ┌─────────────────┐
│    Changes      │─┤                                   └──│   OPA Updates   │
└─────────────────┘ │                                      └─────────────────┘
┌─────────────────┐ │
│Work Performance │─┘
│   Information    │
└─────────────────┘
```

Inputs to the Control Procurement Process

The Contract, Procurement Plan and Procurement Documents are output of the previous processes, which contain details about the terms of the procurement contracts.. Let us not review them again here. You might revisit the previous pages, should you like to review them.

The Work performance data refers to the performance of the suppliers, with respect to meeting their performance objectives against the expectation. Performance Reports are the review done by the Seller about the performance of the seller with respect to the progress and meeting the objectives of the contract.

Approved Changes are any changes requested to the procurement planning, as we are currently in the Manage & Control Process. Change requests are usually raised when something goes wrong during the contract execution process.

Tools Used in the Control Procurement Process

Contract Change Control Process

Whenever there is a change required while managing the contract, the performing organization's Change Control Process comes in handy for the Project Manager. Ideally, changes to the contract may be required due to any issues or problems encountered.

The Change Control Process to the Contract is same as applicable to any other knowledge area.

Performance Reporting

Every Project Manager has the responsibility to report the progress of the project to their senior management and this is achieved by way of preparing a detailed Project Performance review reports. The data received from the Seller is considered a key input in preparing these reports. The template for such reports may vary from every Organization and their information requirement. The performance contains the status in the form of data and narrated description of the progress.

Inspections & Audits

One of the key success factor of every project is to make sure the project is producing product or services that is in accordance with the objective of the project and complies with the customer requirements. This can be achieved by conducting inspection and audits of the actual products and services. Such inspections help take a realistic assessment of the quality of the product or service besides identifying issues in advance

At times, such pre-determination of problems lead to Change Control Process on the Contract.

Performance Review

To make sure, the processes followed by the sellers adhere to the recommend quality process and meets the process benchmark established as per the professional standards, many times the buyer conducts audits of the seller's process compliance. At the end of such process reviews, the buyer might recommend process improvements, which may or may not be agreed by the seller dependent on their business strategy.

Note that the performance review is different from the inspection and audit, since the former is to review the process whereas the inspections is about the product or service compliance.

Payment Systems

Every employee works to make a living. None will be ready to do their work for free. Similarly, each of the seller expect to get paid for all the work done by his project. Such payment system is predetermined by the buyer and the payment policy is strictly followed by way of payment cycles.

Every Contract document highlights the payment terms, specific payment policies and payment cycles in detail, thus eliminating any questions or confusion.

Claims Administration

A Claim may be a demand or dispute between a buyer and seller over some point of content of the contract. It is quite possible that either or both of them disagree on certain aspects of their obligations in meeting the contract.

For example, the buyer has changed his production plan to meet the festival demand and expecting the seller to updates his support plan to cater to this changed scenario. However, the Seller has resourcing issues to meet this request. The Seller do not have required support personnel and need to hire from the market, at higher cost. The buyer is not willing to pay the extra bucks to the seller. This results in a dispute.

In general, every contract has specific clauses or terms to resolve such disputes or claims. Both the buyer and seller are expected to understand this and honor the pre-determined terms of the contract. Note that every signed is legally binding the buyer and seller equally.

Records Management

Communication plays a very vital role in a contract. As we have seen in the Communication Management Planning process, any document that involves exchange of data or information becomes an asset of the specific project. In terms of a project, documents such as bills, invoices, emails, meeting minutes, advises, memos are all samples of records.

Since the contracts are legally binding the buyer and seller, it is essential that all of these records are collected and kept for future reference requirements.

Output of Control Procurement Process

You should be familiar with most of the outputs of the Control Procurement Process. You might review the previous pages of this chapter if required.

Contract Closure Process

Do you think, a successful Procurement process ends with the supply of great products or best available services from the selected vendor?

It is true that every Project Manager want to procure the best products or services for his project, he has little more to do beyond managing the Contract Management Process. A procurement process wraps up only in the Project Closure phase, wherein the Procurement process is formally closed by way of legal, financial and administrative terms.

Necessary procurement audits are conducted to make sure that both the buyer and sellers successfully met the terms and conditions of the contract for the ultimate benefit of the project. All contract related documents including the lessons learnt, best practices followed and feedbacks about the contract are stored in the Organization Process repository for future reference and benefits.

In many instances, either the buyer or the seller may not be fully satisfied with the execution of the contract. However, irrespective of these disappointments, the contract is considered closed when all the expected terms and conditions are met by both.

Let us take a look into the Contract Closure Process with the help of the below diagram.

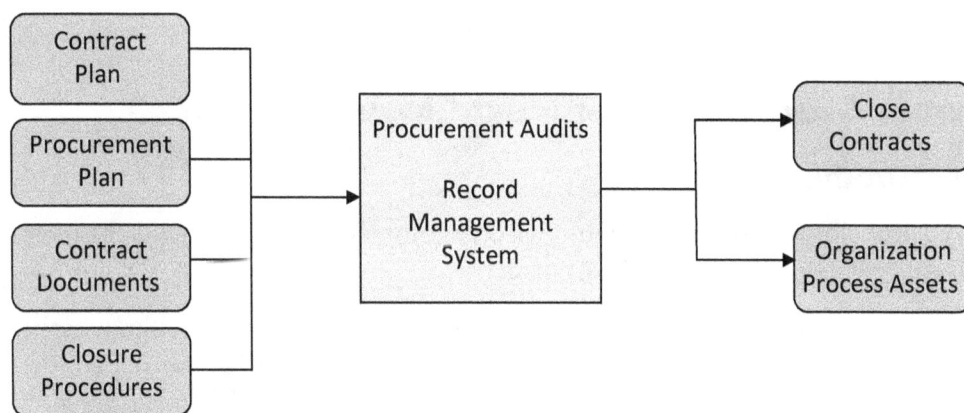

Inputs to the Contract Closure Process

Contract Management Plan

Besides providing details of controlling the procurement process, the Contract Management Plan has details on evaluation criteria and the checkpoints for meeting the contract terms and conditions by both buyer and seller. These are very essential to assess the completion of contract terms prior to contract closure.

Procurement Management Plan

A Procurement Plan contains the details of the Products or Services that were planned to be outsourced besides the original planning ideas, expectations and other terms of the contract. These are essential inputs to validate whether the original plan is met as part of the Procurement Contract.

Contract Documents

Every document that were signed or exchanged as part of the procurement process.

Closure Procedure

Every Organization has its own set of procedures or formalities to be completed with respect to closing a contract. Ideally, many of these procedures are illustrated in the Contract Management Plan document. However, any additional processes to be followed must be available in the Organization's process assets.

A contract can be closed once all the terms of the contract are met by the buyer and seller. The seller complete all the committed delivery of products and services as per the contract while the buyer is expected to meet the payment commitment for the products or services.

Tools Used in the Contract Closure Process

Procurement Audit

A project closure doesn't end with delivery completion and financial closure of all commitments agreed in the Contract.

As a last step of the Procurement process, the Project Manager verifies whether all the terms of the contract are met including the intended delivery of products or services agreed. In addition to this, a detailed analysis is carried to understand what went right and wrong, compliance of the products, their fitness to use.

A detailed document listing the lessons learnt is prepared and uploaded in the Organization's process repository for future reference.

Records Management System

One of the key success criteria for a project is the availability of historic information, expertise available within the organization and documentation available.

Every piece of information related to the projects are vital for the performing organization's capability and its future success. This signifies the documentation of all vital project information such as cost, schedule, risks, contracts, resources, technical, business information and other components and storing them in the Organization's process repository a very important responsibility of the Project Manager and his team.

In fact, a project is not considered closed without the Organization repository updated with all of these information.

Does this make sense?

Output of Contract Closure Process

Closed Contracts

A formal signoff of the Contract upon successful completion of meeting the terms. It is the responsibility of the buyer to send such a formal signoff to the seller that the contract objectives are met by the seller. Such a formal signifies the end of the contract.

Organizational Process Repository

All documents related to the contracts such as Procurement plan, Contract Management plan, contract documents, templates, emails and so on are stored in the Organizational process asset library.

If you could remember, you might have referred a good amount of such historic data from your Organizational process during the course of your project execution.

Key Points to Remember in Procurement Management Process

Non-Disclosure Agreement

A non-disclosure agreement is a declaration signed between the seller and buyer to maintain strict secrecy over the contract and the entire project execution. By signing the agreement, both the buyer and seller agree to respect each other's business strategies and any business and project related information from getting out of their organizations. In today's intense business competency climate, a NDA plays a key role in limiting the leaking of business relation confidential information to the competitors.

I wouldn't hesitate to say that, in case of such leakage of confidential business related information, the damage to the buyer is more than the seller.

Conflict of Business Interests

At times, there may be situations that the seller does business with another company that might involve use of same resources, business strategies and technology. While the seller cannot always be restricted from engaging in any such business tie-ups with buyer's competing companies, it becomes the buyers responsibility to make sure the seller understands and respects the business interests and strategies of the company.

Usually, in many cases special clauses of the agreements clearly defines such risks and make sure the seller is aware of such risks.

Terms & Conditions

The terms and conditions is a very important factor between the buyer and seller. Both of them work on certain understanding and business interests. Every important expectations of the contract and the limitations are clearly included in the terms and conditions clauses of the contract document.

In addition to this, the payment terms are clearly defined in the document, which is legally binding the buyer when it comes to settle the payment for the seller.

EXERCISES

Fill in the Blanks

1. Cost risk is more on the _____ in a Fixed Price bid.

2. The task of convening a meeting of all the bidders to clarify doubts and answer questions on a procurement contract is called _____.

3. In a Cost reimbursement procurement model, responsibility of maintaining quality of the procured product or services lies with _____.

4. Before beginning to work on the procurement management plan, the project manager conducts an assessment of procuring or making the product. This process is called _____ Analysis.

5. RFB in a procurement process stands for _____.

True or False

1. A procurement audit is assessing the efficiency of the company's procurement process, on the lines of the Quality assurance   (**True/False**)

2. Every company has a list of qualified sellers and the procurement bids are invited only among them   (**True/False**)

3. Non-Disclosure agreement is one of the standard procurement document (**True/False**)

4. Project risks are owned by the Seller in a Time & Material contract   (**True/False**)

5. Control Procurement means monitoring the contract implementation   (**True/False**)

Match the Following

*   Contract Closure   :   Contract negotiation
*   Select Seller Process   :   Claims administration
*   Invite Seller Response :   Seller evaluation
*   Control Procurement   :   Procurement Audit
*   Plan Contracting   :   Advertising

ANSWERS

Fill in the Blanks

1. Seller
2. Bidder Conferences
3. Seller
4. Make or Buy
5. Request for Bid

True or False

1. False
2. False
3. True
4. False
5. True

Match the Following

- Contract Closure   : Procurement Audit
- Select Seller Process : Contract negotiation
- Invite Seller Response : Advertising
- Control Procurement   : Claims administration
- Plan Contracting   : Seller evaluation

Test Your Knowledge

1. Richard is a project manager, who is currently engaged in the planning portion of his project. The project is planning to produce specific model of engines that are used in aviation industry. As part of his planning, he is looking at the possibility of outsourcing certain components based on the feasibility. He has a clearance from his senior leadership team to apply his own wisdom to come to a decision on the procurement process. With the management backing, Richard is not sure whether to procure a special type of engine valves for the project. So, he is considering two scenarios. First is the cost of producing the product in-house and the second option is to procure the valves.

   Which task is Richard performing now?

   a) Procurement Management

   b) Plan Purchase & Acquisition

   c) Plan contracting

   d) Control Procurement

2. As part of your procurement process, you are asked by your senior leadership to invite all the proposed sellers to come to the office on the specific day to participate in a session that will provide them insight into the planned procurement, processes , expectations and many more details. This meeting is schedule to demonstrate the organization's fair procurement practice, provide more details and answer every questions of the sellers.

   Which process group are you in?

   a) Execution

   b) Initiation

   c) Planning

   d) Monitoring & Control

3. What among the below is NOT an example of Procurement document

   a) Risk register

   b) Contract Statement of Work

   c) Request for Quote

   d) Description about the product to be procured

4. Diana is the project manager of a very large logistics project being executed for a prestigious customer. She is under very tight schedule and involved in the procurement audit being performed on her procurement plans.

Which process group is she into now?

a) Monitoring & Control

b) Execution

c) Planning

d) Contract Closure

5. Jacqueline is assigned as a project manager for a civil engineering project. She is working for a large and well reputed engineering construction company in the country. Her project envisages setting up a container terminal in the local port. Prior to her begin the planning process, she was invited to a meeting with the company's senior executives. In the meeting, she heard that a part of the workforce is to be outsourced to a local contractor due to resource related problems, the company had while executing the last project. The senior executives asked her to prepare a procurement plan, where the vendor would be charging for the effort each of their staff spent on this project besides the usage of their equipments.

What type of contract is this?

a) Fixed Price

b) Time & Material

c) Cost Plus Fee

d) Costs Plus incentive fee

6. You are in the middle of planning for procuring specific types of components from one of the vendor. Your company has a list of preferred vendor list and decide to go with one of the regular vendor for their outsourcing needs for this project. When you are working on the terms of the contract, you have some questions on the contractual terms and cost liability for the project. You are not sure, what the state law says about cost liability.

Which is the BEST group or person to answer your questions?

a) The customer

b) Project Management Office

c) Your senior management

d) Legal department

7. Which type of contract carries more risks for the buyer than the seller

a) Time & Material

b) Cost Plus Incentive Fee

c) Cost plus % of cost

d) Fixed Price

8. You are working with a vendor to procure specific components, which is critical for your project. Your project is Time & Material type of contract. Prior to signing the contract, you asked the seller to provide the cost of the materials that will be used. Based on the input, you prepared the cost baseline. However, as the project makes progress the seller approach you and want the cost of the material be revised since there was appreciation in the price of the products. You suggest the seller to raise this as a claim to discuss and settle.

    Name the tool, that is used to resolve such problems.

    a) Procurement Management Plan

    b) Claims Administration

    c) Contract Statement of Work

    d) Conflict Management

9. You are managing a structural engineering project and working with a vendor for the supply of critical components. The project is a Fixed Price Plus incentive type of contract. Your project has been going smooth until you heard from the seller last week that he is running out of cash due to unexpected cost on the raw materials used to produced the components to supply to you. This has resulted in the seller having to bear the procurement cost overrun and want the cost be revised for the work being done by them.

    What are the options available for the seller?

    a) Poor planning. Seller can renegotiate with the buyer for revised price.

    b) The seller wanted to quote a competitive cost to take cost advantage and to win the contract.

    c) Seller might have quoted the price intentionally in order to win the contract. Once the contract is signed and work started, the seller organization is acting smart and trying to get the cost revised

    d) Seller has to assume the remaining cost of execution after the project cost hit Point of Total assumption.

10. The primary purpose of Control Procurement process is

    a) Procurement Change management

    b) Claims Administration

    c) Payment management

    d) All of the above

11. You are nominated the project manager of a large engineering project, that aims to produce a prototype. As part of the project procurement planning, you decide to procure certain critical components from sellers. To achieve this, you want to first carry out

a study of the market for the available sellers and the features of the products. You also go through reviews from different organizations, who procured the components from the sellers.

This study is part of

a) Plan Purchase Acquisition

b) Select Seller

c) Invite Seller response

d) Control Procurement

12. Jack is a project manager, who has just got his project execution completed by his team successfully. He has scheduled a scope verification review meeting scheduled with his stakeholders. A majority of the project work was outsourced by his organization through a preferred vendor. After the scope verification process is completed by the stakeholders in the project closure phase, what should Jack do NEXT?

a) Break a bottle of champagne

b) Begin collecting all the lessons learned and upload them into the organization's process repository

c) Perform Contract closure process

d) Release the team and get them redeployed

13. Control Procurement is part of which process group?

a) Execution

b) Monitoring & Control

c) Planning

d) Closure

14. Julia is a project manager, who has decided to procure certain support service requirements of her project from an external vendor to save cost and time. Her main focus is to reinstate confidence of the customer in the business unit. Her focus is mainly to plan and drive the core activities of the business unit. When she begin the procurement planning process, she is not sure when to finalize the Contract Statement of Work.

In which process, the Statement of Work be finalized ?

a) Prior to project charter

b) Request Seller response

c) Plan Purchase & Acquisition

d) Plan Contracting

15. **Force majeure describes**

    a) A force closed contract

    b) Forcing the customer to honor the commitment in a fixed price contract

    c) an unexpected event, such as hurricane or any other natural disaster

    d) None of the above

16. **You are a project manager and outsourced a portion of the project requirement to a vendor. As you carry out an audit of the procurement process, you find that the vendor has overcharged you for the services provided and this amount of significant and done without any prior approval.**

    What is the BEST response you can think of?

    a) Raise the issue in your meeting with the vendor and ask them to adjust the overcharged money

    b) Call the vendor and warn them of contract termination if this practice continued any further

    c) Recover all the overpaid amount from the vendor

    d) Put the issue on hold now until the project is closed.

17. **Monica is a project manager, whose project has a good amount of work being outsourced. After thoughtful examination of bids received, she has shortlisted select vendors and begun contract negotiations with the sellers.**

    Which process is she into?

    a) Request for Seller Response

    b) Select Seller

    c) Control Procurement

    d) Plan Contracting

18. **Name the tasks that are performed in the Close Contract process.**

    a) Scope Verification & Bills payment

    b) Upload Lessons Learned & Contract analysis

    c) Record Management Systems & Procurement Audits

    d) Financial & Administrative closure of the project

19. **You have negotiated and finalized the details of the contract with your preferred vendor for the procurement of certain components and services to support your project requirement. The price is agreed and the supply schedule is finalized. You obtained an approval from your senior executives after providing all the inputs and answers to their question.**

Which document would you send to the seller as an official offer of purchase?

a) Contract Statement of Work

b) Purchase Order

c) Request for Bid

d) Letter of Intent

20. You are the project manager of a project that is aimed at developing a business critical banking software for the ever demanding market. The size and scope of the project is so huge that you decide to outsource a part of the resources from several vendors. The features and design for the application is very unique and you are nervous about the confidentiality. You do not want any of the team members, leaders or experts to disclose anything about the product to anyone ever.

How would you put this expectation in a procurement process?

a) Strictly instruct all the vendors to educate their staff of secrecy of the application and its features

b) Call a meeting of all the team members and ask them not to discuss about the product with anyone both inside and outside the organization.

c) Sign a Memorandum of Understanding (MOU) with every resource in the presence of a representative of the vendors

d) Include a Non-Disclosure Agreement as a procurement document and get acceptance from the vendors.

21. Your project involves installing 25 computers, which will be procured from a vendor for a fixed cost and 10% fee.

This is an example of

a) Fixed Cost

b) Cost Plus Incentive fee

c) Cost Plus Fixed Fee

d) Cost Plus Percent Cost

22. Which process stress the importance of information technology as an effective tool to manage business and procurement process

a) Select Seller Process

b) Control Procurement

c) Plan Procurement

d) Contract closure

23. Which of the following tool is NOT part of the Plan Procurement & Acquisition process?

    a) Expert Judgment

    b) Organizational Process Assets

    c) Contract Types

    d) Make or Buy Analysis

24. Which among the following is NOT an input to the Invite Seller Responses

    a) Enterprise Environmental Factors

    b) Procurement Plan

    c) Procurement Document

    d) Organizational Process Assets

25. You are a project manager for a large construction project. As part of the procurement plan of yours, you have shortlisted few of the services that can be outsourced for effective handling and less cost. You created a procurement management plan, documented all the details about the service requirements and have all the procurement documents. You conducted bidder conferences, invited bids and proposals. You received enormous number of sellers expressing interest and submitted bids for the procurement contract. Now, it is time for evaluating the bids and pick the most eligible seller to supply the services.

    Which process are you into?

    a) Plan Procurement

    b) Plan contracting

    c) Invite seller responses

    d) Select Seller

ANSWERS

1.   **Answer: B**

     Justification: Plan Purchase & Acquiring process is the first step in the Procurement management. The very first task for a project manager to do is to decide whether to make the product or outsource it from an external vendor. An intense analysis is required to come to this conclusion, keeping in mind the cost, schedule and capability of both the buyer and sellers. In this case, Richard is analyzing the benefits and disadvantages of making it or procuring the product. This analysis is called Make or Buy analysis. This process primarily produces a decision whether to make or procure.

2.   **Answer: B**

     Justification: As part of the execution process of procurement management, a bidder conference is one easy way to get all the bidders in one place for providing the required inputs on the product being procured and to answer any questions. Though a product analysis and procurement document might give a detailed view of the product, there should be a collective meeting to address questions. This is called a Bidder conference. Another reason behind holding such conferences is to make sure the potential sellers are treated in a fair manner, transparency and everyone get a chance to have same amount of information about the procurement process.

3.   **Answer: A**

     Justification: Procurement documents are a group of mandatory documents that details the procurement process, products being procured, the evaluation criteria among many other required information for the potential sellers to validate and assess their ability to supply. Prior to inviting interests and bids from the potential sellers, procurement documents are required to be created and shared. However, a Risk register is internal to a project and is created and used by the project manager to identify risks and manage the risks.

4.   **Answer: D**

     Justification: As part of the contract closure procedure, the project manager has to validate the procurement process having met the procurement process objective that it was intended for. A procurement audit is similar to a scope validation process being carried by the stakeholders to validate the project deliverables meeting the objectives of the scope. Any discrepancy, deviations and omissions are to be documented and clarifications required prior to approving the closure of the procurement process. The responsibility of the procurement closure process rests with the project manager.

5. **Answer: B**

    Justification: A Time & Material price contract can also be called Staff augmentation project, in which the vendors supplies the required human resources and the material that are required to execute the project as per the scope. The vendor will not responsible for the scope of the work, quality or any of the project risks, except the ones relating to the human resources and the equipments. The project management mostly rests with the buyer.

6. **Answer: D**

    Justification: It is in the procurement process, the involvement of the legal department is seen mostly in any organization. Since a contract is legally binding and reached with organization that are external to the buyer, the terms of the contracts and agreements to be in compliance with the law. Whenever there is an issue or clarification required, the legal department is the probable best group to address them and help with a resolution.

7. **Answer: A**

    Justification: In a Time & Material contract, the seller's responsibility is limited to providing human resources and the equipments required to execute the work. In all the other three types of contracts listed in the answers, the seller has the ownership of the project and its processes, whereas the buyer is limited to monitoring the progress of the procurement process. Any potential delays or other risks are monitored by the buyer.

8. **Answer: B**

    Justification: A claims administration process is used to resolve any disputes or claims for cost reimbursement and other related issues. Every procurement process has specific references to resolving disputes and claims related issues. Assume a procurement claims process is similar to an insurance claims that we make in our real life. They both are similar in nature, subjected to an analysis, investigation and providing documentary evidence to support the claim. The project manager becomes the deciding authority whether to accept the claim or reject.

9. **Answer: D**

    Justification: The greatest risk for a seller in a fixed cost contract is the cost risks involved. By entering into a fixed price contract, the seller agrees to supply the required product in complete form and guarantees the scope meeting its objectives and according to buyer's satisfaction. Any cost overrun is on the seller. In this case, the seller has hit the Point of Complete assumption of cost. This means, any cost incurred beyond this point for the work committed is responsible for the cost overrun. The seller has very limited chance of a contract revised to have this cost overrun covered. As per the contract, the seller is expected to supply the products or services, irrespective of the cost overrun.

10. **Answer: D**

    Justification: The control Procurement process is part of the Monitoring and Control Process group in the procurement management. The project manager monitors the contract and the work being executed as part of the agreed terms. Any disputes, claims or payment related issues are managed under the claims administration process. In addition to these, any changes required on the procurement contract is raised and managed as part of this process. A claims administration process is similar to other subsidiary plans, in the sense that they all handle the same tasks for the project.

11. **Answer: A**

    Justification: Any activity that is done as part of a decision making initiative falls under the Plan Purchase & Acquisition process. In this situation, prior to decide on the procurement, the project manager does a market study to understand the current trend, advantages and disadvantages of making or procuring the components, the cost advantage, risks involved and the list of potential sellers and their production processes are analyzed. Keeping all these analyzed data as input, the project manager arrive at a decision on Make-Buy the relevant product.

12. **Answer: C**

    Justification: A contract closure process refers to performing a procurement audit, sending a formal notification to the seller that the procurement process is complete besides settling any outstanding payment to the sellers. A contract closure process is part of the administrative closure for every project. The lessons learned and releasing the team and getting them redeployed are part of the closure process, but can be done once the other administrative processes are completed.

13. **Answer: B**

    Justification: A control Procurement is similar to a scope or schedule monitoring process of the respective knowledge areas. The terms and conditions of the contracts are monitored by the project manager as part of the Control Procurement process.

14. **Answer: D**

    Justification: A Contract Statement of Work can be considered final only if every detail about the procurement process, the planned product or services are finalized. In the initial Plan purchase & acquisition process, the details are collected and they are analyzed by the project manager to give a final shape to the statement of work. This SoW is shared with the stakeholders besides other procurement documents. Option (a) is irrelevant to this question since the project SoW is prepared before the project charter.

15. **Answer: C**

    Justification: A ' **Force majeure**' is also called as an 'Act of God.' Every procurement contract signed between a buyer and seller has certain special situations like natural disasters such as hurricanes, earth quakes. Due to uncertainties resulted by these unusual phenomenon, there may be disruption in services or honoring the contract terms by the seller. The buyer lists the liability on the part of such failures.

16. **Answer: A**

    Justification: Ideally, none would want to land in a situation where the other business partner is taking advantage of the service being provided. If that happens, ideally the law mandates the buyer to terminate the contract and take legal action against the seller. However, the buyer should take the commitments, schedule and the project impact into consideration. An immediate course of action is to escalate this issue to the vendor and seek explanation and remedy to contain the damage. In the worst case scenario, the buyer can terminate the contract and take legal action.

17. **Answer: B**

    Justification: Contract negotiation is one of the tool in the Select Seller process. The procurement documents narrate the details of the procurement process, product being outsourced and evaluation criteria. However, the contract negotiation is carried out after the evaluation of the potential sellers are completed and chosen. Details such as schedule, risks, commitments and cost is discussed between the buyer and sellers as part of the negotiation.

18. **Answer: C**

    Justification: In a Record Management System, all details of the procurement process such as cost, issues, risks and schedule level data are documented and stored in the organization's process repository for future reference by other project managers of the organization. A procurement audit validates the objectives of the procurement process against the actual status of the objectives to make sure that the contract is fully honored by the buyer and seller.

19. **Answer: B**

    Justification: In most of the contracts, a purchase order signifies the beginning of the supply of products or service by the seller. A purchase order places the order for products or services agreed in the contract and quotes the quantity in units and price mutually agreed. A purchase order is a legally binding document for both the buyer and seller.

20. **Answer: D**

    Justification: A Non-disclosure agreement is a key procurement document that is to be signed by the seller committing strict confidentiality related to the business, methodologies, data and the strategies of the buyer. A NDA is a legally binding document and is required to be signed by every resource working on the project. As per the NDA, every piece of information related to the project is classified and any failure to honor the agreement result in legal action and penalty for the resource and the vendor in general.

21. **Answer: D**

    Justification: One need to be very careful, when dealing with Cost Price. The terms may be tricky about incentive, fee and per cent cost. In this case, the cost is paid to the seller in the form of cost + certain per cent of the cost. Hence, option D qualifies to be the better choice. Cost + fixed incentive refers to paying the cost and a fixed amount of money as incentive fee.

22. **Answer: B**

    Justification: Since a managing a contract involves several activities, process and protocols to be followed, use of information technology such as hardware systems, software, system tools might make the life of the project manager easier to manage the work with a fool proof administrative setup. Though the use of information technology is seen in every process, it is more recommended in managing the contracts.

23. **Answer: B**

    Justification: A plan procurement & Acquisition process is more about taking a realistic approach towards the particular project and its requirement. Though an organizational process assets are greatly useful in every process and process groups, its usage is minimal in the plan purchase process. A project manager conducts a market research and extensive analysis that will influence the decision making process as to whether make or procure the products and services.

24. **Answer: A**

    Justification: In this situation, the Enterprise Environmental Assets is not of much relevant since the company's policies and forms/templates are taken into account in the earlier procurement process to arrive a decision on the procurement and seller management process.

25. **Answer: D**

    Justification: In the first few processes of the procurement planning, the groundwork is done to decide on the make or buy decision, finalizing the procurement plan, procurement documents and inviting bids and interests from different sellers. Project manager hosting bidder conferences and releasing advertisements through media are part of procurement planning. Once the bids are received, the project manager evaluate each of the bid for cost, quality and schedule feasibility before choosing a seller.

This page is intentionally left blank

Project Time Management

Objectives

At the end of Project Time management, you should be able to understand:

- what is a Time management and its importance in a project
- how time or schedule is related to other components of project
- how project schedule is prepared. What is an activity and how it is defined
- activity resource estimation
- how the duration of each activity estimated
- sequencing the activities
- critical path, networking diagrams, leads, lag and float on a project
- schedule compression techniques
- schedule development and control

What is Time Management?

How would you define Time or Schedule Management in a project environment?

Initially, It might appear easy to define. However, in realistic terms, managing the project schedule is not as easy unless you have exceptionally great Project Management skills. To put it clearer, anything that involves human resources is not so easy because humans can think, take decisions and have their own opinion on everything that they do. In addition, every risk associated with the project impacts the project schedule.

Having said that, schedule is not all about simply managing tasks but it is a time scheduled for individual resources or groups that are assigned these tasks in a project. Developing a project schedule combines multiple activities that are interrelated yet independent, each of which involve great amount of challenges. More than creating a schedule, managing a project schedule is even more challenging since a project manager should be prepared to face unexpected events during the project execution. The efficiency of a project manager lies in developing a realistic project schedule that is acceptable to every stakeholder of the project.

Here might come a question.

Where and when does the schedule appear to be part of a project.

If you are little ignorant with your understanding of Time management planning, you might answer the above question as "Project Planning Group." This is not entirely true.

The Time Management task actually begins in the Project Initiation group. To be more clearer, the Time management activity began simultaneously when you got yourself assigned as the Project Manager of your project. Do you remember the Project Charter that we reviewed in an early chapter of this book. The Project Charter has set overall expectations on the scope, cost and Time for the project manager and his team. If you could revisit the sample project charter that is given in the earlier part of this book, you would find high-level project milestones listed in it. Anything that deals with effort or dates has a lot to do with Time Management.

The overall project objective set by the customer or sponsor is the high level expectation for the team. The expectation may be critical for them and it becomes the primary responsibility of the project manager and the team to honor the expectation and highlight any issues, risks or inability in meeting the schedule is conveyed well in advance to help the customer analyze and get back to you with their views. Managing this critical task of project schedule and meeting the deadline is all that is done in the Time Management process.

The above lengthy definition must be good enough to help understand what is Time management.

Significance of Time Management in a Project

Time Management can be called the nerve center of a project, since many other processes are dependent on Time Management to be able to achieve their own objectives.

For example, Project Cost estimation is done based on the project schedule. Work Breakdown Structure and Time Management are interrelated, since both speak about managing schedule. Human Resource planning is dependent on the project schedule. Similarly, Risk, procurement and every other management planning involves good amount of effort and scheduling required.

In short, if the project's time management is not efficient and accurate, the impact of it will be felt across the project from start to end. Similarly, when something is not going as expected, the project manager should keep an eye on the project schedule, since a schedule is like a ticking clock. The clock doesn't stop for any expected or unexpected problems during the project execution phase.

Is it a fair statement to make?

Time Management Planning - An Overview

Having understood what is Time Management and its significance in a project environment, let us look at what forms part of the Time Management Process.

As defined earlier in the previous pages, a project is all about performing interrelated tasks in a pre-determined sequence and in a sequential order. Each of these tasks have their own objective and produce an unique deliverable or outcome that will enable the project to produce predetermined deliverables Managing project schedule requires good amount of planning done on the part of the project manager. The first and ultimate output is the project Time management plan, that narrates the ways and methods, by which the activities are planned to be executed, tracked and monitored.

If you could recollect what we reviewed in the Scope Management process, we have come across Work Breakdown Structure (WBS) and WBS Dictionary. The Work Breakdown Structure contain details of the individual activities, also known as Work packages, to be performed in the project and listing them in an unique order. The WBS dictionary narrates the objectives and scope of each of these work packages for better clarity and easier understanding.

We will be using each of these lowest level of decomposed activities for the purpose of estimation, execution, monitoring and controlling the schedule of the project. Since the schedule of the entire project is dependent on the decomposed tasks, one need to pay significant amount of focus on these components.

The below diagram explains the tasks involved in the Time Management process for easier understanding.

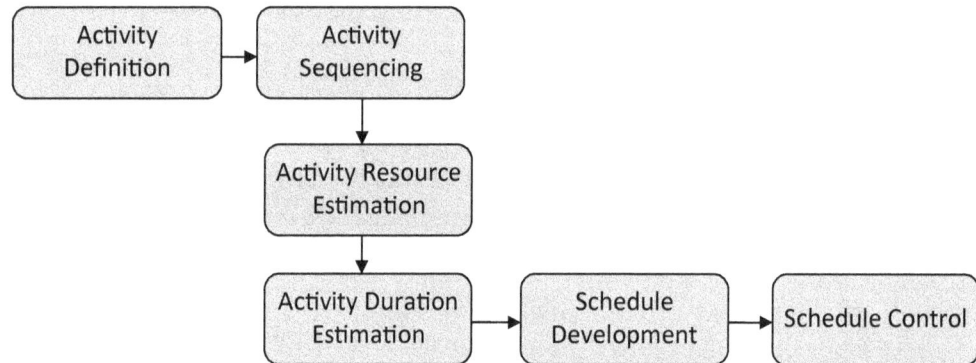

Is it not interesting to note that, several processes are to be performed before the project manager begins to develop his project schedule?

The above six tasks are performed as part of the Time Management process. If you notice, each of these processes are unique with their own objective of producing an outcome.

Activity Definition

Having gone through the above diagram, you might have a question as to what is the difference between the Activity here and the work packages defined in the WBS of the Scope Management Process.

The Activity in the Time Management process is the result of decomposing the work packages that are defined in the WBS task in the Scope Management. A work package is a specific functionality and the functionality is split into multiple manageable activities. At this point of time, the Project Manager's focus is more about defining the activity that is planned to be performed as part of the project and not to worry about the functionality or to identify resources or the start and end dates of performing these activities.

Before you begin working on the scheduling the work packages or activities of a project, it is essential to identify the activities first and this is done in the activity definition process.

The below diagram illustrates the process of Activity Definition

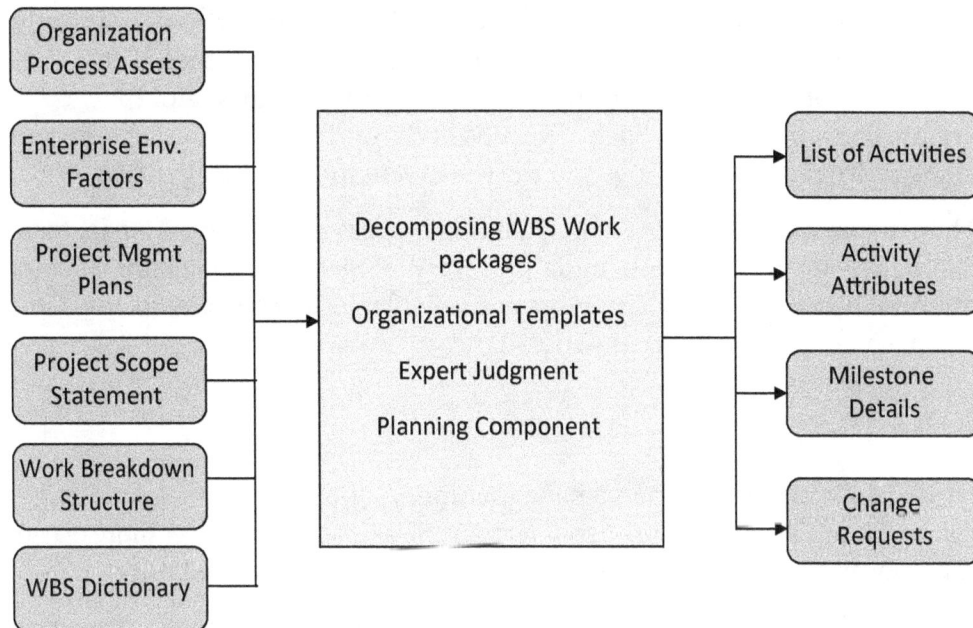

Organization Process Assets

Enterprise Env. Factors

Project Mgmt Plans

Project Scope Statement

Work Breakdown Structure

WBS Dictionary

Decomposing WBS Work packages

Organizational Templates

Expert Judgment

Planning Component

List of Activities

Activity Attributes

Milestone Details

Change Requests

Note on Inputs Used in Activity Definition

Organizational Process Assets

The historic information and other process assets available in the Organizational process repository are very vital input that might offer great amount of information and helpful in identifying the Activity and defining them. Referring to the previously executed similar projects might be even better.

Enterprise Environmental Factors

This repository of Organizational policies and procedures might offer useful guidance on how the performing organization handles Time Management and tasks associated with every project. Not every organization have their project strategies mirroring each others. Due to better quality conscience or issues and risks experienced in the past, some organizations might have additional layers of testing or reviews done before delivering the end product or deliverables to the customers.

To elaborate more, some Organizations might chose to have the testing activities assigned to the dedicated testing team for efficiency, expertise and due to quality factor. Such activities need to be defined in the Activity definition process and estimated.

Work Breakdown Structure

WBS is the most important input to the Activity definition process, since the activities are defined by decomposing each of the work packages of the Work Breakdown Structure. Each of these activities produce unique output to the overall project objective. Such decomposition of activities help the Project Manager to track the activities and the time spent in completing them.

The purpose of working on Scope Planning process before Time Management is because, in the Scope Planning process WBS gets created listing each of the decomposed tasks. These tasks are considered as activities in the Time Management process and estimation done.

WBS Dictionary

The WBS Dictionary provide detailed narration of each of the work packages defined in the WBS. The purpose of using WBS as an input is to get more clarity and information on each of the tasks that are scheduled for the project.

Sometime, referring to the WBS dictionary might provide inputs on creating new tasks or activities.

Project Scope Statement

The Project Scope statement serves as a very good reference point while decomposing the WBS work packages into multiple smaller and easily manageable activities. An efficient way to define the activities is to compare the Work Breakdown Structure, WBS Dictionary with the Project Scope Statement. In other words, WBS is expected to reflect the objective of the Project Scope statement.

Referring to the Project Scope Statement as an input here is to get an idea of the activity to be performed before working on their estimation. In addition to this, the project scope statement might help understand the complexity of the project and its outcome, which subsequently has an impact on the effort requirement of individual tasks.

Project Management Plans

Another important input to defining the Project activities are the Project management plans. While WBS have the work packages defined and listed, the project plans provide more inputs and clarity on the exact nature of the activities performed in each of the process groups, thus helping the Project Manager to identify every activity of each of the knowledge areas and accommodate the relevant activities in the Time Management planning process.

Assume, the quality management plan is going to require a review of the work products by the quality group. This means, this review task is required to be included in the project schedule and estimated for the effort.

Tools Used in Activity Definition

Decomposition of Work Packages

This means, you will consider the Work packages that you defined in the Scope Planning phase and decompose them into easily manageable activities to help in estimating the effort required for completing them.

An important point to remember.

When you are decomposing work packages, the better option is to decompose each of the work package to the lowest level that can be easily managed. This is called **Top-Down approach**. By doing this, it becomes easy handle the definition of the tasks. However, when you do an estimation, whether it be time or cost, always remember that the ***Bottom-up approach*** is recommended for accuracy. Upon completing estimates for all of these tasks they are consolidated and the result is the overall estimation for the project or larger work packages.

Organizational Templates

Like many other knowledge areas, every organization has a repository of recommended templates to be used by their project team. The advantages in using these templates is they complying with the respective Organization's policies, strategies and approach with respect to the specific process, thus making it easier for the Project Manager and his team.

However, it is always good to know and understand the contents of such templates and their significance to the project.

Expert Judgment

Consulting experts and Managers of project that were executed earlier in the same Organization is another great tool that can be used in defining the Activities. Being very critical to the project schedule and cost, one need to be extremely cautious in listing down the tasks and their background.

Planning Component

Though not an accurate methodology, whenever few or many of the activities are unknown in a project, dummy activities are assumed and created in the project's activity list along with estimates for such activities. Remember to place these activities levels above the WBS work packages so as to plan for these unknown tasks that might be coming your way in the future. Whenever such packages are assumed and created in a project schedule, buffer time is added into your schedule to handle these tasks.

The above is called as *Planning Component*. In other words, it is all about planning for certain components that are unknown at certain point of time. As the project makes progress, these dummy tasks can be replaced with real tasks with their schedule estimation. One disadvantage with this methodology is that there are possibilities of differences in the schedule estimation between the dummy tasks and the real ones.

As explained in earlier chapters of this book, making assumptions is an acceptable and recommended practice when certain activities or components are unknown. However, remember that such assumptions are not definite tasks but only imaginary tasks that are communicated to all the stakeholders with the justification.

Rolling Wave Planning

Another important way to handle similar situation as explained above is called Rolling Wave Planning.

When you are managing a project, there are most likely unknown components. Rather than getting oneself stuck into finding these unknown components a better idea is to list the activities that are known and go ahead with planning for the known ones. However, the Project Manager should keep a closer look into unknown or missed components and work on them as and when they become known.

Though adopting to Rolling Wave Plan helps the Project team to stay focused on their schedule and project scope, it equally carries risks of working in vacuum relating to certain portion of the scope. So, it is always recommended to use this methodology unless there are no other alternative solution.

Outputs of the Activity Definition Process

Activity List

Once the activity definition process is complete, what you get is the list of activities that are to be performed in the project. The list include every activity, for which effort is involved and estimated which subsequently has a cost associated with them. The list of activities are the lowest level in the project.

A better way to list the activities is to create an activity tree with logical sequencing of the listed activities. By doing this, it becomes easy to provide estimates for each of the logical branches of the activity tree.

Activity Attributes

If you remember the purpose of having the WBS dictionary in the Scope Planning phase then you will realize the contents of Activity Attributes.

In short, Activity attributes are narrative information on what each of the activities are about and their characteristics such as the activity sequence, predecessor and successor tasks besides any constraint in performing the specific activities.

List of Milestones

Remember that an easier way to track the progress of a project is to take checkpoints at specific point of the project execution. Such checkpoints are called *Milestones*.

Let us assume, you are managing a large project of building a bridge and you have listed all the activities involved in the construction. If you plan to track the project's progress, group all of these activities logically and track these groups. Your senior management may not be interested in knowing the status of each of the lowest level of activities are doing. Rather they would want to know where does the project stand at any point of time.

Is the above definition confusing still?

Let us consider the bridge construction project into six phases namely Acquiring Land, Earth work, Procuring materials and human resources required for the project, planning for the foundations, executing the project construction phase, verifying the quality of the work done. Each of these phases may have one or many activities that are defined in your Activity definition process. This means all of your defined activity are collectively represented by these six phases.

Now, when it comes to tracking and reporting the project progress of your construction project, your senior management would be more interested in knowing whether the initial earth work is complete or not. This phase is called a Milestone and the project is considered making healthy progress if it is able to meet this Milestone within estimated budget and schedule.

Tracking each of the lowest level of activities, their schedule and cost is the responsibility of the Project Manager. The Project Manager need not report these details to the senior management by way of status update on the project, but would be using these lowest level activities to track the progress of his project.

Change Requests

As the Project Manager begin defining the activities of the project, there are chances that the original scope needs an update, though it is not necessary to happen.

Do not worry about the changes to the Scope just because of defining certain activities.

Changes to the original scope doesn't mean you will be building an airport rather than the planned bridge. Changes may be the way you planned to perform the project activities, approach, strategy etc. All details of such changes are key output of the Activity Definition process.

Having reviewed the Activity Definition process, let us take a practice test on identifying potential activities that might required to be performed in a sample project

Verify your Understanding of Activity Definition

You are assigned as the Project Manager of developing an application to support your customer, who are in the Insurance business and providing various insurance products to their customers. The application is expected to create new customers, make updates to the customers, provide options of Home Owner, Auto, Life Cover, Health Insurance and Travel Insurance services. Your Organization has specific strategy to handle application development and delivery.

As per the plan, your team is going to conduct a study of the customer requirements, Business Study, Design, Develop and Test the application. You are responsible for all Quality activities and management of the application development from start to end. You are given a team of business analysts, developers and Testers to get the project executed.

From the above details, could you list all the activities that are required to be performed as part of the project. Use the below blank space to complete your answer.

Activity Sequencing

Having identified the activities that are going to be involved in the project execution, it is time to arrange the order of their execution. While learning about the Activity sequencing, it should be remembered that this is not an easy task but require lot of attention, care and focus while arranging the sequence. To narrate in simple way, the activities are to be related and schedule in a logical sequence. Also note that, dependencies between activities are to be considered while arranging the activities.

To have the list of activities arranged in an appropriate sequence, we would consider the output of Activity definition and process them with appropriate tools to generate the list of activities in a different form. The below diagram narrates the relation for better clarity.

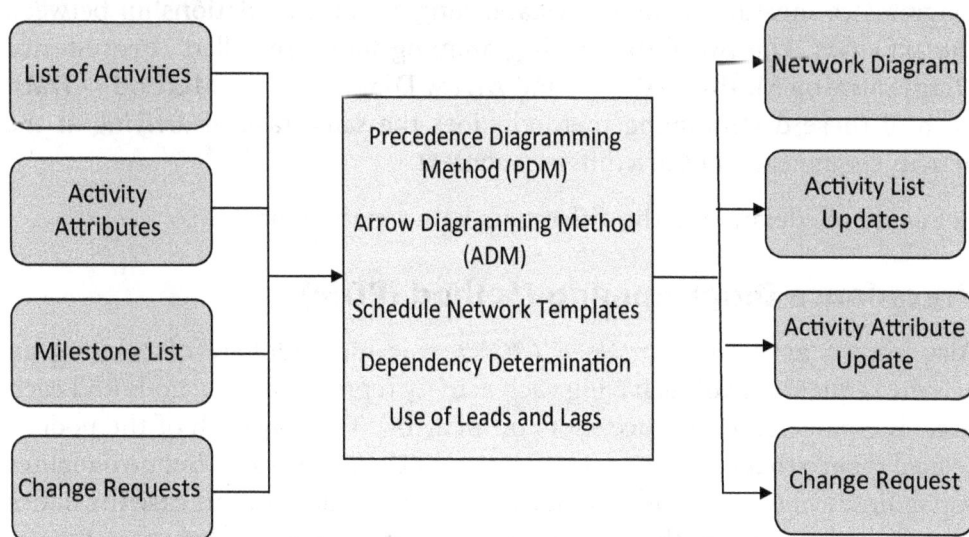

Inputs on Activity Sequence Process

Since all of the inputs are resulted by the previous process, Activity definition, it is not necessary to explain everything again.

Remember that the Activity attributes contain the narration of each of the activity, besides the details of precedence and successor activities and the logical relationship between listed activities of Activity Definition process.

Tools Used in Activity Sequence Process

Defining the sequence of activities is pretty challenging, since it need to be done with logical and more sensible relationship between each of the activities.

As an example, let us consider the same example of building a huge bridge that connects one part of the city with another part. The bridge has become necessary to ease the congestion on another bridge that is built at a distance and farther for a section of the residents of your city. You have the list of tasks that are required to be performed to get the bridge project completed.

When you want to sequence the activities, you are expected to follow a logical and sensible approach so as one task doesn't get overlapped with its dependent task. Similarly, there should be an appropriate relationship between preceding and successor activities. You cannot begin your earth work before the land acquisition is completed. Similarly, water outlets on the bridge cannot be done before the surface floor is laid on the top of the bridge's surface. These are few examples of logical relationship between activities.

Does it make sensible now?

The best way to represent the sequencing of activities is by way of drawing diagrams connecting them and establishing a realistic relationship between the activities. The two forms of diagramming tools are called **Precedence Diagramming Method (PDM)** and **Arrow Diagramming Method (ADM)**. Both of these diagramming methods does the same task of arriving at the activity sequencing, but in a different context.

Let us see the details and the differences between them now.

Precedence Diagramming Method (PDM)

Also known as *Activity-on-Node (AON)*, this methodology of creating an activity sequence involves having each activity represented as a node and each node is connected to its successors by an arrow. The way each of the node is related is such that each Node may have more than one father, but no daughter can indirectly become a father of its own father. Because in this case the nodes represents activities with a duration, one can determine the successor- or predecessor-relation by subtypes.

The PDM has clearly explained the dependency on performing every task in several ways, in terms of Start and End of each tasks. The four different ways to represent this are

• *Finish-to-Start*	:	The predecessor has to be finished before successor can start.
• *Finish-to-Finish*	:	The predecessor has to be finished before successor can be finished
• *Start-to-Start*	:	The predecessor has to be start before successor can be started
• *Start-to-Finish*	:	The predecessor has to be start before successor can be finished

Now, let us refer the below diagram for better understanding of the Precedence Diagramming Method.

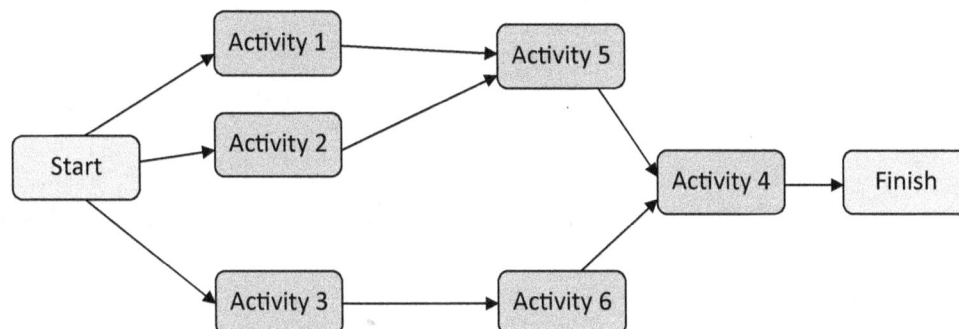

Notes on PDM illustrated above

- Activity 1, Activity 2 and Activity 3 start simultaneously at the beginning of the project. All of these three activities are independent of each other at this point of time

- Activity 5 cannot commence until both Activity 1 and Activity 2 are complete. Even if one of these two activities are complete, Activity 5 should wait for the other to complete before getting started itself.

- Similarly, Activity 6 can be started only after Activity 3 is complete.

- Similarly, Activity 4 cannot commence until Activity 5 and Activity 6 are complete. In a way, Activity 4 cannot commence until all the other activities in the sequence are completed successfully.

The above Precedence Diagram should not be too difficult to understand. Each of the activities are logically related and their dependencies are explained well in the Precedence.

Arrow Diagramming Methodology (ADM)

The same scenario can be used to represent the Activity Sequencing process with the use of Nodes and Arrows. Thus ADM is also known as Activity-on-Arrow (AOA).

In an Arrow Diagramming Method, every activity is represented as an arrow while the Nodes represent the Deliverable states which are connected by each Arrow. Due to the nature of this methodology, only Start-Finish relationship exists between nodes. Every dependencies between the nodes should be represented as dummy activities.

Let us take a look into the below diagram for more detailed view

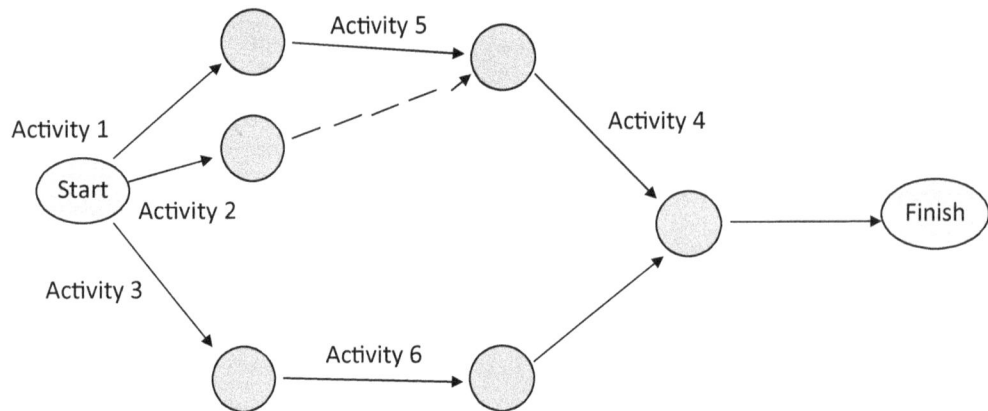

Schedule Network Templates

These are nothing but the templates available in the Organization repository. These templates are validated by the Quality group or PMO of every performing organization.

Using such templates might provide insight into how the previous projects managed to create such network diagrams.

Dependency Determination Methodology

No project can be independent from other factors. There are some sort of dependency present in everything that we do. A project is dependent on many people, resources and other factors for execution. Taking a realistic and sensible approach in determining the dependency between each of the activities and defining the level of dependency.

There are three types of such dependencies that can exist in a project

Mandatory Dependency

A mandatory dependency is a task that must be completed in order to initiate subsequent processes. For example, before the design is approved, the team cannot begin its work on constructing the product.

Discretionary Dependency

A Discretionary dependency is an optional completion of task to get the subsequent dependent tasks kick-started. However, a discretionary dependent task is not necessarily should be completed.

For example, the construction of the product need not wait till the labels are printed.

External Dependency

An external dependency is not directly the responsibility of the project, but influenced by certain external factors but will bear impact on your project.

As an example, if you are laying a railway track between two cities To operate the services between the cities the Railway companies should procure Locomotives and coaches, which is not covered in the scope of your work or project. This is called External Dependency.

Leads and Lags

Lead Time are a specific amount of effort that is intentionally put between a predecessor and the successor in order to balance the schedule and dependency between two activities. The amount of effort that is to be considered for Lead time depends on the nature of the activity and the dependency of the next activity.

For example, when you are building a road project you cannot begin painting the yellow lines in the middle of the road unless all the equipments are cleared of the area. Similarly, during fund raising event for a political party, dinner cannot be served until the chief guest arrives at the event venue and completes his inaugural speech

Let us look at the below diagram to understand more on this

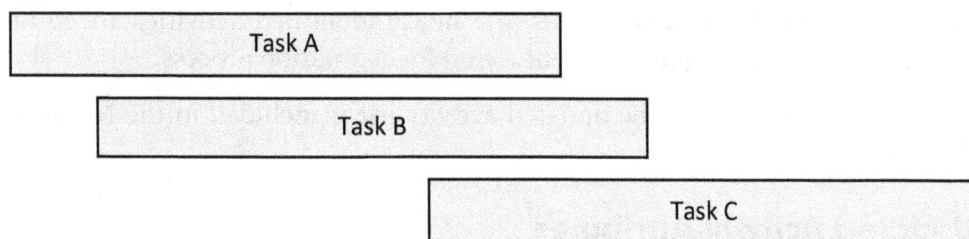

```
┌──────────────────────────────┐
│            Task A            │
└──────────────────────────────┘
     ┌──────────────────────────────┐
     │            Task B            │
     └──────────────────────────────┘
              ┌──────────────────────────────┐
              │            Task C            │
              └──────────────────────────────┘
```

In the above diagram, the tasks Task A & Task B do not start simultaneously. Similarly, there is a significant amount of time between tasks B & C. Irrespective of the reason for this delay, the time before the Task B and Task C is called *Lead Time* in a Schedule.

Lag Time is the amount of time given to a successor task before it can get kick started after the predecessor task is completed.

As an example, even if you are completed with laying the railway line between two cities, the train services cannot be started unless the safety inspections are completed. Similarly, even if the senate completes debating on a new constitutional changes that is aimed at curbing illegal drug trafficking from across the border, it cannot become a law until the President signs it.

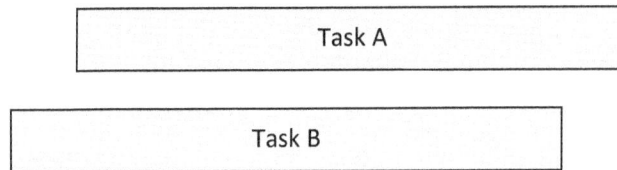

```
┌─────────────────────────────────────────┐
│                  Task A                   │
└─────────────────────────────────────────┘

┌─────────────────────────────────────────┐
│                  Task B                   │
└─────────────────────────────────────────┘
```

In the above diagram, the time given to task A after the Task B is completed is called *Lag time*. This means that Task A completes later than Task B.

Outputs of Activity Sequencing Process

Network Diagrams

The Network diagram can either be Activity on node diagrams (AON), generated by the Precedence Diagramming Method (PDM), or Activity On arrow Diagrams (AOA), generated by Arrow Diagramming Methods (ADM).

The choice between these two is left to the discretion and requirement of the Project Manager and the customers. There is no one type of diagram that is considered to be better over the other. The outcome of the activity sequencing is a list of activity in a logically organized.

Updated Activity List

There are times, you might end up with more activities when sequencing the list of activities. In such situations, the newly identified activities are to be included in the existing list and considered for estimation process.

Remember to make sure the updated activity list is included in the Network diagrams.

Updated Activity Attributes

When you identify new activities during the sequencing of listed activities, the newly identified activities' attributes such as predecessors and successors are to be defined and the overall list of activities are required to be revisited for including these attributes.

Requested Changes

When identifying new activities during the activity sequencing process, the newly identified activities might result in minor to major changes to the original project scope or any other management plans. In order to get the changes accommodated into these plans, necessary change requests are to be raised and reviewed before getting them included in the plans.

The above inputs should help you understand the process of activity sequencing well. Now, take a moment to think whether you are doing these activities in your project. If you are doing it different, you may very well identify the gaps between your process and the one narrated above.

Activity Resource Estimation

Having reviewed the activity sequencing process, it is time to identify the resources required to perform these activities. When I say identifying resources, it means estimating the number of resources to perform all of the listed activities, engaging appropriate resources in terms of skills, efficiency and expertise to perform each of these activities. These are performed as part of the Activity Resource estimation.

At this point, it is important to note that while identifying the resources, the project manager should keep in mind the dependency between activities, since one cannot afford to have same resources doing multiple tasks that are dependent on each others, all of which are on the critical path. This is very important component of the Time Management Process, since such resource and activity dependency would end up depending on the same resource, which is also a risk factor for any project. We will discuss this risk in the Risk Management Plan chapter.

Now, let us look at how the Activity Resources Estimation process is done. Let us look at the diagram below to understand this process.

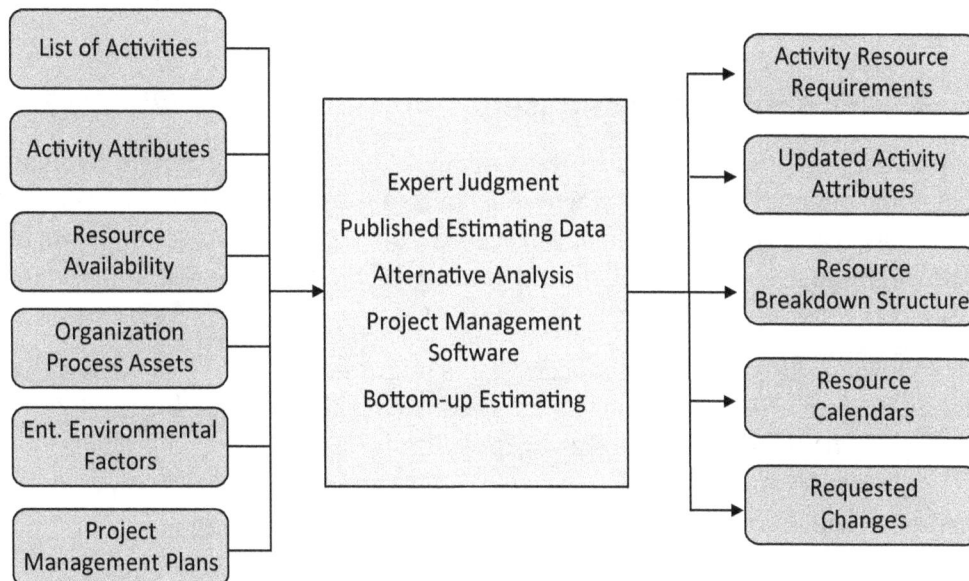

Inputs	Tools & Techniques	Outputs
List of Activities	Expert Judgment	Activity Resource Requirements
Activity Attributes	Published Estimating Data	Updated Activity Attributes
Resource Availability	Alternative Analysis	Resource Breakdown Structure
Organization Process Assets	Project Management Software	Resource Calendars
Ent. Environmental Factors	Bottom-up Estimating	Requested Changes
Project Management Plans		

Inputs of Activity Resource Estimation

List of Activities

To begin with, let us take the list of activities, which were output of the Activity Definition process (the activity list is to be arranged in an appropriate logical sequence to have better visibility on resource utilization). We require this input to map the activities with the list of available resources, which is another input to the Activity Resource Estimation process.

Activity Attributes

Activity attributes is one important input of this process When identifying the resources for executing specific activities care should be taken to understand the predecessor and successor activities and their inter-dependencies between them. If the Project Manager is not careful in estimating the right resources against the list of activities, the project might end up with the same resource executing multiple tasks simultaneously.

Resource Availability

This is another critical input to this process since the outcome of the activity resource estimation process is greatly influenced by the number of resources that are available for deployment in the project.

List of resource availability is not generated by any other processes, but should be available with the Project Manager or with the Resource Management group of your organization.

Organizational Process Assets

The process assets available in the Organization repository might give you guidance on similar situations where resources were mapped against the list of available activities in previously executed projects. The process assets might also highlights the risks and issues faced while estimating the number of resources for specific activities.

In addition to the above, the process assets might help the project manager to know, how the previous managers handled when they were unable to identify the required resources within the organization.

Enterprise Environmental Factors

One may be wondering, what the Environmental Factor has to do with activity resource estimation process. Every organization have their own strategies to utilize resources into project. Some organizations may not support utilization of resources across projects and activities, while some other organizations might attempt to leverage resources' available time to work on multiple projects in order to save cost of hiring new resources. The Enterprise Environmental factors lists the organization's policies and strategies that would be guiding the project manager while estimating the resources to be used in the project.

Project Management Plans

The project plans are basically used as a reference in this process. In addition, any updates required to the resource management plans as a result of the activity resource estimation process.

Tools Used in Activity Resource Estimation

Expert Judgment

Consulting with Project Managers of previously executed projects and other experts having expertise in resource estimation would help in identifying the number of resources, skills required before the Project Manager actually begin executing the work. In addition to the human resources, consulting experts helps in identifying the correct materials that are required to carry out the activity.

In addition to the above, there may be situations when other project managers' might have faced problems identifying the resources on time and within the organization or skilled resources working on another project. Their experiences on identifying such resources and utilizing them without affecting any of their current engagement would be of great help.

Alternatives Analysis

Whenever you plan for certain activities, it is always a good idea to have Plan B as a backup. It will help reduce the risk of the project getting delayed much in advance.

For example, if you couldn't find the required resources within your organization, you should be prepared to hire external resources. To get this done, the project manager should have the resource requirement plan, justification and business case ready to have it approved.

Published Estimating Data

One of the best ways to estimate the resources for activities is to refer to various external resources such as from magazines, journals, books, production data from various other projects across industries. Having these data collected and analyzed will help the Project Managers to arrive at a more realistic resource requirement data for his own project.

Remember that, such data collected can be used only for reference purpose and subjected to change depending on the current project requirements.

Project Management Software

Most of the Project Management software inherit features that help estimate the resources required in performing the project activities. The software generates resource availability calendars based on their estimation that help the Project Manager to have a realistic resource requirement and availability.

Bottom-Up Analysis

Whenever you hear the term "estimation" always remember bottom-up estimation. Using the bottom-up estimation reduces the risk of resource and schedule overrun. In a Bottom-up estimation technique, the activities at the lowest level are considered and assigned with resources before the Project Manager moves up to the other activities above.

The process of doing the estimation from the lowest level of activities and moving on above is *Bottom-up estimation* technique.

Output of Activity Resource Estimation

Activity Resource Requirements

The primary output of the Activity resource estimation process is the list of resource requirements for each of the activities scheduled to be performed for the project. Consolidating these resource requirement information for all activities should get the overall resource requirement details for each of the work packages for the project.

Updated Activity Attributes

When the project manager is working on estimating the number of resources for all the activities, there may be possibilities of changes required to the list of activities. For example, if a specific activity is bigger in size it might be further logically subdivided and created with activities. In such scenarios, the activity attributes might require updates. The possibilities are remote, but cannot be ruled out.

Resource Breakdown Structure

If you remember the Work Breakdown Structure that we learnt in the Scope Management Planning process, the equivalent of it for Resources are the Resource Breakdown Structure (RBS). The RBS has the list of resource details listed in a specific hierarchical structure based on resource type and category. The RBS of a project gives a better and easily understandable version of the Resource requirement of the project.

Resource Calendars

A Resource Calendar is a very important data for the project manager when he is trying to deploy the resources to specific activities or work packages. The Resource calendar provides details of the resource availability period, working period and idle time. The calendar will list schedules for each of the resources of a project.

Requested Changes

When the resource estimation for each activity is done, there may be chances of changes to be carried to the activity resource estimation process itself due to unavailability of resources with specialized skills. In such cases, change process might required to be carried to make sure the resource estimation is more realistic with the available resources. All these requested changes are included in this output.

Activity Duration Estimation

Having identified the resources for executing all the activities of the project, it is time to move on further and estimate the duration of each activity before we arrive at a overall project schedule. Activity duration estimation is an important task to be performed since it gives an insight into the potential effort requirement to complete the identified activities. Once the duration is estimated the project manager can easily come up with overall effort estimation requirement for the project.

Having the overall effort estimation for the project will help the Project Manager to come up with cost estimation for the project. A detailed narration of Cost Management planning will follow this chapter in this book.

At this point, one might have a question "Why should the Activity Duration Estimation be performed after the Resource estimation?"

The answer is pretty simple and straightforward.

The skills, ability and quality of the resources are key factors that will determine the effort required to perform each of the activities. Unless the resources are identified for each of the task, it will be impossible for the Project Manager to arrive at the effort estimation for every activity.

To understand the process of Activity duration estimation, let us take a look into the below diagram.

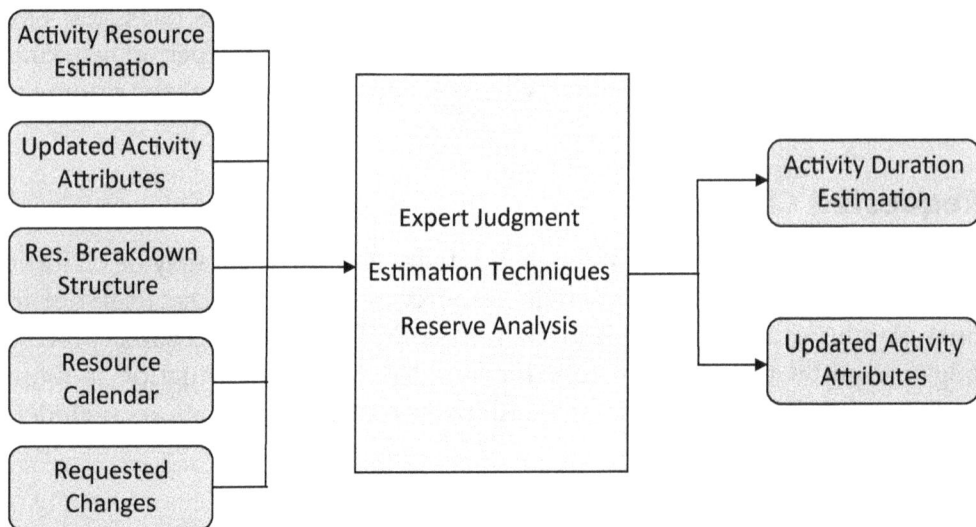

Note on Inputs to Activity Duration Estimation Process

If you notice the above diagram, all the inputs used are resulted by the activity resource estimation process. Since we have reviewed these in the last few pages, let us proceed to the tools that are used in the activity duration estimation process.

Tools Used in Activity Duration Estimation Process

Expert Judgment

As always, consulting the project managers of previously executed projects and experts with expertise in handling such projects are precious source of information that will help the project managers to estimate the effort requirement for every project.

In addition to their expertise, they may be aware of any unknown risks or issues that are hidden while executing these activities. As an example, let us assume a resource is scheduled to work on a specific component of the development project for a banking application. Based on the original scope, the resource is responsible for coding the component. However, at a later stage it is noticed that one additional validation is required to be performed, which is determined by the resource while working on the program. This validation will take time to get executed due to dependency on another component being developed by another resource. Unless the validation portion is completed, the original component cannot be tested and termed it complete. This dependency is going to inflate into the effort estimated already.

If, for any reason, the Project Manager is not able to realize this dependency ahead of time he will end up having to revise his schedule to accommodate this requirement. People having worked on similar project or situations can able to identify such risks ahead of time. This justifies the use of Expert Judgment as an important tool in identifying the activity duration in a project.

Estimation Techniques

No estimation is possible without following certain techniques and involvement of some calculations. Estimating the effort duration is no exception to this. There are three types of estimation techniques that can be used to achieve this purpose. They are

Analogous Estimation technique uses the historical data in addition to expert judgment, in arriving at an activity duration estimation. In other words, assume you are managing a large mechanical project that is about to build a huge boiler for the upcoming power plant in your neighboring town. You identified a supplier that supplies critical electrical components required for your project. You never worked with this supplier ever but your company has experience working with them. You refer to your Organization repository to pull historic data about the past contracts signed with this supplier and seek the assistance of another project manager, who outsourced electrical components from the same supplier last time. He could able to provide his inputs, risks and issues of working with this supplier and you get the benefits of planning your procurement plan better.

Parametric Estimation technique uses specific estimation software or formulas that were arrived based on the performance of the past executed projects. Data about the current project is fed into the software or formula, which will analyze and provide the rough order of estimation for the current list of activities for the project. The one disadvantage of this method is the results cannot be called accurate since it just resembles the outcome of previous projects.

Three-point Estimation technique produces three sets of estimations, which are possible in any project based on different situations. The first result is classified as *Realistic*, which means the estimation may be most likely to be realistic. Second result is *Optimistic*, which may not be realistic but potentially possible case scenario. Third estimation is *Pessimistic*, which represents the worst-case scenario of estimation technique.

The final numbers of estimation is the average of all these three case scenarios.

Reserve Analysis

Every project has known and unknown risks inherited into them. To handle such risks, it is always a good idea to have reserve time allocated against specific tasks or overall project buffer. The *Reserve Analysis* is all about computing the amount of buffer time and how this buffer time is represented in the estimated results of the project.

The reserve can be parked against human resource utilization, components and any cost planned for the project.

Output of Activity Duration Estimation Process

Activity Duration Estimates

The ultimate and important output of Activity duration estimation is the list of activity and the estimated effort for each of the activity. In most project scenarios, the estimations are given in terms of work hours. However, the estimation technique is not limited only hours but more flexible to days or weeks, depending on the project requirement.

At this point, it is to be noted that the estimation doesn't provide any start and end date for any of the project activities, but merely give only the effort estimation numbers.

Activity Attribute Updates

Whenever you work on certain estimation, you tend to come across new information, scope or activities relating to the particular project or components. Whenever you find new piece of information, it is not to be ignored but updated into the Activity Attributes of the particular activity. Hence, the Activity Attribute update becomes the second output of the Activity Duration estimation process.

Tidbits

Who should ideally be doing the estimation for each of the activities?

Is it the Project Manager or the team member, who is assigned the activity?

It can be either doing the estimation. Since the team member is working on the work package or activity, some might argue the respective team member should estimate his work. This is sensible too. In some cases, the project managers or anyone assigned by the project manager understand the complexity of the work packages, dependency and the ability of the assigned team members. So, the project manager also can do the estimation and inform the respective team members.

Both can be possible.

Schedule Development

The most important objective of the Time Management Process is to develop a schedule for the project from start to finish. So far in this chapter, we have seen how the activities are defined, sequenced, resources are estimated and duration of each activity is calculated. Considering all of these as inputs, we are now ready to develop the project schedule, which will become the baseline upon approval from the sponsors and all stakeholders. The developed schedule will have all the activities lined up in a specific order, start and end date for each activity that the resources are identified.

Once the schedule is complete and available, it should give the Project Manager a fair understanding of the possibility of meeting the committed deadline to the customers. If the developed schedule overshoots the agreed deadline, then the Project Manager might need to squeeze the time estimates for few of the activities so as to bring the schedule to meet the deadline.

Thus the schedule will become the guiding force for the Project Manager and the team in meeting their activity deadlines. In addition to this, the developed schedule becomes a critical input for estimating the cost of the project work. We will understand this in the Cost Management chapter.

Let us now see, how the schedule development process is represented in pictorial form.

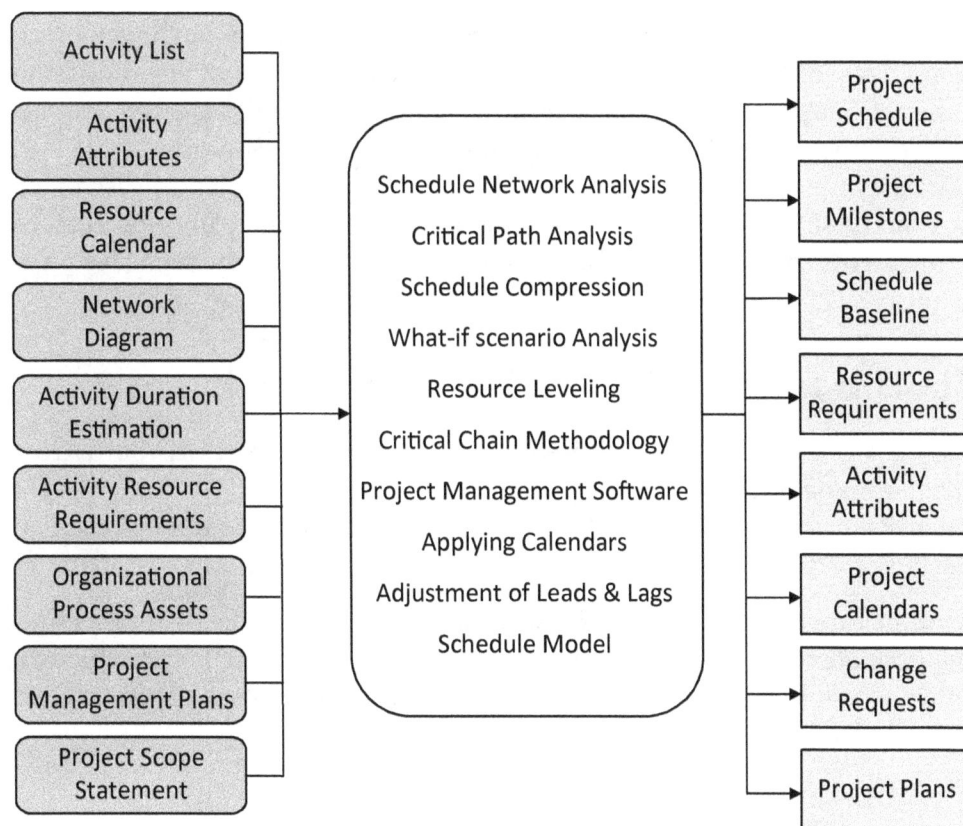

Inputs	Tools & Techniques	Outputs
Activity List	Schedule Network Analysis	Project Schedule
Activity Attributes	Critical Path Analysis	Project Milestones
Resource Calendar	Schedule Compression	Schedule Baseline
Network Diagram	What-if scenario Analysis	Resource Requirements
Activity Duration Estimation	Resource Leveling	Activity Attributes
Activity Resource Requirements	Critical Chain Methodology	Project Calendars
Organizational Process Assets	Project Management Software	Change Requests
Project Management Plans	Applying Calendars	Project Plans
Project Scope Statement	Adjustment of Leads & Lags	
	Schedule Model	

Inputs on Schedule Development

If you notice the above diagram closely, you will find that all the output of the previous processes of Time Management are considered as inputs to the Schedule Development process. This is due to the fact that the Schedule Development is the consolidation of all other processes of Time Management to arrive at a Project Schedule.

Since we have reviewed the first six inputs of the above diagram in the earlier processes, let us not repeat them again here. You may turn back to the previous pages of this chapter, should you require to review them again.

Organizational Process Assets

At times, you may want to refer to your Organizational process repository for vital inputs about the estimation process and how it was done in earlier projects. In addition to this, since the scheduling process involve more about human resources and their availability, their calendars, holiday plans and shift schedule are to be considered as inputs. These inputs form part of the Organizational Process Assets.

Project Scope Statement

The purpose of referring to Project Scope Statement is to know the important milestones of project tasks, definitely to-meet dates and any important assumptions and constraints identified for the project. These become very critical input when you develop the project schedule. The project manager should make sure that these mandatory dates are not missed. In case of any possibility of missing the deadlines due to any dependency or other reasons, adjustments to the resources utilization, dates need to be made at this phase of the project.

Tools Used in Schedule Development

The Network Diagrams that we prepared in the previous processes (both Arrow Diagramming Methodology & Precedence Diagramming Methodology) is extensively useful and helpful in preparing the schedule for the project from the bunch of available data.

Extreme care is to be shown when assigning dates to the individual tasks since the attributes of these tasks shouldn't conflict with each other, failing which the entire schedule might result in chaotic situation at a later stage of your project.

Critical Path Analysis

One of the most important way to develop a project schedule is to establish a Critical Path of activities. A critical path is a list of activities that begins when the project begins and ends when the project closes. The critical path is the list of activities that takes the longest duration than any other path of the network diagram, yet each of these activities are interconnected and dependent on one another. In addition, remember that each of the activities on the critical path are logically dependent on one another.

The most important point to remember is that, if one activity on the critical path falls behind the schedule, it will cause delay on the entire project schedule. An example of a Critical path is illustrated below

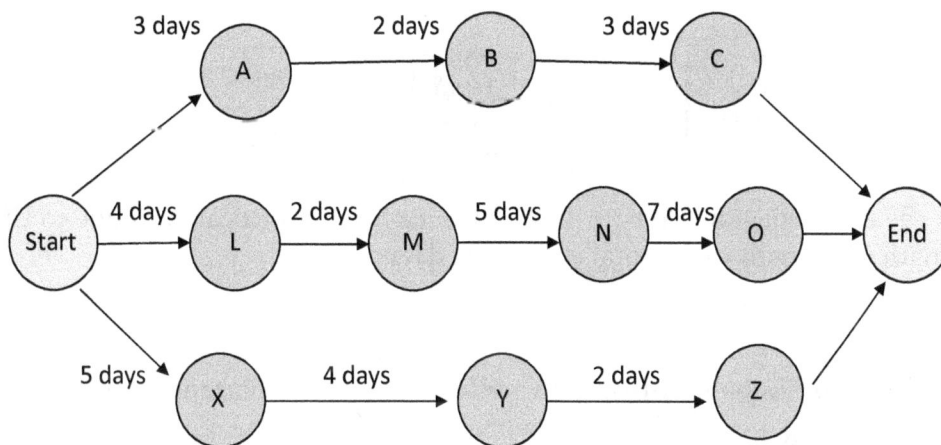

In the above diagram, the path Start-L-M-N-O-End is the critical path, since this path requires the highest amount of effort to complete.

The major advantages of analyzing the critical path is, if an activity is on the critical path and is delayed, it alerts the Project Manager to take remedial actions to bring the path back to normal. Similarly, if an activity is not on a critical path but is delayed, it will not cause panic. If such a task is complete within a reasonable delay, it will help the Project Manager to utilize the available time of the resources to work on the critical path to save time and catch up with the schedule.

The critical path need not be straight line in a network diagram. It can branch out from any of the activities listed in the diagram. Let us look at an example network diagram below.

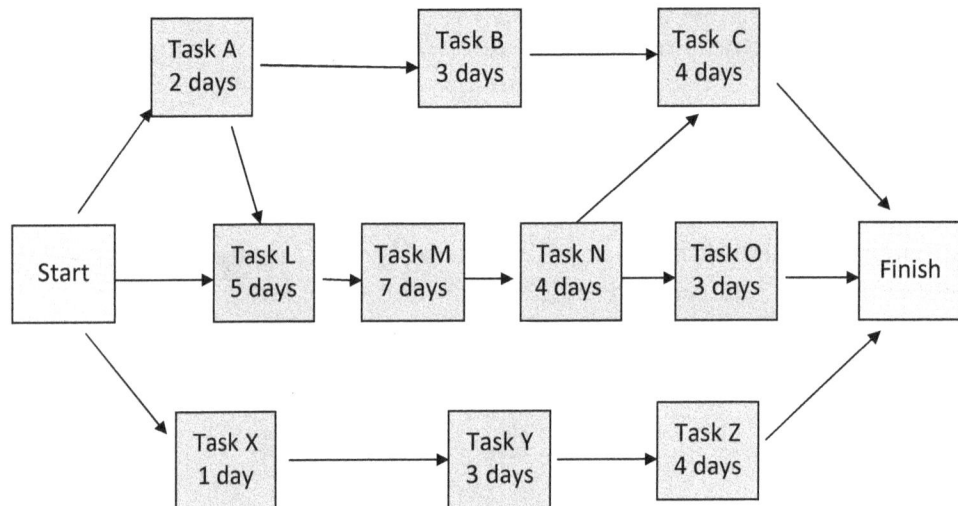

In the above diagram, Start-A-L-M-N-C-Finish is the critical path due to the length of the path with a total effort of 22 days.

Float

When we speak about Critical path methodology, it is important to know about Float.

A float is a duration between activities. It is the amount of effort your project can afford to miss before it begins to impact your overall project schedule. So, how to identify the float of an activity? Let us consider the same diagram given above to illustrate the float

Total planned effort on the critical path (Start-A-L-M-N-C-Finish) is 2+5+7+4+4
= 22 Days

Total planned effort on the path Start-A-B-C-Finish   = 2+3+4   =   9 days

Total planned effort on the path Start-X-Y-Z-Finish   = 1+3+4   =   8 days

As explained earlier, the float permitted on the critical path is zero.

The difference between the planned effort on critical path and non-critical path becomes the float of the non-critical path. In the above example

Float available on Start-A-B-C-Finish   = 22 - 9   =   13 Days

Float available on Start-X-Y-Z-Finish   = 22 - 8   =   14 Days

The above calculations indicate that the activities on the path Start-A-B-C-Finish can collectively slip the schedule upto a maximum of 13 days, before it begins to delay the project schedule. Similarly, the activities on path Start-X-Y-

Z-Finish can collectively slip the schedule upto a maximum of 14 days before the project gets delayed.

In other words, a float is the amount of extra time some of your project activities may have before you can actually hit the panic button.

Does the above makes sense?

Schedule Network Analysis

While referencing the schedule network diagrams provide the list of activities to be executed, the activity attributes should provide the dependency between each of the activities. Analyzing these two data should list the sequence of activity execution besides which activity should go first and which should wait (due to dependency on another activity). It would be helpful, if you recall the Leads and Lags that we reviewed earlier in this chapter.

Having the sequence of activities and their dependency on hand means, the Project Manager can identify the tasks that can start early and late or finish early and late.

An *Early Start* of an activity is the earliest time an activity can begin to execute. To get this activity started, all its predecessors should have been completed. If there is any delay in any of the preceding activity, it will result in delay in the subsequent activities as well. In a network diagram, if a job in the path slips from its original schedule, it will have its impact till the end of the finish. This is due to the dependency factor between activities. To understand more on this, refer to the diagram below

Similarly, *Early Finish* is the earliest date that an activity can finish. To get this activity finished, all its predecessors should have started earlier and finished earlier or on time.

Late Start and Late Finish

Late Start is the latest date, an activity can begin but still can finish on time without causing any delay to the project. *Late Finish* is the latest date, an activity can finish without delaying the overall project schedule. To understand this in detail, let us refer to the diagram below

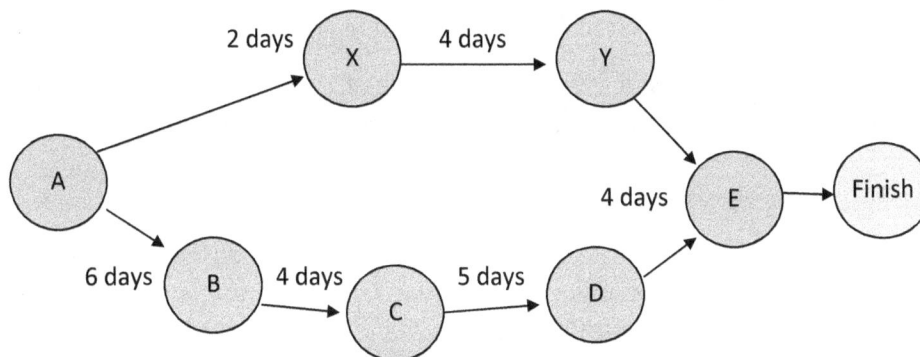

In the above diagram, the critical path of the diagram is A-B-C-D-E-Finish = 6+4+5+4 = 19 days

The effort for activities	B+C+D	= 6+4+5	= 15 days
The effort for activities	X-Y	= 2+4	= 6 days

The above numbers means, activity X can have a late start of 9 days but still can meet the deadline of starting the activity E. Similarly, the activity Y can finish 9 days later than its originally schedule finish date before it kickstart the activity E.

(*Note: The activity E can be started only when both the paths are successfully completed. If either of the path is delayed beyond acceptable level, it will result in late start of activity E*)

More on Schedule Network Analysis

Critical Chain Methodology

We have already seen how a critical path is arrived and managed. It is a list of activities that takes the longest duration to complete and resources are assigned to the activities on the critical path.

However, in a critical chain methodology, the resource dependency and availability is used to determine the critical path. Once the critical path is established, buffer resources are added backward from the committed delivery date, wherever the resources are required at important phases. This will ensure the project meets the agreed milestones without having any major concerns on the delivery.

Resource Levelling

It is very common that some of the project has greater dependency on a single or group of resources due to their expertise or ability to handle difficult tasks. However, it is a risk as well, since such dependency might put the project in deep trouble when the resource is not available for any reason. Sometime the same resource might be handling two different activities, both of which are on the critical path.

When such situations arise, the critical path itself might require to be revisited to accommodate this dependency and minimize the impact.

Applying Calendars

When developing the schedule, another most important factor to be considered is the availability of all resources. Of course, you would have considered their vacation plans in the form of Resource Calendar. However, external factors such as local holidays and weather condition related plays a critical role in influencing the critical path.

As an example, let us assume you are working on a project that designs a internal combustion engine for a propeller. The team that is designing is located in the United States and two locations in Europe. As a Project Manager, you are developing the project schedule. While developing, you should verify if there are any local holidays in each of the locations that might required to be factored into your schedule.

Adjusting Leads and Lags

Leads and Lags can come in handy when the Project Manager is trying to develop the schedule. At times there may be adjustments required on the Leads and Lags that are already identified for the activities. This is to make sure the project schedule do not get distorted.

Project Management Software

Often, the Project Management Software helps the Project Managers to derive the project schedule from the network diagrams. If you ever used any of the Project planner software, you might understand how easy to prepare a Work Breakdown Structure of a project from the list of tasks.

Similarly, the Project Management Software picks data from the network diagram and creates a tentative project schedule with the list of tasks, dates and effort involved. Thus it becomes easy for the Project Manager to work on a readily available skeleton version of the schedule and input his updates and other data.

Schedule Model

A sample model of project schedule can be created with the collection and consolidation of all data, including the list of activities and the activity attributes using any available Project Management Software. Such a sample model can help the Project Manager to have a visual representation of how the schedule might be with these data before he could go on and finalize his project schedule.

What-if Scenario Analysis

Believe it or not, the What-if analysis is a very efficient tool in developing the schedule of the project.

The What-if analysis can be equated with the Risk Management planning of the project since you will sit back and imagine every potential scenario that could result in unexpected situations of the project execution phase. In other words, the Project Manager would sit back and think about what could potentially go wrong in the project much in advance and begin planning for such unexpected turn of schedule related events.

As an example, imagine you are managing an event management project in your town for the customer. When you develop a schedule, you might potential consider the following situations and ask yourself some questions such as

- What if the customer decide to push the start time by 30 minutes?
- What if the Chief guest arrives 1 hour late due to traffic jam, generated by this event?
- What if 50% of the invitees do not turn up to the event?
- What if it rains heavily during the event?

The What-if Analysis helps the Project Manager to consider similar potential troubles that might come his way and analyze the impact of such troubles on the project schedule.

Schedule Compression

Now, let us come to the most important and interesting tool to handle schedule development. That is compressing the schedule to meet the agreed deadline of the customer.

Imagine you are part of your company's Research & Development department and working on a project that is to develop a prototype of a new series of auto and to test the prototype. Your responsibility is to manage the design, development and testing of the new model, that is planned to be launched in the market in four months time. You developed a schedule and got approved by the sponsor and all the stakeholders. The sponsor happen to be your company's senior management, which is closely monitoring the progress of your project.

In the middle of the project, unexpected scope changes forced the project to slip the schedule. Your project is already three weeks behind schedule. Your management has already committed to launch the new model in the market in four months. So, they want you to do whatever it could take to get the prototype developed and tested as per the committed schedule.

Now, what are your possible options? How would you handle this situation?

It is not very difficult to handle, but needs some wise thinking and analysis of the situation to arrive at a solution.

There are two better options available for you to overcome this trouble. First is, **Crashing** and **Fast-tracking** the schedule. Let us review both of them in detail

Crashing the Schedule

When you are behind your schedule and desperately required to meet the deadline, Crashing the schedule is a possible solution to you. This means, you will be adding more resources to the activities that are part of the critical path or moving resources between non-critical path and critical path to handle the important tasks.

However, this technique has one disadvantage. Adding more resources adds to the cost. If your management is not going to approve the additional budget, then Crashing the schedule may not be the right choice for your project.

Fast-tracking the Schedule

When you are behind your schedule and want to get the project back to its track another option worth considering is to Fast-track the project schedule.

Closely analyze the project resources and their work schedules. Look at the possibilities of doing two activities simultaneously. For example, your team can prepare the test data while carrying testing with those data simultaneously.

There are a couple of risks in adapting to this methodology. First, the project team might have to redo some part of their work. Second, there may be some quality issues coming up, since the project manager's focus is now shifted to meet the deadline. Fast tracking might work well, if these two risks are handled carefully.

Output of Develop Schedule Process

Project Schedule

The ultimate and most important of all the output of the Develop Schedule process is the Project Schedule itself.

Collecting all the effort and resource related information and consolidating them provides a project schedule to the project manager. The schedule contains the list of each activity of the project, effort required and start and end dates for each of the activities. At this point, the Project Manager should have a rough idea about when he can have his project completed and will be in a position to compare the committed delivery date of the project with the realistic picture on schedule.

Let us take a look into the sample project schedule given below. The schedule is only for illustrative purpose.

Project Title   Project Schedule

Start Week	Jan 5, 2014

Week	1	2	3	4	5	6	7	8	9	10	11	12	13	14	15	16	17	18	19	20	Notes
Starting	Jan 5	Jan 12	Jan 19	Jan 26	Feb 2	Feb 9	Feb 16	Feb 23	Mar 2	Mar 9	Mar 16	Mar 23	Mar 30	Apr 6	Apr 13	Apr 20	Apr 27	May 4	May 11	May 18	
Phase One	Quality Assurance Plan																				
		Project Plan																			
			Plan Review																		
Phase Two				Draft Requirements																	
				Capacity Planning																	
					Project Test Plan																
					Acceptance Test Plan																
							Final Requirements Specfications														
							Phase Review and Approval														
Phase Three								Draft Design Specifications													
								Configuration Management Plan													
									Architecture Design Plan											
								Define Interface Requirements												
										Shared Component Design										
										Integration Test Plan										
											Define Project Guidelines									
												Final Design Specifications								
													Phase Review and Approval							

(column 7 shaded: Milestone, additional funds; column 20 shaded: PROJECT END)

List of Milestones

Another important output of the develop the schedule process is the list of milestones and the dates that are associated with each of the milestones. A milestone is not entirely an activity that is executed as part of the project. However, a milestone can be a phase of the project, which is tracked with a targeted date.

When the milestone data is shared with the sponsor, the Project Manager has a responsibility to provide status updates to the sponsor for each of the milestone. Whenever the senior management of the project performing organization questions about the status, it should be remembered that they are referring to the milestone status.

Schedule Baseline

When the project schedule is fully developed and approved by the sponsor, it becomes the schedule baseline of the project. Any future status of the project schedule is tracked against this baseline.

Other Outputs of Schedule Development Process

When you are working on the project schedule, there are more than likely that you might need to carry updates to many components such as resource calendars, activity list, activity attributes, change requests and other *project management plans*.

These changes are updated accordingly and considered as a key output of the Schedule development phase.

Schedule Control

Having developed a Project Schedule and got it approved from the sponsor and other stakeholders, currently we have the Schedule Baseline. Let us assume the team is executing the construction phase of the project and the project manager has the responsibility to monitor the project's progress and be on top of his project to *monitor and control* the changes that might come.

So, what comes next on Time Management?

Having a project schedule developed doesn't guarantee everything will go according to the schedule and the Project Manager will have the deliverables on the date defined in the schedule on his table.

Unless the Project Manager is alert and careful, the project schedule might take the project weeks behind its original plan, thus derailing the entire project and the cost incurred on the project becoming a wasteful expenditure for the sponsor. The major factor that might carry this risk is the need for changing the project schedule.

The primary responsibility of the Project Manager is to identify the factors that might cause the changes required on the project schedule and make sure that the project is meeting it's committed delivery schedule.

The Project Manager monitors the project schedule on a daily basis, by getting updates on the listed activities and comparing the original data with the project's schedule baseline. Any request for change is scrutinized very closely and carefully before taking a decision whether to go ahead with the change or reject it.

To understand more on the Schedule Control process, let us look into the process diagram below

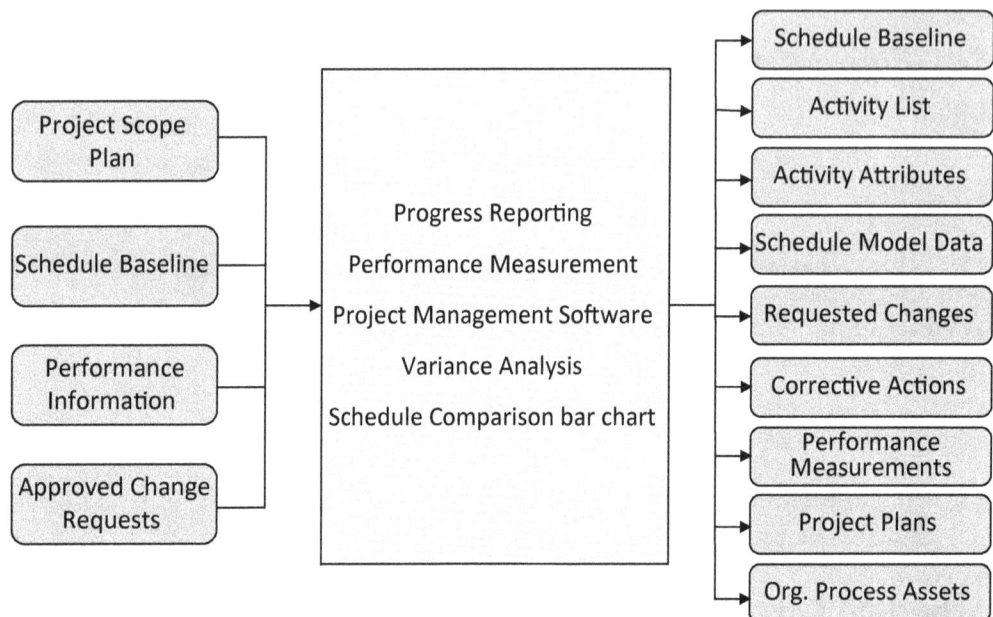

```
┌──────────────────┐                                      ┌──────────────────────┐
│ Project Scope    │                                      │  Schedule Baseline   │
│ Plan             │                                      └──────────────────────┘
└──────────────────┘      ┌─────────────────────────┐     ┌──────────────────────┐
                          │  Progress Reporting     │     │  Activity List       │
┌──────────────────┐      │  Performance Measurement│     └──────────────────────┘
│ Schedule Baseline│      │  Project Management     │     ┌──────────────────────┐
└──────────────────┘      │  Software               │     │  Activity Attributes │
                          │  Variance Analysis      │     └──────────────────────┘
┌──────────────────┐      │  Schedule Comparison    │     ┌──────────────────────┐
│ Performance      │      │  bar chart              │     │ Schedule Model Data  │
│ Information       │      └─────────────────────────┘     └──────────────────────┘
└──────────────────┘                                      ┌──────────────────────┐
                                                          │  Requested Changes   │
┌──────────────────┐                                      └──────────────────────┘
│ Approved Change  │                                      ┌──────────────────────┐
│ Requests         │                                      │  Corrective Actions  │
└──────────────────┘                                      └──────────────────────┘
                                                          ┌──────────────────────┐
                                                          │  Performance         │
                                                          │  Measurements        │
                                                          └──────────────────────┘
                                                          ┌──────────────────────┐
                                                          │  Project Plans       │
                                                          └──────────────────────┘
                                                          ┌──────────────────────┐
                                                          │  Org. Process Assets │
                                                          └──────────────────────┘
```

Input of the Schedule Control Process

Project Scope Plan

You may be wondering, what the Project Scope Plan doing in the Schedule Control process.

The question is very genuine since we are not doing any updates to the project scope in this process. However, since the Project Schedule control is all about keeping the change requests under control, it is essential to look for areas which might cause changes to the project requirements, which will ultimately have an impact on the project schedule.

This justifies the inclusion of Project Scope Plan in this process. Whenever you hear about requested changes or change management, it ultimately means one or more of the stakeholder of the project has requested for changes to the project scope. Unless the change requests are scrutinized carefully, it will result in blowing up your project schedule, much to the displeasure of the customers.

Schedule Baseline

Whenever there is a changes are required to the Project schedule, the ultimate document to refer is the Schedule baseline to understand the current schedule estimates before including the updates to the schedule.

Performance Reports

One of the critical input of the Schedule control is the Performance report. The performance report provides vital inputs on the project performance that helps the Project Manager to look for performance improvement initiatives. These improvement initiatives help reduce the need for changes to the project scope and schedule.

Approved Change Requests

Any changes that are requested by any of the stakeholders get scrutinized by the Project Manager first. Once the CR is required to be included in the project scope, CCB is approached for approvals. All approved change request details are available in this input.

Remember that not every requested changes need to get approved. The purpose of having a Change Control Board is to validate the requested changes to analyze its need, impact and urgency before taking a decision as to whether proceed with including this change in the project or reject.

Tools Used in Schedule Control Process

Progress Reporting

If you have good amount of experience as a Project Manager, then you would be aware of what Progress Reporting is all about and you would have done enough of it in different contexts. In the case of Schedule control, you are more concerned about the start and end dates of the project activities, the effort spent so far and where is the project milestone compared to where we wished it to be.

In addition to the above, you should be able to provide details of the unfinished portion of the project activities. The consolidated details should give a clearer picture on the project's overall status and how much more it will take to get the project completed. The progress reporting is used to highlight any risks, issues and accomplishments by the project team and its positive or negative impact on the project's schedule.

Performance Measurement

One of the reason for having changes is due to the review of the project's performance. If the project is slipping in its schedule, the Project Manager might be required to review the project schedule and take suitable corrective actions. Whenever the project schedule changes, the Project Manager is responsible for collecting the performance data and update the customers.

When the Project Manager is tracking the performance of the project, his primary focus should be to collect the variance details also known as Schedule

Variance (SV) and the Schedule Performance Index (SPI). These two vital data provides insight into how the project is progressing at that point of time.

Let us learn more about calculating Schedule Variance (SV) and Schedule Performance Index (SPI) in the Cost Management Planning chapter.

Project Management Software

There are many software that are readily available in the market has the capability to analyze the project schedule, the progress and the estimated schedule of the remaining tasks and generate neat reports. These software can be used by the Project Managers to utilize the various features that it offers.

Variance Analysis

A variance analysis is obtained by comparing the planned schedule dates with the actual schedule dates. The result is the variance in the project schedule. Finding the Schedule Variance (SV) is one important task of the Project Manager during the project's Monitoring & Controlling phase. Project performance information act as a vital input in finding the variance details.

If the variance in the schedule is bigger, it conveys serious trouble for the project and might need to be looked into immediately.

Schedule Comparison Bar Chart

If you have prepared enough of project charts based on real-time data, then it shouldn't be difficult for you to prepare schedule chart for the project. The bar chart has two bars, one to highlight the planned schedule for each activity while the other represents the actual data.

Output of the Schedule Control Process

Schedule Baseline

Whenever the schedule is being monitored, there are always possibilities of new updates to the project scope and other plan components possible. Such changes result in revising the project schedule that was already planned. After the changes are effected on the other project plan components, the schedule baseline needs to be updated.

Thus the output of Schedule Control finds a revised Schedule baseline.

Activity List

As explained earlier, when schedule is monitored there are possibilities of new tasks getting added to the list of activities that are already identified. The new activities gets added to the existing list and result is a fresh list of activities.

Activity Attributes

Subsequent to the revised list of activities, every new activity has its own attributes and impacts the attributes of existing activities (the predecessor and successor activities will see updates due to the inclusion of new activities).

Requested Changes

The list of changes that were requested and subsequently approved by the Change Control Board for inclusion in the project plan.

Schedule Model Data

A sample model of project schedule created with the collection and consolidation of all data, including the list of activities and the activity attributes using any available Project Management Software. Such sample model provide insight into the current trend of the project schedule planning process, thus helping the project manager to make adjustments, wherever necessary.

Organizational Process Assets

Remember that whenever you are carrying updates to any of the plan components, sometime the details of the issues or updates might required to be captured as a Lesson Learned, as part of the Project Management process requirement. These provide as a very vital information for the performing organization and other project managers, who may be managing similar projects in future. Thus, this becomes one important output of the Schedule Control output.

Performance Measurement Data

As we use the Performance Measurement as a tool to do the Schedule Control process, we tend to collect much of data related to the project's schedule performance. These data are consolidated and shared with the stakeholders, who will be interested to know how the project is performing at any given point of time.

As a project manager, you might require these data to keep track of the milestones and provide updates to the sponsor.

Corrective Actions

As part of the project monitoring and control phase, project schedule might undergo updates due to change requests raised and approved. Details of all the changes carried is consolidated and shared as list of corrective actions.

Impact of Change Requests on Schedule

Often people do not pay much importance to the Changes requested to the Scope. They do not realize the impact of receiving changes to the original scope of the project. Of course, Changes cannot be avoided or turned back blindly since it may be important for the customers.

However, unless the proper Change management process is followed, the Project Manager might end up blowing up his original schedule, thus impacting the cost, scope, quality and what not? A change requested may appear to be minor and might require few hours of effort or even no additional effort too. However, it is the responsibility of the Project Manager to get the impact assessment of the impact done before giving a go ahead to carry out the change request.

Assume you managing a project that is about managing a cultural event in the downtown. You are fully prepared with the events lined up and all the rehearsals done. The compeering is prerecorded and automated. On the day of the event, you are being approached by the event organizers to include an martial arts event to be performed by an young artist. This little performance will not take more than few minutes of time.

As a manager of this project, you look at the possibility of including this request but find that all the participants are given clear instructions on their turn of events, time schedule and expected duration of their respective events. Moreover, since the compeering is prerecorded, you cannot insert this requested event anywhere in the middle. Unless you take a realistic approach of this change request, your project cannot go smooth and successful.

So, being a Project Manager is not so easy task but full of responsibilities, accountability, ownership and confidence in taking decisions.

EXERCISES

Match the Following

Activity Definition   :   Assess the effort required for each
                                           activity in the list

Activity Sequencing   :   Prepare the project schedule from the
                                           activities list

Activity Resource Estimation   :   Monitor the schedule and control the
                                           changes

Activity Duration Estimation   :   Rearrange the activity list in a logical
                                           sequence

Schedule Development   :   List of activities to be performed de-
                                           rived from WBS

Schedule Control   :   Assess the resource requirement for
                                           each activity

True or False

1. Time Management is an evolving process and can be updated as the project makes progress (**True/False**)

2. Project Schedule is a key input to the Cost Management Plan (**True/False**)

3. Schedule Control means controlling the project schedule and keeping it within baseline (**True/False**)

4. Fast Tracking the project schedule might result in quality issues (**True/False**)

5. Work Packets in WBS are same as Activities in Project Schedule (**True/False**)

Briefly Answer the Following Questions

1. What is the difference between an Activity attribute and WBS Dictionary?

2. What is the difference between Project Schedule and Schedule baseline?

3. How would you differentiate outputs of Activity definition and Activity sequencing processes?

4. If a task on the critical path is running behind its schedule, what is the best way to bring it back to schedule?

5. How do you explain What-if Scenario while developing the schedule?

ANSWERS

Match the Following

Activity Definition	: List of activities to be performed derived from WBS
Activity Sequencing	: Rearrange the activity list in a logical sequence
Activity Resource Estimation	: Assess the resource requirement for each activity
Activity Duration Estimation	: Assess the effort required for each activity in the list
Schedule Development	: Prepare the project schedule from the activities list
Schedule Control	: Monitor the schedule and control the changes

True or False

1. False
2. True
3. False
4. True
5. False

Test Your Knowledge

1. You are in the middle of developing your project schedule. You are able to list all the activities that are planned to be executed in your project. While developing the project schedule, you find that one of the key resource in your project will end up handling two activities, both of which are on the critical path. Even worse is both of these activities are dependent on each other.

   Unfortunately, both these activities require a specialized skill on certain technology, which is not available with other resources. Confused as to what to do, you approach your supervisor and explain him the dilemma and seek advice. Your manager ask you to do Resource leveling to overcome the issue.

   What does the Resource Leveling means?

   a) When several resources are available in your project, it is a very good idea to identify the brightest among them and use them as backup the original team member to complete both the tasks, that are on the critical path.

   b) Assign the tasks on critical path to all the resources equally to eliminate schedule risk

   c) Resource leveling refers to reviewing the critical path, when the same resource is assigned more than one task, which are on the critical path.

   d) Have buffer resources available to balance schedule risks on the critical path.

2. Robin is managing a project, which is part of a program. He has already completed defining the scope of the project and currently working on developing the project schedule. He just completed high level schedule development and find that the effort requirement may be 20% more than expected for his project. When he raises this during the project review meeting, his program manager says he cannot afford to get the cost blowing over the budget. So, he asks

   Robin to review the schedule completed before creating a final draft of the schedule.

   Robin is not sure, whether he heard his program manager right, since he spoke about 'blowing the cost budget' when he was discussing about his developed schedule. Could you help Robin with an clarification?

   a) Robin should better check with his program manager before he begin working on the revision.

   b) Schedule development is a key input to the cost planning process. So, his program manager was right in making that statement.

---

c) Robin could consult the Project Management Office (PMO) to understand what is the organization policy says about schedule and cost planning.

d) The program manager made that statement by mistake, probably due to stressful project schedule.

3. **A Lead time in a project schedule refers to**

a) It is the amount of time available between a predecessor and successor tasks to balance their dependency

b) The amount of effort that the project is ahead of its schedule

c) The time taken by the project to reach the current phase since the start date

d) None of the above

4. **Lisa is managing her first project for her company, which has enormous amount of faith in her skills and ability to drive the project and the team successfully. She amazed every stakeholder and her boss by completing the scope definition successfully and on time. She is now planning to develop the project schedule and currently working on defining the activities that are involved in the project execution. As she makes progress with the activities, she find that there are many unknown components in the project and finding it difficult to define them. She is more concerned about these unknown ones, since it will be challenging to estimate effort for these components.**

    When she raises this concern in the regular meeting with her boss, he suggest her take the Rolling

    Wave approach.

    She is now more confused since the term 'Rolling Wave' is unfamiliar to her and she is hesitant to ask her boss. Could you help her with an explanation?

a) Rolling wave is about keeping the project rolling without worrying about the missing components, since it is not the fault of Lisa to have so many unknown components

b) She must ask her boss to explain what a Rolling Wave approach means

c) Rolling wave is a strategy to dummy components in place of unknown ones.

d) Rolling wave planning is about working with the known components while waiting for clarity on the unknown ones.

5. **A float in a project refers to**

    a) A float means the amount of effort that is available between two tasks

    b) Making sure the team doesn't float any of the policies or law while working on the project

    c) Float refers to the time, when the team is going to complete their construction phase and float the deliverables for acceptance testing

    d) None of the above

6. **You are running late with your project schedule and worried that you are most likely to miss the development schedule of your project due to longer than estimate effort requirement. As the customer is not ready to push the target date for delivery, your senior management asking you to adopt to schedule compression techniques.**

    What are the schedule compression techniques available to you?

    a) Take off tasks that are not critical among your deliverables

    b) Focus on tasks that are on the critical path and get them completed on schedule

    c) Let your customer know that there were some unexpected schedule overrun and the team cannot complete as per the original schedule.

    d) Look for crashing the schedule or fast track the project.

7. **In the Schedule Development process, what does a late start refer to**

    a) Late start is the amount of time, a task can be delayed

    b) It is the amount of effort the project began behind its original schedule

    c) Late start means amount of effort a specific task began behind its schedule

    d) Late start means the amount of effort the next start can begin late

8. **Which of the following is a tool used in activity duration estimation process**

    a) Organizational Process assets

    b) Reserve Analysis

    c) Critical Path Analysis

    d) Resource Leveling

9. **A discretionary dependency refers to**

    a) An optional dependency between tasks that are on the critical path

    b) The dependency that is left to the discretion of the project manager, who makes an analysis of the task

    c) An optional dependency between two tasks, where one task need not necessarily wait for the other

    d) None of the above

10. You are attending an organizational meeting involving every project manager working in your office. You are in the learning phase of project management and is very excited about this meeting, since you get a chance to meet and interact with many project managers and share their experience. In her speech, one of the participant speaks about the importance of using networking diagrams while scheduling the project. Having a networking diagram in a project simplifies the effort spent on the project scheduling and makes the life easier for the project manager.

    Now, you are not sure having used networking diagramming technique in your project though you are aware of what it is. Can you name the process that generates network diagrams in a project schedule?

    a) Activity Sequencing

    b) Activity Duration Estimation

    c) Schedule development

    d) None of the above

11. A revised schedule baseline is an output of

    a) Schedule definition

    b) Schedule Control

    c) Schedule development

    d) Activity Sequencing

12. You are managing a construction project and is in the execution phase. You were able to produce a great scope, schedule and cost estimation, which were approved by the customer. You identified a great team of engineers, who work hard to get the project move on as per the schedule. However, due to a dependency in the form of supply of some critical components by your customer's vendor, your team is now running one week behind the schedule. You are now worried about this delay and afraid that the schedule gap might widen even further, since there are some more risks that are expected.

    To recoup the time lost due to this delay, you decide to crash the project schedule. However, your organization has shot the idea down instantly saying it is unacceptable for the company's business reasons. What could be the possible reason for this refusal?

    a) Probably, the company is not fully aware of the background of the issue and the schedule risks.

    b) Company always follows a very disciplined and strict approach when accepting such requests

    c) Schedule crashing involves deploying additional resources, which impacts the cost and profitability

    d) Your organization must be for fast tracking the project, instead of crashing the schedule.

13. Candice is working on developing a schedule plan for her project. She has listed all the activities that are derived by decomposing the work packages. One day, her customer invites her for a meeting to discuss the effort requirement for the project. In the meeting, the customer wants to know the approximate effort requirement to complete the project. The customer require this information to report to his boss. Since Candice is well aware of the scope of the project and the complexity, she gives a rough estimate for the development phase.

    However, when the team works on the execution phase she find the effort requirement was far more than she predicted because of complicated development tasks, dependency and wait time. Her actual schedule was about 50% more than the rough estimate she gave to her customer. The customer is not happy with this amount of effort and feel the team spent too much more time than it should have, even though the effort required to complete the development is justified for its complexity.

    Candice is confused and not able to understand where and what went wrong with the development? Do you mind helping her with your inputs?

    a) Candice is not to be faulted since she was aware of the project scope and the complexity. It is the fault of the team not to live upto her expectation.

    b) The customer was given only a rough estimation of schedule. It is their fault to track the project based on a rough estimate.

    c) The external dependencies are the cause of all this

    d) She should have taken a bottom-up approach to estimating the project for much more realistic effort to track.

14. **A contingency reserve refers to**

    a) Adding extra time for tasks in the project schedule

    b) Reserving a specific resource to work on a project task

    c) Using the optimizing technique to make sure the resources meet the schedule estimation

    d) None of the above

15. **Three point estimation is about**
    a) Providing project schedule estimation at three different stages of the project to have a realistic schedule numbers for the customer
    b) Reviewing the project schedule at three different phases and make required adjustments to bring the schedule to an achievable target
    c) Taking three different approaches to schedule estimation such as Realistic, Optimistic and Pessimistic
    d) All the above are incorrect, it's something else

16. **One of the important requirement for a critical path is**
    a) All the tasks should be of high importance
    b) Critical path cannot have any float
    c) No two tasks on the critical path MUST be assigned to the same resource
    d) Only tasks that are critical to the business can be on the critical path

17. **When is a variance analysis performed in a project?**
    a) During Schedule control process
    b) Planning phase
    c) Execution phase
    d) Project Closure

18. **You are in the middle of developing your project schedule. As agreed with your customer, you schedule a meeting with your stakeholders to review the schedule as you make progress with the schedule. One of the stakeholder asked whether you applied resource calendars into the schedule or not.**

    What would you understand from this question?
    a) Applying calendars refers to considering resource availability and external threats that might have impact on the schedule
    b) It means scheduling the tasks to each of the identified project resources
    c) Requesting the resources to provide their estimation for their tasks
    d) None of the above

19. **A Lag refers to**
    a) A schedule delay in a project
    b) Schedule buffer
    c) Project reserve
    d) Amount of time given to a successor task

20. A Network diagram is useful
    a) In establishing a network of tasks
    b) To determine critical path, lead, lag and float between tasks
    c) To establish a project schedule
    d) All of the above

21. Your project is running behinds its schedule and the customer is worried about the potential delay in the delivery. The cause of the delay is on the customer end and due to unclear requirement and numerous unknown tasks in the original requirement. After setting all these right, your project started late by 3 weeks. The total schedule for the project is 18 weeks. The customer wants you to make up for the lost time and is willing to bear any additional cost, if it is justified. At the same time, you have to make sure the quality is not compromised.

    What would be your approach?
    a) Crash the schedule, since the customer is willing to bear the additional cost
    b) Tell the customer that nothing can be done since the delay was not your fault
    c) Keep continuing with the project work at the same pace as it progressing now. You can assign outstanding tasks to resources that gets freed up at a later stage of the development phase.
    d) Fast track the project

22. You have created a list of activities and asked your team to provide an estimation for their respective tasks assigned. After a week, each of the team member revert with their estimation in terms of hours. Since you are familiar with the bottom-up approach to estimation, you consolidate all of these effort and arrive at a overall project estimation.

    What might be missing in your approach to estimation?
    a) Nothing. You just followed the bottom-up approach to estimation.
    b) You should not let the team members do estimation.
    c) Bottom up approach is not effective when the team does the estimation
    d) Contingency reserve is not included in the estimation

23. Rebecca is assigned as a manager of a railway project. She is working to get the project scope defined. Her organization has already assigned few of the key project, who are experts in executing such railway projects. After having these staff onboard, she cannot utilize them since the scope is not approved yet. This is a perfect example of

    a) Mandatory dependency

    b) Schedule overrun

    c) Poor planning skills

    d) Schedule reserve utilization

24. Which of the below is true about the critical path

    a) All tasks are critical

    b) Longest path

    c) Only critical resources are assigned to tasks on the critical path

    d) A maximum of 6% float is permissible for the critical path.

25. Having dummy tasks in a project schedule is permitted because it is required as per

    a) Project contract

    b) Reserve analysis

    c) Planning Component

    d) Mandatory project buffer requirement

ANSWERS

1. **Answer: C**

    Justification: Using the same resource to develop multiple tasks on the critical path pose several risks to the project. The primary among them is a potential schedule risk and resource dependency. If such a dependency cannot be avoided, the project manager should carefully review the entire critical path and attempt to eliminate such risks.

2. **Answer: B**

    Justification: It is the Time and Cost Management planning that have very high rate of dependency on each other. Every project spends a significant of money on human resources and the effort of resources are handled in the Time management planning process. So, any schedule overrun would have serious cost impact on the project.

3. **Answer: A**

    Justification: A lead is usually the effort intentionally put between a predecessor and successor task. The purpose of having such effort may be anything, including a potential dependency between those two tasks.

4. **Answer: D**

    Justification: A rolling wave planning is normally not a highly recommended practice in managing a schedule, since the project manager will be working in vacuum with unknown components. The Rolling Wave approach should be adopted only when it is unavoidable.

5. **Answer: A**

    Justification: A float is a result of the project scheduling, wherein multiple project paths are established and some of the tasks on these paths have buffer time available to start or complete due to certain dependencies between tasks in their path. When a wedding is planned, there may be time between preparing the food and serving them to the guests. This time is called a float.

6. **Answer: D**

    Justification: Crashing the schedule and Fast tracking the task completion are two schedule compression techniques available for a project manager. Crashing the schedule means adding extra resources to complete the tasks as per the schedule baseline. The disadvantage with this approach is increasing cost due to deploying additional resources. The other technique is fast tracking, which means taking up multiple tasks simultaneously. The disadvantage with this technique is a risk on the quality of the output.

7. **Answer: A**

   Reason: At times, tasks on non-critical path may have the luxury of having some amount of buffer time before the whole path can be completed. Such buffer time gives the luxury to the core team members to play for their task start depending on their other tasks. At this moment, it is to be noted that the tasks on the critical path cannot have a buffer time or late start.

8. **Answer: B**

   Reason : When activities are planned and estimated, it is essential for the project manager to do an analysis of the schedule reserves to take care of any risks or contingencies. If any of the task has more risks, it may be good to have contingency reserves planned for such tasks. Ideally, a total project reserve can be upto 8% of the overall project estimation.

9. **Answer: C**

   Reason: At times, there may be some tasks which have dependency on one another, but they need not wait for each other to complete before getting kick started. When a development team is working on creating a attractive multimedia gaming software, they do not need to wait for the outer box to be printed to proceed to completion. However, the software cannot be launched in the market unless both these tasks are completed before the estimated time.

10. **Answer: A**

    Reason: Having a networking diagram while sequencing the listed activities help establish a clear relationship between tasks. Two types of network diagrams are Arrow Diagramming Method (ADM) and Precedence Diagramming Method (PDM). The network diagrams help decide on the critical path of the project schedule and to plan for effort requirement for each of the task on the project.

11. **Answer: B**

    Reason: One of the important task during a schedule control is to look for change requests that might influence the project schedule. Though a change request means additional work for the project manager on top of the project schedule, it cannot be avoided. Whenever a change request gets approved by the Change Control Board (CCB) the scope, schedule and cost baseline need to be updated and the resultant output of the schedule control process is a revised schedule baseline.

12. **Answer: C**

    Reason: Crashing the schedule results in additional cost for the customer and the performing organization. IF the cost impact can be absorbed by the contingency reserves, it may not be difficult to get it approved. However, if the contingency reserve is used then the project would have to be executed without a contingency reserve, which is a cost risk for the customer or performing organization. Fast tracking the might not have cost impact but carries a risk on quality.

13. **Answer: D**

    Reason: When a project manager is performing an estimation, using the bottom-up approach is always recommended. The trouble for Candice is due to the fact that she gave a high level estimate for the entire development phase without thinking much about the effort requirement for individual tasks considering their complexity, resource capability, risks and dependencies. The better way she could have handled this issue is to get the all the project tasks estimated individually before summing them up and adding a contingency requirement for the development phase. The numbers arrived so would be much more closer to the realistic amount of effort involved.

14. **Answer: A**

    Reason: There may be certain tasks in a project, whose requirement may not be clear or carry some amount of risk factors due to dependency factors. In such situations, a project manager can add some amount of effort as contingency reserve in anticipation of risks in future. Not every task in a project can have a contingency reserve and the total contingency reserve can be between 5-8% of the overall project effort requirement.

15. **Answer: C**

    Reason: When a project manager is working on estimating the duration of each of the project activities, one of the method of having the estimate done is to consider three different possibilities of scenarios based on the scope requirement and the dependencies and risks. A Realistic estimation is more about considering a best case scenario based on the possible turn of events. Second option is to have a optimistic approach, which refers to taking an optimistic view of the dependencies, complexity and risks and arrive at an estimate. The third technique is pessimistic estimation, which considers the negative possibilities before arriving at the estimate.

16. **Answer: B**

    Reason: This being the most appropriate choice of answer, the critical path is also known as the longest path in a project schedule. The critical path is established by considering the tasks with highest amount of effort involved and the dependency factors. Thus, a critical path cannot have a float to itself. In addition, all the other paths are expected to be complete, when the critical path reach its completion stage. It is also true that it carries a high risk to have the same resource with two tasks, both of which are on the critical path.

17. **Answer: A**

    Reason: As the name indicates, a variance analysis refers to finding the amount of effort variance found over a project task. Such analysis is obviously performed when the project manager is monitoring the progress of the tasks. A variance analysis help the project manager understand the root cause of the issue and take immediate steps to fix the issues.

18. **Answer: A**

    Reason: When working on a project, one of the risk is about the availability of the resources or external factors such as nature, holiday calendars which might have serious impact on the project schedule. Considering such factors during the schedule development reduces the risks of schedule overrun at a later stage of the project.

19. **Answer: D**

    Reason: Lag Time is the amount of time given to a successor task before it can get kick started after the predecessor task is completed. Even if the election voting is completed in the election, the new government cannot assume office until the results are declared and are invited by the Head of the state to form a government.

20. **Answer: D**

    Reason: The primary purpose of using a networking diagram is to facilitate developing a project schedule. To have a project schedule developed, the project manager should identify the tasks, sequence them, identify resources for each of the task, estimate the effort requirement and consolidating the effort using the bottom-up approach before adding a contingency reserve to arrive at a final project schedule requirement. The networking diagram plays a crucial role of establishing the relationships between the tasks that aids in developing a schedule.

21. **Answer: A**

    Reason: If you read the question carefully, it becomes imminent that the customer is willing to bear the additional cost but wouldn't compromise on the quality of the deliverables. This should help identify the correct answer to the question. Crashing the schedule might involve deploying additional resources, but fast tracking involves high quality risks on the deliverables.

22. **Answer: D**

    Reason: Having a contingency reserves for critical and high risk project components is always a recommended practice for the project managers to balance the risk factors for any task. After the task level estimations are done, the project manager should add contingency reserves before arriving at a project schedule estimate.

23. **Answer: A**

    Reason: The issue here is the presence of mandatory dependency. The project scope is not yet approved, which means the team do not have an objective or have tasks scheduled for them. Unless these dependencies are removed, the team can begin working on their respective tasks.

24. **Answer: B**

    Reason: A critical path is also the Longest path in a project schedule. Among all the tasks identified in the project, the paths with more amount of effort and dependencies among themselves are listed as critical path. A critical path cannot have any buffer time and should never miss its schedule deadline.

25. **Answer: C**

    Reason: The concept of planning component is useful when the project manager is working on the schedule. The planning components enables the manager to implant dummy tasks in place of the unclear or undefined ones. The project cannot be held back for the sake of few unknown requirements. These dummy components are replaced as and when the requirements and clarifications are obtained for the unknown ones.

This page is intentionally left blank

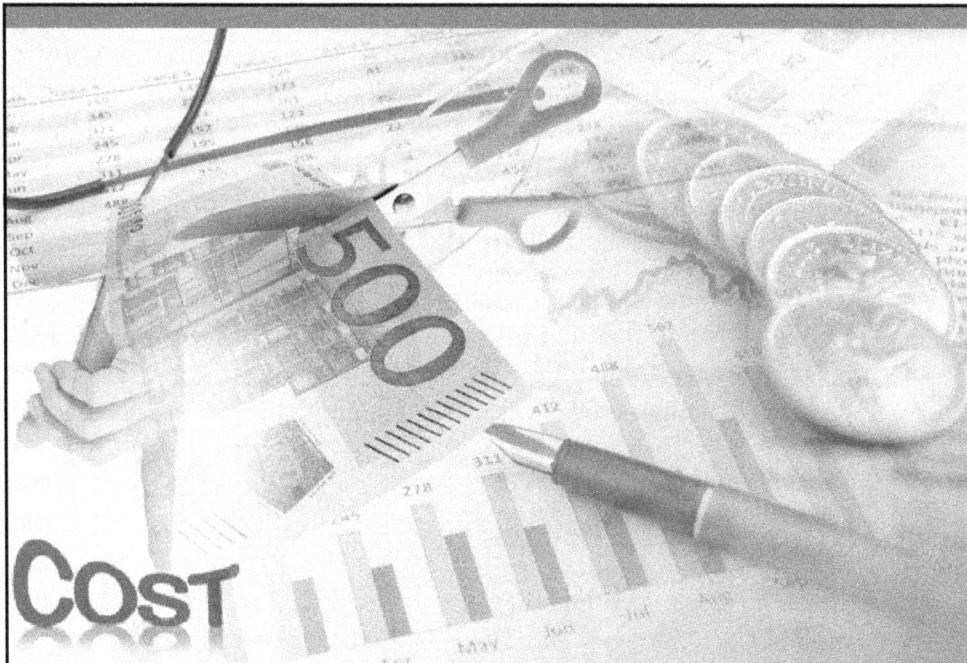

Project Cost Management

Objectives

At the end of Project Cost Management chapter, the reader should be able to:

- understand the significance of Cost in a project execution
- classify different costs in a project
- understand different types of costs involved in a project execution
- know how cost is estimated in a project and what goes into this estimation
- understand how the cost is consolidated into a single budget
- know about cost baseline and its significance on project
- know about Cost controlling techniques
- understand how changes are handled in cost management
- know different formulae that are used in cost management processing

Every organization has a financial interest behind taking most of their decisions. Every business wants to make profit and willing to spend sensible amount of money to execute projects, investing in innovations and new initiatives to gain market advantage and profits. Unless the organizations get a decent amount of return on their investments, none will be willing to spend money on their project. To have a decent return on projects, the project manager has the responsibility to manage the cost effectively.

Unless the managements are convinced that the money to be spent on their projects is reasonable and justified for benefits in return, it would be difficult for the project managers to get approval for their projects. The project Cost Management is a disciplined approach of managing the cost of executing a project.

Cost Management Process

The Process of estimating, managing and controlling the cost of a project together is called Cost Management. The Cost Planning of a project is a critical task of a project manager, since the outcome of an entire project will not be acceptable to the performing organization or to the client unless the project is completed within the estimated budget.

Having a new multimedia based gaming software developed is always a dream of every software company, but if it cost three times more than their competing company's product, the performing company will not get any significant advantage of the entire project itself.

The role of the project manager is not to plan for the cost of executing the project alone, but also to manage the cost and to keep the project cost under control and complete the project within the approved cost estimates.

What are Classified as Costs?

Every organization has its own way of identifying and accounting the costs. It might be unique to companies or industries and services.

Any expenses or cash outflow that is incurred as part of the project planning and execution is classified as cost. In other words, any direct cost involved in the project is classified as project cost. Having said that, you should also remember that some of the expenses such as administrative purpose are not always part of the project cost unless the cost is entirely incurred for the project alone.

In general, three types of costs involved in a project are
* Human Resource Cost
* Material Cost
* Services Cost (depending on the type of project being executed)

A *Human Resource Cost* is any expense incurred in hiring and paying for the Human resources that are part of the project. Normal categories of such costs include hiring cost, salary, allowances, performance incentives etc.

A *Material Cost* is any expense that are incurred towards procuring materials and services for the project. Imagine a situation when a medical research facility is working on a project to develop new vaccine for a deadly disease. Any raw material required for this project is classified as a material cost.

Are these the only material cost for this project?

Not exactly. Other possible expenses include buying equipments, research facilities, medical equipments, computer devices, stationery and even the places that are used by the research associates are charged to the project. All of these components are used only for this project and they are to be classified as project cost.

In addition to this, there are certain types of administrative costs too. For example, if any of the project team member is required to travel to another facility or customer locations for any project related requirement, the cost of travel and using the booking facilities might be classified under administrative cost.

Does it make your understanding clear?

Types of Cost

There are two different types of cost possible in a project execution.

Fixed Price   :   A fixed price cost is one, where the entire product or service procurement is done for a fixed price agreed between the buyer and seller. Such a predetermined fixed price would include cost of material, human resources and any service requirements in producing the product.

Variable Price :   In contrast to the Fixed price, a variable price is charging the buyer for the product or services being offered. Such a price need not be same throughout the project phase but keeps changing according to material or human resource cost. Unlike Fixed price contracts, there are different types of contracts possible under the variable price bids.

We will be learning more on the cost, when we review the procurement management planning.

The Significance of Cost Management Planning

The ultimate goal of every project or initiative in an organization is aimed at carrying business to generate income. The ambition of every business in this world revolves around market leadership, reputation and profits. The process of planning and tracking the expenditure of the business is handled by the *Cost Management process*. The Cost management process help balance the amount spent against the benefits carried by the project execution.

A project can proceed only when you complete your cost planning and get approved. No organization is going to give a blanket permission without knowing the cost involved. The objective of every organization is to gain maximum benefits at a reasonable cost and this cost is planned and made available only by way of the Cost Planning. In every organization, majority of the cost is incurred by way of human resources and materials.

If you recollect what we reviewed while creating the Work Breakdown Structure (WBS) under the Scope Management Plan, you can understand how the cost is planned and tracked in the Cost Management Planning process.

Critical Points to Remember

Unlike other planning processes, Cost is not only very critical but also very tricky and needs a lot of attention and focus while planning. The primary reason is because Cost talks about numbers and not descriptive assessment or analysis. Unless the numbers are close to reality, the cost forecast is not going to get approved by your management. If the cost forecast is not going to get approved, you cannot begin working on your project.

It's as simple as such. This indicates the criticality of the Cost planning process.

When you do an initial estimation of Cost, do not worry if you cannot have the precise and accurate numbers. It is pretty natural that lot gets changed as the projects begin making progress. While the cost of the materials and other physical resources such as cost on cubicle and computer machinery may remain static, the human resource cost might see significant changes.

The numbers at the time of planning can only be an estimated or approximate cost. Thus this estimate is called as *Ballpark Estimate* or *Rough Order of Estimation*. In other words, the Ballpark Estimate is nothing but the approximate cost of project execution, which may be revised at a later date.

Whenever there is a significant amount of deviation or difference from this baseline cost, you need to do an analysis to understand the reason and make appropriate amendments to the cost baseline. This process should be narrated in the Cost Management Plan.

Cost Management Processes

Once you complete going through this Cost Management Planning chapter, you will realize that the process is similar to Schedule Management Process in several ways, whether it be estimation or controlling them. In simple terms, Time or Schedule Management Process is all about effort involved while the Cost Management Process is all about converting the effort into project cost and managing the cost of the project.

As is the regular practice, whenever you want to execute an activity, you first plan on how you going to handle it, then execute and control the outcome. Cost Management Process is no different than this. There are three types of Cost Management Processes are

•   Cost Estimation

•   Cost Budgeting

•   Cost Control

In the *Cost Estimation process*, the Project Manager will be estimating the cost for each of the work that is planned and done in the project. The details of the work is already listed in the Work Breakdown Structure. The cost is primarily related to the time and any materials that may be used in performing the work.

During the Cost *Budgeting Process*, you sum up all the estimated cost for each of the work packet being performed and arrive at a Cost baseline for the entire project. Such budget should take care of the schedule, materials and any other factors that may be influencing the cost of the project. Cost baseline is prepared in the Cost Budgeting process.

In the *Cost Control process*, you monitor and track the work being performed against the budgeted cost for each of the work package. Any deviation from the cost baseline for each of the work packet should invite a strict scrutiny to understand the reason and any review requirement. Change Management process to the Cost is used in Cost Control process.

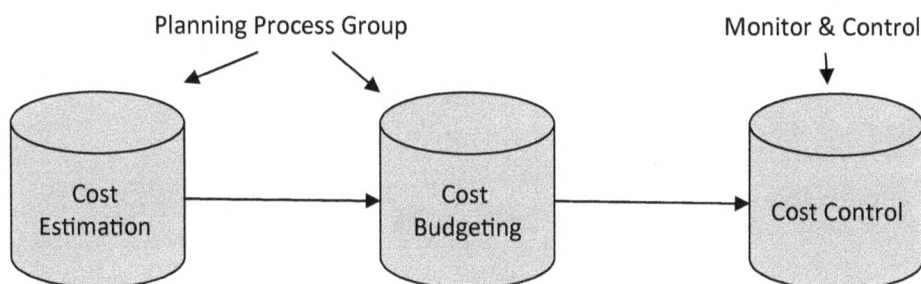

Cost Estimation

In the Project Initiation process group, you might have done a very high level cost planning to get the project charter approved. The estimated cost of the project is an extension of the cost given in the project charter, though may not be exactly the same.

Before you begin your project, the most important task to be completed is to get a formal signoff on certain plans. One of them is the Cost Budget Plans. It is needless to stress that unless the Cost budget is prepared and approved by the sponsor, the project is not going to start.

To have the cost budget plan, one need to have an estimation of cost involved in executing a project. So, in the initial phase of Cost Management, whatever the cost that you may have is only an estimated cost of individual components such as human resource cost, physical resources and any cost that is involved in the project execution. In this Cost estimation process, the cost for each of the activity or components are estimated individually. At this moment, we will not have the overall cost estimates for the entire project.

I am sure, after reviewing the Time Management chapter, you must be familiar with the three different types of estimation techniques namely Analogous, Parametric and Bottom-up estimations.

Now let us take a look into what forms part of the Cost Estimation process. Refer to the diagram illustrated below

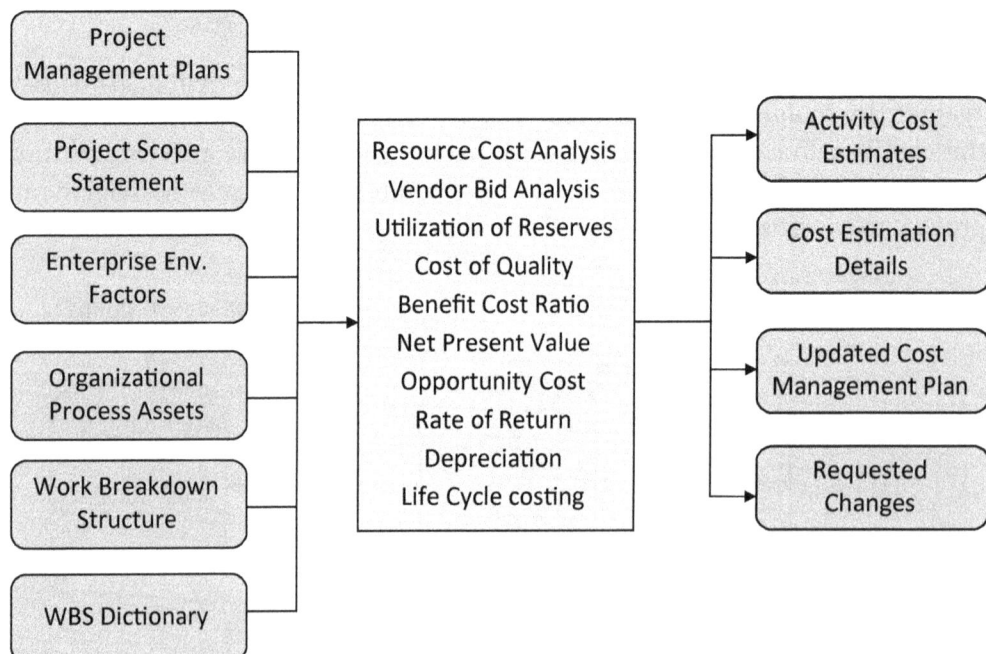

Among other inputs, the *WBS* or *Work Breakdown Structure* is one key input for the cost management planning process since the cost is calculated based on the effort, resources and time. WBS Dictionary has the details of the work products or packets that the resources are assigned to. The WBS Dictionary is useful for reference purpose in this process.

One of the easier and convenient way to arrive at a Cost Estimation is by referring to the past projects for useful inputs. Since every project has been executed according to the *Organizational policies and process assets*, it might ease the work of the Project Manager to estimate the cost of the tasks and resources.

Other *Project Management Plans* provide vital inputs in arriving at the effort in executing the project. For example, each of the resources effort is tracked by the Time management plan and Work Breakdown Structure is part of the Scope Planning process. Similarly, the *Project Scope Statement* provides insight into the complexity of the tasks, which has a direct bearing on the cost involved.

Are the inputs remain same for every project executed, across all industries and services?

Not necessarily.

As I repeatedly say, the project planning process is customizable to every project and industry according to the specific needs.

In the case of Cost Estimation process, the above diagram is specifically for human resource intensive business, say Software Development sector. The business involve limited amount of material procurement done but most of the cost is towards engaging human resources.

However, take the case of a automotive manufacturing unit. Here every project executed involve certain amount of materials being procured and the cost of materials surpass the cost spent on human resources. In such scenarios, the project cost estimation might require to take into account the material cost as input.

Tools used in the Cost Estimation Process

Let us now take a look into the tools that are used in arriving at the Cost estimates for a project

Resource Cost Analysis

As explained earlier in this chapter, the cost of hiring a human resource is one of the critical cost that influences the overall cost of the project. Hence, it becomes very important to assess the cost of engaging each of the resources and the return on them.

Similarly, every material that you will be using in your project comes with a cost and this cost is to be charged to your project. For example, if you are working on a software support service department that is responsible for executing a project, every desktop, networking devices and even the cubicles that houses the team members comes with a cost. These costs need to be charged to your own project and the same is tracked by the Project Manager.

Let us assume, you are executing a scientific research project that has a definite objective and target dates to meet. While trying to identify the resources to work on the project, you are not able to identify a specific area of stem cell research. This forces you to go to the market to identify and hire a resource.

Who will bear the cost of hiring?

Ideally, the cost of hiring a resource should be borne by the organization and not charged to the project, unless the organization's policy speaks otherwise. Whenever a resource is identified to work on a project, they are first hired into the organization and assigned to the project. The cost is company's until the resource is hired and then the project bears the cost. Once the project is completed, the resource gets released from the project and redeployed to another project.

Does it make sense?

Vendor Bid Analysis

These days many organization have developed a strategy to outsource their work or manpower requirements to external vendors who have expertise or available pool of resources at their disposal. The advantage of outsourcing is to reduce the cost by way of inviting bids from multiple vendors or using expertise from external agencies.

The best way to choose the best resources is to invite bids from multiple vendors and picking up the best bet that will fit the performing organization's bill and the expectations. Analyzing all these vendors and the services they offer is done using *Vendor Bid analysis*.

Utilization of Reserves

Not every project gets executed according to the plans and cost estimates. In most projects, unexpected risks might result in schedule and cost overruns. This means, unless the Project Manager makes a sensible planning on the project and the cost, he will not be able to control the cost overrun, which will not be taken lightly by any management.

When any critical task is performed as part of a project, there should always be a cost reserve required to be maintained in case there is a need in future. The utilization of reserves is all about how the cost reserve is maintained.

When a project manager is planning on having a reserve for his project, what would be the ideal limit of having it?

Usually, the reserve is expected to be between 5-8% of the overall cost of the project budget.

To remind again, a reserve is only to meet contingent expenses and need to be within certain limit, failing which the project budget will hit the roof, thus making it difficult for the project manager to justify the cost of executing the project.

Cost of Quality

What is your thoughts on the cost of quality in a project?

Is it the money spent towards engaging a representative from Quality group to support or testing effort spent to ensure quality of the deliverables?

Certainly not either. Then, what is it all about?

Cost of quality refers to the amount spent towards doing things, the right way. This is very important component in a project since the cost of poor quality deliverable would be catastrophic for the project and the performing organization. The cost of great quality project goes far beyond achieving the objectives of the project. A project executed well within the schedule, cost and quality gains the confidence and trust of the customers about the ability of the performing organization. It brings more business, money and customers. In addition, such successful executions bring expertise to the performing organization.

On the contrary, the cost of poor quality of a project and deliverables is exactly opposite to all of these and much more. The money spent on resources, materials and planning is sensible for the project only if it delivers the desired results, which meets the customer expectation in every sense.

Besides these above tools used in the cost Estimation, there are few more tools that are used in analyzing and deriving the cost estimation for the project. Let us see them now.

Cost Benefit Ratio

None wants to invest in a project with no objective. Either an organization's objective is for better return on their investment or to gain a market advantage over its competitors. The Cost Benefit Ratio is the amount, the project is expected to make Vs. the amount invested in executing the project. If the return on investment is higher than the cost, it is considered a profitable investment.

Net Present Value (NPV)

The NPV of a project is the value of the project at any given point of time during a project execution. This value is derived after removing the money spent on the project. The primary purpose of finding a NPV is to assess the worthiness of executing the project, before investing more into it.

Opportunity Cost

Though this is not very common in most organizations, it is good to be aware of opportunity cost. When an organization has two project to choose, the amount of money being lost on turning down one project in favor of the other is called an Opportunity Cost.

Rate of Return

An internal rate of return is the per cent of return on investing in a project. The return rate is computed by the funding organization to justify the execution of the project.

Depreciation Cost

In many situations, the outcome of a project begin to lose its original value as the time passes by. For example, you are managing a project that builds a new ship. The value of the ship begin to lose its original value as the time passes. This is called Depreciation.

Lifecycle Cost

A Lifecycle cost is the amount of money to be spent to develop, maintain and support the output of the project. This includes phases such as development, installation and the cost of maintaining it after being installed with the users.

The Output of Cost Estimation Process

Activity Cost Estimates

As explained earlier, each of the component of the projects, whether it be human resources or materials and facilities used in the execution of the project comes with a cost and these cost are charged to the respective projects for easier cost management.

In the Cost estimation process, the cost for each of these components are listed and is considered an input to the next related process, Cost budgeting process. So, do not worry much about the Cost estimates at the project level now. You will be handling this task in the Cost budgeting process, that is to follow next.

Cost Estimation Details

The Activity Cost estimates will contain only the name of the task and the cost associated with those tasks. At times, it doesn't make much sense to just read the numbers related to cost. So, obviously it becomes necessary for the Project Managers to substantiate those numbers with the narration of the details to help anyone to understand the task and the justification. Remember the WBS dictionary that you created in the Scope Management Process. The Cost Estimation details are similar to it.

Updated Cost Management Plan

As you make progress with your project execution, you might have learnt some valuable lessons that might force you to make changes to the way you have been tracking the cost of your project tasks or the materials. Imagine a situation, when your vendor has revised the cost of the outsourced resources by 5% to support the increasing cost. It is not only just the numbers that get updated but also how you tracked this cost till now. You might even have missed a reserve cash for your project or your reserve cost is not in commensurate with the reality of the project.

All these updates to the Cost Management techniques are illustrated in the Cost Management Plan.

Updated Change Requests

As we have seen in the earlier chapters, every change requested in the project involves certain amount of cost due to additional work to be performed or extra resources. Whenever such changes are requested, the cost and schedule of the project is definitely bound to change. Thus the updated change details are considered as an important output of the Cost Estimation Process.

Cost Budgeting Process

Once you are done with the cost estimates of individual tasks and materials that are going to be part of your project, then comes the critical of consolidating and budgeting the overall cost of your project. You now have the estimated cost of all the tasks that are to be executed as part of your project.

As described earlier, Cost budgeting is nothing but the initial step of setting the cost baseline of the overall project. The baseline is set once your cost budget is created and approved by the sponsor of the project.

Now, take a moment to remember the bottom-up approach that we used while creating the activities to be executed. For example, if you want to group your activities by design, development and testing phases you would have estimated cost for each of the activities under these phases. Adding the cost of each of these activities would give you the overall project cost as well as for each of the phases.

Now, to understand the cost budgeting process, let us refer to the diagram below

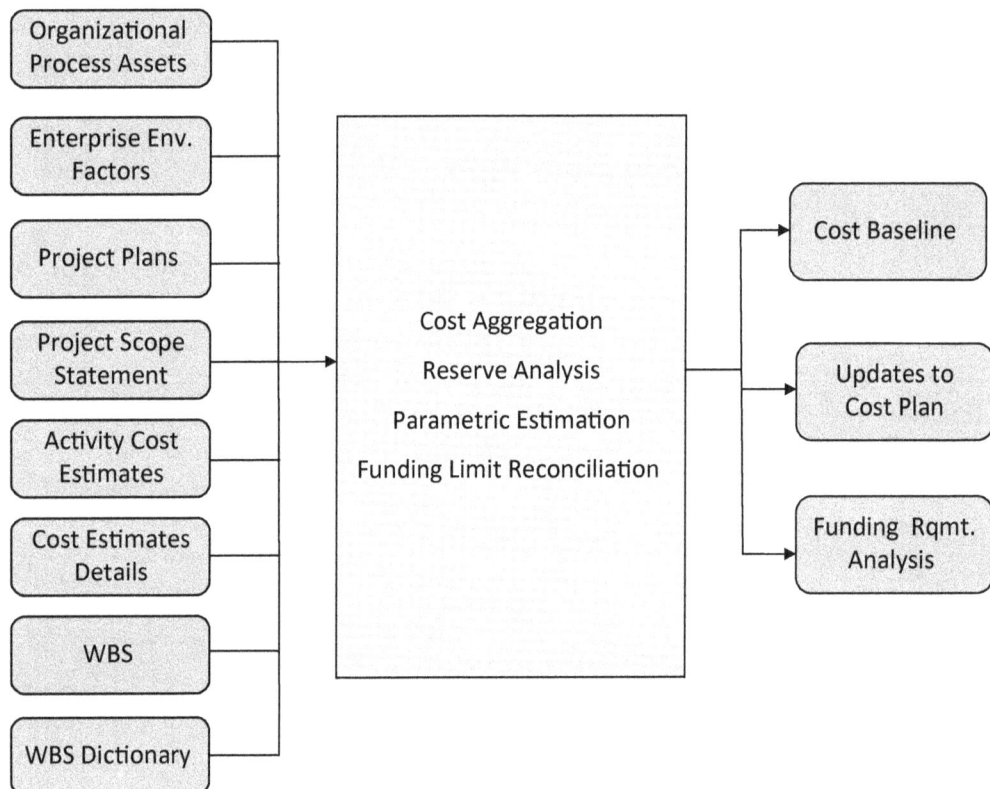

Notes on the inputs to Cost Budgeting Process

Among others, we use the output of the Cost Estimation Process as inputs to the Cost Budgeting process. The *Activity Cost Estimates* contain the estimated costs of individual tasks such as Human Resources Cost and any material cost. As explained already, these costs are added in the Cost Budgeting process to arrive at a overall project budget.

Similarly, *Cost Estimates Details* narrate the details of individual tasks and materials defined in the Activity Cost Estimates.

Work Breakdown Structure (WBS) and *WBS Dictionary* are used primarily for reference purpose in the Cost budgeting process. Whenever there is a need for more clarification on any individual tasks, WBS and WBS Dictionary comes handy for the Project Manager.

Organizational Process Assets might be of great help as reference point to understand how the cost budgeting was done in the earlier projects. Such references might help eliminate any errors before they could occur.

Similarly, *Enterprise Environmental Factors* offers the Project Manager guidance to the Organizations policies and processes relating to the Cost budgeting methodology. Every Organization has its unique way of estimating and managing the costs. Referring to the Enterprise Factors might help the Project Manager understand the boundaries and limitations.

Similarly, Project Scope Statement and Project Management Plans are primarily used for reference purpose in the Cost Budgeting Process. This means, these components do not necessarily gets updated in the Cost Budgeting Process.

Hope, the above make perfect sense in understanding.

Tools used in Cost Budgeting Process

Having understood the inputs of the Cost Budgeting process, let us now move onto the tools used in the cost budgeting.

Cost Aggregation

Having compiled the cost of each of the work package or material, now it is time you consolidate the cost of each of the work packet as you feel convenient to do. You can consolidate the cost of the project by phases or tasks or even function.

Reserve Analysis

An intelligent project manager assess his risk plan to identify the critical risks that requires more attention and allocate some cash surplus to utilize if the risks really happens in his project. This cash surplus is not to be utilized for any other purpose except handing unexpected events during the project execution. This cash surplus is called Project Reserve.

Parametric Analysis

A Parametric Estimation is a technique of comparing the project budget with that of the other projects that were executed by the performing organization in the past. The primary objective of this task is to bring the project budget on par with the reality.

As a word of caution, when I say the project budget to be more realistic you should also note that every project is unique in its own way. The project budgets need not be exactly same. There are many factors that influence the projects such as human resource cost or material cost. So it is quite natural to have some differences in their budgets.

Project Budget Funding Reconciliation

Before the Project Manager begin planning on the project, he should be aware of the maximum funding his organization is willing to spend on the project. This maximum limit includes all project spending, reserves and any other cost related to the project. The cost budget of the project should be within the spending limit set by the performing organization.

In case of any deviation from the project spending estimation (such as blowing up the project spending threshold set), the Project Manager is expected to revisit his project schedule and cost to revise the cost or work with the sponsor for revising the spending limit.

Output of the Project Budgeting Process

Create a Cost Baseline

Once Project Manager is done with consolidation of the entire project cost, including the project and management reserves, what is on hand is the overall Cost of the project. There is no definite format set for this cost baseline. The cost baseline is the estimated cost of executing the project for the performing organization.

Hold on.... the project cost baseline is not ready yet.

Once the cost estimates and budget is available, the same is to be shared with the sponsor to get their written approval for the project cost. When the sponsor approves the project cost, the project is considered to be ready to begin. In many organizations, all the stakeholders are notified of the cost estimates. However, it is the sponsor who takes a final call on approval or refusal.

Funding Requirement Analysis

As explained above, the cost of every project is arrived in two ways. First is the overall cost of executing the project and second, cost of each phases of the project. Both these are to be shared with the sponsor while seeking their approval.

While tracking the project cost, the cost by phase comes very handy to analyze and understand the health of the project in terms of cost. Such tracking helps the Project Manager to understand whether there is any serious deviation in the cost estimates Vs. the reality. Similarly, the Project Manager should make sure that sufficient cash is available to him to support the project cost during any time of the execution. This can be possible only with definite commitment of support from the management.

Updated Cost Management Plan

Once the Cost budget is approved by the sponsor and the funding requirements are known, the Project Manager updates the Cost Management Plan on all the details along with any known issues, assumptions and risks that were identified during the Cost planning process. This will help in tracking the unexpected issues and risks along the way. Now, let us look at how the cost budget is arrived at. Refer the diagram below to know more

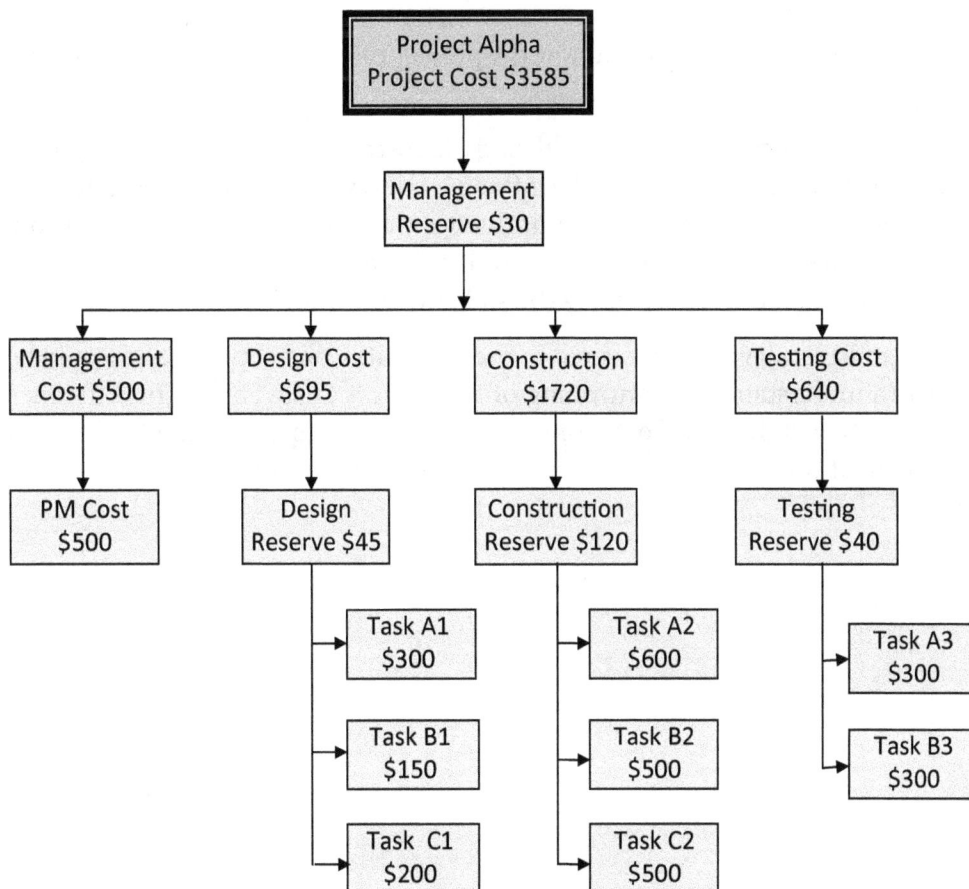

```
                    ┌──────────────────────┐
                    │   Project Alpha      │
                    │ Project Cost $3585   │
                    └──────────────────────┘
                              │
                    ┌──────────────────┐
                    │   Management     │
                    │   Reserve $30    │
                    └──────────────────┘
                              │
   ┌──────────────┬──────────┴─────────┬──────────────┐
┌──────────┐ ┌──────────┐      ┌──────────────┐ ┌──────────────┐
│Management │ │Design Cost│      │ Construction │ │ Testing Cost │
│Cost $500  │ │  $695     │      │    $1720     │ │   $640       │
└──────────┘ └──────────┘      └──────────────┘ └──────────────┘
     │            │                    │                │
┌──────────┐ ┌──────────────┐  ┌──────────────┐ ┌──────────────┐
│PM Cost   │ │  Design      │  │ Construction │ │  Testing     │
│$500      │ │Reserve $45   │  │Reserve $120  │ │Reserve $40   │
└──────────┘ └──────────────┘  └──────────────┘ └──────────────┘
                   │                  │                │
              ┌──────────┐      ┌──────────┐     ┌──────────┐
              │Task A1   │      │Task A2   │     │Task A3   │
              │$300      │      │$600      │     │$300      │
              └──────────┘      └──────────┘     └──────────┘
              ┌──────────┐      ┌──────────┐     ┌──────────┐
              │Task B1   │      │Task B2   │     │Task B3   │
              │$150      │      │$500      │     │$300      │
              └──────────┘      └──────────┘     └──────────┘
              ┌──────────┐      ┌──────────┐
              │Task C1   │      │Task C2   │
              │$200      │      │$500      │
              └──────────┘      └──────────┘
```

Notes on the Above Diagram

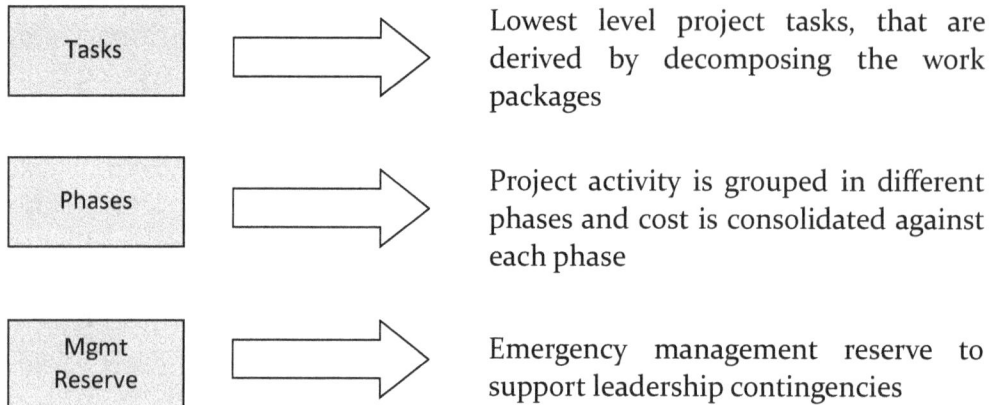

| Tasks → | Lowest level project tasks, that are derived by decomposing the work packages |

| Phases → | Project activity is grouped in different phases and cost is consolidated against each phase |

| Mgmt Reserve → | Emergency management reserve to support leadership contingencies |

Cost Control Process

We started off with understanding what is a Cost Management Process and how we estimate the cost of individual tasks, materials and phases. Then we followed with budgeting the cost of the whole project and submitted to the sponsor and stakeholders for their approval. Once the Cost was approved, we began working on the project.

Now, it is time we take a look at how the project cost is performing against what was planned in the earlier processes.

Cost Control process is about monitoring the cost as per the plan and controlling the changes, that might potentially influence the revision in project cost. Ideally, Changes are the major factors that influence the cost of the project execution. So, it becomes primary responsibility of the Project Manager to keep an eye on the changes that are requested by the stakeholders during the project phase.

If you could recall what we covered in the Schedule Control process, it would be easier to understand the controlling of the Project Cost. The major difference between Schedule and Cost Controlling processes is that Schedule speaks about effort involved along with the dates, while Cost Controlling is all about the cost of execution. To understand the Cost Controlling Process, let us refer to the diagram below

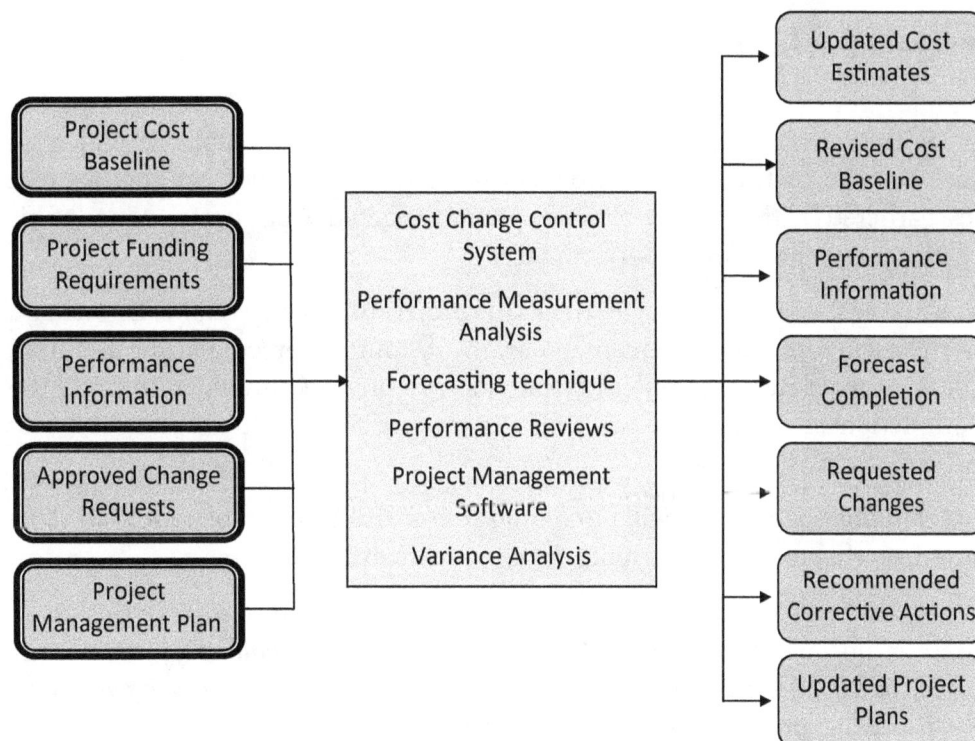

Notes on inputs of Cost Control Process

Let us now review each of the inputs to the Cost Control Process.

Cost Baseline

Probably, Cost Baseline document is one of the two most important inputs to the Cost Control Process. This is because, whenever we want to track the cost, we should first have the original plan on hand and this cost plan is available in the form of the Cost Baseline. The Cost Baseline contains the cost details of every component of a project such as human resources working on the entire project lifecycle besides the cost of every material and services being utilized during the project execution phase.

The Project Manager will be tracking the actual cost of each of these components against the respective Cost Baseline and investigate if there is any variance in the Cost Planned against the Actual cost of the respective component.

Project Funding Requirement

This input contains details of the Cost plan and requirement of the project by phases. This is an excellent piece of information to track the health of the project since it would be much easier to diagnose the project health by phases before arriving at an overall analysis outcome of the project as a whole.

Decomposing the project cost by phases and tracking them highlights variance before the project cost blows up out of control.

Project Performance Information

Besides the Project Cost Baseline, the Project Performance Information is another critical input that helps in analyzing the health of the project in terms of the cost. In other words, Performance Information are metrics that are gathered by the Project Manager about the actual work performance of his team against the planned performance.

Whenever the Project Manager tracks the project progress, what he has on hand is the task completion percentage against planned percentage. In addition, the forecast date of completion and the resource requirement towards the completion of each of the tasks. This data can be used to measure the cost incurred against planned.

Later in this chapter, you will be coming across various ways to arrive at the cost numbers that are vital information help tracking the progress.

A note on Project Performance information : As explained earlier in this book, there is no definite format or template prescribed for collecting the project performance information since each of the projects are unique in their own ways. So, it is recommended to refer to the Organizational repository for templates used in previous projects or creating a new template depending on the project requirement.

Similarly, the WBS can be altered and reused to track the project performance information. The WBS provides the vital inputs on the task list, resource data and the effort involved, thus making it a base document in the Cost estimation process.

Approved Change Requests

As explained earlier in this book, Change requests play a very vital role in deciding the success and failure of the projects. Besides this, they decide the acceptance of the outcome and conformance to the requirement of the customers.

When the Project Manager monitors the execution Cost of the project, Change details are one key component that needs to be tracked. In most cases, once the Changes are approved by the stakeholders, the scope, cost and schedule baseline gets realigned to reflect the approved change. However, the details of the approved change requests throws more light on the details of the Change requests and subsequently justifies the Cost factor.

Project Management Plans

The use of Project Management Plans is to refer to them for additional information on the individual plan components and the performance of the project against the planned performances.

For example, if the Project Manager wants to refer to the list of open risks of his project, he ideally refers to the risk register and Project risk plan for any planning related inputs on risks.

Tools used in the Cost Controlling Process

Cost Change Control System

Cost Change process is similar to any other Change Management process that defines, tracks and monitors the Change Processes for the respective knowledge areas. Primarily, the Change Process to the Cost is defined according to the needs of the project and approved by the stakeholders. In general, the Cost of the project is impacted due to the scope or schedule updates. However, in some cases the cost itself gets updated, in spite of no impact on the schedule and scope.

Such changes to the cost is also handled with the help of Cost Change Control System.

Performance Measurement Analysis

The Cost performance of the project is one very critical component and the responsibility of the Project Managers while monitoring and controlling the project execution. Unless handled carefully, the performance of the project might derail the whole project out of proportion.

Analyzing the performance of the cost is done with the help of various mathematical formulas, which are not very difficult to understand or remember. The process of analyzing the actual project performance is collectively called as identifying the Earned Value of the project. To find the project performance, you should first find the Planned Value of the project and compare it with the Earned Value to find. It should be remembered that the analysis is required to be done at frequent intervals or at any duration that is mandated by the customer and project requirement and the details of the analysis to be shared with the stakeholders as mandated in the Communication Plan.

Now, let us find out how to calculate the Planned Value of the project.

To know the Planned Value, you should first have the total budget estimate for your project. This is called Budget At Completion (BAC). This budget doesn't involve any calculations. Just simply refer to the project budget that you prepared and got it approved by the customer.

Budget At Completion (BAC) = $ 12000

Now, you should get the details of where the team is expected to have been with respect to their progress. To get this detail, you should refer to the original schedule that you prepared for the project. Your schedule says your team should have spent about 200 hours of work out of the scheduled 500 hours. So, the Planned % Complete is 40%

Planned % Complete = 40%

Simply multiply the BAC with Planned % Completion and the result is Planned Value.

PV = BAC x Planned % Complete

PV = $ 12000 x 40%

Planned Value = $ 4800

This is the Planned Value of the project at any given point of time during the project execution. I am sure, this is not difficult to find out.

For the sponsor or a customer, $ 12000 is the value that is set as value expectation from the project. This amount is the Project budget for the Project Manager. Planned Value is the amount of value, the project was expected to have delivered till date against the overall target.

Calculating the Earned Value

Earned Value of the Project is the actual value the project has delivered at any point of time against the project budget.

If you are able to understand how we arrived at the Planned Value of the project, then it is very easy and straightforward to arrive at the Earned Value of the project.

To know the Earned Value, consider the total budget estimate for your project.

Budget At Completion (BAC) = $ 12000

Now, you should get the details of where the team stands with respect to their progress. To get this detail, you should refer to the original schedule that you prepared for the project. During your discussion with your team you understand that your team has completed about 250 hours of work. So, the Actual % Complete is 50%

Actual % Complete = 50%

Simply multiple the BAC with Actual % Completion and the result is Earned Value.

$$EV = BAC \ x \ Actual \ \% \ Complete$$
$$EV = \$ 12000 \ x \ 50\%$$
$$\textbf{Earned Value} = \$ \ \textbf{6000}$$

This is the Earned Value of the project at any given point of time during the project execution.

Now, comparing the Planned Value with the Earned Value gives you the cost status of the project. In other words, the Earned Value is the amount of value the project has performed against the original cost budget.

To calculate, if your project is ahead or behind schedule, you can use different ways. One of the method is to find *Schedule Performance Index (SPI)*

Schedule Performance Index = Earned Value/Planned Value

If the SPI is less than one, then you are behind your schedule. You might need to investigate the cause of slipping the schedule and cost estimate. If the SPI value is greater than one, you are ahead of schedule.

To find out the Schedule Variance, simply subtract Planned Value from Earned Value.

Schedule Variance = Earned Value - Planned Value

In the above example, the project's actual performance is better than the planned performance. On the contrary, if the project's actual performance is less than the planned performance target, then the project is considered to be delivering lesser value to the customer against the budget.

More on Performance Measurement Analysis

Whatever we reviewed above is not all about Measuring the project performance. There are several ways of finding the performance relating more to actual cost of performance.

The Actual Cost (AC) of performance is the amount of value your project has consumed so far.

Cost Performance Index (CPI)

To find the Cost Performance of the Project, the formula is same as finding Schedule Performance Variance. You just need to replace Planned Value with Actual Cost.

Cost Performance Index (CPI) = Earned Value / Actual Cost

Cost Variance (CV)

To find the Cost Variance of the Project, the formula is same as finding Schedule Variance. You just need to replace Planned Value with Actual Cost.

Cost Variance (CPI) = Earned Value - Actual Cost

If the CPI is greater than one and CV is positive, your project is in better shape and you are within your Cost budget. On the contrary, if the CPI is less than one and CV is negative, it invites an investigation for overshooting the cost budget of the project.

In short, the larger the Schedule Performance & Cost Performance Indexes, the project is in better shape in terms of Cost and Schedule deliverance.

Forecasting

Having reviewed the current status of the project cost and schedule above, it is time we look at forecasting of the project when it is really get completed. In other words, Forecasting is a method of using the Cost Performance Index and Schedule Performance Index to identify how the project will perform when it is complete.

Forecasting is equally important data for a project manager, who has the responsibility to report significant amount of metrics to the senior management to convey the current status of the project and the expected numbers when the project is completed.

A Forecasting technique is another set of analysis and few more mathematical formulae that are used along with the current status of the project in terms of the cost, emerging trend that are highlighted by measuring Earned Value besides the experience of the Project Manager managing the project tasks at any given point of time.

As an example, if the project trend at any given point indicate a cost overrun, then the Forecasting methodology will help realize the estimate cost overrun of the project at completion.

Estimate at Completion (EAC)

Estimate at Completion is one technique of using the current cost trend of the project to find out how much your project would cost at the time of completion. This is one good forecasting tool that helps identify cost related risks in advance before they begin to cause a greater concern.

Estimate At Completion = Budget At Completion / Cost Performance Index

Just substitute the BAC & CPI with the respective numbers and the result is your Estimate at Completion.

More Tools to Find out the Monetary Value

A couple of more tools would be helpful to you, when you are looking for the approximate monetary value of your project cost at the time of budget. The tools are namely *Estimate to Completion* and *Variance at Completion*.

As their name speak, Estimate to Completion (ETC) is a tool that gives you the approximate funding requirement of the project from any point of time in a project till its completion. To calculate the ETC, you just need to have the Estimate at Completion (EAC) and Actual Cost (AC) of the project.

Estimate To Completion = Estimate At Completion - Actual Cost

Similarly, to find the expected *Variance at Completion*, you require the Budget and Estimates at Completion. The formula for finding the Variance at Completion is

Variance At Completion = Budget At Completion - Estimate At Completion

The above formula will give the expected Cost Variance at the completion of the project. The use of having the Estimate and Variance at Completion is to prepare to fix any expected cost overruns before it really happens.

Using the above simple formulae, it shouldn't be much difficult for you to find out the Actual Cost of the project upon completion. To make it simple and easier to refer, each of these terms, their descriptions and formulas are given in the below table

Term	Description	Formula of Calculation
Budget at Completion (BAC)	The total budgeted cost of the project execution	
Planned Value (PV)	Planned Cost of the project at any point of the project phase	PV = BAC x Planned % Complete
Earned Value (EV)	Actual Cost of the project at any point of the project phase	EV = BAC x Actual % Complete
Actual Cost (AC)	Overall cost of the project budget	
Schedule Performance Index (SPI)	Performance of the project schedule at any time	SPI = EV/PV
Schedule Variance (SV)	Variance in the actual schedule against targeted	SV = EV - PV
Cost Performance Index (CPI)	Performance of the project cost at any time	CPI = EV/AC
Estimate At Completion	The estimated amount when the project is completed	BAC/CPI
Cost Variance	Variance in the actual cost against targeted	CV = EV - AC

Project Performance Reviews

The reviews are the best ways to analyze and understand the performance of the project components at any given point of time. The reviews are usually done by way of convening meetings of the project team and other stakeholders, depending on the need of the project.

While meeting with the team and other stakeholders to carry out a review of the project performance, the metrics relating to the Earned Value and Planned Value besides having details of the Forecasting numbers are to be kept handy to share with the team and understand the current status at any given point of time, variance in the cost performance of the project and potential risks in completing the project phases as planned.

Such review meetings provide an excellent platform to analyze the project status and the emerging trend.

Project Management Software

Another way to understand and analyze the current cost status of the project is by using Project Management Software that are available in the market or with the performing organization. Such software help understand the emerging cost trend in the project and highlight any potential risks, issues or trouble that are ahead in the project.

Since the Cost Management involves a whole lot of numbers, the Project Manager should pay utmost care and focused in reading and understanding the numbers and their significance. Referring to historic data of the past project executed by the performing organization or discussion with other Project Managers might be of great help as well.

Variance Analysis

When the Project Manager is managing the project execution, one of his primary task is to keep track of the project progress and comparing the actual performance information with the planned performance expectations. Whenever there is a variance observed in the project, the Project Manager needs to dig in and analyze the cause of the variance and take necessary measures to control the cost before the project cost actually overshoots the project budget.

Output of the Cost Control Process

Updated Cost Estimates

The Cost Estimates can undergo change due to various reasons. Some of them are Change requests to the original scope, internal and external factors that cause a deviation from planned schedule and any other factor that require a review of the cost.

Updated Cost Baseline

The updates to the Cost baseline is influenced by the Change requests that are raised during the project execution phase.

Performance Information

These are metrics tracked and collected by the Project Manager during the project execution phase. These data provide very vital source to understand the health of the project and highlights any risks or trouble ahead of the Project team much in advance.

Forecast Completion

An outcome of the Forecasting of cost task, this provides estimates of the expected cost of the project based on the current trend. Earned Values details are considered critical tools that help arrive at the forecast cost of the project upon completion.

Requested Changes

List of all Changes that were requested along the project execution. These changes influenced the cost baseline that were initially set by the Project Manager during the Cost Management process.

Recommended Corrective Action

Whenever there were defects that were found as part of the review process, the same is followed by corrective actions to fix these defects. The defects and their fixes are monitored by the Project Manager and the list of defects and their fixes forms part of the Cost Control process.

Since the defect fixing forms part of the quality process there is a cost factor attached to it. This justifies them being included as an output of the Cost Control Process.

Risks Associated with Cost

When I speak about Cost risks, you might be wondering what types of risks can be there relating to the cost.

Let us now recollect the Fixed price cost of a project that we reviewed earlier in this chapter. Assume, you are representing a seller's organization and executing a project to supply specific components to a larger buyer. Your organization has decided to sign a fixed price contract with the buyer to supply the components. The cost includes human resource effort, materials, Shipping and handling cost behind certain administrative cost of the project.

While you are in the middle of executing the project, you find the material cost has increased by 3% and the resource cost by 5%. When you revisit the cost baseline, you realize that this increases will inflate your cost budget by about $12350.

How would you handle such a situation?

In a typical business environments, there are very limited options available in a Fixed Price contract. The seller is expected to have included such cost related risks while signing the contract with the buyer.

In a *variable cost bid*, the cost risk is on the buyer, who pays the seller for the human resources and the material requirement for the completion of the project.

How to Control Overshooting Costs of Project?

The best way to keep the project costs under control is to limit the changes requested on the project after the team begin working on the project deliverables. While changes cannot be avoided and not all changes can be denied, an intelligent planning would reduce the need for more changes from coming after the project execution phase begun.

One of the best way to reduce the number of changes being requested is to spend little more time while planning the project. It all begins with identifying the stakeholders, who are going to be part of the project from start to end. Spending more time to understand their requirements and updating the scope before getting everyone's concurrence is another possible way to eliminate the cost from overshooting. Third option is to have sufficient cost reserve for all risks and getting this cost approved from the sponsor.

Another major factor that impacts the changes and subsequently the cost is not paying much attention to assumptions and unclear scope. It is true that not all projects have the privilege of having the entire scope defined before the Project team begin working. At times, it may require some assumptions made relating to the scope. A careful analysis of the assumptions would possibly reveal the magnitude of the unclear scope. If the unclear part is significant, it would not be a wise decision to jump into the project execution without highlighting the assumptions and scope clarity to the stakeholders.

The reason being, if there is a need to include a larger updates made to the original scope at a later phase of the project, the impact of such updates might invite huge cost on the overall project and might push the completion date and resource requirements beyond the original plan.

Does Having Larger Project Reserve Help Reduce Cost Overshooting Risk

Not necessarily always.

Having a large project reserve is definitely good for a project manager. But, it also signifies trouble for him and the project.

Assume that a Project Manager has estimated the overall cost of $100,000 for his project, out of which 20% goes towards contingency funding or project reserve to handle any potential risks. Unless the risk is really huge, most likely to happen and the impact of which is significant, this 20% reserve cannot be justified. Having 5% to 8% of the project cost as contingency fund is more sensible and sounds reasonable. However, having a 20% reserve points to the lack of planning efficiency of the project manager, even if the project doesn't utilize most of it. Having a large contingency funding result in huge overall cost of the project, which influences the sponsor to think twice before approving the project cost.

Similarly, a project cannot always have contingency funding to handle any potential changes that is anticipated. The cost of changes are required to be handled outside the original project cost and that is why we have the Change Management Process.

Unfortunately, many of the organization tend to overlook the impact of the requested changes, which balloons into a significant resource cost and overrunning the committed deadline. Unless the Change Management process is effectively setup and followed strictly, with no exception, it will always result in a cost overrun for the project.

Now, take a moment to think how many projects gets completed on the agreed deadline?

You would find that 70% of the projects executed miss their originally committed deadline, no matter which industry or which region they get executed in.

If you take a closer look into the cause of this overrun, the primary reasons would be poor planning and indiscriminate number of changes that were requested throughout the project phase, which resulted in schedule, scope and cost overrun.

Does this make sensible?

Impact of Cost on Quality

If you could remember the Triple Constraint Diagram that we reviewed earlier in this book, any significant changes in Cost would have serious impact on the quality of the project and its outcome. One cannot just ignore the impact at any point of time in the project.

Imagine a situation, you are executing a project and about 100 hours behind schedule. Your client was expected the project delivered in the next two days. Obviously, you cannot push the client expectation on delivery date. Ultimately, you begin thinking of adding extra hands to get the work done on time. This means adding more cost to the original. If you fail to do your project outcome need to be delivered without the quality review, which might have serious impact.

What would be your strategy in this situation?

EXERCISES

Fill in the Blanks

1. _____, _____ and _____ are the three processes of the Cost Management Planning.

2. A cost baseline is finalized after the _____ process.

3. _____ represents the difference between the planned cost and the actual cost incurred by the project.

4. _____ means the total budget of the project cost

5. _____ is the amount of value the project has earned against the baseline at any point of time during the project phase.

Match the Following

- Schedule Variance : Project performance at completion
- Cost of Quality : Earned Value / Actual Cost
- CPI : Contingency fund
- Forecasting : Expenses on Reviews, audits and Testing efforts
- Project Reserves : The difference between the schedule baseline and actual

True or False

1. A cost is not dependent on any other project subsidiary plans (**True/False**)

2. Cost Closure is not part of the Project Closure process group (**True/False**)

3. Project reserve is used to substantiate the overshooting cost of the project (**True/False**)

4. Having a larger project reserve helps the project manager since he/she need not worry about any sudden change requests coming the way (**True/False**)

5. Cost baseline is the estimate that is impacted upon fresh change requests (**True/False**)

ANSWERS

Fill in the Blanks

1. Cost Estimation, Cost Budgeting and Cost Control
2. Cost Budgeting
3. Cost Variance
4. Budget at Completion
5. Earned Value

Match the Following

- Schedule Variance : The difference between the schedule baseline and actual
- Cost of Quality : Expenses on Reviews, audits and Testing efforts
- CPI : Earned Value / Actual Cost
- Forecasting : Project performance at completion
- Project Reserves : Contingency fund

True or False

1. False
2. True
3. False
4. False
5. True

Test Your Knowledge

1. You have been nominated as a project manager of an engineering project of your organization, replacing another project manager. The previous project manager had trouble with managing the cost of the project and was replaced by you. Your senior executives have high hopes in your ability and talent and asked you to take ownership of everything about the project. Your priority should be to resolve the open issue left by your predecessor. When you began investigating into the issue, your find that there was a change request raised by the customer, who wanted the change be included in the scope without fail. However, the previous project manager couldn't accept the change since it involves huge cost impact with several weeks of additional effort. But the customer insisting that your organization has a legal obligation to honor every change raised.

    What type of contract are we talking here?

    a) Cost + fee reimbursement

    b) Fixed Price

    c) Time & Material

    d) Cost reimbursement

2. You are the project manager currently working on consolidating all the cost details for each of the project components such as human resource effort cost, materials and service cost. Once you consolidate all of these, you are planning to add your cost reserve and bring the cost plan to a proper shape. Which process are you into now?

    a) Cost Estimation

    b) Cost Consolidating

    c) Cost Budgeting

    d) Cost reimbursement

3. Which of the following statement is true about a cost risk in a project?

    a) Time & Material contract means cost risk for the buyer

    b) Fixed Price puts the cost risk on the seller

    c) In a Cost reimbursement contract, the seller accepts no responsibility of the project work

    d) None of the above

4. Your organization is in the information technology business and specializing in banking and financial service industry. Your company has received business proposals from two banking companies that are fiercely competing with each other. Both of the business proposals are very attractive but your organization has chosen to

go with only one of the proposal for some unknown reasons. Once the management has taken a decision on which customer to go with, they direct you to find the opportunity cost of this decision.

What do you understand by 'Opportunity Cost'?

a) Opportunity cost is the amount of revenue expected by the decision made

b) Opportunity cost is the amount of business expected from other customers operating in the same domain

c) Opportunity cost means the amount of money to be spent to explore more business opportunities for the organization

d) Opportunity cost is the loss of business resulted by the decision

5. Dan is just assigned as a project manager for a civil engineering project and he has started working on the cost planning for his project. As he is still in the initial stages of preparing the cost budget for the project, one of the stakeholder approach him and wanted to know whether he can provide a ballpark estimate for the project cost.

What is a ballpark estimate in terms of the cost?

a) A ball park is the cost of executing the project given as a break-up of phases.

b) Ballpark estimation means sharing information on how the cost estimation is done.

c) Ballpark estimation is the high-level estimation on cost, when the details are still being worked out

d) Ballpark estimation means providing the details cost budget for every task.

6. **In which process, the cost baseline gets updated?**

a) Cost Estimation

b) Cost Budgeting

c) Cost Management Planning

d) Cost Control

7. You are a project manager on a software development project for one of your prestigious customer, with whom your company has been doing business since over a decade. The relationship has been very cordial all through these years. However, this time there has been some concerns about the cost of the project and your supervisor wants to know the planned value of the project in the middle of the execution. Your total project budget (BAC) was $120,000 and the project should have finished about 40% of the planned work by now.

However, your project is behind schedule and is only 25% done at this moment of time.

Your supervisor wants to take a call as to whether how to get the project cost back on its track and the Planned Value data will be a key input in this regard. From the data given above, what is the planned value of the project at this point of time?

a) $48,000

b) $120,000

c) $30,000

d) $78,000

8. Considering the same scenario narrated in Question 7, can you able to find the Earned Value of the project at this point time?

a) $120,000

b) $30,000

c) $78,000

d) $150,000

9. You are managing a massive event management project in a large city, which has a population of over 2 million. You have prepared a sales calendar to sell the 40,000 tickets planned for the event. During the middle of your busy sales schedule, you schedule a review of the status of the planned sales. As per the target established for yourself, you should have sold about 70% of the tickets by now. But, you are finding the total sales at 45% of the total tickets. Your senior management is concerned about this shortfall and wants the variance in the sales in numbers.

What is the variance in the ticket sales Planned Vs. Actual?

a) 28,000

b) 18,000

c) 31,500

d) 10,000

10. Your project team is busy with their construction activity. Your excellent project management skills ensured the project scope, cost and schedule planning done at the right time and within the expected target dates to get them approved. Your project had an actual budget of $300,000 and was expected to be executed within 12 weeks. Exactly halfway into the project schedule calendar, you find that the project has surpassed the schedule target and is 60% completed, thanks to the hard and smart effort of the project team.

Based on the above details of the project status, what is the SPI of the project at this point of time?

a) 12.0

b) 1.0

c) 1.2

d) $30,000

11. For the situation narrated in Question 10, what is the Schedule Variance of the project at this point of time?

a) $30,000

b) 1.2

c) 150,000

d) 180,000

12. Your review of the project's cost performance during the mid-term review reveals that the project's Budget At Completion is $40,000 and the Cost Performance Index is $28,000 and the project has another 4 weeks to meet its schedule deadline.

What is the Estimate At Completion target for the project?

a) $12,000

b) 1.2

c) $68000

d) 1.42

13. Sarah is a project manager, who is tracking the cost performance of the project as part of the monitoring & Control process. During her review, she finds that the cost performance of the project is on the negative side and she is finding it difficult to balance it. The cost performance of every individual tasks are more than her budgeted cost even though the scope has not changed.

When she contact the Project Management Office (PMO) for guidance, the PMO member reviews her overall estimation technique and observes that she has followed Analogous estimation technique and this has been the root cause of all her cost trouble.

What is an Analogous estimation in a cost planning process?

a) Using a top-down estimation approach

b) Using Bottom-up estimation approach

c) Estimation cost for every phase

d) None of the above

14. Robert is managing a construction project for his organization and has done an excellent cost planning for the project. However, during the review of the cost performance in the middle of the project execution, he finds that the Cost Performance Index (CPI) of the project is far below 1% and his supervisor has started to raise serious concern about the completion of the project within the planned budget.

What does a CPI below 1% means for Robert?

a) Cost performance is healthy for the project since it is below 1%

b) Cost performance is average

c) Project's cost performance is below expected performance level

d) Robert should check Cost related risks in the risk register for a fix.

15. In which phase of the project, the Ballpark estimates are given to the stakeholders?

a) Initiation

b) Planning

c) Execution

d) Closure

16. You are assigned as a project manager for a project that envisage setting up a new assembly line for an engineering company that plans to manufacture earth moving equipments. The project is very huge and the cost involved is into hundreds of millions of dollars. As part of the initial infrastructure requirement, you plan for essential equipments, infrastructure, facilities, computer systems and software requirements for your project.

Such costs are the perfect example of...

a) Variable Cost

b) Fixed Cost

c) Cost Reimbursement

d) Time & Material

17. When you are in the middle of your project , your customer has called you over the phone and asking you to provide Cost forecast for the project at completion. Which project process group are you likely to be in now?

a) Execution

b) Closure

c) Monitoring & Control

d) Initiation

18. **Which among the below is an example of direct project cost?**
    a) Cost incurred towards buying pipes and machineries for the oil pipeline project
    b) Cost of office supplies at the corporate office
    c) Retirement benefits to the team members
    d) All the above are direct project costs

19. **Which among the following uses Trend analysis in a cost management**
    a) Earned Value (EV)
    b) Planned Value (PV)
    c) Budget at Completion (BAC)
    d) Forecasting

20. **Pick one of the following, which is a good example of Forecasting**
    a) Estimation at Completion
    b) Actual Cost
    c) Earned Value (EV)
    d) Schedule Performance Index (SPI)

21. **You are the manager of a project that is mandated to develop an application software for the retail sector. You have planned all the project plan components and the project kick started on time. The project has been going well till last week. However, due to some dependency related issues, the project resources had a weeklong wait time for another program to be completed to check the interface and data integrity. This has impacted the project schedule and the project is likely to be now pushed by a week. When you discuss the issue with your supervisor, you are asked to provide the approved cost details for further discussion.**

    Which data you are expected to use for the planned discussion?
    a) Cost baseline & Cost performance data
    b) Cost Estimation
    c) Cost Budget
    d) Schedule performance data

22. **A Schedule Variance is**
    a) the Budget At Completion (BAC) divided by Actual Cost
    b) the difference between Earned Value and Planned Value
    c) Schedule Performance Index (SPI) divided by Cost Performance India (CPI)
    d) None of the above

23. EV-PV = 0 means
    a) The project is ahead of its schedule
    b) The project is behind schedule
    c) The project is exactly on schedule
    d) None of the above

24. **The level of risk of following an Analogous cost estimation is**
    a) High
    b) Low
    c) Moderate
    d) Does it make any difference?

25. **A project's Cost Budget is**
    a) same as Cost estimation
    b) sum of cost estimation for individual tasks, material and reserve
    c) Estimation of cost for individual tasks
    d) Project reserve

ANSWERS

1. **Answer: B**

   Justification: From the narration of the situation, it is very clear that your organization has signed a fixed price contract with the buyer. The biggest disadvantage of working on a Fixed Price project is the cost risk is on the seller. In a fixed price bid, the seller undertakes to execute the project for a certain cost and within the stipulated time. In many cases, any additional changes or updates to the same scope is to be borne by the seller organization. The project performing organization has to be very careful at the time of negotiating for the contract and define the boundary of the scope of the project, in order to stand any chance of renegotiating the contract at a later stage, if there are any significant scope changes to the project.

2. **Answer: C**

   Justification: A cost budgeting process has the cost of all the tasks, materials and services consolidated using the bottom-up technique of estimation to arrive at the overall cost of each phase, such as development, project planning and so on. After the consolidation is done, the project manager adds the cost reserve for the project and come out with a cost budget for the project. This cost budget becomes the cost baseline of the project upon approval by the project sponsor.

3. **Answer: B**

   Justification: If you can understand the situation narrated in question 1, you could easily answer this question as well. In every Fixed price contract, the seller accept all responsibility for producing a product or service. As long as the project progresses without any major surprise, the seller do not find any risk. However, if the project goes off the track or additional changes surfaces, the risk gets triggered for the seller.

4. **Answer: D**

   Justification: In the first look, the term 'opportunity cost' might sound misleading. However, an opportunity cost is the amount of revenue lost when the project performing organization decide to turn down a project proposal in favor of another. The reasons behind the decision may be varying.

5. **Answer: C**

   Justification: It is very common that some initial level estimation details are required by the project manager, performing organization and customers that will be used to arrive at some decisions about the overall project cost or schedules. A project manager is expected to have an initial estimation done on his project based on the initial scope and understanding of the work involved. A ballpark estimate is not considered very accurate.

6. **Answer: D**

   Justification: Whenever you see terms such as 'Revised baseline,' you are most likely to be working on the Monitoring and Controlling process group. Based on the work being performed and the cost performance of the project, project managers tend to take a relook into the cost baseline which was earlier approved. In addition to this, any change requests that has a significant amount of additional updates on the scope is most likely to impact the project cost. After the change request gets approved, the project cost baseline undergoes an updated as well.

7. **Answer: A**

   Justification: A planned value is the value of the work that was planned to be accomplished at any given point of time in a project. The planned value is derived from the overall project budget and the planned amount of work completion of the project tasks. In this case, the project's overall budget was $120,000 and the project should have completed 40% of the work at this moment. This transforms into $48,000, which is the amount of value the project should have provided at this moment.

8. **Answer: B**

   Justification: In contrast to the Planned Value computation, the Earned Value calculation refers to the amount of value the project has generated for the customer against the planned value. In other words, an Earned value is the reflection of realistic situation of the project performance in terms of the cost. In this case, the project has generated 25% of the total targeted value of the project budget till this point of time.

9. **Answer: D**

   Justification: The variance between the Planned Value and Earned value is the difference between them. In this case, the total targeted ticket sales was 40,000 and the project has targeted a sale of 70% which works out to 28000 tickets till date. But, the actual sale of tickets is 25%, which is 18000 tickets. The Variance between the planned and actual is 10,000 tickets.

10. **Answer: C**

    Justification: If you read the question carefully, the project is halfway through and the performance of the cost is 60%, whereas the expected performance was 50%. Schedule Performance Index is obtained by dividing Earned value with the Planned value. Based on the cost performance of the project, the SPI works out to 1.2, which is a positive sign for the project.

11. **Answer: A**

    Justification: The schedule variance is represented in terms of $ value and is derived using the total project budget and the planned and actual performance of the project at any given point of time during the project execution. In this case, the project had a total budget of $300,000. The performance of the project is better than expected at 60%, which works out to $180,000. This means the project has generated a value of $180,000 against the planned $150,000. The difference between them is the Schedule Variance of the project.

12. **Answer: D**

    Justification: An Estimate at Completion (EAC) is the estimated value of the project, when the project is completed. The Estimate at completion is the result of Budget At Completion divided by Cost Performance Index.

13. **Answer: A**

    Justification: An analogous estimation technique involves estimating the overall project estimate and then estimating the individual phases and tasks and bring them all equivalent to the project budget. An analogous estimation is not very accurate, since every individual task may be unique to itself with specific dependency, resources and risks. For the sake of understanding, it is good to be aware of the analogous estimation technique.

14. **Answer: C**

    Justification: A cost performance Index below 1% means that the project's cost performance is not meeting the targeted level. If the CPI is 0.60 it means the project is delivering 60% value out of the expected 100% value at any given point of time. A frequent analysis of CPI at different stages of the project helps the project manager to look for remedies and to bring the cost back on track.

15. **Answer: A**

    Justification: A ballpark estimate is also known as Rough Order of Estimation. As the name indicates, a ballpark estimate is taking a rough estimation of the project's cost estimation. The project manager usually does the cost planning in the Planning process group of the project. A final cost budget of the project will be available only when a detailed cost planning is completed. This justifies providing a ballpark estimation, when the project is in the initiation stage.

16. **Answer: B**

    Justification: The cost given in the question are one time cost incurred during the initial stage of the project, also known as setup cost. They are mostly fixed cost in nature, unlike the resource cost or services cost.

17. **Answer: C**

    Justification: A forecasting of cost performance is done based on the current trend of the cost and using some formulae to arrive at cost details for future, usually the end of the project. The Forecasting is done as part of the Monitoring & Control process group.

18. **Answer: A**

    Justification: A direct cost is one, which is spent in order to achieve the objectives of the project. In this question, the project is about laying a new oil pipeline between two points of a country or city. The essential components required for the project to meet this objective is the utilization of human resources and material resources. Pipes, infrastructure and machineries required are direct expenses on the project.

19. **Answer: D**

    Justification: A forecasting of cost performance means using the current trending project performance information to calculate the future performance. The current cost performance of the project can be calculated various modes such as identifying Earned Value, Planned Value, Cost and Schedule Performance Index etc. Using these data to identify Estimate to Completion and Estimation at Completion is called Forecasting.

20. **Answer: A**

    Justification: A forecasting means finding the future performance of a project cost. Among all the choices given, Estimation at Completion qualifies to be the only answer

21. **Answer: A**

    Justification: Whenever a discussion on the cost performance and re-planning the cost for the project is done, the most appropriate piece of information required is to have the planned cost for the project and the current performance data. This will help the project manager and other stakeholders to understand the cost trend to forecast the cost estimation at completion. Once the project manager and other stakeholders are convinced of an imminent cost overrun, the cost gets re-planned and to update the cost baseline.

22. **Answer: B**

    Justification: A variance is calculated when you have two different values of the cost available. In this case, the Earned Value indicates the project's earned value for the customer and the Planned Value is expected value. Their difference gets the Schedule variance.

23. **Answer: C**

    Justification: A null difference between Planned and Actual project cost performance indicates that the project is meetings its performance expectation. A current healthy performance trend of a project do not guarantee a healthier trend in future. So, the project manager should pay attention to the remaining scheduled tasks and also the risk registers for any potential risks that might have significant cost performance risk on the project.

24. **Answer: A**

    Justification: As illustrated earlier, an analogous cost estimation is not a recommended cost estimation practice since it carries a huge cost risk on the project.

25. **Answer: B**

    Justification: A Cost budget is arrived using the outcome of cost estimation and adding management reserve to the numbers. The cost estimation helps the project manager identify the cost of individual tasks, materials and services. AS is a normal practice with estimation, a small amount of reserve is added to handle any unforeseen risks.

This page is intentionally left blank

This page is intentionally left blank

Project Quality Management

Objectives

At the end of Quality Management chapter, you should be able to understand:

- What quality is about in a project environment
- Objective of the quality process
- How quality planning is done in a project and the processes being performed
- Quality audits and quality assurance processes
- Tools used in quality planning and control processes
- Cost of quality and the impact of not following quality processes

What is Quality?

If you are asked to define the lifeline of a project in one word, what would you define it as?

I would say "Quality."

Obviously, we expect quality in everything that we buy. Similarly, an outcome or end result of a project will not be acceptable to the customer unless it meets their expectations and this expectation is guaranteed by the effective Quality process being followed by every organization. In short, Quality is the greatest selling point of this modern world, which has no dearth of tough and vigorous competition among rivals in business.

Quality is about doing the right thing, the right way.

Is it a fair statement to make?

In a project environment, Quality signifies the importance of every other plan that you have for your project. Recollect the triple constraint diagram that we read in the *project framework* chapter of this book. Scope, Cost and Schedule have a direct impact on the quality. Intelligent Project Managers know how to effectively balance the Scope, Cost, Risks, Resources and Schedule to produce an end result, that conforms to the customer expectations. At the same time, having the deficient quality process would have serious bearing on the quality of your product.

The Significance of Quality

Many people have wrong opinion about quality. People equate quality with testing. It is not totally correct.

When you perform testing of a product, you are just making sure that the product is performing its intended action or producing an expected output. However, quality process is to make sure that the product is to be produced according to conformance of requirements and meets customers expectation.

When you speak about quality, we need to remember two things. The quality of the product and the quality of process. Though both of these appear to sound similar, they handle two different tasks in different contexts but still interdependent. Here is how

The quality of the product is what reaches the customer. If the product doesn't perform what the customer paid for, then there is a defect in the product itself. In other words, the product has failed the quality test. If only one product failed to meet its expectations of the customer, then you need to investigate the product for any defect. However, if all the deliverables miss this quality test, then you need to revisit the quality process that you followed in your project execution.

Is it clear?

Take an example of Barbara inspecting the production line that produces shoes two shifts a day. As per the original plan, the morning shift is scheduled to produce one batch of shoes while the second shift is expected to produce different batch. There is a break of half hour between the shifts.

When she inspected the production line and the end product in the morning, it was producing the shoes as per the plan.

However, when she goes for inspecting the production line shortly before leaving the office, she notices some inconsistency in the production line that produces incorrect batch of shoes with defective specification. After a careful scrutiny of scheduled tasks, she realizes that the quality process was overlooked by some of the staff at the production line.

As a production manager, she understands the consequences of such mistakes. She recalls the early morning meeting with the senior executives, wherein she agreed to meet the production target set to her for the current week. She cannot afford to miss the production target and is desperate to fix the issue.

She immediately refers to the quality plan to realize that the design program has a minor glitch, thus producing unacceptable result. She takes the issue with the appropriate group to get the glitch fixed. The next day, she works with the technicians at the production line to make sure the output is meeting the quality expectation.

Quality of a product or process should mean producing an end product or result that was agreed between all the stakeholders. Producing an end result, that was never expected, is not going to convince anyone of the stakeholder.

Let us assume your production department is expected to produce Product A as per the specification. However, at the end of the day you end up with Product B which is of better quality than Product A, do you think your management is going to be impressed by the production department's delivery of Product B.

Certainly they won't be impressed and may fire the department head for inefficiency.

This is because, every organization has commitments made to their customers or other vendors on the delivery of certain supplies. Delivering a different product, even if it is of better quality, is not going to fetch you any single dollar.

The quality of a product can be classified in three ways.

- Meeting customer expectations
- Conformance to requirement
- Fitness to use

Quality

- Customer Expectations
- Conformance to Requirement
- Fitness to Use

There is no single one of them to be more important over the other, but all the three components are equally important for a customer.

All these three are interdependent, which are guaranteed only by superior quality process being followed. In other words, the customer has clearly stated what their expectations are about the end product. Your customer has stated the expected features of his product in the contract

Based on this expectation, you have defined the product requirement in the scope and design. You obtained the concurrence from the stakeholders for this scope (now you could understand the importance of stakeholder management process in defining the scope of the product). If the end product meets this scope, then it is considered as conforming to product requirement agreed with the customer. Similarly, the product should be fit for use, failing which the product is of no use to anyone, even if it meets the physical features.

This might sound a bit confusing as you may think that if the product conforms to the original requirement, it should be fit for use. That is pretty sensible question.

Let us assume a situation. You are managing a project to lay a road that will provide direct connectivity to two towns which are separated by a huge hill. So far, the hill has forced the trucks taking longer route to transport materials from one town to the other. Once you complete your project, the trucks can save about 78 miles of distance to ferry goods between these towns. This project is considered very important strategically since it provides easier and cost effective connectivity.

Once your project is completed and the traffic is opened, a serious problem is noticed. The gradient of certain sections of the road is too high that trucks with over 5 tons of materials find it impossible to climb the mountain with their load. This forces the drivers to avoid this road for fear of getting stuck with their cargo on the hilltop. The local councils of the two towns are disappointed with the project itself since it served nothing for them. Since they feel the road cannot be altered they declare the road unfit for use for heavier trucks.

As a project manager, you might argue that you captured the scope from every stakeholder, got their concurrence and the entire project was executed within the budget, cost and according to quality processes agreed by the customers. The road is laid with super good technology. But, the road doesn't serve the purpose of its sponsors.

Who Decides the Quality of a Project?

In short, Quality is the responsibility of everyone in the project. Unless everyone do their job as per the predetermined objective, the project is not going to produce an end result that is in conformance to client requirement and is acceptable to the customers.

There is no single person who can decide the quality of a project, since the quality is inherited into a project by default. However, it is the project manager who plans and owns the Quality management process for the project and monitors it.

As is the practice, a project manager is the owner of the outcome of the project and is held accountable, if the produced product or service is not meeting the intended expectation of the customers.

The Quality Processes

To achieve superior quality objectives of every project, there are three different processes that make sure the project delivers the desired output that conform to customer expectations. The three processes are

- Quality Planning
- Quality Control
- Quality Assurance

While the Plan Quality Management and Quality Control is specific to the project's quality objective in particular, quality assurance is about taking a step backward and make sure your quality process itself is assessed and to make sure it is capable enough to deliver the intended objectives of the project. In other words, you are performing an audit of your own quality process that you planned. This is to eliminate any known defects in the process itself.

Among the above three processes, Planning Quality Management is done in the Planning Process group, while Quality Control and Quality Assurance are part of the Monitoring & Control Process group.

Quality Management Planning

Planning for the quality of a project is the primary and first step in quality management. The primary objective of this process is to plan on handling any potential quality issues before you actually begin your work. When one speaks about Quality Planning, he is referring to planning for preventive action.

Remember the fact that the better quality planning of every project makes sure you need to spend lesser time on fixing problems at a later phase of the project.

Let us take a look into the below diagram to know more on the quality management process

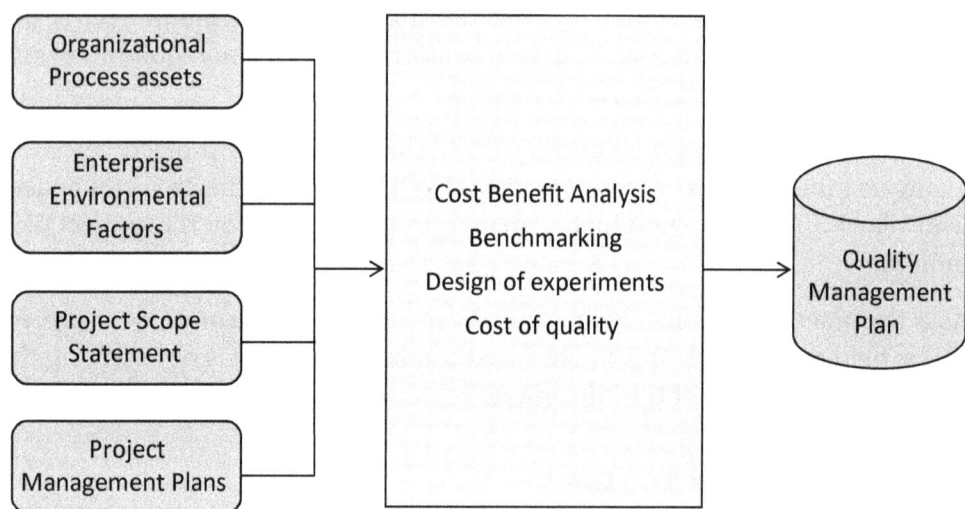

In the above diagram, *Organizational Process assets* should help the project manager with an insight into the quality planning undertaken in the projects executed in the past. It would always be a good idea to take a look into the quality planning of the other projects for any risks or issues. Even better is to find out, if there were any similar projects executed by the organization. This strategy might throw potential risks and issues in advance, to help you plan for them before they can occur.

Enterprise Environmental Factors details the organization's quality policy and a guidance to the project manager on the specifics of quality expectations.

The reason for considering Project Scope is to make sure your quality process is in conformance with the desired scope of the project. You can easily understand the importance of the Project scope statement, if you remember the three processes of quality that we discussed earlier in this chapter. The reference of Project scope statement makes sure the project delivers outcome, which is according to customer expectation and fit to use.

The Project Management Plans are used as input here to make sure the dependency on individual subsidiary plans on the quality of the project is taken care of.

Tools Used in the Quality Planning

Cost-Benefit Analysis

There are two ways to handle the quality of an outcome or end result. An analysis is carried out to find out which is more economical in terms of the cost and effort before deciding to choose one.

First is option is to spend effort and resource to ensure quality of the product. To put it more clear, many organizations keep their quality group or specialists involved in a project, who support the project manager in defining and managing the quality process and verifying the quality of the produced product or service. The cost of this option is not difficult to find. It involve resources and schedule.

Second option is the feasibility of redoing them. In some companies, which have high ratio of success in their objectives, they prefer to spend less on quality assurance and instead prefer to spend on replacing faulty products. This is in keeping the company's track record of quality products.

The biggest disadvantage of this option is that, quality is not guaranteed even if the product is redone by the project team. The primary reason is, nothing changes with the quality process when adopted to this option.

Benchmarking

If you are not aware, where to begin with the quality monitoring or how to measure the quality conformance, the best place to start is to refer to the previous projects' quality score. Such quality information of previous projects are found in your Organization's project repository. The Quality group or Project Management Office (PMO) of your organization should be able to guide you to these details. These scores can be set as a benchmark for your project and you can begin to track the quality conformance of your project further on.

When you set any specific project's process or data as a benchmark, that project's plan becomes critical input for your project's quality plan.

Design of Experiments

One of the best ways to implement quality process in a project is to design sample experiments. Based on the project scope, samples are tested for desired outcome. Such random samplings are common in many production environments.

As an example, when you are working on a project to produce certain type of battery for specific needs, you can pull samples from every batch and test them to make sure the device meets the desired quality requirement. Quality measures are run against these samples to make sure the quality process works fine in your project.

While the random sample testing is common in the production environment, the IT industry has a formal testing activities carried out on every deliverable produced by the project team. This is called various types of testing such as Unit testing, integration testing and User acceptance testing to make sure the deliverable meets the customer expectations and accepted.

Cost of Quality

To help remember the cost of quality, that we reviewed earlier in this book. The cost of not meeting the quality standard is catastrophic for an organization, since it defeats the very purpose of executing a project. This means, quality do not come free for a project, but good amount of energy and effort goes into defining the quality process, planning and managing them.

Most organizations find it difficult to justify the cost of quality when they manage their project execution for the clients. It is like, who pays for the quality. While the customers expect the deliverable to meet the agreed quality guidelines the performing organizations want to charge for the quality support. Since the quality process of an organization doesn't produce any output, it becomes tricky to measure the benefits of quality. The efficiency of a quality process results in lesser rework or defects.

Let us not get into discussing who is right among the two.

A quality process doesn't necessarily mean the effort and cost spent on testing activities after the deliverables' construction is completed. Any effort spent on preventing and inspection of defects, documentation, defining quality standards, benchmarking, verifying, reviewing the work products and the quality processes are all part of the effort and cost spend on quality.

Output of Quality Management Process

Even though Quality Management Plan is considered the output of the quality planning process, there are multiple other outputs related to the quality is produced. They are

Quality Checklists

A quality checklist is a list of tasks that you will use to verify the quality processes. Such checklists helps determine mistakes before they turn into defects. The list is predetermined by the Project Manager and is closely linked to the project defect prevention technique. Another use of such quality checklists is to determine whether the deliverable meets the customer needs and specifications.

Process Improvement Plan

A Process Improvement Plan is one of the most critical component of a project. This is closely associated with the project's processes. Every project manager must use their experience, expertise, knowledge and the specific needs of his project to define a quality process that results in a high quality product or outcome that meets the customer expectation.

A process improvement plan is to define ways, how you will follow improvements to the quality processes that is being followed by your project to make sure your quality process results in producing a superior quality product. The actual idea of the process improvement plan is to fine-tune the existing processes and bring them to deliver the best of the results.

Quality Baseline

A quality baseline is the initial quality expectation that is set by the Project Manager. It is against this baseline that the Project Manager will compare the actual metrics collected from the quality verification activity to analyze the efficiency of the quality process. If there are any major deviation from the quality baseline, then it becomes the responsibility of the Project Manager to initiate change process and review the baseline to make necessary amendments, wherever required.

Quality Metrics

Quality metrics are the data collected during the quality inspection or verification process. The details of the metrics is mapped against the quality baseline and help measure the efficiency of your quality process. Some of the quality metrics include the number of defects identified as part of the testing process or the review comments and their severity against the benchmark.

When a quality process is run against a trial running on a high speed railway track that was recently laid, if the results of the quality inspection produces uneven results at a specific stretch, this data helps the Project Manager to eliminate issues that may be causing the quality issue.

Updated Project Management Plan

As the Project Manager begin working on the initial version of the project's quality management plan, there may be situations he might require to carry amendments to other project plans.

Imagine a situation, where you had to make significant amount of updates to your quality management plan, while you were doing a quality verification of the outcome of your project. Your changes to the quality management plan is certain to impact all these three other subsidiary plans (Do you now remember the triple constraint diagram, where quality is directly related to schedule, cost, scope and risks)

So, due to this updates to the quality plan, you have to update one or many other subsidiary plans. Hence, this becomes an important output of the quality management process.

Once the project quality planning is completed, you will be having quality baseline available for measuring the quality of your objective. In addition, the initial metrics is available along with checklists of tests that your team is expected to carry as part of ensuring quality.

Not all the project plans may be used as input, while you work on the quality management plan of your project. However, some of the plans may prove to be useful when you plan for quality. As described earlier in this chapter, ensuring quality of a project involves cost attached to it. This cost is incurred by the way of resource utilization as an example. Does this require referring to *cost management plan*?

Similarly, when you have quality planning done, you should get approval from the stakeholders. The communication channel, mode and ownership are defined in the communication plan. Is it not? So, you need to refer *Communication Management Plan*.

Similarly, you need to plan for the resources that will be performing quality tasks. Such quality control can be achieved by way of testing or reviews, which involves resource planning. Such resource planning is done in the *Human resource management plan*.

Project Quality Control Process

Once you are done with planning for your quality management, the most important task of performing quality control comes into picture. It is during the quality control process, you make sure your project is producing results that is according to your quality plan and produces end results that conforms to the standard and meets the customer expectation.

There are several ways one can ensure project outcome meets the quality expectations. While the quality metrics offer an excellent way to measure your project's progress according to your quality management plan, another best way to make sure your project produces according to your quality plan is to consider the outputs of quality planning process and run them against certain tools or methodologies to assess the efficiency of your quality process and the quality of the end result.

Let us consider the below diagram, that lists the quality control process in pictorial form

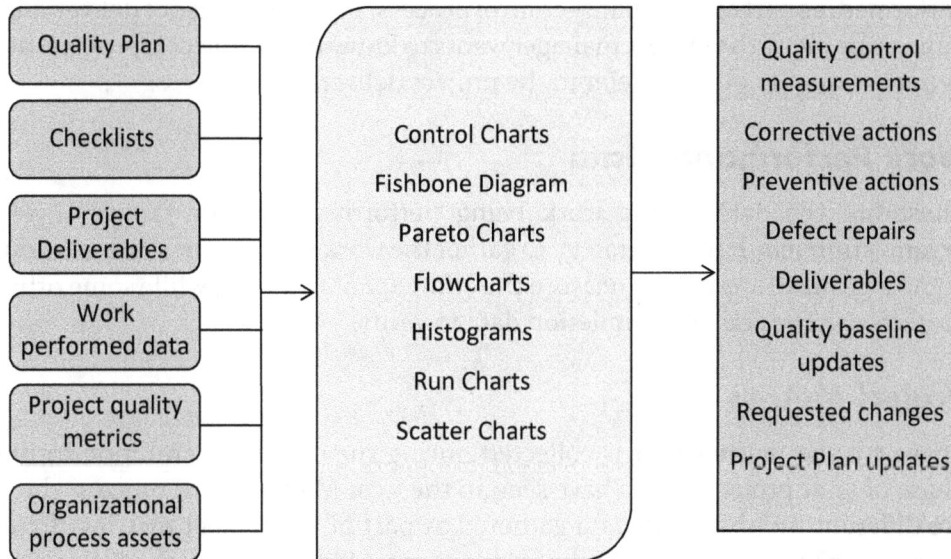

Inputs	Tools & Techniques	Outputs
Quality Plan	Control Charts	Quality control measurements
Checklists	Fishbone Diagram	Corrective actions
Project Deliverables	Pareto Charts	Preventive actions
Work performed data	Flowcharts	Defect repairs
Project quality metrics	Histograms	Deliverables
Organizational process assets	Run Charts	Quality baseline updates
	Scatter Charts	Requested changes
		Project Plan updates

Inputs used in the Quality Control Process

Quality Plan

Your initial quality management plan that you prepared during the planning phase of your project. The purpose of using the Quality plan is to identify the quality control plans and measures to help yourself assess the progress of the project and measure how the quality process being followed.

Checklists

The checklist of tasks or points you have listed and that can be used to perform the quality verification process. As we have noticed in the Quality Planning process, one of the ways to ensure quality of an outcome or product is to list down the components that are identified as critical and expected to meet the customer requirements. This checklist of components is very critical input to the quality control process.

When the scope verification process is done during the project closure phase, these tasks are verified against the actual end result to make sure the deliverables meet the project objectives.

There are some organizations, who help the sellers by providing the test data they will be using to verify the scope of the deliverables. This is definitely an advantage for the project manager since the team will have the test data available with them in advance to verify the deliverable even before the client does. In addition, this strategy will also eliminate human errors, especially when creating test data to test the products.

Project Deliverables

The most important components of the quality control process. Every activity performed, as part of the Quality control process, involves the use of deliverable. As an example, if the project manager wants to know if the project is progressing as per the quality plan, he refer to the project deliverable to assess.

Work Performance Data

These are the data of the work being performed by your project. Every organization may have its strategy to gather the work performance information. Some organizations might measure the effort spent to assess, while some other projects use the activity completion data to verify.

Project Metrics

These are the metrics that is collected during the execution and monitoring phase of your project. As we have seen in the Cost Management process, there are different numbers and data gathered as part of the project metrics. Some examples of the metrics are Schedule Variance, SPI, CPI, Planned Value and Earned Value.

Organizational Process Assets

These are very vital inputs in most of the project planning activity. You can use historic data to determine the quality baseline, benchmarking and many other key data to have a better understanding of the quality control process and to eliminate any other known issues encountered during the quality control process.

Brief Review of the Tools used in Quality Control Process

Control Charts

Also known as *Rule of Seven*, the control charts are one of many best ways to analyze the efficiency of your quality process as you make progress.

Assume you are monitoring a sorting facility in a logistics company that handles huge volume of shipments every day. The facility use conveyor system to sort the shipments according to different regions of destinations. The conveyor belts are programmed to sort in a specific sequence depending on the destination. However, the other department has reported issues of malfunction. You are monitoring the computer graph that shows the sorting activity in the form of a graph. You have set a minimum and maximum limit on this chart and you expect the consignments fall between these minimum and maximum ranges. These ranges can be called as thresholds of tolerance.

However, you notice that there is a pattern emerging on the graph where the data point fall outside of these threshold limits occasionally. If the data point falls beyond the limit once or fewer times, it may be acceptable. However, if there are seven instances of continuous pattern beyond the threshold limit, then this is considered to be out of control.

This process of rule of seven is narrated in the above diagram for your clarity.

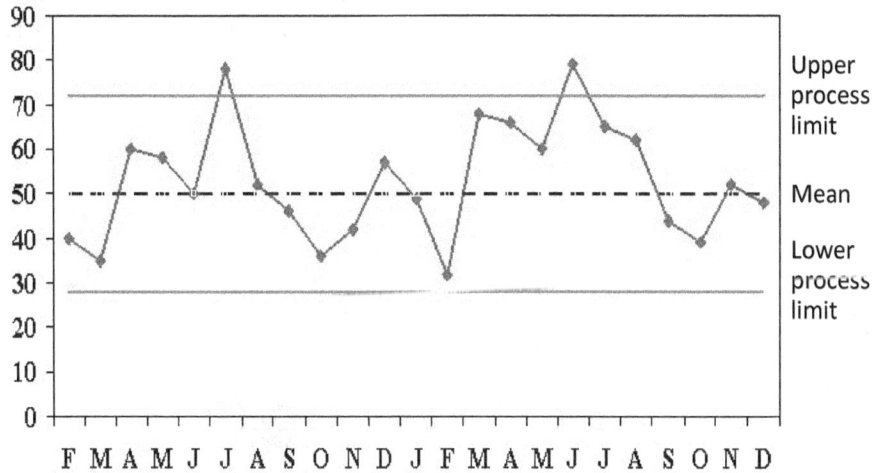

Fishbone Diagram

Also known as *Ishikawa diagram* or *Cause and effect diagram*, the defects are classified in the form of causes. To arrive at this diagram, you need to list all potential categories where defects can happen. Once you classified multiple categories, you can list down specific reasons that might cause the defect from your analysis.

A sample fishbone diagram appears like the below diagram. Since the diagram appears like a Fish, it gained its name as Fishbone diagram.

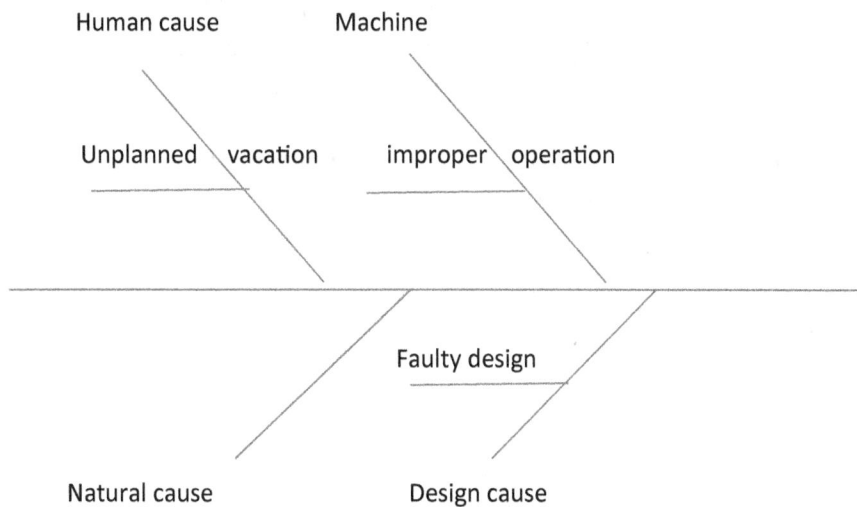

In the above Fishbone diagram, the vertical lines represent the category of defects while the horizontal lines are root causes of the defects. Representing your analysis as a Fishbone or Ishikawa diagram will help you categorize the problems in easily understandable format.

Flow Charts

Flow charts are easier way to represent the functioning of processes in a visual form. They also define the interdependencies between tasks in a structured way. Such charts help anyone to understand the processes without much hardship.

A sample flow chart is given below

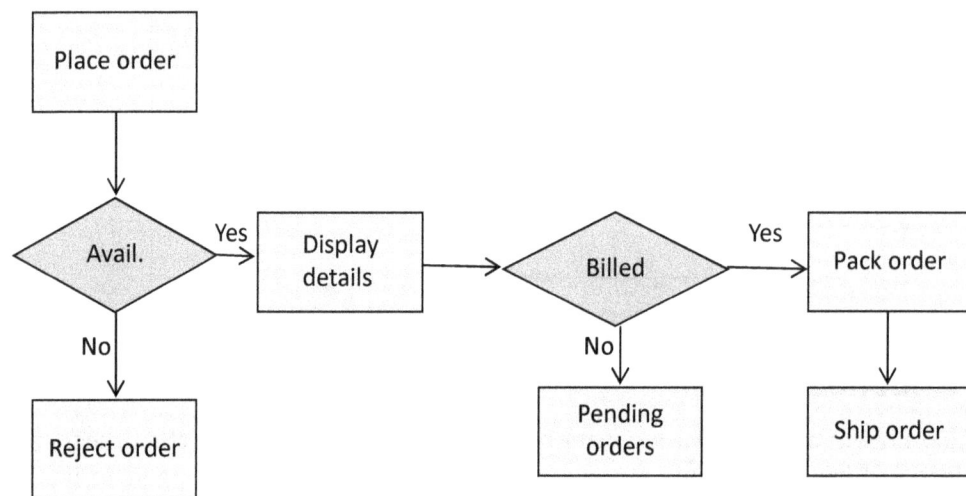

Pareto Chart

If you take a closer look into problems that existed in any project of your Organization, you will notice that most of the quality issues must have been caused by smaller number of causes. In other words, 80% of project defects are caused by 20% of the reasons. As an example, in a textile spinning unit, most of the problems of malfunctions might have caused a spate of quality issues of unacceptable output. Your quality process might be top class and you may have excellent resources. But, if the machine is not maintained properly, it is bound to put your project into trouble.

This is called *80:20 rule*. The quality review data need to be represented in the form of a graph, which will highlight the area that needs more attention due to the volume of problems in them.

A sample Pareto chart is given below for your reference.

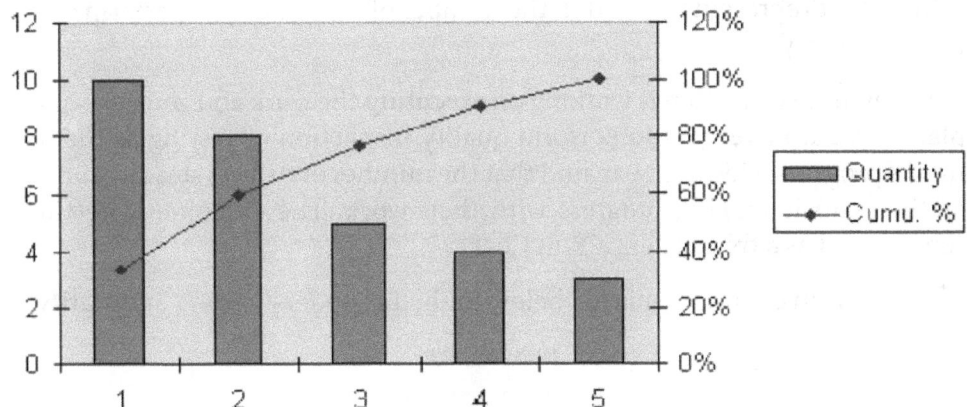

Classifying the causes of defects and their subsequent impact on the final outcome of the project is called 80:20 rule. This helps the Project Manager to target the major causes in order to eliminate most of the quality issues quickly within lesser amount of time.

Histograms

Histogram is another form of data representation in the Quality Control Process.

Let us say, you are working on testing activities and you find about 150 defects in the overall project from all the team members. It need not be all critical defects. The defect count is overall to your project. Histogram helps you classify the defects based on their priority. Usual classification of defects are Critical, High, Medium and Low. Tracking each of the defect against these classification will give better idea on which one to be fixed on priority basis and which ones can wait. Usually, most defects in a project fall under Low priority, thus helps the Project Manager to fix the critical and high prioritized ones using the Histogram.

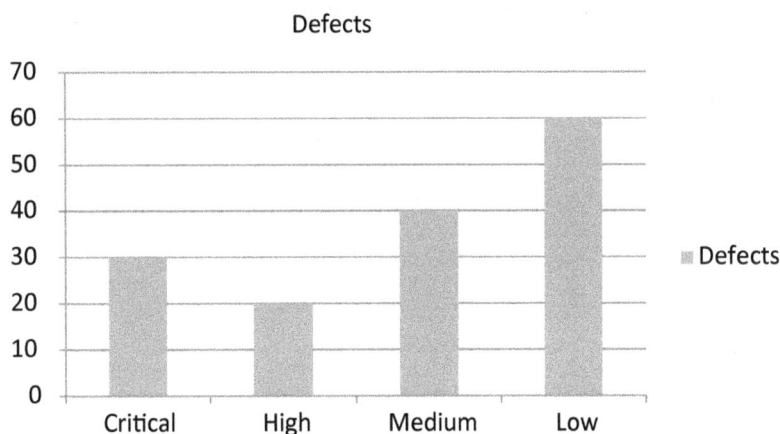

Run Charts

A Run chart represents a trend in the number of defects as you perform certain type of activity.

Let us assume your team is working on executing the work and you have quality plan that mandates you to perform quality inspection or testing as the team makes progress. However, you find that the number of defects steadily climbing as the team is making progress with their work. The outcome of testing is represented as a trend using a Run Chart.

A sample Run chart is displayed below for better understanding and clarity.

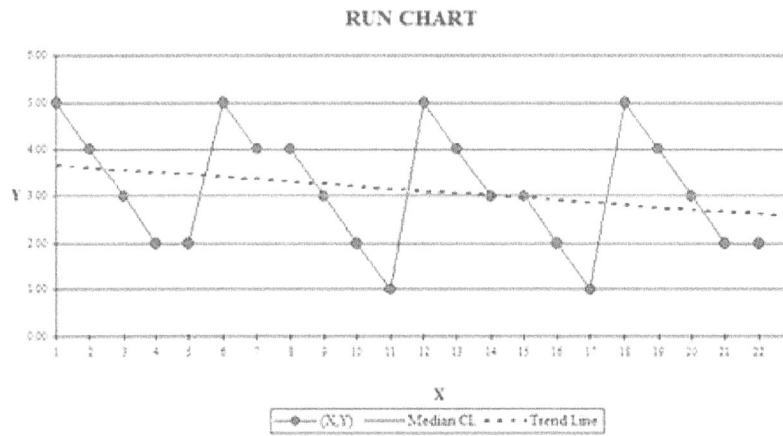

Scatter Charts

A scatter chart is a another form of collecting and tracking data, which is represented in a graphical form.

When you are carrying out tests, you record the findings of your testing task and record them in a scatter chart. When you add more test cases and redo the testing, there are going to be fresh set of test results. When you correlate both these sets of results and record in a scatter charts, you will normally find fewer defects with more test cases than the numbers that you identified earlier.

A sample scatter chart is displayed below for your reference.

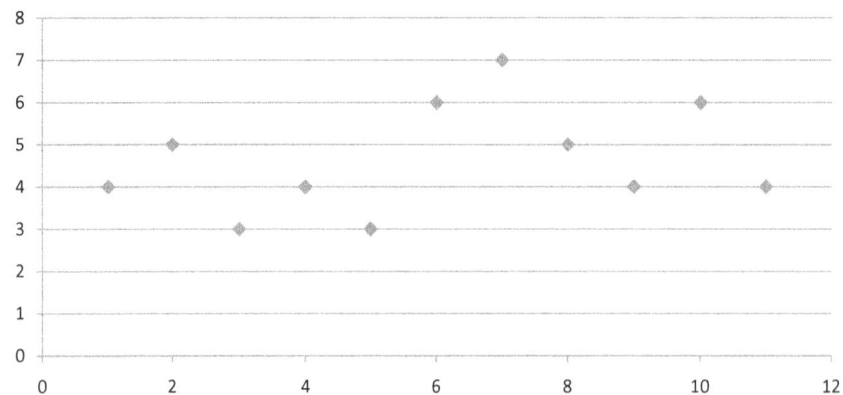

Outputs of Quality Control Process

Quality Control Measurements

The Quality control measurements contain all the data related to your quality inspection. The details include total defects identified, testing details, classification of defects and locations and further.

Corrective Actions

A corrective action is the outcome of identified quality issues as part of the quality control measure. In other words, Whenever a defect is identified in a project, necessary fixes are to be made and a root cause is to be analyzed to prevent recurrence of such defects in future. This is otherwise called as a reactive measure of defect fixing.

Preventive Actions

The opposite of Corrective action is to prevent defects from occurring. Whenever there are any patterns of problems are identified in a quality inspection process, a deeper investigation might throw more light on a potential quality process. Performing a root cause analysis of such issues might help prevent such problems from occurring in future. This preventive action is also referred as proactive handling of problems.

Defect Repairs

A defect repair is the details of all defects identified, their fixes and other relevant data associated with the details. This is one key output of the quality control process to demonstrate the efficient quality control process of the performing organization.

Validated Deliverables

The ultimate and expected output of the quality control process is the validated or corrected deliverable, which is free of all defects, conforming to standards and according to customer expectations.

A better practice is to have a Work Product Review (WPR) on each of the deliverable to capture the defects, their impact and potential cause of such defects. Such WPRs are stored as part of the Organizational process assets and historic information, that act as a critical input to future projects. Such WPR process is not restricted to any particular industry, but can be effective across all spheres of projects.

When you complete fixing all the defects that were identified as part of the quality process, all you get is the validated deliverable which are good for delivery. Necessary work product reviews are carried that identified defects and

- **Quality Baseline Updates**
- **Requested Changes**

Continuous Improvements

One of the key success factor of a quality planning is to constantly look for improvements to the process and the way the projects are managed. Though there is no definite rule to adopt to such methodology, a continuous improvement is takes a revisit to the way projects are executed and this extensively uses the real time data to analyze how the quality process works in the project execution and make necessary changes and improvements, wherever required and to make the quality process more efficient.

Differentiate Quality Control Vs. Quality Assurance

Take a moment to identify the difference between quality assurance and quality control?

In brief, quality control is to enforce the quality process in your project. In other words, the project manager and the team follow the quality processes that are already in place while executing the project. These quality process was planned by the Project Manager, who shared and got it approved by all the stakeholders. The quality process guarantees an acceptable outcome of the project that is in conformance to requirement and meeting customer expectation. Some of the components of the quality process is by testing strategy, test cases, reviews and verification of the outcome. The primary goal of the team is to produce an end result that passes the quality verification

However, quality assurance is to make sure your process is fool proof and doesn't produce defects or faulty outcome. This quality assurance process is not dedicated to any single outcome of a project but overall quality process as a whole.

If there is a fault in your process, it will continuously produce faulty results. This will end up spending more money on fixing problems. Instead, an intelligent Project Manager acts proactively and focuses on quality assurance process verification done on the project.

Quality Assurance Process

Having understood the quality planning and quality control processes, let us now move onto review the quality assurance process.

Unlike all other processes, quality assurance might involve another external group, Quality Management team of the organizations. The primary responsibility of the Quality management group is to make sure all the projects adhere to the strict quality processes and conduct frequent audit to validate the quality processes.

To understand how the quality assurance process works, let us look at the diagram below.

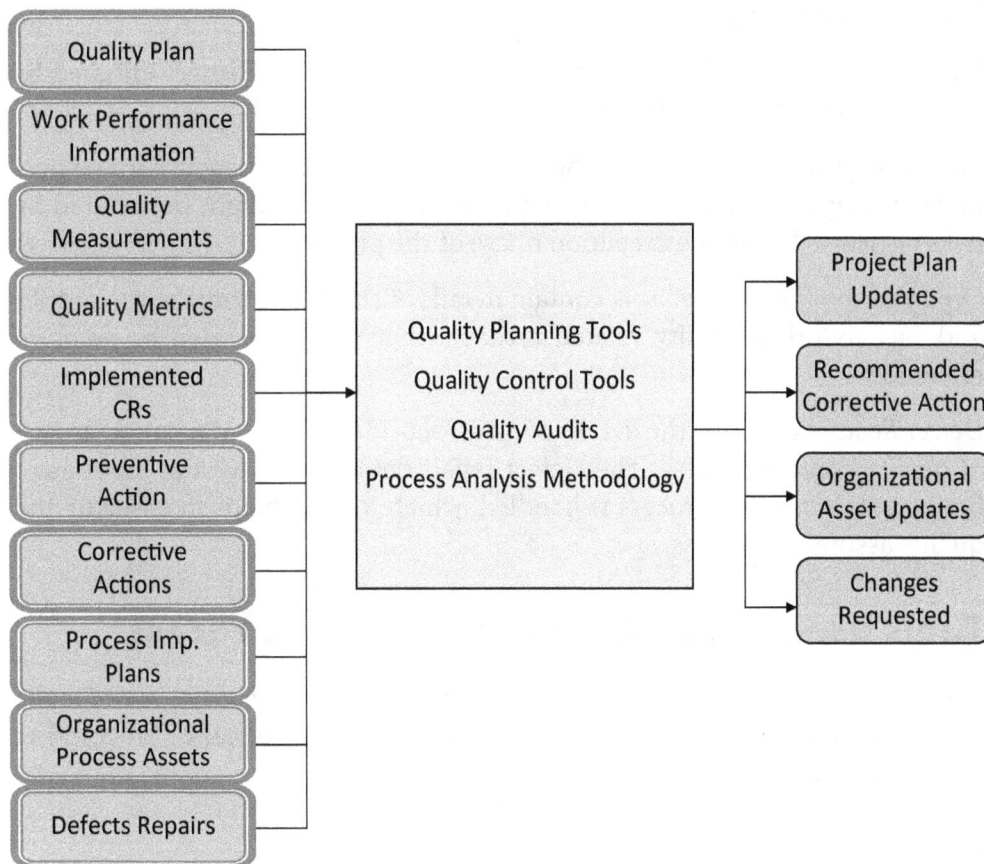

Quality Plan

Work Performance Information

Quality Measurements

Quality Metrics

Implemented CRs

Preventive Action

Corrective Actions

Process Imp. Plans

Organizational Process Assets

Defects Repairs

Quality Planning Tools

Quality Control Tools

Quality Audits

Process Analysis Methodology

Project Plan Updates

Recommended Corrective Action

Organizational Asset Updates

Changes Requested

Inputs used in the Quality Assurance Process

The quality plan is mainly used to understand the planned quality aspects of the project. This quality management plan reflects the strategy and plan of the project manager with respect to the quality.

Work Performance Information, Performance Measurements & Quality metrics are real time data that is collected by the Project Manager from the project team and his own effort.

Implemented Change Requests are the requested Changes by various stakeholders. All the requested CRs undergo the regular Change Management Process and the list of approved CRs are considered as input in the Quality Assurance process. The purpose of using the Implemented CRs is to make sure how the Change Management process were followed in getting these change requests implemented.

Preventive Actions & Corrective Actions are some of the measures initiated by the project managers as a response to defects or issues.

Process Improvement Plans are the plans of the project managers with respect to enhancing the project management processes, which might be resulted by risks or issues during the execution phase of the project.

Organizational Process Assets contain details of the quality processes, metrics and various other quality related artifacts that might be used as point of reference.

Defect Repairs contains the details of all defects identified and repaired as part of quality control process. The Defect repair details provide vital input as to how the defect fixing process is handled, which in turn helps in ensuring the quality assurance process.

Tools used in the Quality Assurance Process

While we are very familiar with the *Quality Planning* and *Quality Control* tools, we have a couple of new tools being used in the Quality Assurance Process. Let us review them now.

Quality Audits

Quality audit is an excellent process to make sure your project is following fool proof quality process and complies with organizational and business requirements.

Of late, most organizations in this world have realized the importance of having quality audits to ensure projects follow strict quality assurance processes and to look for gaps in the process compliance. The primary objective of such Quality audits is to reassess their quality processes and also to take an external view of the gaps besides keeping the processes updated with any new innovative ideas or processes resulted by any other projects.

Usually, an organization's quality team is in charge of such quality audits. Even if no quality audits are performed in your organization, a Project Manager can initiate one to make sure he is following a fool proof quality process to deliver a great product or outcome. The output of such quality audits is a report on the current quality compliance status and process improvement plans.

Process Analysis Methodology

As explained earlier in this book, every project is expected to be aligned with the goals of the performing organization. The same applies to the outcome of every project being executed by the organization. The quality process guarantees the final outcome of the project. If the outcome doesn't meet the organizational goals, it leads to review of the quality process itself. The process improvement plan is to be considered to compare the outcome of the project with the Organization's set objectives.

If any deviations or discrepancies are noted, the Organization's process repository is required to undergo an update to reflect the change. This *Process Analysis* is one key quality assurance techniques being followed globally.

Output of Quality Assurance Process

Obviously, the outcome of any audit involves recommendations and updates to the existing process. *Recommended corrective actions* are the prescribed fixes to the current processes being followed to fine-tune them for better efficiency.

Based on the recommendations of the Quality audit, few or many of the *project management plans* might undergo updates.

To make the updates and process improvements permanent, the Organizational Process Repository must be updated to benefit the future projects' of the performing organization.

Any changes requested as part of the Process improvement and assurance process is listed as another output here.

What are Quality Documents?

The quality of a project can be ensured by various ways. The most common strategy to ensure quality is by way of conformance to quality standards set by the project managers and through reviews.

Most of the organizations in this world have their organizational repositories filled with various best practices, quality documents and templates. It is a common practice for every organization that requires their project teams to use these templates for any process requirements. Good amount of metrics are collected with the help of these documents that will help analyze the health of the project at any point of time.

Can you list down five such templates available in your organizational repository and the purpose of them in the below box?

Template Name	Description

Some of the quality documents include:

*   *Work Product Review*
*   *Test Plans*
*   *Testing Strategies*
*   *Root Cause Analysis*

You could find out, if your organization has any of these documents used and the contents of them for better understanding of the quality process.

The Significance of Templates

The usage of Organizational process repository is most useful when you are working on the quality management than ever. Insuring quality of your deliverable involves follows certain quality guidelines, reviews and testing the deliverables. Each of these tasks involves preparing documents as a result of completing these processes.

When it involves documentation, the first place to look for is the Organizational repository. The repository contains plenty of documents which were used in the previously executed projects and proved successful. Using these documents instantly keeps the project team in an advantageous situation of using templates which were already approved elsewhere.

Further, it is to be noted that the organizational repository of documents and templates are only recommended practices in all organization. This means the templates are customizable to suit individual projects. However, it is recommended to take the quality group or Project Management Office into confidence and have their approval while you customize these templates to your project needs.

Who Should Drive the Quality in a Project?

As narrated earlier in this chapter, Quality is the responsibility of everyone in the project team. Unless everyone are committed to the quality process, the final outcome will not meet the customer expectations.

However, the Project Manager is responsible for making sure that the quality plan is strictly followed by the team. A proper quality control process is to be strictly enforced by the Project Manager. In addition, the Project Manager handles all the communication between the project team and the end user group. All quality related issues and communications are to be tracked to understand any deviation or defects identified during the verification phase of the project.

EXERCISES

Match the Following

* Quality Assurance   : Work Product Review
* Pareto Chart   : Cause and Effect diagram
* Ishikawa Diagram   : Auditing the quality process
* Quality checklists   : 80:20 rule
* Quality document   : List of criteria to verify to assess quality compliance

Fill in the Blanks

1. _____ means taking proactive actions to eliminate any potential defects in future

2. Rule of Seven are also known as _____ which refers to a continuous pattern of seven instances falling on one side of a graph.

3. _____ is about assessing the advantages between spending effort on quality process and redoing the work

4. Planned   Value   and   Earned   Value   are   examples   of _____.

5. The cost incurred on utilizing a specialized quality professional can be classified as _____

True or False

1. Quality Control means controlling the quality related issues and preventing it from causing damages to the project objective   (True/False)

2. Quality planning means planning on how the quality process will be managed   (True/False)

3. Quality assurance process refers to assuring the customers that the product quality is assured   (True/False)

4. One of the follow-up action of a defect identification process is a Corrective action   (True/False)

5. A quality baseline is used to assess the quality compliance of a product (True/False)

ANSWERS

Match the Following

- Quality Assurance   : Auditing the quality process
- Pareto Chart   : 80:20 rule
- Ishikawa Diagram   : Cause and Effect diagram
- Quality checklists   : List of criteria to verify to assess quality compliance
- Quality document   : Work Product Review

Fill in the Blanks

1. Preventive Action
2. Control Chart
3. Cost Benefit Analysis
4. Quality metrics
5. Cost of Quality

True or False

1. False
2. True
3. False
4. True
5. True

Test Your Knowledge

1. **Pick the most appropriate statement that best describes Quality Management**

   a) Quality is always not about fixing problems with the deliverables but is more about planning to do things, the right way.

   b) Quality Management offers various templates to fix problems

   c) Quality Management results in additional cost to the project budget

   d) Redoing the work is always the best option than spending effort on quality

2. **Steve is a very talented member of your team. He is working along with another dozen members in constructing his deliverables. Out of faith in his ability, you are planning to engage him in verifying the deliverables and check if they meet the scope. You have created a resource utilization plan for Steve through the end of the project closure.**

   How would you describe Steve's planned responsibility in this project?

   a) A team member capable of outsmarting others

   b) An efficient leader

   c) Work Product Review

   d) None of the above

3. **The responsibility of Quality rests with**

   a) Project Team

   b) Project Manager

   c) Project Management Office

   d) Stakeholders

4. **You are a project manager asked to assist another project manager who is managing a very highly visible project. Due to the criticality and sensitivity of the project, your organization wants to give utmost importance to the quality of the deliverables. So, they have asked you to manage the quality part of the project. With your expertise in delivering quality products to the customers, you begin planning for your project. As you begin planning, you have multiple meetings with the other project manager, the team and several stakeholders to understand their expectations and accomplishments. After completing all the deliberations, you are expected to set your quality expectation to the project.**

Which one would get your highest vote among the below options?

a) Conformance to requirements

b) Fitness to Use

c) Customer Satisfaction

d) All of the above

5. Upon successful completion of which process in a project, do you call the quality process as complete.

a) Quality Management Planning

b) Quality Assurance

c) Quality Planning

d) Scope verification

6. You are managing a project, that has produced specific range of electrical generators for the consumer market. After the construction is completed by your team, it is time to inspect the quality. As a strategic way of verifying the quality of the deliverables you decide to adopt to random sampling method of quality inspection.

What does an Random Sampling methodology does?

a) Among a huge number of products produced, samples are picked randomly and verified for quality

b) Using select test cases to verify the quality of the product

c) Picking some samples and sending to the customer for scope verification

d) None of the above

7. You are a project manager currently in the planning phase of your project. During the quality planning, you want to be extremely careful about customer satisfaction and give importance to setting your quality standards in the project. As part of your strategy, you decide to create a methodology that identifies each of the causes that result in quality issues. Against each cause, you list the effects that causes quality impact.

How would you describe this methodology as?

a) Control Charts

b) Pareto Charts

c) Fishbone Diagram

d) 80:20 Rule

8. Among the below list, which option is TRUE about Gold Plating?

    a) Gold plating is considered a defective deliverable.

    b) Gold Plating should be avoided at all times.

    c) Gold plating is not an acceptable form of quality practice, even if the customer approves the deliverable

    d) All of the above

9. Andrea is a project manager, who is managing her first project in her organization. She has completed the scope, schedule and cost planning for her project and is in the process of identifying her project team. Being new to the project management environment, she decide to refer her organization's process repository to identify any suitable quality processes of projects executed in the past. She could now manage to have a quality planning in place for her project.

    However, when the team begin producing deliverables, the quality inspection process begin throwing too many quality issues and this has become a serious concern for Andrea, who want to get it fixed. She feel there may be problems with her quality process.

    What would be your suggestion for Andrea to overcome this trouble?

    a) Add more resources to get the deliverables verified and capture defects before the deliverables are delivered to the customer

    b) Get her quality process inspected by Project Management Office or Quality group in her organization

    c) Instruct the team to follow the quality process very strictly and warn of strong action, if more defects continue to surface with the deliverables.

    d) Quality issues cannot be avoided in any project. She must arrange for quality training to the team to be more alert to defects.

10. It is found that 80% of projects problems are caused by 20% of the reason. This is called 80:20 rule, in which the quality review data are represented in the form of a graph with defects specifically highlighted to represent more attention. This method of having a bar graph representation is also called

    a) Pareto Chart

    b) Histogram

    c) Control Charts

    d) Run Charts

11. Your project team has just begun working on their construction phase and you are overseeing the project risks, schedule and cost factors of the project. During one of the business unit meeting, you overhear another manager speak about planning to have the quality inspection performed on the deliverables once all of his team members have completed their construction activities.

    He claims that he has implemented this innovative idea in order to reduce defects resulted by dependencies on uncompleted deliverables.

    Do you approve of this 'innovative' initiative?

    a) Yes. It really sounds innovative since the reason seems justified

    b) No. It is always a good practice to have the quality inspection performed as soon as the deliverables are completed.

    c) Yes. What is wrong with supporting innovative initiatives.

    d) Yes. I would rather wait and see how this new initiative works.

12. Among the below choices, what is TRUE about Quality Control Vs. Quality Assurance

    a) They both are same. Quality Assurance is about planning for Quality while Quality control is enforcing it

    b) Quality control is to enforce quality process on projects and deliverables, while Quality assurance is to get the process audited

    c) Quality Assurance assures quality deliverables to the customers

    d) Quality Control imposes strict control over defects, while quality assurance is planning for quality process

13. Process Analysis strategy is part of

    a) Quality Planning

    b) Quality Control

    c) Quality Assurance

    d) Quality inspection

14. You are currently managing a highly sensitive project for an important customer. You have a quality process established for your project. As part of the process strategy, you have various ways to verify the quality. As per one such strategy, you decide to create a checklist of points that you want your team and quality specialists to focus on while verifying the quality of the deliverables. This is to make sure, all the defects and quality issues are captured and fixed before delivery.

    Which process group are you in?

a) Planning

b) Execution

c) Initiation

d) Monitoring & Control

15. Which among the below are part of the Quality Management Planning process?

a) Benchmarking

b) Design of experiments

c) Cost Benefit Analysis

d) All of the above

16. You are working on a project and your team is working on their construction activities. Some of the deliverables are ready for customer verification. However, as part of your quality strategy, you plan to have an internal verification performed on all the completed deliverables. You plan to get your available team members to perform this internal validation. As the team begin working on validation, some of them report similar quality issues which is not resulted by the construction. The deliverables are completed as per the scope. Upon investigating into the root cause of these quality issues, you notice that there may be some process issues causing these errors. You begin working on getting these fixed.

Which process group are you in now?

a) Execution

b) Monitoring & Control

c) Closure

d) Planning

17. Jack is a project manager assigned to manage a construction project. He has been known in his organization for his project management skills. He is considered to be having sound knowledge on quality processes. In his latest project, he planned well for the scope, cost and schedule well. However, when it comes to quality planning, he gives more importance to internal testing activities by deploying specialized testers. He goes pretty soft on quality planning, since he do not want to put pressure on the team with quality compliance expectations. His argument is that since the scope verification is done before delivering to the customer, it shouldn't be a problem for his organization. This theory of him has found some supporters in his organization.

How do you view Jack's strategy?

a) His approach is sensible, since his delivery reaches the customers after undergoing one round of internal validation. The customer should not complaint about how he approach his delivery commitments.

b) His strategy is not correct. He should follow only the standard practices of his organization and cannot practice his own

c) His strategy is not acceptable since he seem to be focusing more on defect fixing than prevention. Quality is not all about testing but adopting strategies to eliminate problems before they occur.

d) If Jack's boss do not have problem, he can continue with his strategy.

18. **Which of the following statement is TRUE about Kaizen theory**

a) 80% of the project issues are caused by 20% reasons.

b) Flowcharting is one of the important strategy that guarantees quality oriented delivery

c) Rule of Seven

d) Kaizen theory is about constantly introducing small incremental process improvements in a business in order to improve quality

19. **Jackie has successfully completed her mortgage project execution and her team had done a great job. In fact, they even proactively designed some report templates, which they considered to be better than what is already approved by the customers. Jackie made sure no data requirements are missed out in these reports or Gold plating in the project. During one of a casual meeting with the stakeholders, she showed the attractive templates with better features, The stakeholders remarked the templates looking attractive. Based on this feedback, the team replaced the approved templates with these new ones and completed the development phase.**

During the scope verification process. the stakeholders raised concerns about these templates and refused to approve the deliverables since they considered the deliverables not to be in accordance with the approved scope. What do you consider as trouble area in this issues?

a) The stakeholders are to be faulted since they cannot appreciate proactive work of the team with better looking templates and with same features as approved.

b) Jackie should have obtained consent of the scope changes from the customer before changing the template design. Quality grade is the area of contention in this case.

c) Jackie should request the stakeholders for a review of their decision with proper justification

d) Stakeholders are at fault since the team included the new templates in place old ones only after showing to the stakeholders.

20. **Which one among the below are TRUE about Histogram**

a) A Histogram is part of quality control process and used to represent defect data in graphical form

b) Histogram is one of quality planning tool

c) Histogram is used in the Quality assurance process

d) None of the above

21. **Choose the answer from the below, that best describes Just in Time (JIT) methodology**

a) JIT is all about doing the right work at the right time to ensure quality of the deliverables

b) JIT guarantees the project execution according to the schedule.

c) JIT is used to monitor all the components of the triple constraints

d) JIT means zero inventory and storage cost.

22. **From the below list, what BEST describes the advantage of conformance to quality processes**

a) Customer satisfaction

b) More business

c) Increased business confidence

d) All of the above

23. **Corrective Actions & Preventive Actions are key strategies of**

a) Quality Planning

b) Quality Control

c) Quality Assurance

d) Quality Management

24. **Using the quality data of similar projects of the past to arrive at a baseline for the project is known as**

a) Quality Planning

b) Quality Checklists

c) Quality Assurance

d) Benchmarking

25. **Cost of non-conformance results in**
    a) More lessons learned
    b) Better quality product
    c) Rework
    d) Performing organization gets to straighten its quality process

ANSWERS

1. **Answer: A**

    Justification: There are many wrong opinions about Quality management. Most people mistake Quality as doing testing. Of course, testing is part of a quality process. It is about defect fixing methodology. But, Quality is more about proactively preventing issues and problems. Having a quality process defined in advance educates the team on various factors, right from designing their applications till generating the deliverables. Once these quality processes are taken care, it will reduce the number of defects with deliverables. Needless to say, Prevention is better than cure.

2. **Answer: C**

    Justification: Work Product Review is part of a quality process, wherein the completed deliverables get reviewed by another team member, project manager or another expert. While the quality process mandates the team to develop a quality output, a completed deliverable cannot be delivered to the customers without undergoing a review. The document that is used to record all the review comments is called Work Product Review. In most organizations, the WPR details are shared with the customers as an indication of their determination to quality process.

3. **Answer: B**

    Justification: The responsibility of the quality rests with the project manager and his team. However, the ownership of the quality process is with the project manager, who plans, executes and monitors the enactment of his quality policy. The project manager's responsibility begins with defining the quality process for his project, train the team on the process, making sure the team follows the process till coordinating with the stakeholders, who perform the validation of the deliverables.

4. **Answer: D**

    Justification: The motto of every organization's quality policy should be to meet the customer expectation to produce a product that is in conformance to requirement and subsequently the product is fit to use. The customers pay to get the projects executed only with these expectations in mind. The responsibility of the project manager is to design the quality process with these objectives in mind. No customer can compromise on any of these three expectations.

5. **Answer: D**

    Justification: Even though the project manager has an excellent quality process in place, getting the team trained on the processes and the importance of following the quality process and getting the deliverables tested before delivering to the customers, it is only during the scope verification process the deliverables get verified for conformance to their requirements. It is true that the quality process might have been shared with the stakeholders, but that doesn't guarantee them of quality deliverables. Hence, the scope verification assumes significance.

6. **Answer: A**

    Justification: When an organization is generating huge number of outputs every day, it may not be possible to test the quality of every component. Such organizations give utmost importance to setting up quality processes and goals that is considered fool proof. Some examples of soft drinks manufacturing companies, which produce hundreds of thousands of bottles a day. Besides strict quality processes, these business adopt to random sampling methodology to test its products to make sure the products are produced according to the quality guidelines.

7. **Answer: C**

    Justification: A fishbone diagram is also called as Cause-Effect diagram. Another name for this is Ishikawa diagram. While performing quality validation, every defect identified are classified under specific causes and their effect. In other words, when a project produces a huge machine, the quality process might reveal problems in the electric circuits, which result in uneven functioning. In this case, the electric circuit is the cause and the effect of it is uneven function which is not acceptable as per the quality policy.

8. **Answer: D**

    Justification: Gold Plating refers to producing a product or outcome, which was not approved by the stakeholders or sponsor. When a product is produced not according to the planned objective, it is considered a defective scope as per the quality management processes. At times, a customer may even approve such a product or outcome, but still it do not comply with the quality processes being followed globally. A better way to manage such 'extras' is to follow change management policy to include them as formal scope.

9. **Answer: B**

    Justification: Globally, it is recommended and acceptable practice to refer the organization process assets while preparing the quality process. However, it is also essential for the project manager to make sure such a process is in line with the quality requirements of the current project. In this case, Andrea had exactly this mistake done. She used the process assets to have her quality policy, but failed to verify the conformance of the process to her project. The best option for her is to have quality assurance performed by the quality group or PMO.

10. **Answer: A**

    Justification: A pareto diagram is also called as 80:20 rule, which means most of the project's problems are caused by smaller number of issues. Once the project manager focuses on the most important of these causes, the quality process can be easily resolved for the project.

11. **Answer: B**

    Justification: The work product review activities of every deliverables should be taken up after every deliverables are ready. Identifying potential quality issues in advance is always good since it gives enough time for the team to fix to eliminate other dependency related issues. In addition, it reduces the last minute pressure on the reviewers scrambling to complete their reviews.

12. **Answer: B**

    Justification: As the choice B narrates, Quality assurance is all about performing an audit on the quality process to make sure the process is capable of producing intended results for the project. Remember that quality processes of every project is unique and no two projects can have same processes. This indicates the requirement of quality process in line with the project's requirements.

13. **Answer: C**

    Justification: One of the tool that is used in the quality assurance is analyzing the process being followed by the project. This will make sure the process is reviewed and to make sure the process requirements meet the intended objectives of the project and capable of producing desired results.

14. **Answer: B**

    Justification: Checklists is one of the quality management tool that is used to validate the quality of the deliverables. Having a checklist of evaluation criteria is one of many strategies a project manager can have to manage the quality of the deliverables. Hence, this qualifies to be part of the project management planning.

15. **Answer: D**

    Justification: All of the options listed are qualified to be part of the project quality planning process since they are some of the strategies to be adopted by the project to manage the quality process and drive the project towards success.

16. **Answer: A**

    Justification: The issue listed in the question is the result of not so-effective quality process being followed for the project. This definitely requires an audit on the process itself, as part of quality assurance.

17. **Answer: C**

    Justification: When it comes to professional world, proactive approach is recommended and practiced by every organization. In this question, what Jack's approach is reacting to problems, which come in the form of defects in the deliverables. When defects are identified he deploys the testing team to fix them. This strategy has forced him to deploy specialized testers and quality specialists, which carries a cost burden on his account.

18. **Answer: D**

    Justification: Kaizen can be implemented in organizations by improving every aspect of a business process in a step by step approach, while gradually developing employee skills through training education and increased involvement. The principle in Kaizen implementation are:

    1. Human resources are the most important company asset,
    2. Processes must evolve by gradual improvement rather than radical changes
    3. Improvement must be based on statistical/quantitative evaluation of process performance.

19. **Answer: B**

    Justification: The issue narrated in the question is resulted by the team giving surprise to the stakeholders by creating a new template, even if it is attractive and include all the features of the approved one. Every requirement of the customers and strategy of them may have some reasons behind them. When a scope statement is approved, the customer begin to exact the approved solution only and nothing more or nothing less.

20. **Answer A**

    Justification : A Histogram is one of the quality control technique used to track the quality process on the deliverables. When performing quality control process on the deliverables, the defect details are collected and consolidated and used as a chart in graphic form to classify them based on defect criticality. Thus the Project manager gets a priority list of defects, which can be planned more effectively.

21. **Answer: D**

    Justification: The primary purpose of following Just In Time (JIT) methodology is to save the inventory cost as well as the cost of storing them. This methodology requires high degree of planning and involve high amount of risks involved, since the availability of components is very key to have the production schedule. The quality of the processes plays a very critical role behind the successful adoption of JIT technique.

22. **Answer: D**

   Justification: The answer is pretty simple and straightforward. In these days of increasing competition, every organizations wants to establish their supremacy over the other and this supremacy can be assured only by the quality. An organization that insist on superior quality process always stand to gain the confidence of the customers, increased business, more opportunities, new customers and brighter future.

23. **Answer: B**

   Justification: Quality control refers to enacting the quality process, which was planned in the initial stages of the project. When the quality process is followed, there are possibilities of defects being identified, requirement of corrective and preventive actions.

24. **Answer: D**

   Justification: Having a benchmarking is same as setting up quality baseline for the project's quality objective. In order to assess the quality performance of the project, the data from the previous similar projects are considered as baseline. The project manager performs his own analysis to arrive at a benchmarking for the current project.

25. **Answer: C**

   Justification: The cost of non-conformance refers to the quality process being not formulated according to the standards or not following them. In either case, the result is the effort spent on rework in fixing project problems. There are many more risks for the performing organization and the project manager in the form of loss of customer's faith and increased cost on the project.

This page is intentionally left blank

This page is intentionally left blank

Human Resource Management

Objectives

At the end of Human Resource Management chapter, you should be able to know:

- Importance of managing human resources in a project environment
- how the human resources planning is done
- how resources are identified
- the relationship between WBS & human resource planning
- what is staffing plan and RACI chart
- advantages and disadvantages of having virtual teams and co-located teams
- Team building activities such as motivation and conflict management
- different types of leadership qualities of a PM on his team control
- organizational policies and its impact on teams

Significance of Human Resource Management

We have been reading several management components that are all equally important for the successful execution of a project. That's fine and alright.

Have you ever thought, what is the most challenging job for a Project Manager from start to end of his project?

If you ask me, I would say It is engaging and managing the Human Resources in a project environment.

Unlike other factors, the Human Resources can think, act, have opinions, communicate, react, has likes and dislikes and many other characteristics that may prove positive or negative for the project. In a project environment, Project Manager cannot take every single decision and impose it on the team, thus the team can only do the job they are told to do. Imagine the impact of a project manager of a construction project asking the team to begin working on the construction, while the team is awaiting the design review.

What can a project deliver without the involvement of manpower? I would say Nothing.

No project can be successful unless the project has a great team, good working environment and commitment from every member of the team. In many projects, the project manager is expected to obtain a buy-in from the team before the actual execution phase can begin.

During the different phases of the project, the project team is required to communicate between each other, take decisions and carry out their assigned responsibilities. They need to be motivated and any conflicts should be resolved without any impact to the project. Having to handle all these responsibilities becomes a critical and challenging task for a Project Manager, besides planning for his entire project and having to manage stakeholders and their requirements.

In addition to the above, since the human resources are the most important factor in a project execution, it becomes the major risk that require great amount of attention from the project manager.

Does this sound sensible?

No wonder, Human Resource Management is highly challenging for any Project Manager.

Different Types of Human Resources in a Project

In a project, there are different types of resources exist, each of which perform different types of activities.

Project team	:	Comprising of hardcore technical team that executes and tests the projects/products.
Management Team	:	Team of people, who manage the work of their respective projects and team
Other stakeholders	:	A group of people, who are positively or negatively impacted by the execution of the project, who approve the funding, provide the overall project requirement, providing clarifications on project scope and track the progress of the project.

How each Resource Management Processes are Related?

From the other knowledge area components that we have reviewed so far, every process has a specific relationship with each other.

We begin each of the knowledge area by planning and then track the plan during the Execution phase and then in the monitoring and controlling phase. The Human Resource Management is no different from them.

Let us look into the below diagram to understand more

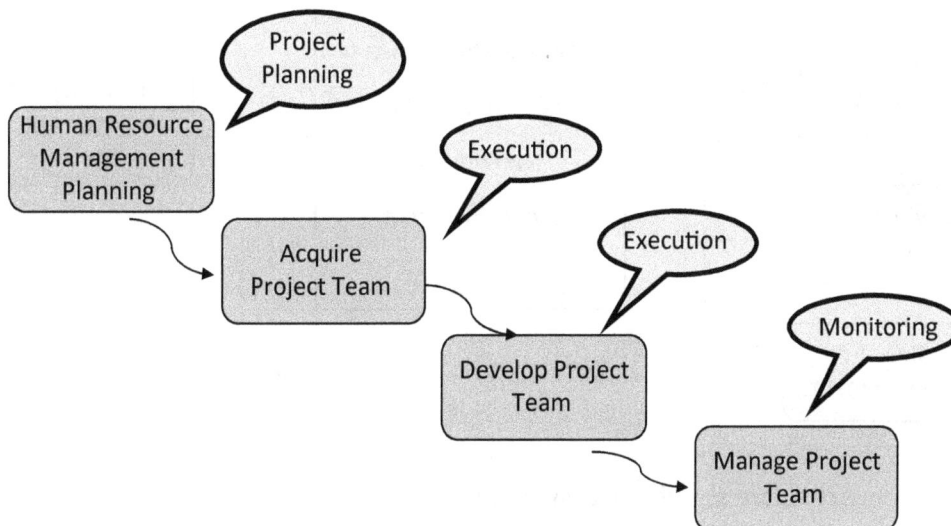

We begin with the planning process for Resources in the Planning Process group. This is followed by the Execution phase, where we acquire the project team and develop the team. Finally, in the Monitoring & Control phase of the project life cycle, we manage the team and resolve issues surrounding the acquired team.

Let us now understand all of these activities in details

Human Resource Management Planning

The most important of all the Human Resources processes is the planning phase, where you will do the estimation of resources. If you could recollect what we reviewed in the Time and Cost management processes, you would realize that those two knowledge area processes are followed by human resource management. In the Time Management, we estimate the amount of effort involved in executing the project activities whereas in the Cost management we estimate the cost factor of involving the project execution. In Human resource management, we plan for managing the human resources for the benefit of the project and the performing organization. This phase is very critical considering the fact that unless the resource planning is done sensibly, subsequent phases of handling the identified resource would fail.

Now, let us take a look into how the Resource planning, also known as Staffing plan is executed with the help of the below diagram

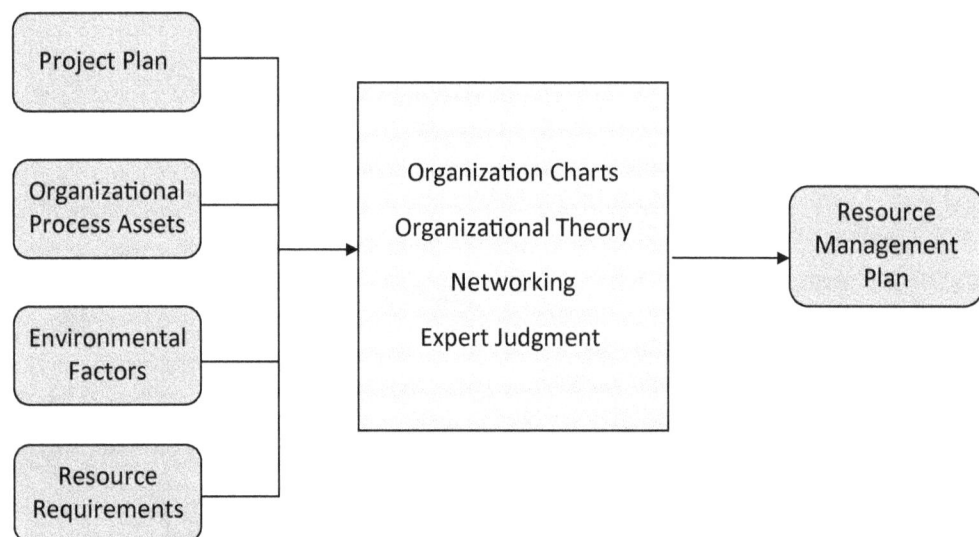

The above diagram should be easy to understand.

Inputs to the Human Resource Management Planning Process

Project Management Plan

The primary purpose of having the Project plans as an input to this Human Resource Planning process is to understand the resource requirements for each of the activity to be performed in the project. When the staffing planning is being done, the Project Manager should take into account, the total number of activities, types of activities, activity attributes, resource requirement for each activity into consideration.

Can you identify why do the Project Manager required to consider the types of activities in the staffing plan?

The purpose of identifying the activity type is to classify the activities so that it becomes easier for the Project Manager to plan for the resources performing the activities. For example, when you are managing a project that is going to develop a banking application, you might require a specialist designer and subject matter expert with expertise in banking application to support the design phase. Similarly, the application review process may need to be reviewed by these experts. A technical guy may be able to review and support only on the technical aspect of the project, but need not be on the application support activities. Similarly, if the project is going to have a dedicated quality expert, the same is included in the staffing plan.

To put it easy, the project scope will only provide details of what has to be done, but it is in the Human Resources phase, the project manager decides how to get the project scope into a realistic outcome and who are all going to be part of the effort.

The Human resources planning refers to, how the project is going to be engaged with different types of resources doing different tasks. So, care should be taken in classifying the resource requirements of the project.

I hope the above makes sense.

Organizational Process Assets

When the Project Manager is working on the staffing plan of his project, resource plans of previous projects come in for his aid more than any other planning component. The reason is process assets in the Organizational repository doesn't only contain the issues and risks related to the resources but also have details of the resource requirements, which resources were identified, their skills, expertise details and how the resources were deployed in the project.

In addition to the above, all lessons learned highlights the issues encountered and how they were resolved. Remember that most of the organizations have details of each of their staff and their background information so as to refer and to make the life of project managers easier, while identifying suitable resources for their projects.

When using these historic information, the Project manager has the advantage of identifying potential risks in advance and eliminate them or mitigate them before they could hit the project.

Enterprise Environmental Factors

This is another important component that needs the attention of the Project Manager while working on the staffing plan.

Every organization have their own resource utilization policy. For example, some organizations might want testing activities handled by their dedicated testers for reasons of expertise and efficiency. Similarly, many organizations want to engage the resources from the quality group as stakeholders of their projects.

The enterprise environmental factors has the details of the organization's policy towards identifying and utilization of resources for their projects.

Resource Requirements

One of the important input required to plan for the Human Resource Management is to highlight the resource requirement and their utilization schedule in the plan. While listing the resource requirement, it is essential to highlight the skills required, when the resources are required and the duration of their engagement. These vital input help plan for acquiring and utilization of the resources in an effective manner.

Tools used in Human Resource Management Planning Process

Organization Charts

When planning for the Human Resources to be part of the project, using the Organization chart is very essential considering the fact that the Project Manager is trying to setup his own Project Organization within the Organization itself.

Before identifying the project organization, it is essential to understand what is already available on hand and then analyze to plan for what sort of project organization to be formed. To get all of these happening, the best tool to refer is the Organization Chart or the list of available resources for utilization.

At times, referring to such Organizational charts and other projects' organization chart will help the Project Manager to get some ideas on what type of organization is practiced elsewhere in the organization. While planning for resources for the project, the manager should remember that each of the position created for the project should be closely aligned with the project scope statement. For example, if the project scope mandates an extensive responsibility for a subject matter expert (SME) and a testing professional with specialized skills, the project organization should have positions for such resources planned.

Organization Theory

Organizational theory is about referring to already proven strategies and organization's policies while planning for the project organization for individual projects. Every organization has its own policies and recommended practices with respect to utilizing human resources as part of the project team. In general, organizational policies reflect their business strategy as well.

The policies and resourcing strategies of organizations are mostly influenced by their past experiences of deploying and managing resources.

Networking

Networking is similar to Expert Judgment, wherein the Project Manager consult every available resource, experts, documents in the Organizational repository and magazines to understand the happenings around the organization and industry and stay on top of his project human resource planning.

Remember that an intelligent Project Manager keeps his mind open and receptive to ideas, no matter from where and how it comes. There are plenty of innovations and strategies being planned and managed around the business world, which result in a greater success for the performing organization.

Expert Judgment

One of the very important tool that will help the project manager to arrive at a meaningful Resource Management Plan is to consult experts and other managers. Often such consultations and meetings help identify better strategy and eliminate risks and issues before they occur. Consulting external sources such as articles that appear in magazines, seminars and newspaper columns are great source of information that could potentially help develop a resource management plan.

Tidbits

> *If part of a project is outsource to an external vendor, how would the project organization chart be impacted? What type of authority, a project manager can have on the resources of the vendor organization?*
>
> *Well. I would say, it depends on the type of contract that is signed. We would be reviewing more on the contracts, when we get into the procurement management chapter.*
>
> *In a fixed price contract, the responsibility of the vendor is to deliver the intended product or services as set out in the contract. If a vendor is expected to supply motherboards for a computer manufacturer, the vendor takes complete ownership of his task and control the resources and their responsibilities. The buyer will have limited power on such resources.*
>
> *However, in a variable price contract, all project resources are normally listed under the project organization of the buyer for reasons of project ownership and accountability*

Output of Human Resources Management Planning

A Human Resource Management Plan can be in different format and some of them are listed below for your reference.

Organizational Chart

The ultimate outcome of the Human Resource Planning process is the Organizational chart, that defines the type of Organization the project is going to have and how the team is structured within the overall Organization. It is expected that such a project Organization fits into the overall organizational structure in every sense and meets the Organization's strategies and policies with respect to deployment and utilization of human resources.

A sample Organization Chart is defined as below

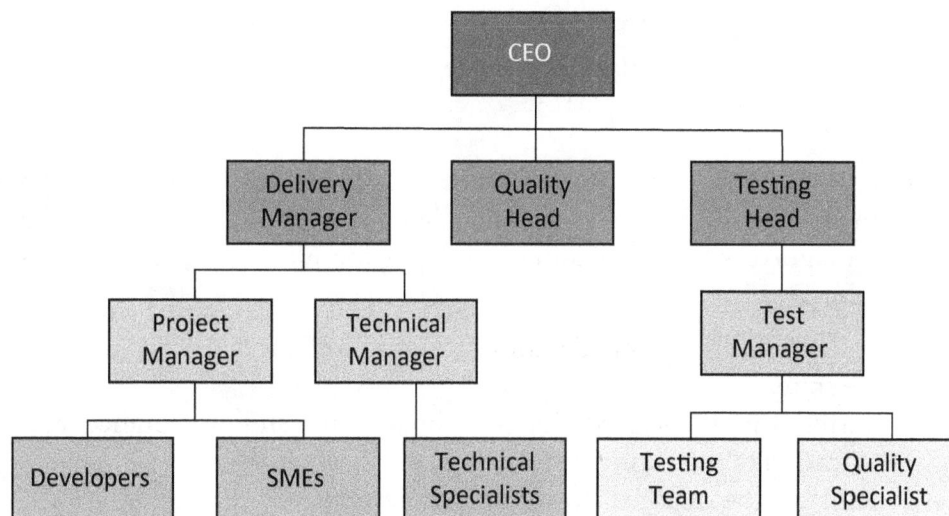

Do not get confused to see the CEO, Heads of specific groups in this organization chart. The primary purpose of having this organization chart is to have a better visibility on where each of the project resources stand within the organization.

Staffing Plan

The strategies of the Project Manager with respect to utilization of the identified human resources is explained in the Staffing plan. Note that a staffing plan is not only critical but also tricky that require more attention and focus.

In general, the Staffing Plan will provide details of the resources that are to be part of the project, when each of them are required in the project and what skills are expected from them in supporting the project requirement. The staffing management plan also speaks about how the project manager is planning to develop the team and resolve any issues faced.

Further, a detailed resource requirement schedule, the training requirements of the team members, how the team will be recognized and rewarded for their contribution to the project are explained in detail in the Staffing Management Plan.

A sample Staffing Plan is seen below:

THE STATE ELECTION COMMISSION
Staffing Plan for Mid-term Elections 2015

Overview

The State Election Commission is required by the law to complete the implementation of the new voting machine systems procured through the contract signed with the vendor, M/s FairGame Electronics Inc., during March 2015.

- Coordinate voting system demonstrations in 6 of the 8 election districts in the state
- Prescribe the rules for adoption, operations and acceptance and certification of the voting system
- Promulgate the rules for fair voting in the state
- Facilitate the training and support of the newly adoptable voting system in each of the counties

Staffing Plan Proposed

The overall project will be carried out under the supervision of the State Election Commissioner (SEC) and his office. The SEC will set the rules and guidelines that is required to be strictly followed by every member of the project.

The Station Election Commissioner will have the liberty to nominate anyone from his office to oversee the project execution and provide written report to his office.

The State Election Commissioner will be at his liberty and discretion can request, deploy and release the election officials based on the requirement mandated by the State Election policy.

Organization Plan

Project Manager : Kenneth Wayne PMP will be managing the overall project team. He will be operating out of the State Election Commissioner office. The Project Manager will provide the leadership and his expertise to implement the project execution and validate the new voting machine system.

Project Team

The entire project team will be split into three components each of which will have specific responsibilities such as execution, Technical support and Testing. The team will be identified by the Project Manager, who will be leading the team.

The above staffing plan is only for sample purpose. The original staffing plan can be according to the individual project requirement. As illustrated in the description of the staffing plan, the project manager can include every component as required and planned.

Roles & Responsibilities

The R & R definition is a key component of the Human resources Planning process since lot might go wrong in the project unless the roles and responsibilities of all the resources are not defined clearly. The Roles & Responsibilities document clearly narrates every individual position's roles and expected responsibilities, their boundaries within the project.

RACI Chart is one important chart that is produced as an output of the Human Resources Planning process. RACI stands for Responsible, Accountable, Consult and Inform. The best way to define the Roles & Responsibilities is to define a table with as much details as possible and clearly.

A key responsibility of the project manager is to create the RACI Chart, as part of the staffing management plan, distribute the chart to every stakeholder and get their concurrence. This would help a clarity on who has what responsibility. Pay as much attention as possible towards this chart, as it might help troubleshoot potential issues in future.

A sample RACI chart is found below:

Tasks	Account PM	Account DM	Functional PM	Functional DM	MSS Focus Group	Training Team	Remarks
Technical Competency Building	I	I	R	A	C	C	Support group will perform this task
Technical consultancy	I	I	A	I	R		Tech Support will perform this task
Project Management	R	A	I	I	C		Delivery Organization to perform
Design Activities	R	A	I	I	C		Delivery Organization to perform
Execution	R	A	I	I	C		Delivery Organization to perform
Testing	R	A	C	I			Delivery Organization to perform

Acquire Project Team

No project will be successful unless the project is supported by the best of the resources who have necessary skills, motivation, determination and commitment. While acquiring the team is a critical task of the project manager keeping the team motivated is another important task that should happen all through the lifecycle of the project.

Being the most important factors of a project execution, the project manager should be focused on availing the best of the resources and at the right time, who can support his plan and understand their responsibility. Acquiring project team consists of some simple tasks but very important ones.

The process is illustrated in the diagram given below

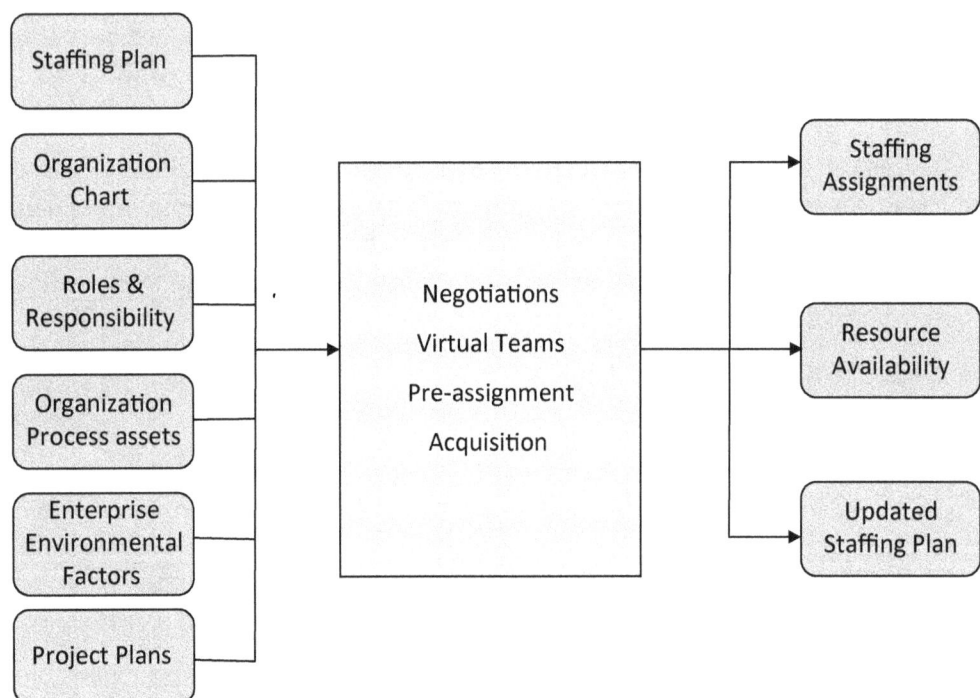

Inputs to the Acquire Project Team Process

From the above diagram, you may notice that many of the inputs of the Acquire Project team process are the output of the previous process. So, let us not repeat reviewing Staffing Plan, Organizational Chart and Roles & Responsibilities again.

Organizational Process Assets

When planning for the Human Resources for the project referring to the process assets help significantly in identifying past risks and how they were handled by the previous managers. Similarly, lessons learned will highlight the kind of issues that need to be prepared for. If the project manager is looking for a resource with specialized skills, he might consult the available project artifacts in the organizational process repository.

When referring to the similar projects for input, there are more likely to identify business or technical experts. Not having the right resource is same as having the wrong resources for the project. The impact of both these is going to be catastrophic.

Enterprise Environmental Factors

Every organization has its own policies and strategies in deploying and utilizing resources for their projects. As an example, in view of keeping the cost under control, some organizations might resort to deploy people with lesser experience in their project, who are backed by few highly experienced human resources.

Similarly, some organizations has it a habit to insist for quality professionals to be part of the project team. Such professionals will involve themselves in every aspect of the project to make sure the project produces the best outcome possible.

Project Management Plans

Referring to other project plans will help the Project Manager to identify resources with specific expertise to support the project need.

For example, when referring to the Scope Management plan, the Project Manager might realize that the project require a Subject Matter Expert due to the complex nature of the requirement.

Tidbits

HALO EFFECT

When working on acquiring the project team, one of the most important point to be considered is a Halo effect.

What is a Halo effect?

Halo effect is to utilize the wrong resource for doing the job. Just because someone is good in a technical job, does not certify the person to be very good as a Project Manager. At times, in order to motivate and retain some resources, organizations tend to give such resources other opportunities that are not familiar to them.

Motivating the project team members is always good and helps keep the spirits of the team high, but such generosities will do good for none. This will result in the failure of the person and doesn't benefit the Organization.

So, the project manager should be extremely careful when identifying resources to do certain jobs, especially for leadership roles.

Tools used in Acquire Team Process

Now, let us look into the tools that are useful in acquiring the project team.

Negotiations

Having to negotiate with other managers is one most important aspect of acquiring the project team. To execute a specific activity of your project, you might need a particular resource, that has expertise and knowledge on the technical or functional part of the activity. But, if the resource is engaged into another project or part of another functional group, the only option for you is to negotiate with those managers and use the resource for your project.

Often in business environments, especially in the informational technology industry, it is a common problem to have technical or functional experts readily available. This results in negotiations between managers to utilize the resources' time. At times, such resources might be partly utilized and billed between both projects.

Remember the fact that, hiring a new resources is not going to be cheaper. Hiring a new resources involve cost of hiring, training cost and time taken to get the resource engage actively in the project. So, negotiation is always a better option to keep the cost under control.

Virtual Teams

A virtual team has become unavoidable in many industries, especially in information technology, finance and market research sectors. Having all the resources available in the same location is always good, but it is not so easy to have the team available in the same location.

In order to overcome this trouble, virtual team is one suitable option. The technological advancements of the modern world comes in handy when working with virtual teams. The team members may not meet each other every day, but they communicate with each other through emails, telephone devices, instant messaging and any other mode that will help them to stay in touch with the rest of the team.

Remember that having a virtual team has some disadvantages too, since they may not meet each other and may not be aware of what happens at the other end, unless one care to explain the other.

Pre-Assignment

Have you ever had the luxury of being guaranteed of some specific resources without having to negotiate?

If yes, you would probably have to include the work assignments for such resources in the staffing plan of your project. As an example, if you refer to the sample staffing plan given in this chapter you would notice that Kenneth Wayne PMP is identified and assigned as a project manager of this project. This means he is blocked for this project and there is no need to negotiate with anyone for using him.

Acquisition

When there is no way out to identify a project team from within the performing organization, the last option to chose is to acquire the team from the market. This means, the project manager need to work with the Human resources and Resource Management groups of the performing organization to approach contractors and manpower consulting agencies to hire project resources.

Output of Acquire Project Team Process

Staffing Assignments

The ultimate outcome of the Acquire project team process is the list of assignments that are identified for the project team.

As the project manager completes the acquire team process, he will have the list of all activities and resources are identified and assigned for each of the activity in the list. An intelligent project manager will highlight the % availability of the resources against each activity and make it more clear for all stakeholders.

Resource Availability

A resource availability document is the calendar of every individual resources, who are assigned to the project.

In other words, the available dates and time of each of the resources are captured in the calendar and shared with every stakeholder of the project. If a specific resource is available only 50% of the time for this project (as we discussed earlier, resource sharing between projects is common in the business environment for optimization of available resources).

Similarly many organizations do not prefer to lock its resources to their projects unless they are required full time from start to finish of the project. As an example the technical designers may not be required during the whole of the project phase but only while preparing the technical design phase and

---

to validate the final outcome of the project to make sure the project outcome meets the desired project objective.

All such criteria are highlighted in the Resource availability calendar. Take a look into a sample calendar that I have created for you.

Resource/Week	Week 1		Week2		Week3		Week4		Wk5
Joshua									
Monica									
Robert									
Jane									

The above chart will provide a pictorial representation of the availability of each resource of the project team on a weekly basis. Work assignments can be shaded for easier readability.

Update Staffing Plan

Now, let us revisit the Staffing Plan that was prepared during the previous process, Human Resources Planning due to various reasons. It might be too early to have all the information available in the Human Resources Planning process.

However, when the Project Manager begin working on acquiring the team, there might come many developments and updates to the original plan. Sometimes, the identified resources may not be available fully or even partly. There may need to be alternate plans to replace such resources. All such up-to-date information are updated in the Staffing Management Plan and make it a live document for reference.

Tidbits

Do you require a change management process to get the staffing plan updated at any time of the project?

Not necessarily.

A project's staffing plan is not an independent entity but dependent on few other components such as Schedule, Cost and Scope of the project. Any significant change on these three component will have impact on the planned staffing for the project. As such, a staffing plan cannot independently undergo changes for any reason.

Does this make sense?

Develop Project Team

Now that we have planned a project team and acquired it do not guarantee the successful execution of the project. Remember that, what we have done is just planning for the project resources and identified them. The most important task of a Project Manager during the entire Project Execution phase is to manage the resources of the project, their expectations and needs.

Unless the project resources are well managed, motivated and heading in the direction that the manager has planned, there are more possibilities for the team not to have their focus towards achieving their objectives and goals of the project but result in a chaotic situation unless the manager has a great control over the project.

As explained earlier in this project, what the project manager dealing with are human resources that can talk, think and take decisions independently. Human resources might become sensitive and emotional at times that need to be handled tactically by the project manager. Considering all of these factors, I wouldn't hesitate to call the developing team process to be the most complicated work for a project manager.

These above issues signify the importance of the Develop Project Team process. Now, let us look into how the process works with the help of the below diagram.

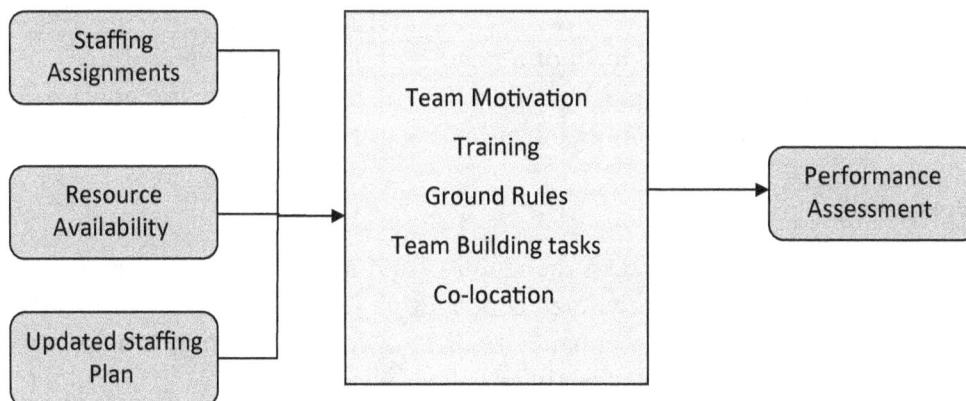

Inputs to the Develop Project Team Process

All the three inputs to this process are the output of the previous process, Acquire Project Team. Hence, let us not repeat the discussion on these again here.

One must understand that clarity in the definition of activities, roles and responsibilities of the project team is very critical for the successful development of the project team. Let us now see how the process works.

Tools used in Develop Project Team Process

Motivation Technique

Assume yourself to be a team member of a project and given a huge application to develop. How would it feel, if you have keep working on your assignments for weeks together without anything else. When you see that some of your friends have got better opportunities to work on other projects and are getting rewarded for their hardwork. Would you still feel interested to stay on the project?

When it comes to developing the team and managing their efficiency, your goal is to motivate the team in every possible way and occasions. Not every expectation can be set for the team and monitored. It deliver nothing for the project.

Some of the most important motivation techniques available are to recognize the talent and contribution of the individual resources and to reward them suitably. Even a simple email appreciation goes a long way to keep the team up in high morale and give them energy to achieve their objective. Every organization have their own unique way to recognize the talents and reward the best performers thus motivating others.

Unless the team believes and have faith in the human resource strategies of the performing organization, it would be very difficult to expect much productivity from the team.

The rewards can be in the form of a raise, allowances, cash rewards and any other possible ways. Such motivations make the team believe they are treated with special interest by their organization.

Training

Having the team get trained on their subject and areas of operation is another way to encourage the individual contributors and keep them motivated. Everyone have ambition to enhance their knowledge, that might help them nurture their future growth. Training can be used as a great motivating tool for a project manager.

If any of the team member is not skilled enough to perform the job, it becomes the responsibility of the project manager to get the resource trained. This helps the organization to realize its project objective besides giving the resource chance to have its skills developed.

Ground Rules

Having the ground rules set in advance for the project team enables the project manager to define a perfect working condition for the project team. Having the rules and regulations defined earlier helps the entire team realize the expectations and work accordingly. Once the ground rules are set, it becomes easy for the project manager having to just oversee if everything is progressing according to the objectives of the resource planning.

Another advantage to have the ground rules set helps eliminate conflicts among the team members.

Co-Location

If you understand the concept of virtual teams, then you can call co-location to be the exact opposite of it. It is true that having a virtual team has certain advantages with itself such as flexibility to identify suitable resources for the project, not having to depend on one single location for the resources. A project manager has larger boundary to look for a suitable team member for the project. However, virtual team has disadvantages too.

While the virtual teams help the organizations to identify the best of the skills to be part of their projects, the co-location helps improve the communication among team members. Besides improved communication, co-locations help the team to develop a sense of community among themselves and engage in multiple skills and personal development initiatives.

An improved communication results in more exchanges of ideas and opinions relating to the project. A co-location technique is also called a *war room*. This name is given due to the fact that a co-located team result in huge amount of communication, exchange of opinions and arguments.

Leadership Qualities of a Project Manager

So far, we have seen various ways to identify the team, develop them and keep them working towards their goals. Does this all prove the Project Manager to be a great leader?

Not necessarily.

To be a leader requires much more than just having the ability to manage the work. To be a leader require a significant amount of efficiency and skills on the part of the project manager. Skills refers to soft skills and ability to lead the team by example, knowledge and influence. Every project manager is expected to possess the influence and power on their team. Unless the team has its faith in these power of their manager the project manager would fail by himself.

So, what empowers the Project Manager to be a great leader? Let us look into the powers now.

Legitimate Power

A legitimate power is the authority, the project manager is given while she was made the manager of her project. It would be good to recall the Project charter that was prepared and handed over to the Project Manager in the beginning of the project.

The very purpose of the project charter is to authorize the manager to lead the team, assign work and manage the project and all its phases from start to finish. A smart project manager is expected to take ownership of the project and responsibility of the work being executed by her team. It becomes her ultimate job to make sure everything is under her control and the team has the right guidance and direction to proceed and execute a great project.

This authority helps the Project manager to assign work to her team, track them and resolve any issues on the way to completing the work.

Reward Power

A reward power is a very worthy motivation technique available for the project manager to keep the team motivated and work towards achieving its goal.

A reward can be in the form of cash allowance, gifts, vouchers or any other form practiced by the performing organization. However, the project manager should be very careful to chose the right person and reward them in the right sense. This is because any unfair practice in choosing the resources will result in disenchantment among other team members, thus causing disappointment. While the right person is rewarded for his hard work, it is also essential that only achievements get rewarded and not a universal rewarding system.

A more realistic and sensible approach to reward can do wonders, if it is tied to specific expectations or goals for the team members. The rewards announced by the Project Manager should be truly rewarding every deserving team member rather than being vague in the meeting criteria of the team.

For example, if the Project Manager announces a reward for the team member who completes their work packet first will only end up being branded unfair. It's a very basic fact that work packets assigned to different team members have different levels of complexity and it would be unwise to equate them as one when announcing the reward.

On the contrary, if the reward system carries a cash award of $500 to every team member whose work packet passes the acceptance test in the first attempt and on time, it would be truly motivating and meaningful.

Does this make sense?

Expert Power

Everyone has a specific skill and talent inherited in them and the Project Managers are no exception.

An expert power is the respect that the team has on their Project Manager for his expertise in a specific area. As we discussed earlier in this book, the Project Manager is not necessarily be a technical nerd. He may have exceptional capability in team building, motivating, ability to drive the project out of critical situations, on time delivery capability, risk handling, great co-ordination capability with all stakeholders or leadership capability.

Such *expert power* is inherited into great leaders.

Referent Power

Let us take an example that you are assigned the project manager of a large project, which is considered by your organization as a critical one in terms of strategy and returns on investment. The outcome of the project is so important that your organization will stay ahead of its peers, if the project is executed successfully.

Out of faith in your ability and expertise, the CEO personally nominates you to this position and authenticates you to take any decision to make sure the project objectives are met on time and according to conformance to customer requirement. In a more realistic term, you are representing the CEO of your organization in front of the team.

This authority given to the Project Managers are called *Referent Power*.

Punishment Power

Least popular and not recommended among all of the authority, the Punishment Power means taking tougher actions against errant team members in order to bring discipline, meet the deadline or project objectives. While the punishment power helps the Project Managers in extraordinary situations, it is always advised to use this technique as the last option to manage the team.

In addition to the above caution, the project manager should be extremely cautious on how this power is used. If the manager decides to use this power, it should be done more privately, such as speaking and warning the team member in private rather than in front of other team members.

More on Motivation

Unless the work environment is pleasing and satisfactory none of the project team members are going to like what they do in the project, no matter how much expertise they have or gain. Motivating the team thus becomes most critical aspect of the project manager's role.

Some of the important facts to be known about team's expectations and motivating issues are:

Maslow's Hierarchy

Every team member have needs of different magnitude. They expect their least of the needs met by their organization. As an example, the team expects simple stuff such as coffee machines, easy access to printers, flexible work hours as basic needs. Unless these are met, they do not wish to think about higher rewards such as increase in salary, bonus and so on.

Before the organization think about rewarding the team big, it should make sure basic needs are taken care first.

McGregor's Theory X & Theory Y

Not every Project Managers are alike. Some managers do not trust their own team, even if they were chosen by the manager himself. These types of managers are classified by McGregor as Theory X category of managers.

However, some managers have trust in their team when it comes to delivering their best and according to set goals. Such managers fall under Theory Y category.

According to McGregor, Theory X managers tend to micromanage the team and project due to this lack of faith in their team. Remember that having or not having faith in the team itself becomes a critical motivating factor among the team. This means, even if the project managers do not trust their team, they need not show it in front of the team.

Herzberg's Motivation Theory

Some people give preference to healthy work condition, cordial relationship with everyone in their organization and a good personal life. Unless these conditions are met, they wouldn't care much about any motivating factors of the organization.

One of the most important motivating factor is to have a very healthy and professional working culture in the organization.

Expectancy Theory

Similar to the rewarding system of motivation, the Project Manager has to set expectations among all the team members with a fair and realistic rewarding system to keep the team motivated towards their goals.

No member of the team would be interested in the rewards, if the project manager expect the team to complete their construction within half of the estimated hours.

McLeiland's Achievement Theory

Often the team like to achieve something in their career and projects, want to have power to do more within the organization besides having influence and affiliation of being part of a great project or organization with cordial relationship with everyone in the project or organization.

Not everyone in this professional world wants to keep changing their organization too often. Significant number of people look for growing with their respective organizations and it is the organization to utilize their skills and interest in its favor.

Output of the Develop Team Process

Performance Assessment

The ultimate output of the Develop Team process are the ways, the project manager keeps the team motivated to perform well and achieve their goals. A very fair and honest review of the performance is essential from the Project Manager in making his project successful and the team motivated.

In many organization, a performance appraisal system plays a very critical role in deciding the work culture and conditions. A wrongly conceived performance appraisal system might prove fatal for its operations and subsequently result in exodus of key resources. A fair and honest appraisal system turns out to be a great motivating factor.

Manage Project Team

Having planned for the team, identified them and developed the team and its capabilities is all fine. Still a Project Manager is not guaranteed of the best of the team's power, ability and delivery excellence when it comes to meeting its goals or project objectives.

A larger responsibilities lies in addressing various human resources issues that might come up during the manage & control process group of the project. In fact, the responsibilities are equally critical as developing the team's ability since a major portion of the risks rests in managing the project team and the issues among them.

Let us now look into how the Manage Project team process works with the help of the below diagram

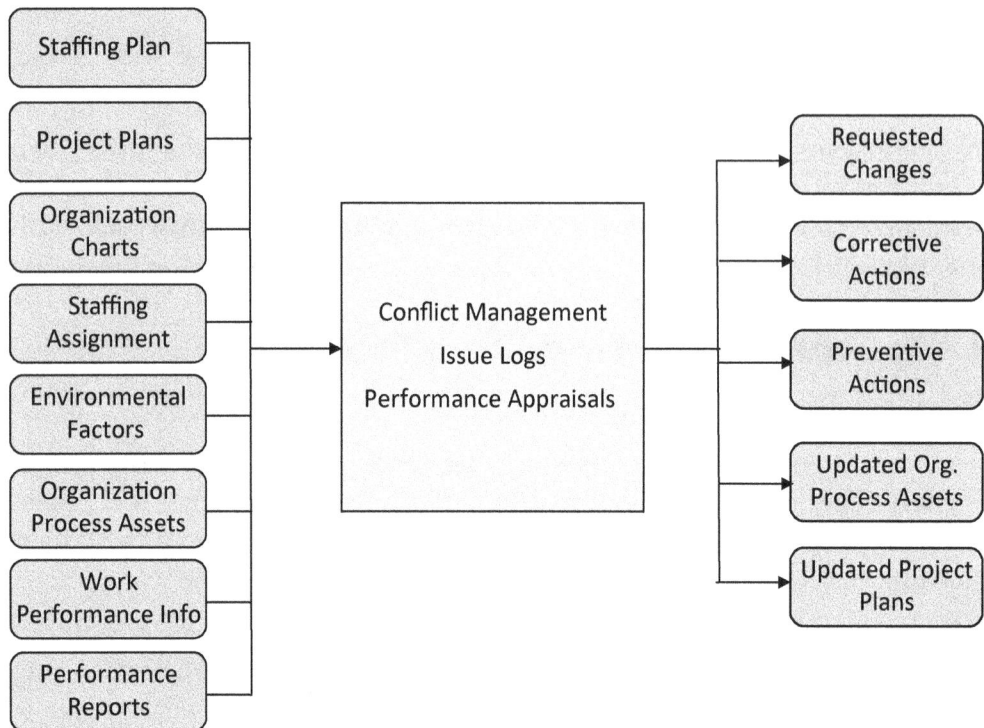

Inputs to the Manage Team Process

From the above diagram, the first six of the inputs should be familiar from the previous processes discussed in this chapter. Let us not review them again but review the remaining two inputs below

Work Performance Information

When the Project Manager is trying to get a hold of the project team, managing them and their work, having the Work Performance information comes in handy since it is a direct reflection of the team's ability to meet their goals expectation.

The format of collecting the work performance information is left to the discretion of the project manager and the other stakeholders of the project.

Performance Reports

Can you take a step back and identify the difference between the Work performance information and Performance Reports?

Well. The work performance information speaks more about the performance of the team against the work packet assigned and the efficiency in completing it. In short, it is about how the project is performing against the predetermined objectives. However, performance reports are inputs about the attitude, pro-activeness, knowledge, initiatives and various other individual qualities and traits of the team members that helps them to complete their work assignments efficiently.

The performance feedback of the individual team members are very essential information to be gathered by the Project Manager during the monitoring and controlling phase of the project.

Tools used in Managing the Team

Conflict Management

Conflict is anything that brings disenchantment or displeasure among the project team members for whatever reason. Some of the most common causes of such conflicts include resources, schedules and priorities.

Resources are those physical resources that are essentially required by the team members. Some examples of resources are tidy work space, coffee machines, copier or even office supplies that are scarce.

Besides the above reasons, there are possibilities of personality conflicts among the team members.

When there are multiple people involved in doing some activities there are bound to be discussions, expression of opinions on technical issues, differences in opinion on project related components such as cost and scope among team members since each have the right to have their own thoughts on the activities being performed.

The Project Manager can set the expectations and goals of the team with task completion dates, quality standards and work hours but he cannot set expectations for the team members' right to express their opinion.

In such a scenario, the efficiency of the Project Manager in handling conflicts between the team members becomes very critical. How does the Project Manager handle such conflicts between his team members.

Primarily, there are five recommended ways to resolve conflicts. They are

Confrontational (or Problem Solving Strategy)

Though the term 'confronting' might sounds misleading, it is indeed the best approach when it comes to problem solving. Confronting means the Project manager investigates the conflict on hand and performs own analysis of the issue to identify the root cause and fix it. Unless the project manager faces the issue and determined to get it fixed, the project may not move forward and its impact will be far reaching at times.

If the newly built home appear unstable, the best approach to take is to look at the foundation of the construction and fix the issue rather than looking at the quality of the paint.

Does it make sense?

Compromise

When two resources are tied in a conflict situation and if they decide to forge a compromise at both the ends, it means they are giving up something at either end or both. The efficiency of this strategy lies in what is being compromised. Though compromising appears to be establishing consensus among people, it should be adopted as the second option.

The primary strategy of the Project Manager should be to confront the problem and fix the root cause. Compromise can be considered only if the above strategy doesn't yield a acceptable solution for the project manager.

Smoothing

When there is serious conflict between two people, any decisions taken in urgency might prove to be counterproductive. Doesn't it?

In a project scenario, when there is conflict between two members of the team, one of the strategy adopted by Project Managers is to pretend as if there is no serious issue in existence. It might appear unacceptable for many. But, playing down such issues gives time for both the resources to keep their differences down. Once there is a return of cordiality among the team members, the Project Manager takes his view and analyze the actual issue and find a way to fix it.

Forcing (a solution)

At times, when there is no other way out to resolve a conflict, the Project Manager need to act tough and take a decision to force end the conflict. This means the Project Manager imposes his decision on both the resources.

This is not a recommended practice for the Project Manager since such forcing results in a favorable ending for one while the other resource feel being let down by the Project Manager.

Withdrawal

Assume a situation where there is a conflict between two resources that results in an unending argument between them. The Project Manager tries his best to patch up between the two resources but fails in his attempt.

Out of distress, he decide to pull himself from the conflict and stay away. What would be the outcome of such an action?

Such withdrawal strategy is not going to solve the problem, which will remain between the team members. Ultimately, it will affect the project.

This means withdrawal is not a recommended practice to resolving conflicts among the team members.

Issue Log

Issue log doesn't need to be restricted only to tracking project related issues and record the resolutions.

Issue logs can also be used to track conflicts between resources, track the progress of the resolution and record the resolution in a formal document. The issue longs can also be used to record issues encountered during the project execution. The final issue log gets updated into the Organization's process repository for future reference by other Project Manager.

Remember that this issue log is different from the delivery based issue longs in the sense that this need not be shared with the team but to be kept confidential for future references.

Performance Appraisals

Another most important tool available to manage the project team members is to carry out assessment of their performance.

In a performance appraisals, the Project Manager is expected to take a very honesty and transparent approach to analyze the performance of the resources, identify the strengths and weakness, suggestions for improvement and providing his honest feedback to the resource.

In most of the work environments the performance assessment process becomes a very critical factor that either motivates or disappoints the resources. Hence the Project Manager need to exercise extreme care and caution in what he discusses with the team members and substantiate his points with valid and acceptable facts.

Output of the Manage Team Process

As the project makes progress and the Project Manager is managing the team, there are more likelihood of him coming across many issues, conflicts and other performance related issues.

Each of these might result in updates to various plan components or how the processes are working. Every update is carried out in the project plans and the Organization's process repository is updated with the lessons learnt and issue logs. Recommended corrective actions and preventive actions are documented by the Project Manager and tracked to closure.

Human Resources Related Risks
in a Project Environment

When one speak about planning for the Human Resources and managing them, it is equally important to analyze the risks that are related to Human Resources in a project environment. Resource related risks play a very vital role in a project environment since losing a critical resource will have significant impact on the project.

Similarly, not able to identify a suitable resource for a project will impact the project schedule and cost significantly. It is always a very good practice for a Project Manager to keep looking for resource related risks of every possible kind. Attrition is inevitable in a business environment, but having the attrition when the project is at a critical phase cost a lot for the project. Similarly, non-availability of resource at a crucial phase of the project execution carry certain risks.

Motivating the resources and conflicts between resources need to be addressed with high importance. Some of the good practices that might help an organization can be listed below

Open door policy	:	Ability for the resource to express their issues and grievance without fear of retaliation
Performance assessment	:	One of the most important issues for resources is the feeling of being treated unfair by the organization. Having a transparent and fair assessment of performance and helping the resource with communicating a honest views and suggestions for improvement ideas
Motivation	:	Motivating the project team with available opportunities, rewards and help develop their skills

Considering Cultural, Ethnic, Regional and
Emotional Issues while Handling Human Resources

Some of most trivial issues that might arise while working with multiple resources from different geographies (at times within the same geographies) are related to culture, ethnicity and political issues.

For example, political developments in the other part of the globe might have influence on the resources. Same goes with cultural differences might result in conflicts or differences of opinion among project team members.

While the successful project execution should be high on the agenda of a Project Manager, he should also take a honest and unbiased view in approaching such sensitive issues and resolve issues before it begins impacting the project.

EXERCISES

Fill in the Blanks

1. _____ strategy is always recommended when it comes to resolving conflicts among project's human resources.

2. One of the motivation technique that recommends setting realistic and achievable expectations for the project resources and a reward system is called _____ .

3. The least recommended power of exercising a Project Manager's authority is _____ .

4. Since Jack is not able to identify his technical experts from the same project location, he went to hire few of his resources from another town. The team will be split between the locations but constantly interact on phone for project related updates. This team arrangement is known as _____ .

5. Janet is a project manager who has just completed with her project. In order to recognize the technical expertise of one of her resources, she decide to recommend the resource to manage a project, without realizing the resource's poor project management capability. This is an example of _____. .

True or False

*   Great project managers always insist for team's co-location, no matter what   (True/False)

*   Herzberg's Motivation theory is about setting realistic goals and expectations for the team and achieving their objective gets them great rewards   (True/False)

*   In a conflict management strategy, forcing a solution is not recommended unless it is essential   (True/False)

*   When there is a conflict of opinion between two team members over some technical issues on their activities, the project manager is not expected to involve but to stay away and let the team settle their disputes   (True/False)

*   Performance Assessment is the only outcome of the Develop Team process.   (True/False)

Match the Following

- War Room   : Setting the Do's and Don'ts for the team
- Expert Power   : Roles & Responsibility table due to his expertise
- Ground Rules   : Negotiations
- Acquiring Team strategy : Team's faith in the project manager
- RACI Chart   : Co-located Team

ANSWERS

Fill in the Blanks

1. Confrontation
2. Expectancy theory
3. Punishment Power
4. Virtual Team
5. Halo Effect

True or False

*   False
*   False
*   True
*   False
*   True

Match the Following

*   War Room : Co-located Team
*   Expert Power : Team's faith in the project manager due to his expertise
*   Ground Rules : Setting the Do's and Don'ts for the team
*   Acquiring Team strategy : Negotiations
*   RACI Chart : Roles & Responsibility table

Test Your Knowledge

1) Tom is a project manager and is leading a team of about a dozen resources. One day, he notices a couple of team members in a meeting room arguing over something. When he checks into the room, he realizes that they have some difference of opinion on certain functionality of their respective activities, which are dependent on each other. Since the discussion is getting serious, Tom decide to leave the room as he has a regular scheduled meeting.

   What strategy Tom has adopted in this situation?

   a) Confronting

   b) Withdrawal

   c) Compromise

   d) Smoothing

2) If a project manager is negotiating between his team members, who are in a conflict over some issues, to stand down and give up their opinion.

   What sort of strategy is this be called?

   a) Smoothing

   b) Confronting

   c) Withdrawal

   d) Compromise

3) Kate is a newly nominated Project Manager to take over the project and move forward. She has a team of 20 resources. In her first meeting, she informs the team that she has been handpicked by the company's Executive Director, whom she worked with in a similar project in the past and completed successfully. She also claims that the company's leadership has strong faith in her capability and has authorized her to take all decisions required and drive the project.

   What type of authority she is exercising here?

   a) Referent Power

   b) Legitimate Power

   c) Punishment Power

   d) Reward power

4) Stewart is a project manager for his engineering design project and has a team of 12 engineers part of his team. Due to his bad experience with his previous project team, he is not believing his current team much and validate their feedbacks, opinions and comments with other experts before accepting or turning it down.

What kind of approach is he following?

a) Herzberg Motivation Theory

b) Expectancy Theory

c) McLeiland's Achievement Theory

d) McGregor's Theory X & Theory Y

5) The Production Management project of ABC Motors is planning to produce a specialized earth moving machinery of world scale and the team of 50 are working hard at the production shop. Since the team is based together, there are no dearth of confrontation, discussions, debates, expressing individual's opinion and arguments. The work is progressing as per the plan but there are chaotic situation at times that makes their senior leadership wonder what is going on with the production team.

What would you call this situation as?

a) Healthy work environment

b) Halo Effect

c) War Room

d) Virtual team

6. Peter is a member of a software development project. He and his manager go out for lunch on a Friday and happen to meet a friend at the restaurant. During their discussion, his friend asked him about his job and responsibilities. As he claimed himself as a senior member of his project, he was asked where does he stand in his organization in terms of position. Peter is not able to give a clear answer to his friend.

Why is Peter having trouble in defining his position in the organization?

a) Peter is honest worker and not having enough time to pay attention to this

b) His manager hasn't shared the organization chart that he prepared for the project

c) Peter doesn't want to reveal his position to his friend

d) None of the above

7. Sarah is the newly nominated Project Manager of a project that is planning to build a massive ship for a overseas customer. She has graduated in mechanical engineering from a very reputed university. Since this project is strategically very important for her organization, they wanted to bring in Sarah and use her expertise in getting this project completed. The organization is expecting to secure several other similar project from that part of the world.

Sarah has setup her team and grouped technicians and construction workers based on their expertise and experience. In her meeting with the team, she asked her team members not to hesitate approach her, if they are stuck in any technical issues as she has executed similar projects in the past and can try her best to answer their question.

How do you describe Sarah's approach to the project?

a) She is trying to show herself as an expert for own benefits

b) She is a team player and want to keep the team motivated

c) She asked her team to approach her only as a last option.

d) She is using expert power as a motivation technique.

8. Sam has been managing his project since a year ago and the team has been doing great work. However, the team's productivity seems to have gone down as the team is feeling increasingly unsecure about their position in the organization. The team has serious concerns about the annual raise they received four months ago. During one of the meeting with his team members, Sam observed that the team feels the organization is trying to remove some of them and using its policies to brand them as not efficient.

What could be the reason behind this insecure feeling of the team?

a) The team is not very impressed with the way their annual performance assessment was conducted by Sam.

b) The team's concern is unjustified and Sam should not take it seriously

c) Team members are trying to cover-up their delivery failures

d) Sam should not take it seriously as he is just enacting company's policy in everything he does.

9. Nominating team members for a professional development and leadership training is part of

a) Organization's strategy to identify suitable leaders

b) Organization trying to save hiring cost and look for their next PM from within

c) Motivation technique

d) To compensate for their poor performance assessments

10. What is the most common causes of conflicts in a project environment?

    a) Resources, priorities and schedules

    b) Someone's ego clash

    c) Unsatisfied performance assessment & rating

    d) Unsatisfied with raise given

11. Sylvia is a very efficient project resources, who can successfully complete any assignment given to her. She has been on the organization's list of technical expert in her area . She has been assigned to a high profile project that has a huge potential to grow and bring more dollars to her company. She has been doing very well to assist the team with her technical expertise. Bill is her project manager. In one of the team meetings, there was a serious discussion about meeting the scope requirements among team members and Bill. During the course of the discussion, Bill is upset and frustrated with Sylvia's remarks on certain technical issue. In order to set the expectations straight, Bill asks Sylvia not to step out of her role and decide on schedule, which is his responsibility to plan. Both Bill and Sylvia were upset about each other for the rest of the meeting. The next day, Sylvia approached her Technical Manager to move her to another project since she feel the current project environment is not very impressive. What could have convinced Sylvia to stay with her current project?

    a) A better role, raise and authority over the project

    b) She must have authority to take important decisions.

    c) Bill should have called Sylvia for a one-one meeting to express his displeasure and frustration over her remarks rather than expressing it in front of all the team members.

    d) Sylvia may not be interested to work with Bill due to his arrogant outburst in the team meeting.

12. Nominating a team member as Organization's Star of the Month program is part of

    a) Rewards & Recognition technique

    b) Team building activity

    c) Regular work of a project manager

    d) Meet the nomination target for the program manager

13. A project manager cannot enforce any of his motivation technique in his project in a functional organization. This is because
    a) There is no need to motivate since it is a functional organization
    b) it is Human Resources group's responsibility
    c) The team do not report to the Project Manager
    d) Team is well motivated by their Functional Manager

14. Janice is a project manager and has about 24 members in her team working on construction activities. During a regular meeting with her team, she finds two members of the team arguing on certain technical issues. As the members keep arguing and never ending, she find that the time is running out to come to a conclusion and cannot wait for an understanding. She finally decide to instruct both the members to work according to her instruction to be sent by an email shortly after this meeting.

    What approach Janice has taken to address this conflict?
    a) Confrontation
    b) Forcing
    c) Withdraw
    d) Compromise

15. You have been nominated as the project manager of a life sciences project that involves collecting analysis data from different part of the world. Your organization is funding the project and has given you the authority to identify the team and take the project further. Since the project objective involve studies conducted around the world, you decide to setup virtual team and planning to engage several voluntary organization, who have been engaging in similar studies in the past. You just started working with these organization now.

    Which process are you engaged in now?
    a) Human Resource Planning
    b) Manage Project Team
    c) Acquire Project Team
    d) Develop Project Team

16. **A War room is**

    a) where project decisions are made by the project manager and his stakeholder

    b) a room where the project managers meet their team members to conduct their performance assessment process

    c) A room where conflicts are resolved

    d) None of the above

17. **A 'Halo Effect' is**

    a) An organization promoting someone as a project manager, because they are good technically.

    b) An impact resulted by poor rating given to a team member

    c) Very healthy project environment motivated by a very understanding manager

    d) Result of heavy attrition in the project team

18. **In the middle of the project execution, Robert found a lot of confusion among his team members over who should do what. This type of situation is the result of**

    a) Everyone wants to outsmart others

    b) there is no Roles & Responsibilities defined by Robert

    c) Such confusions are common in any project environment

    d) Poor human resource planning

19. **What among the below list BEST describes a motivation technique**

    a) Nominating someone for a leadership training

    b) Gift voucher in appreciation of excellence in performance

    c) Nominating to a seminar that takes place in another town

    d) All of the above

20. **When Steve is not able to make two of his team members arrive at an understanding, he lets them discuss and sort the issue among themselves. This is an example of**

    a) Forcing

    b) Withdrawal

    c) Confronting

    d) Compromise

21. You are a project manager working on a telecommunication project. A part of the work has been subcontracted to a vendor, who has deployed 20 of his resources to work on this project. The team and their work is being managed by another project manager. When you hear about a conflict with the vendor's team, your responsibility as project manager is

    a) confront

    b) compromise

    c) minimal

    d) withdrawal

22. All of the below listed are responsibility of a Project Manager EXCEPT

    a) Preparing Organization chart

    b) Hiring someone for the company

    c) Developing team

    d) Resolving conflicts

23. The highest level of authority, a project manager can expect in the following type of organization

    a) Projectized

    b) Functional

    c) Matrix

    d) All of the above

24. Cindy is assigned as the project manager and is now in the process of planning for her team. In her previous project, the teams were based at four different locations and this made difficult for Cindy to handle some of her team management responsibilities. Having learnt lessons from the earlier project, Cindy has decided to set expectations for the team. This is an example of

    a) Team building

    b) Motivation

    c) Ground Rules

    d) Healthy work environment

25. Brenda is managing a large telecommunication project, that has over 100 members and several dozen stakeholders, who are directly or indirectly being impacted by her project. The project budget runs into multimillion dollars and this makes the project very highly visible and important for her organization. During one of her regular meetings with her senior management, the Executive Director of the organization is not able to understand the Roles & Responsibility of each of the project stakeholders and the project team. So, he asks Brenda to prepare a Roles and Responsibility chart and share with the senior management.

What document would help define the Roles & Responsibilities in a project?

a) RACI Chart

b) Organization Chart

c) Staffing Plan

d) Resource Management Plan

ANSWERS

1. **Answer: B**

    Justification: Withdrawal is one of the conflict management technique. As a project manager, withdrawing from a situation of this type is not recommended, especially when it involves situations about the manager's own project. At times, the topic being argued may not be important for the project manager, but in such case, smoothing a situation so as to buy time to seek a resolution be recommended. Having a conflicting situation among the team members is a risk for any project, that require a plan of action.

2. **Answer: D**

    Justification : Either the project manager is compromising or have one of the team member to compromise, both of these involve someone giving up something they have been insisting for long. Compromising is not a recommended practice for a project manager, however if the problem solving do not work, a project manager can resort to other option such as compromising.

3. **Answer: A**

    Justification: A referent power is when someone is using others' name or position to assert their authority within a project environment. Though this is not a forbidden authority level, it is not the very best approach in a professional environment. In this question, Kate is trying to assert her position and the influence in order to get complete cooperation and support from her team during the term of the project.

4. **Answer: D**

    Justification: It is very normal for different project managers to have different approach when it comes to managing their teams. Type X managers have the tendency not to trust their team but take all the decisions themselves and micromanage their project. On the contrary Type Y managers have faith in their team and let the team work independently, validate their results and approach their project managers only when some issues are important or need assistance.

5. **Answer: C**

    Justification: One problem arising out of teams co-located is such chaotic scenes, though it is not very common and with every organization. When people tend to work together at the same location, there are bound to be several discussions, exchange of information, expression of opinion and so on. A project manager need to handle all of these wisely to prevent them become a risk. Setting up ground rules for the team would help overcome such issues to some extent.

6. **Answer: B**

    Justification: One of the important task of a project manager, when handling the human resources planning process, is to prepare an organization chart and share it among the stakeholders and the team. This will help understand the hierarchical structure of the project performing organization besides the team to be aware of where they stand in the organization. At times, such organization charts help understand the authority and escalation points, whenever needed.

7. **Answer: D**

    Justification: The best option for a project manager to use their authority is to bring the confidence among the team with their knowledge and ability to drive the project. In this case, Sarah has expertise and experience in the technical area of her project and might have used the expertise in setting the scope and customer expectations. It becomes her responsibility to support the team on technical issues, whenever required. From the narration of the situation, it appears her to be using her power effectively for the benefit of the project.

8. **Answer: A**

    Justification: A performance assessment is one of a critical tool that helps develop a team and keep them motivated. Though such assessment helps the organization identify superior performances and reward them appropriately, any poor handling of such assessments would backfire on the organization with every staff losing faith in the organization's policy, transparency and openness. Even if there is a need to provide negative feedback to any of the team member, it has to be done with supporting evidence and facts to reduce the negative impact on the staff and the team.

9. **Answer: C**

    Justification: Motivating the team can be done in several ways, depending on the organization's policies and the choice of the project managers. The same organization can have different ways of rewarding their super performances. In general, offering raises and cash rewards are known motivating techniques. Besides them, nominating people to training and career development programs help the team stay motivated and have increased confidence in their organization about people care.

10. **Answer: A**

    Justification: Most or all of the conflicts in a project involve the resources. Be it ego clashes or dissatisfied with project decisions, a conflict has negative impact of different magnitudes in different situations. Some of the project related conflicts include unrealistic schedule or lack of rewards and benefits.

11. **Answer: C**

    Justification: Handling human resources is not very easy but very challenging. Everyone have their own priority, expectations and preference. In case of disagreements over some remarks or decisions made, it is always a better idea to schedule a one-one meeting to discuss the issue and sort things out. Expressing in front of the rest of the team will prove fatal for the project. In this case, Sylvia is very efficient and intelligent team member and Bill should have considered that as a risk before expressing his frustration in front of the team. A one-one discussion could have caused lesser or no damage to the project.

12. **Answer: A**

    Justification: As explained earlier, every organization has its own way of rewarding and recognizing talents within the organization to keep their staff motivated. Programs such as 'Star of the Month' can be a coveted recognition within the organization, which is effectively utilized by this project manager to recognize someone's hard work.

13. **Answer: C**

    Justification: The problem while working in a Functional Organization is very limited power to the project manager. The PM do not own the project or the team. They need not pick or release their teams. They just do administrative work in most projects. Thus it becomes the responsibility of the functional manager to manage the team and their needs, which includes keeping the team motivated throughout the phase of the project.

14. **Answer: B**

    Justification: In this situation, what Janice doing is forcing a decision on her team members. She gave chance to her team members to come to a consensus on a technical issue and waited for their decision. When such a consensus do not forthcoming, it is natural for a project manager to take a decision in order to have the project moving. Though forcing a decision is not such a bad idea in a project environment, it is not a very good idea either. A project manager should adopt to this strategy only as the last option.

15. **Answer: C**

    Justification: In this question, you are in the process of identifying the team members and their work location details. This means, you are in the project planning phase. Negotiations are part of the acquire team process.

16. Answer: D

Justification: A team, which is co-located in the same location is called a war room. In general, wherever the team is co-located there are bound to be plenty of exchange of opinions, ideas, data and discussions taking place. The advantage of a co-located team is better control over the team and easier access to people.

17. Answer: A

Justification: As part of a motivation and rewarding technique, there are some organization which promote some of their staff to manage projects. The reason : they are technically efficient and good. Such strategy wouldn't work all the time, since these employees lack management skills even if they can be technically good. Such decisions cause more harm to these staff than doing good, since they might even potentially fail in their new roles.

18. Answer: B

Justification: As part of the project planning, Robert should have prepared a Roles & Responsibilities charter that clearly defines the roles, responsibilities and boundaries of all the stakeholders. A RACI chart is an example of such Roles & Responsibilities charter.

19. Answer: D

Justification: Cash rewards, offer towards career development, nomination to training programs, providing chances to staff to showcase their knowledge in the form of seminars, gift vouchers, movie tickets, bonus, wage raise and letter of appreciation are some of the examples of keeping the team members motivated.

20. Answer: B

Justification: Whenever some conflict surfaces among project team members, it becomes the responsibility of the project manager to find a solution. Such finding solution can should confrontation, which means understanding the problem and solving it. What Steve has done in this situation is, since he is not able to solve the problem, he walks away and force the responsibility of solving the issues on the team members. This is not a commonly recommended practice.

21. Answer: C

Justification: The situation and the problem may appear trivial but is possible when working with vendors. In this case, the project has two managers and a part of the work is procured from a vendor. This means the responsibility of managing the team and delivery rests with the vendor. You cannot resolve the conflicts, since the team do not report to you. Your operational jurisdiction may be limited to your own team and with the project manager of the vendor. However, such a tricky situation is a risk for you, which need to be addressed and handled by you.

22. **Answer: B**

    Justification: The operational boundary of a project manager is mostly limited to his project and its objectives. There is no necessity for the project manager to be involved in the hiring process for his organization. The scope of such hiring doesn't fall within the scope of his project. IT is true that most organizations engage their own technical and managerial staff to identify talent from the market for future deployment. In this situation, we are talking about the project scope and the manager's responsibility alone.

23. **Answer: A**

    Justification: Except in a Projectized organization, the project managers cannot expect complete level of authority for themselves elsewhere. They have the least level of authority in a functional and weak matrix organizations. In a balanced and strong matrix, they share their authority with the functional managers.

24. **Answer: C**

    Justification : Establishing ground rules is a recommended practice for a project manager since it sets the expectations in the initial stages of the project and the team is well aware of their responsibilities and boundaries. Such ground rules are expected to be fair and acceptable to everyone in the team, since the primary goal of the rules is the smooth execution of the project. Planning for the project processes is a well known example of such ground rules, since the manager defines the plan for each components in advance.

25. **Answer: A**

    Justification: A RACI Chart is a Responsibility Assignment Matrix in a project that is to be prepared and shared with all the stakeholders of a project in the project planning phase. The RACI Chart stands for *Responsibility, Accountability, Consulted* and *Informed*. A RACI Chart is especially useful in clarifying roles and responsibilities in cross-functional/departmental projects and processes.

This page is intentionally left blank

This page is intentionally left blank

Project Communication Management

Objectives

At the end of the Communication Management chapter, you should be able to:

- understand how the managing stakeholder process works
- understand the importance of communication in a professional environment
- different types of communications taking place in a business
- understand the importance of communication mode, channels and feedback
- differentiate between verbal and non-verbal communication
- differentiate between formal and informal communication
- understand the significance of various communication documents
- realize the importance of information distribution, control communication process.

The Power of Communication

Have you ever thought, what it would have been, if no communication takes place anywhere around you ever? Have you ever imagined, how you would feel if you happen to watch a movie, that doesn't have a single conversation from start to finish?

Certainly, you never want to be there? Would you?

In today's world, communication has become the lifeline of humans and the world moving and a happening place.

Do you think, this above statement is exaggerated?

However, none will like if too much of communication or irrelevant and senseless communication takes place for no reason. Similarly, communication is expected to take place between people that are appropriate and in right quantity at the right time can make miracles. Often, medium of communication and quality of the exchanged information has more influence than the quantity of the communication.

To make the learning on communication little more interesting, let us begin with an example of a possible real life situation

It was a Friday night. Joe and his wife, Laura, had just gotten into their third argument of the day and were now giving each other the silent treatment, vowing not to be the first one to speak to the other.

However, at bedtime, Joe realized that he would need his wife, who always woke up at 4:30 am to wake him at 5:00 am for golf with his friends. Not wanting to lose the battle of wills, Joe wrote on a piece of paper,

"Laura, please wake me at 5:00 am."

The next morning, Joe woke up at 9:00 am, having missed the golf game with his friends. Furious, he was about to go and see why his wife hadn't woken him, when he noticed a piece of paper on the bedside table.

It read,
"Joe, its 5:00 am. Wake up."

If you are in the situation as that of Joe, how would have felt or reacted to this.

In the above, who is at fault? Laura or Joe? What could have gone wrong then?

In short, neither of them are right or wrong. It was poor handling of communication requirement between each other, especially when the need is important.

In real life, such experiences might be considered a very good piece of humor. However, in a business critical environment, communication plays a very vital role and a moving force driving the business every day. Not only the communication is important, but where, when, how and what is being communicated becomes even more critical.

Assume you are managing a large event management project for your organization. The event is given topmost priority by your senior management, since the event will open new avenues of opportunities and scope for expansion. In addition, the event has gained enormous publicity in the local town since a popular Hollywood artist is participating.

Considering the sensitivity and importance of the event, your organization has handed over the responsibility to you and asked you to manage the whole event from start to finish.

As a project manager, the management looks at you for any information and status of the event. This makes the communication very critical for the organization. Whatever you provide as information becomes the deciding factor for the management to know the status of the event as well as your managerial skills.

Let us now move on.

How Important is Communication to a Project?

The Project Management Institute (PMI), the apex body of the Project Management professionals around the world, says Project Managers spend over 90% of their time in communication. A communication need not be talking over phone or attending to some meetings. Anything that involves exchange of information or data is considered a communication. A communication involves more than one person, wherein a sender conveys some information in an encoded form. The other people decode the message and understand. In every communication a media is essential thru which message is transmitted.

Is it confusing?

Take the case of a business presentation in the corporate world. You are ready with your colorful presentation with good amount of details about your project. You have a group of people sitting in the conference room and you are with your computer and the projector in front of you. In this case, You are the sender and the rest of the audience are the receivers. The computer, presentation and the projector are the media, that are used to carry the message. When you begin speaking your words get encoded and reaches the audience, where it gets decoded and reaches the audience, who understand what you are trying to present in the meeting.

Does it make sense?

Managing Communication Vs. Stakeholders

If you are able to understand the relationship between the communication requirement and the stakeholders management in a project environment, it will help you understand a lot more about managing projects.

Let us consider an example now. You are working on a project that has objective to build an airport in a city. As part of project planning, you are working on communication management planning. You begin with identifying people, who are going to be part of your project. This includes anyone, who are directly or indirectly impacted by the execution of the project. They are called Stakeholders. A Stakeholder need not be individuals but can also be a department or larger group such as community, which is represented by an association or authority.

After identifying the list of people or groups, you work on the communication requirements such as what need to be communicated, when, frequency of the communication and mode of communication. Once all of these details are finalized, what you will be having is a plan that helps manage the stakeholders and their communication requirements?

In a normal project environment such as this airport project, the key stakeholders can be the project manager, project team, project sponsor, city council, vendors and anyone who are directly or indirectly impacted by the project. However, it is the project manager and the team that is directly working on the project on a daily basis. The rest of the stakeholders have limited role to play in the daily activities of the project team. It is the responsibility of the project manager to keep them updated with progress, issues, risks and delays in the project.

How does a project manager achieve these information requirements of all the stakeholders?

The obvious tool that helps the project manager is the communication. Having this mind, is it appropriate to call Communication Management as managing the stakeholders and their communication requirements?

Without the involvement of stakeholders, a communication management plan can be only discussing about communication channels and techniques. So, whenever you speak about communication, always remember the stakeholders. In other words, communication and stakeholders are inseparable.

Is it unfair to say so?

Does everyone who are involved in some form of communication with the project manager or team be called Stakeholders?

It depends on their role and what is being communicated between them.

If a project team member has some technical issues to be clarified and is engaged in a discussion with a technical team or specialist, then this team or specialist is not considered a stakeholder since their involvement is not specific to the project execution but only limited to providing some information to a project team member.

However, if there is an exchange of information or data between team member, who is trying to get their work reviewed by a quality control group, then the quality group or its representative is considered a stakeholder of the project.

I am sure, you are able to understand the boundaries of communication.

Where Does Communication Happen in a Project

Can you answer this question from your knowledge and understanding of the project management?

If you had answered "everywhere from start to end," you are perfectly correct.

Communication is not restricted only to the Planning process group or while preparing Communication Plan. In every phase of the project communication takes place in one way or the other. Preparing a Project Charter is one form of communication, sharing it with others is another. Similarly, preparing a Human Resource Plan is a documented communication that is exchanged between stakeholders.

Likewise, everything that the Project Manager or Team involves is one or the other form of communication something between stakeholders. In other words, whenever there is exchange of some information happens, that is called communication.

What are Different Types of Communication?

Whenever you speak about communication remember the two categories of communications.

• Formal communication

• Informal communication.

There are several forms of communications take place in the business and personal world. Some of the examples are body languages, signs and so on. These are classified as informal communication. We will be knowing more on them later in this chapter.

What are the Differences Between Them?

A formal communication is mostly used in business environment. Use of business language, following communication protocols and etiquettes are all form part of such formal communication. It is strongly recommended when you are interacting with the senior leaders of your own organization or with any of your customers. Sufficient amount of data and justification in a well-documented mode is to be shared with supporting answers to any question that may be raised.

Informal communication is a casual interaction and a way to exchange information. When I say casual communication it doesn't mean sharing incorrect information. Take the case of you want to speak to one of your co-worker working in another department, whom you meet over lunch often or take a walk around. When you speak to him you do not need to be too formal in discussions. You can still be his friend while getting the response that you are after.

Is it clear?

Components of Communication Process

Communication between two sources involves several components. Let us take the case of a verbal communication.

To have a sensible verbal communication take place, what are all you need?

You require two people to communicate. You need something to share, communication channel, mode of transmission. Is that all? Let us look at the below list for further information on these

Sender : Sender is the person who initiates a conversation with another person on some specific subject. The subject may be in the form of a question or exchange of information supported by some data. Any sort of exchange of information is communication, as we have seen earlier in this chapter.

Receiver : Receiver is another person who is going to receive the information conveyed by the sender. The receiving information may be a question or some clarification.

Channel : A communication channel may be anything that helps the conversation or exchange of information takes place. It may be a telephone instrument, in-person conversation, a

		meeting or an email. The channel aides the communication to be happening and complete.
Encoding	:	When a speaker wants to convey something to the receiver the message gets encoded into an audible form and travels to the receiver. The encoding may be in any form. Unless the encoding takes place, the receiver cannot receive the message.
Decoding	:	The opposite of encoding is the decoding. When the receiver is ready to receive the message conveyed by the speaker, the encoded message is decoded and reaches the receiver in the form of an understandable message.
Feedback	:	A feedback is a response from the receiver who receives a decoded message from the sender or speaker. Assume you attending a meeting with your boss to discuss some issues in your project. He has many questions or observations about the progress you have been making. Whenever he speaks on certain points, you are expected to react to it as and when it requires. A feedback need not be in the form of a lengthy answer but a single word or even nodding head is one form of feedback. Unless there is a feedback from your end, the entire conversation is not going to be effective.
Noise	:	Noise is some form of disturbance that happens between communications.

Communication Management Process

Like every other knowledge area, communication management requires planning as well. One may wonder, what is there to plan for communication. Certainly it does require planning. A plan on how you are planning to handle the communication, channels, protocols and what is going to be shared between stakeholders.

Communication planning involves establishing a communication management plan, information distribution, Control communication and Managing Stakeholders.

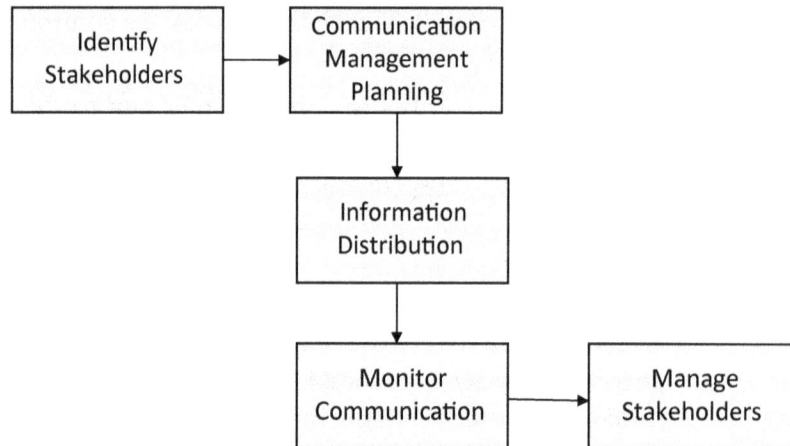

The above diagram is pretty much self-descriptive. The Project Manager has the responsibility to distribute the project related information during the execution phase, while the team is busy in the project execution.

Similarly, managing changes, communication and project performance are the Project Manager's primary task during the Monitoring and Control phase of the project. Unlike many other components, Communication has its influence right from the beginning of the project phase till its closure.

Does it make sense?

Identify Stakeholders

If you are asked to name the most critical activity in a project management, what would you choose?

I wouldn't hesitate to say Identifying stakeholders decide the fate of the entire project and its success. We had already seen the importance of identifying stakeholders and understanding their requirements. Let us not repeat them again here. However, it would be a good idea to understand how the stakeholder identification process works. Let us take a look at the diagram below

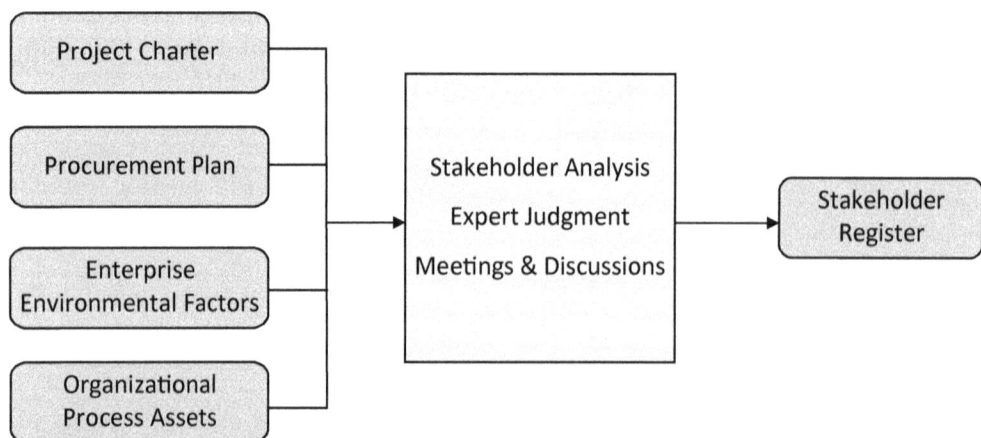

Inputs of Identify Stakeholder Process

As we have understood already, the best phase to identify the stakeholders is in the very beginning of the project. Since the project is in its initial stage, there are most unlikely to be much inputs and details about the project and its objectives. In most situations, the project manager will end up with just a *project charter* as input. However, the project charter should be a good starting point for the project manager as the project charter gives an overall objective of the project and key stakeholders that will be involved in the project.

Though it is not mandatory to have Procurement Plan as an input in identifying stakeholders, there might be decisions made in the initial stages of the process about outsourcing certain components or services to external vendors. In such eventuality, having a procurement plan decision might be of good help in identifying key stakeholders from the vendor end.

Does this justify the need to focus on the procurement planning in the very initial stages of the project?

As narrated earlier, the identification of stakeholders is done in the very beginning of the project. If a part of the project is outsourced through a procurement contract, how could a project manager identify all the stakeholders at the vendor end, especially when the scope is unknown yet?

This situation might be tricky for the project manager, especially if the procurement contract is NOT a fixed price bid.

However, the primary objective of the identify stakeholder process is to collect the requirements of the customer. Thus, having key stakeholders would suffice for the project manager that will facilitate the requirements understanding.

Enterprise Environmental Factors and *Organization's process assets* are standard inputs to the Stakeholder identification process as they help the project manager to understand the organization's policy and practice with respect to stakeholder management process. At times, referring to stakeholder registers of projects executed in the past might help the project manager with vital inputs.

Tools used in Identify Stakeholder Process

The most important tool that will help complete the identify stakeholders process is the use of *meetings and discussions* with the customer organization that will help understand the primary beneficiaries and those groups that will be directly or indirectly affected by the execution of the project. There is no specific tool that will automatically help pinpoint the stakeholders. Only extensive communication and meetings help.

Stakeholders Analysis is another useful tool that help manage the stakeholders. One of the important factor to be considered as part of this analysis is to identify the power and influence of the identified stakeholders, that might positively or negatively affect the project. Similarly, it is also a good idea to identify those stakeholders that will approve the acceptance of the delivered project.

Expert Judgment is an ever helpful tool that will seek opinions from experts about stakeholder identification and managing them.

Output of Identify Stakeholder Process

The single output of the identify stakeholder process is the *Stakeholder register*.

Similar to the Risk Register, the stakeholder register lists all the identified stakeholders, their role in the organization, level of authority and their influence on the project It would be always a good idea to share the identified stakeholder list with the customer and get their concurrence on the identified list.

Unless the stakeholders are completely identified, the project manager is not advised to proceed with the communication planning, as the communication plan uses the stakeholder information extensively to establish communication links, protocols besides the individual communication requirements.

Communication Management Planning

As explained earlier, the project manager plans on how the communication is going to be handled in the project. It is done in the communication management planning process. An uncontrolled communication might result in chaotic situation in the project. It might derail the very purpose and objective of executing the project itself.

Let us now understand how the communication management planning is done. Take a look at the below diagram to know what goes in and what comes out of the communication management planning process.

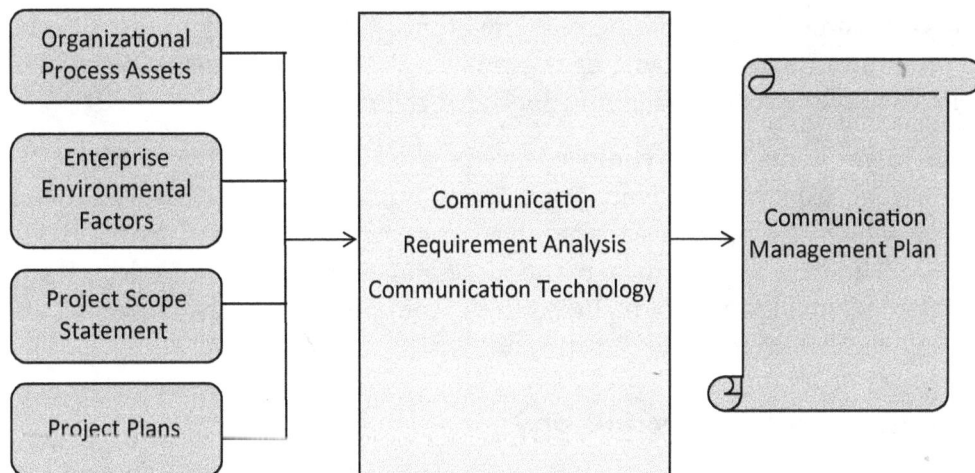

```
┌──────────────┐
│ Organizational│
│ Process Assets│──┐
└──────────────┘  │
                  │    ┌────────────────────────┐      ┌──────────────────┐
┌──────────────┐  │    │                        │      │                  │
│  Enterprise  │  │    │     Communication       │      │  Communication   │
│ Environmental│──┤──► │  Requirement Analysis    │ ──► │ Management Plan  │
│   Factors    │  │    │                          │      │                  │
└──────────────┘  │    │ Communication Technology │      │                  │
                  │    │                          │      └──────────────────┘
┌──────────────┐  │    └────────────────────────┘
│ Project Scope│  │
│  Statement   │──┤
└──────────────┘  │
                  │
┌──────────────┐  │
│ Project Plans│──┘
└──────────────┘
```

In the above diagram, the *Organizational Process assets* have the communication management plan that were created as part of the earlier projects executed by the performing organization. This historical information would help the Project Manager to refer and define the communication plan as detailed and accurate as possible. I would still recommend you to validate with your customers, if they have any special communication requirements. Communication requirements vary significantly between customers and projects.

Enterprise Environmental Factors contains the Organizational strategy with respect to Project Management methodologies. An example is defining the company policy on communication protocols while executing the projects. At times, such protocols would help clarity on responsibility as well. In some organizations, project managers are expected to route important communication to senior leadership of the customers through their senior leaders.

The *Project Scope* helps understand the communication needs of the team. In addition, the project scope sets the objective of the project and the team. For example, if the project scope speaks about carrying out a testing and review activities by specialized teams such as test teams or Quality group, these two groups become stakeholders of the project and need to be included in the communication management plan.

Project Management Plans help understand the various communication needs as required and defined in these plans. For example, the quality management plan narrates how the quality planning is going to be managed and this subsequently results in some form of communications. Same goes with Human Resource plan and so on.

Tools used in Communication Management Plan

Communication Requirement Analysis

There are no tailor-made tool available that helps the Project manager define the communication requirement of the project. The only way to identify the communication requirement of the project is through extensive discussion with each of the stakeholders and analyzing their needs.

One might tend to get confused about this tool. The Project Managers knowledge, expertise on identifying the communication methodologies comes very handy in defining the communication management plan. Identifying all the stakeholders is very critical in the successful execution of the project. If any of the stakeholders are not included in the communication, the impact would be anywhere from major to catastrophe.

Communications Technology

A communication technology is how you want to pass the communication to every stakeholder of your project. Often you might realize that not all the communication need to be sent to every stakeholders. This might overwhelm them besides wasting their time with irrelevant information. So, having a communication technology helps in defining the communication plan and who should receive what.

Some possible communication technology includes having all the communication uploaded in a website or creating a project repository to have all project resources and communication. Can you able to think of any other possible communication technology from your project experience? Use the below box to list them down.

Formal Verbal

When you meet your clients or any senior leaders from your own organization, it is always recommended to use the formal verbal communication supported by documents, presentations and facts. At no point of time use of casual communication is recommended.

Some examples of formal verbal communication is addressing a meeting of stakeholders and client leadership. In short, anything that reaches out to the customers or your senior leadership can be formal verbal communication.

Formal Written

Some examples of formal written communication are PowerPoint presentations, project proposals, legal documents, presenting papers in seminars, meeting minutes, status reports and project management plans.

These documents are prepared with carefully chosen words and language that convey the right and required information to all the recipients with the right tone. A formal written communication has specific language and terms to be used. No casual words or languages are ever used in a formal written communication. A formal written communication can take place within the project itself, such as status reports and meeting minutes.

Can you list known examples of formal written and verbal communication methodologies in the boxes given below?

Formal Verbal	Formal Written

Some of the examples, I can think of are listed below. You may validate your list with mine

Formal Verbal	Formal Written
Press conferences and Corporate communication	Business presentation or company performance report
Status meetings	Test plans and strategies
Addressing seminars	Project forecast reports
Discussion on project risks in a team meeting	Contract documents
Sharing project status and important communication to stakeholders or to the senior leadership	Important project documents such as assumptions, risks and watch lists

Informal Verbal

An informal verbal communication is something wherein you meet your co-worker at his desk to get some questions answered or issues addressed. Such meetings are not planned and no minutes are to be captured to circulate. At times you might meet a member of another team, whose work has dependency on yours, and discuss some emergency fixes that may be required.

Similarly, telephonic conversation with another team member to resolve a technical issue falls under informal verbal communication methodology.

Informal Written

Similar to informal verbal communication, informal written communication is an informal email without adopting to much of the email etiquettes. Such informal written communication takes place between team members working on the same project or with other projects. In an informal written communication etiquettes are not required to be stressed.

As per the Project Management Institute, such informal communication, both verbal and written, works effectively within the same organization and among team members. While interacting with customers or leadership, it is always strongly recommended to use formal verbal and written communication methodologies.

Can you list known examples of Informal written and verbal communication methodologies in the boxes given below?

Informal Verbal	Informal Written

I have listed down few examples of informal communication that are possible in a real life environment. These are samples, but you can verify your understanding of the informal communication with the list below

Informal Verbal	Informal Written
Discussing project related stuff with colleagues over a Friday lunch	Responding to a clarification request of a teammate
Calling another team member to get clarification on a test plan	Forwarding emails with technical details to the rest of the team
Proposing a meeting of the team to discuss important issues	Seeking input from a stakeholder while preparing a legal document
Discussing new risks with the project manager	Sharing the details of the new risk with the rest of the team

Non-Verbal Communication

Not all times, you need to speak or write something to communicate your thoughts or ideas to others. Too often, your body language and facial gestures convey the message to others. If you have you noticed, when someone is talking in a television interviews, the camera focuses on their facial expressions or hand gestures too often. The significance of doing this is to show to the viewers on the thinking of the speaker.

Similarly, when you are engaged in a meeting or discussion with your customers, your gestures convey a lot more than what your voice or presentation does. In fact, your gestures and body language conveys the messages clearer than your voice.

Doesn't it sound interesting?

Paralingual Communication

A paralingual communication is somewhat similar to non-verbal communication. The tone and modulation in voice have their significance during conversations. They convey the speaker's understanding and thoughts on the subject of discussion.

When you are attending a stakeholders meeting and you hearing serious issues and concerns from one of the stakeholder about the progress of your project, it naturally rings an alarm bell for you. This nervousness of yours is reflected in your tone and pitch of your voice when responding back. Such changes in tone are capable of conveying your real thought about the issues being discussed.

Feedback

One of the best way to make a communication process meaningful and sensible is by providing feedback. Feedback doesn't necessarily mean writing an email. It is an indication of active listening on the part of the people engaged in a conversation. When a speaker is conveying some inputs or updates in a meeting of stakeholders, it cannot be a one-way communication. If it is so, it will benefit none. The speaker will keep talking and he may not have any idea whether his speech was making any sense to anyone in the meeting.

Feedback can be even nodding head or saying a simple "Ok" or asking some questions whenever the listener feels as appropriate.

Output of Information Distribution

Updated Organizational Process Repository

You will not be generating any specific report as part of the information distribution. In other words, an Information distribution process is a way to exchange information to all the stakeholders of your project, who are directly or indirectly impacted by its execution. However, your experience and data in this project is recorded in your Organization's process repository for future reference.

Requested Changes

Requested changes is another output of the information distribution process. Can you step back and think why this is an output of Information distribution process?

The reason is, during the planning phase of your project, you obtain a sign off on all the plan components from the stakeholders. Any updates to the planned processes needs to be routed in the form of changes. When you carry out changes in your project and communicate the updates to the stakeholders, you are expected to supplement such communication along with the source of the changes. Hence, it becomes quite natural to have the requested changes as an output of the information distribution process.

Monitor Communication Process

As we are now done with finalizing the processes of Communication Management Planning and Information Distribution, it is now time we go ahead with distributing the performance reports. The output of the Execution phase becomes the input for this Control Communications process. The primary reason for this being, your responsibility as a project manager is to keep all the stakeholders updated with the current progress, planned targets, risk updates, forecast completion and any other updates that may be required by the stakeholders. All of these are the output of the Execution process.

Identifying the right people to receive the right information is very critical for the success of any project. Providing too much of information to too many people is a risk as well since it leads to more questions and confusion. So identifying the stakeholders and the communication management planning becomes very important for reporting the performance information. As we have the communication plan decided and signed off already, it makes the job of a Project Manager a lot easier.

Let us take a look into the below diagram to understand more on the *Control Communications* process.

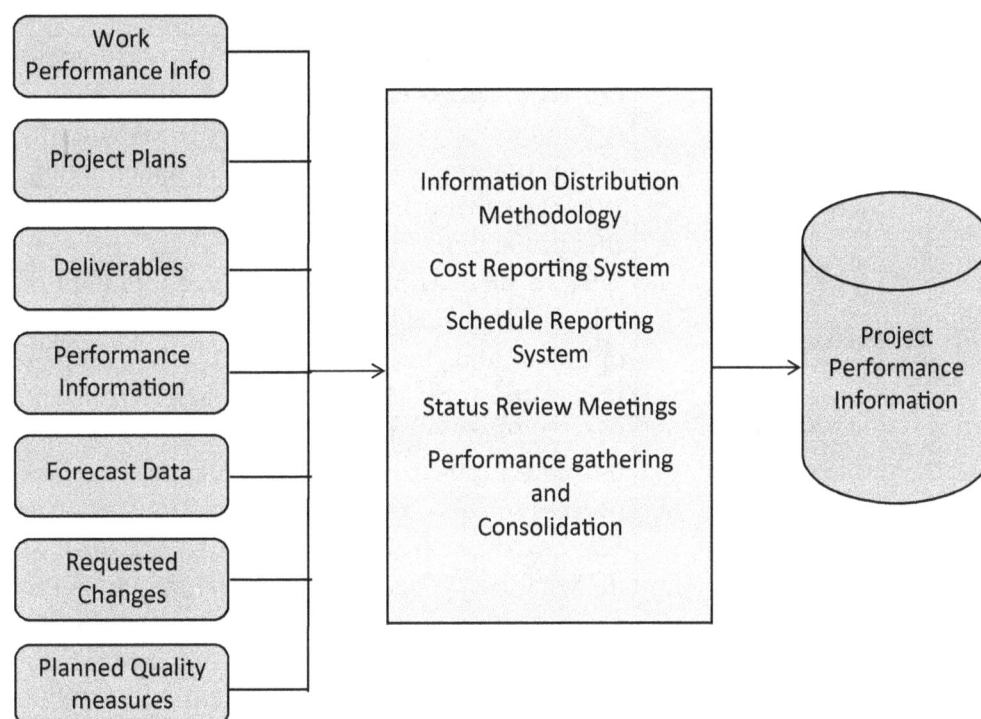

In the above diagram, Project Management Plans and Planned Quality measures are the only components that come out of the Planning Process group. The rest of the components are either output by the Execution Process group or Monitoring & Control Process group.

Inputs for Monitor Communication Process

If you notice the inputs of the Control Communications process, all the data relate to what type of information and reports are expected to be circulated among the stakeholders of the project. More interestingly, these inputs might have been already planned as part of the communication management plan and agreed by the stakeholders of the project.

Let us take a look into the details these inputs below

Input component	Description of the input component
Work Performance Information	A Work performance information is nothing but project progress card with details of individual components, the statuses, issues, risks and any details that may be relevant to the stakeholders.
Project Management Plans	When distributing performance reports of the project, it may be required at times to refer to or distribute the plan components of relevant knowledge areas. However, this is only optional and not mandatory. Note that the Communication Management Plan is part of the Project Plan. So, the Project Plans become an ultimate input to the Control communications process
Deliverables	The outcome of every project is in the form of deliverables. When updating the status of the project progress to the stakeholders, deliverable becomes the most critical input that conveys the health of the project.
Performance Information	The financial health and expected cost of the project is calculated by the EMV of the project. This cost related information is shared with the stakeholders as part of the information distribution process. This data gives the stakeholders, a fair detail on any potential cost or schedule overruns.
Forecast Data	Forecast data is critical information that gives an idea about the expected completion of the project or phases. A forecast data can convey critical details about the forecast cost or schedule of the project when completed. This data helps the stakeholder to plan for tasks from their end.
Requested Changes	When distributing information about the project components or statuses, requested changes play an important role to analyze and understand the changes that has been requested and carried out by the project team upon stakeholders' request.
Planned Quality Measures	Proposed quality measurements to ensure the worthiness of the components that are being worked on.

Tools used in Monitor Communication

Information Distribution Methodology

The way you want to distribute the communication of the performance of your project should have been narrated, agreed and approved in your Communication Management Plan. Ideal modes of communication of performance information are to upload the performance data in a central repository with all the stakeholders having access to it. Other modes of communication are by email, printing and exchanging of hardcopy of the performance and your organization's intranet.

Cost & Schedule Reporting Systems

Cost Reporting and *Schedule Reporting* are two different forms of reporting the cost and schedule related information. How the cost and schedule are planned to be analyzed and finalized is narrated in the Cost and Schedule Management Plans (Now, you must understand why Project Management Plans are used as inputs often in many processes).

Status Review Meetings

Having meetings with all the stakeholders at specific intervals to review the project progress and status is one way to manage and provide the project performance based information. Besides reviewing the status, such meetings help review the status of the risks, any additional issues or risks to be considered etc. Usually, agenda is sent as part of the invitations to such review meetings. It would be a good idea to include the latest status of all components and risks in the form of a report and attached to the agenda.

Some of the documents that are produced by such meetings can be

- Status Reports
- Meeting Minutes
- Issue Logs
- Risk Analysis Reports

Performance Gathering and Consolidation

Again, the gathering of information about the project performance is narrated and discussed with the stakeholders in advance. The project manager is responsible for consolidating the collected information in the form of a Microsoft Project Planner or any equivalent tool.

I am sure, the above information helps understand the way communication takes place, its components and the different channels of communication techniques. Can you list down other information that you would expect yourself to share with your stakeholders of your project?

You may use the below table to complete your response.

Information	Purpose

Having understood the communication process till now, let us consider ways to make the communication process work very effectively so that the project gets maximum benefits and without much risks

The stakeholder management process is not just a process but an art of handling the people, who are positively or negatively impacted and how to handle their needs and communications.

Manage Stakeholders Process

When it comes to managing stakeholders, it all begins with the identification of stakeholders. The details of the stakeholders are already seen in details in the earlier chapters. Let us revisit the details in brief before getting into the details of managing the stakeholders.

Having identified the stakeholders, the next step is to decide what you are planning to share, how and at what interval. If you are able to share the right information at the right time with the right people, you consider your project to be less risky. This statement may look overconfident, but certainly not exaggerated.

Let us look at the diagram below to understand the stakeholder management process.

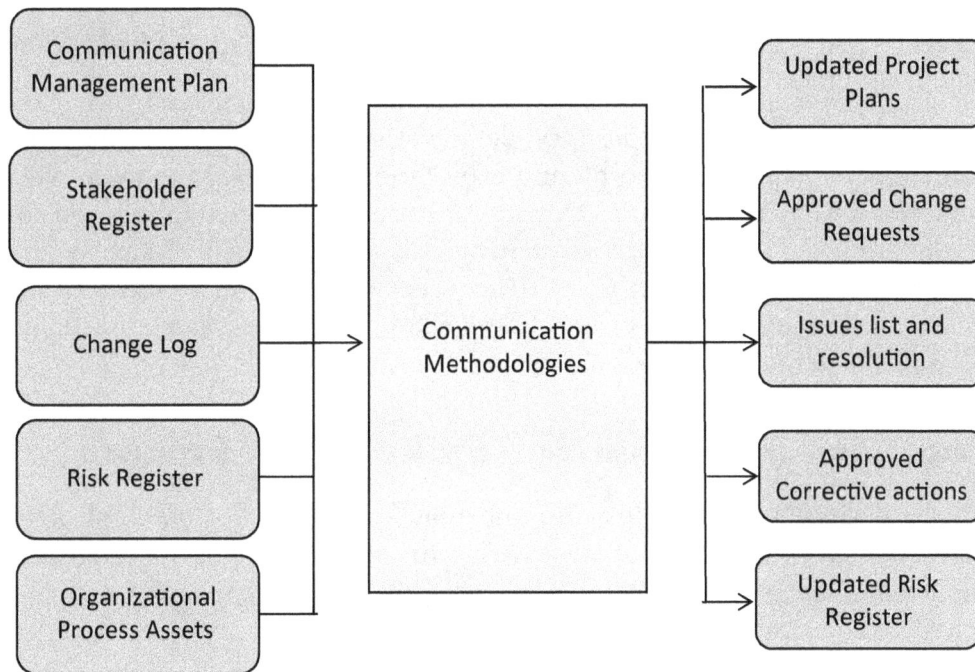

Inputs on the Manage Stakeholder Process

Stakeholder register contains the list of all stakeholders, identified by the project manager, their stake in the project, level of authority and responsibility. For any discussions involving stakeholders, the register becomes a critical input.

The *communication management Plan* should have clearly defined how the communication requirements are planned to be managed, including who are communicating and what is being communicated. The frequency and modes of the communication are clearly defined in there.

Change Log contains the list of all changes requested and their current status at any given point of time. As we discussed earlier in this chapter, the stakeholders are not engaged in daily execution and monitoring of projects. Their engagement is limited to occasional review meetings and to discuss changes requested. Thus, Change Log becomes a critical input for the Manage Stakeholder process.

Risk Register is another key input used in managing the stakeholders and their needs. A risk Register is required to be reviewed as much as possible during every phase of the project due to their criticality and potential impact on the objectives. Any threat or risks in meeting the project objectives need to be highlighted much in advance to the stakeholders.

Organizational Process Repository defines the performing organization's communication policy, protocols and expectations with regard to the project communication requirements. This might include templates to be used for communication, reports and logs exchanged. The Total Quality Management methodology has stressed the need for every organization to follow strict quality and documentation protocols and comply. All these templates should be available in the Organizational Process repository.

Tool used in the Manage Stakeholder Process

If you notice the above diagram, the only tool used is Communication methodologies. However, it can refer to any of the communication methodologies such as one-on-one meetings, teleconferencing, formally scheduled meetings, project kick-off meetings and so on.

The project manager can refer to the communication management plan to understand what is planned and agreed between the stakeholders. The project manager's management and communication skills play a vital role in managing the stakeholders and their needs.

Outputs of the Manage Stakeholder Process

About the outputs of the manage stakeholder process, there may be much more to the ones defined in the diagram. Some of the examples are status reports, activity logs, meeting minutes and so on. The details of the outputs can be referenced in the communication management plans or contract, where the expected deliverables are defined in details.

Updated Issue Log and Risk Register are important documents that gets updated as a result of managing stakeholder process. We will be reviewing the issues in much details in the next pages of this chapter.

Does this make sense?

Who Carries out Communication in a Project?

The answer to this question is "Everyone."

Anyone who interacts with another about the project planning, execution, change management, closure, issues and risks are considered to be communicating with each other on their need. Whenever there is a critical project being executed, communication becomes the key element that can influence the outcome of the project. If there is a chance of missed communication, the result may be catastrophic.

As a Project Manager, it becomes your responsibility to make sure no stakeholder is missed out in important communication. One of the easier way to achieve is to count the number of communication lines. In real term, it may be not feasible to track the communication lines manually. There is a mathematical way to count the potential number of communication lines. It is not that every Project Manager should do this counting religiously, but it is an easier way to eliminate communication issues.

If 'n' is the total number of stakeholders in your project, who are all need to informed of the progress, it is mandatory that every one of them are able to interact with each other depending on their need. Then the total number of communication lines can be established thru the simple mathematical formula

Total lines of communication $= n \times (n-1)/2$

Assume there are 6 stakeholders in your project. Then the total lines of communication channels will be

Total lines of communication $= 6 \times (6-1)/2$
                                  $= 6 \times 5/2$
                                  $= 30/2$
Total lines of communication $= 15$

I am sure, this is not very difficult to understand. Again note that, a project manager is not required to count the total number of communication lines in his project. You can use this to make sure there are no broken lines among the stakeholders.

If you observed earlier in this chapter, a project manager spend 90% of the time goes into some form of communication. It might naturally bring a question in your mind as to why should be worried about communication involving the rest of the team.

Communication in a project is not restricted only to preparing project reports, planning, statuses and collecting metrics. Every piece of data and information forms communication, which are all significant for the project. While the project manager takes responsibility for the planning and project management related communication, he assumes complete ownership of every other communication and exchange of information taking place in the project.

Controlling Stakeholder Engagement

If everything goes well with the stakeholders and meeting their needs, everybody will be obviously happy and relieved.

Unfortunately, it may not be the case always. At times, there are likelihood of managing the stakeholder process going bad, which might impact the overall project execution and meeting the project objectives. How would you handle this? Let us look at the list below

- Have all their requirements (both project and communication needs) and obtaining a sign off help eliminate most of the troubles.

- One of the important task of the project manager is to aim at improving the relationship with each of the stakeholders right from the beginning of the project.

- Building trust and resolving conflicts using negotiation skills, communication skills

- Need to communicate the issues/bad news and risk statuses in timely manner by giving as much information as possible

- Engaging project sponsor, whenever it is appropriate and required.

Which of the Communication Mode is more Important?

There is no definite answer to this. The communication mode and channel are to be decided based on the need and understanding between the project manager and the stakeholders. Sometime a phone call to discuss certain issues might yield a quicker solution. Whenever you interact with your clients, a formal communication is strongly recommended.

An intelligent project manager plans a lot more than just his reports and frequency of distributing the information. A formal communication management plan lists the modes of communication, stakeholders' expectations on communication, what devices are to be used. Risks are to be identified in terms of broken networks or communication devices and necessary mitigation plans are to be identified in advance.

What if a Project Executed Without a Communication Plan?

It will lead to chaotic situation in the project and the project will take a fasttrack approach towards collapse. This is because unless one communicates with another nothing can happen in a project. Even if there is some communication taking place, it should happen between appropriate people at the right time failing which there will be utter lack of clarity that will lead to confusion.

A Communication Management Plan considers all these risks and presents a formal way of establishing the expectations and managing the communication plan as agreed and approved by all the stakeholders.

Defining Benefits at Higher Level

In today's business environment, the senior executives do not have time to read pages of write-ups and data to understand the happenings in their organization and the projects that are being executed by their organizations. When you want to highlight the advantages of executing your project to your senior management, remember the following points in mind

- *Provide accurate data* : *Remember only accurate data with justification gets a buying in from the sponsors for approval and funding. The presented data needs to be clear and represents a bird's eye view of the cost benefits.*

- *Provide quantifiable information:* *Whatever information submitted to the managements, it need to be quantifiable in terms of benefits and have sufficient pictorial representation rather than never ending statements in a PowerPoint presentations. Ambiguous data with no justification gets nothing. Few lines of sensible information, data and plans is far better than a page full of confusing write-ups and data.*

- *Include graphs* *Representation of data in graphical format is another technique to attract attention to key points of your project. There is a famous saying which goes "a picture is worth a thousand words."*

Important Communication Documents

Besides performing all the processes of project management, it is also worth learning few very essential information that is exchanged in a project environment.

In fact, these information are so critical that they decide the fate of the project in many cases. As an example, assume that the team is working hard on their construction activities. As their project manager, it becomes your responsibility to provide updates to the stakeholders on the progress being made by your project. So, you decide to share a status report on a weekly basis with all the stakeholders. If the status of work packages are unclear to the stakeholders, the result would be lack of clarity, faith and confidence in the outcome of the project and in your leadership.

Is it a fair statement to make?

Assumptions & Constraints

Assumptions and Constraints are two of the most critical factors that is worth paying significant amount of focus in any project. In fact, I wouldn't hesitate to equate the assumptions with Risk management, since both of them mean working with uncertainty or unclear information.

A project cannot be executed in a vacuum. However, there may be situations, the project managers will most likely end up with unclear scope or information with certain section of the project (At this point, it is worth recalling the definition of a project speaks as being progressively elaborated). It is acceptable to make assumptions in such situation. However, it is the responsibility of the project manager to make sure such assumptions are closer to a possible reality and also all assumptions are conveyed to the stakeholders in written form and obtain their concurrence.

Project contingency reserves come in handy when working on assumptions. In many projects, assumptions are supported with a portion of a project budget allocated to handling such assumed factors.

Similar to Risk handling, the project manager has to keep a close watch on the assumptions made and consistently make efforts to get the ambiguous assumptions clarified by the stakeholders. Unless the assumptions are cleared at an earlier stage of the project, it might potentially become a bigger risk as the project heads into advanced stage of execution.

Constraints are nothing but limitations with which the project team has to work with.

For example, if the project team is working on constructing an oil pipeline between two cities, which are about 80 miles apart. The project is very critical as it would be financially saving more dollars for the oil company in transporting oil between the towns. Your company is given the task of executing the pipeline project and you are assigned the project manager to execute it.

As you are making headway into the project planning, you come across details of strong opposition from the community, who are opposed to the pipeline being laid through their neighborhood for safety and other reasons. There were multiple protests carried out by the community in the past. This is a cause of concern to you as any further opposition or disturbance would result in a delay in the project execution. As a project manager, it becomes your responsibility to include such risks in the constraint document and make your customer aware of your limitations in resolving such issues, as it is outside the scope of your project. Such constraints should be conveyed at the beginning of the project phase and get a written acceptance from the customers.

Take a look into the sample Assumptions & Constraints document below as reference.

ABC Corporation LLC 17212, Marine Drive, Philadelphia PA 17232 November 14, 2014		
Project Sigma - Assumptions & Constraints		
Assumptions	**Date**	**Status**
1. It is assumed that Sigma Petroleum ('The buyer') will make available required single point of contact to support the design team with clarification on existing functionality and product specification requirements	11/01/2014	**Open**
2. It is assumed that The Buyer will nominate the stakeholders, who will be part of the project and are directly and indirectly impacted by the Project Sigma.	11/12/2014	**Open**
Constraints		
1. It is assumed that The Buyer will settle all civilian and legal disputes before the project schedule and cost estimations are submitted for approval. Failure to settle such disputes will result in delay in project schedule and escalation of cost.	11/01/2014	**Open**

Is it possible to use project's contingency reserve to supplement project constraints?

NO. It is not possible to use project reserve to supplement constraints.

A constraint is an uncertain situation, which is outside the scope of your project. Hence, the project's contingency reserve cannot be utilized to support constraints, which are not under your control.

Issue Logs

No project can get completed without issues. Even a well planned project might have some issues, smaller or larger in size and at different stages. However, how the issues are handled decides the fate of the project and the customer satisfaction.

However, if the issues are handled in an efficient and planned manner nothing is impossible for a project manager. Thus planning to handle issues becomes a key responsibility of a project manager. Like any other planning process, issues require some amount of planning and brainstorming between all stakeholders.

Issue handling strategy differs between organizations. In some projects, issues are communicated to other stakeholders through emails and a lengthy discussions takes place, involving multiple stakeholders. This might sound like a good idea. However, it has one disadvantage in the sense that numerous email exchanges might result in confusion and, in many cases, people tend to lose track of the issues and their updates. So, let us consider another better way to handle such issues.

To begin with the planning process, it is a very good idea to have a issue management register or issue log in place. As part of the communication management planning, handling issues require the commitment and concurrence of the stakeholders, especially when it comes to issue response commitment from the customer. A formal issue list template can be put in place and published to all of the stakeholders.

Whenever an issue is encountered in a project, the issue list gets updated for the new issues and the owner is assigned to handle it. A start and target dates would be a good idea, besides the criticality and impact level of the issue. The description column of the issue list narrates the details of the issue and its resolution requirement.

Handling issue logs is similar to handing Risks of a project. Both these elements are to be focused and tracked closely for any further updates and developments. During the periodical meeting with the stakeholders, the status of each of the issues are to be assessed and updated. Whenever there are issues that require an immediate attention, the dependency and impact is to be explained to all the stakeholders for quicker action. The process is required to be continued until the issues get resolved thus limiting its impact on the project schedule.

Now, let us see the difference between having a issue register and exchange of email communication.

Issue Logs	Using Email to resolve issues
All issues are consolidated in one document	Individual email communication takes place for every issue and the email chain continues till the issue is resolved or scrapped
Easy to track the issues and their latest updates	Too many emails might complicate their tracking
Easy to get the resources and dates assigned for individual issues	Require the assignment and dates to be done manually in emails
Unlikely to lose visibility on every issue	Easy to miss updates due to complicated communication protocols being followed
Easy to record the issues in the organization repository after the completion of the project	Difficult to get all the emails documented and uploaded into the organization repository

Let us now look at a sample issue log below

Iss. No.	Issue Description	Impacted area	Owner	Assigned	Date raised	Targeted Date	Status	Update History
1.	Delay in providing customer details might delay application testing	Client Master Maint.	Dave Dillon	Rob Davey	06/12/13	06/18/13	Open	**06/15** - Rob to provide an update by COB 06/13 - Issue raised and followed up
2.	Test data not yet ready for validating Production master application	Product Maint.	Nick Cook	Laura Davis	06/13/13	06/22/13	Open	06/15 Data to be available by 06/17 06/13 - Issue raised and assigned

In the above issue log, issues are listed and assigned the owner and responsible person for resolving the issue besides the date details.

The update history column contains all the latest updates for this particular issue, which is collected by the project manager. Having the history of update in the same document help consolidate all the required information in one single document, thus reducing the risk of missing updates by way of multiple email communication.

Work Product Reviews

Remember that when someone is talking about quality, they may be referring to Work Product Reviews (WPR) as well.

As we learnt earlier, Quality is all about planning for doing the right things the right way. However, once the work product or construction is completed, the work needs to get reviewed to make sure it meets the predefined objectives. The methodology to validate this is achieved by following a Work Product Review.

What is Contained in a WPR?

Ideally, a WPR should have a detailed description of the defect or bug found in a work product, its impact and severity besides the details of the project team member that worked on the work product, the person who reviewed the work product.

The *impact* of the defect or bug refers to the consequence of the defect upon the work product or the intended final outcome of the project.

For example, if a team member is building an electric circuit as his responsibility of a project that is to produce a larger electric installation for a power plant. When the work product review finds that the switch of the electric circuit is not functioning as it is expected, this becomes a defect. The impact of this defect would be high since unless the electric circuit is essential to operate the entire electric installation at the power plant.

A *severity* of a defect is the criticality of the defect on the reviewed work product or the overall project outcome.

In the same example given above, the severity of a non-functioning switch in an electric circuit is certainly catastrophic since the project cannot proceed further unless the electric circuit is functional. To have the electric circuit functional, the switch should be made operational.

Hope, the above is clear.

Some points to remember about the WPR

* *A WPR need not have target dates assigned for fixing the defect, unless the project requirements expect to have a definite target date due to dependency. When the project manager plan for the project schedule, the dates for review as well as rework efforts are estimated and defined against specific resources. This means, the owner of the work product is expected to comply with the defect fixing as per the planned project schedule.*

- *Every work product should have a separate review and a review record prepared for future clarification and efficiency of defect fixing.*

- *A WPR document is a key deliverable in most of the project environments as it showcase the efficiency of the project performing organizations ability and the project team's capability.*

Let us look at a sample Work Product Review document below

ABC Corporation LLC., 17213, Marine Drive, Philadelphia, PA 17434				Review Date : 06/12/2014		
Work Product Review						
Defect Id	**Defect Description**	**Work Product**	**Impact**	**Severity**	**Remarks**	
IN1012	Faulty switch in the electric circuit that connects the interface with the main compressor	DJI1137	High	Catastrophic	
IN1016	Unstable reading recorded when the circuit is connected to interface	DJI1137	Moderate	Normal	
IN1021	Noise level is more when the compressor was fired using a overriding electric circuit	DJI1137	Moderate	Low	

As I repeatedly say, every template and documents produced as part of the projects are customizable according to the project requirements. The above sample document should be considered for sample purpose only.

Status Reports

If there is one document that can tilt the entire project's progress upside down, that would definitely be called the Status report.

The project manager should be extremely careful with what goes into the status reports. A status report do not just contain the work products and its current status but it should have details of any potential issues, action items, work product start and target dates, their status and dependencies for every work product and the project.

The status report is the bible of the project, which provides the latest information to every stakeholders, who might be influencing the direction of the project based on the current status. In several project environments status report and meeting minutes are combined to be a single document, which is produced as an outcome of the regularly scheduled project meeting. Needless to say, a status report is a live document, which gets updated frequently.

A status report should provide all the project information in a nutshell. The project manager need not write a long story of the work product and project status, but a few lines in brief should help the stakeholders understand the progress.

Let us now take a look into a sample status report

ABC Corporation LLC., 17213, Marine Drive, Philadelphia, PA 17434					Date: 06/12/2014
Project Alpha - Weekly Status Report					
Work Product	**Description**	**Current Status**	**Start Date**	**Target Date**	**Remarks**
IN1013	Accepts supply from interface and connects to the circuit to generate high voltage energy	In-Progress	06/12/14	06/30/14	Progressing as per the schedule
IN1014	Validates the data before passing the control to the interface	In-Progress	06/10/14	07/01/14	Dependency identified with data requirement

Action Items						
Action Item	**Description**	**Owner**	**Status**	**Assigned Date**	**Target Date**	**Remarks**
1	Data to validate the circuit is to be provided by the circuit monitoring group	Jack Taylor	Open	05/30/14	06/27/14	

Project Risks					
Risk Id	Risk Description	Status	Work Product	Impact	Owner
ID703	Delay in providing production data might impact the validation schedule of the constructed work product	Open	IN1014	High	Mark Spencer

In the above status report sample, all essential information that are required to understand the progress of the project and track it are included with ownership, impact, criticality and dates assigned for every individual tasks, issues or risks.

I am sure, you must be already familiar with the status reports of the project. The above sample is just another version of what could be included.

Meeting Minutes

Meeting minutes are one of the important tool that keeps the projects running smoothly. A meeting need not be convened only to discuss the project's status but can be any discussion including brainstorming sessions, to resolve specific issues and questions, addressing risks and so on.

Minutes are written record that reminds people of what was discussed and agreed upon. In addition, minutes help track the issues and problems that are being discussed.

A sample Minutes of meeting template can be seen below

ABC Corporation LLC., 17213, Marine Drive, Philadelphia, PA 17434			Date : 06/12/2014
Dial-in Number : 1888 888 8888		**Pass code : 1234567#**	
Robert Langdon	X	Michael Davey	A
Jack Dillon	X	Sarah Chambers	X
Rebecca Dawson	X		
Project Alpha - Meeting minutes			
1. Explain the current status around the creation of test data to test IN1014 - Robert Langdon			
2. Dependency of data creation with downloading from tape - Sarah Chambers			
3. To check with interface team on removing the dependency to enable data creation - Sarah Chambers Target date of closure - 06/14/2014			
4. Development of circuit to continue pending data availability for testing - Rebecca Dawson			

Action items can be listed in the same meeting minutes and ownership assigned along with target dates of closure.

EXERCISES

Choose the Right Answer

1. An email sent to another member of the project
   - Formal Written
   - Informal verbal
   - Informal written
   - Formal verbal

2. A presentation to the senior management of the customer
   - Formal Verbal
   - Formal Written
   - Informal Written
   - Informal verbal

3. Meeting Minutes prepared and shared with the stakeholders
   - Informal Written
   - Formal Verbal
   - Informal Verbal
   - Formal Written

4. A speech on the capability of the performing organization
   - Formal Verbal
   - Informal Verbal
   - Informal Written
   - Formal Written

5. A discussion with a project team member at the cubicle
   - Formal Written
   - Informal Verbal
   - Formal Verbal
   - Informal Written

True or False

1. Identifying number of communication channels is essentially required in a project (**True/False**)

2. A feedback in a communication process means passing performance feedback in a formal way (**True/False**)

3. A status report should be formally written, even if it is circulated within the project team (**True/False**)

4. Body languages are considered methods of communication (**True/False**)

5. When sharing information with the senior management within the performing organization, the communication can be informal (**True/ False**)

Match the Following

*   Sender   : Tone of the speaker
*   Encode   : A discussion with your teammate while taking a walk
*   Informal Verbal   : Email
*   Paralingual   : The person who speaks
*   Communication Mode : Sender's message gets transformed to reach the receiver

ANSWERS
Choose the Right Answer
1. Informal Written
2. Formal Written
3. Formal Written
4. Formal Verbal
5. Informal Verbal

True or False
1. False
2. False
3. True
4. True
5. False

Match the Following

- Sender   : The person who speaks
- Encode   : Sender's message gets transformed to reach the receiver
- Informal Verbal   : A discussion with your teammate while taking a walk
- Paralingual   : Tone of the speaker
- Communication Mode : Email

Test Your Knowledge

1. Mike is a project manager, who has been managing his construction project and is associated with his organization for several years. Due to his lengthy association with this project and customer, Mike has made several friends at the customer's end. Recently, his organization has received a request for bid from the customer for a high profile contract worth millions of dollars. Out of faith in Mike's talent and proximity with the customer, his senior management has asked him to showcase his company's capability with the specific type of work to make a bid for the contract.

    Mike has scheduled a meeting with the senior management staff of the customer and sent invite to them. On the day of the meeting, Mike took the discuss with ease and presented his company's ability in an informal way without any written slides or data to support his speech. After the discussion, the Executive Director of his company approached Mike and expressed his displeasure with the way he ran the meeting and presented the organization's capability.

    What is the Executive Director so much upset about?

    a) He might have expected Mike to be even more casual due to his close association with the customer

    b) He was upset that Mike approached the meeting in an informal mode

    c) He might have been upset that the customer was not showing any signs of approving his organization's ability

    d) None of the above

2. An email sent to a team member is an example of

    a) Informal written

    b) Formal verbal

    c) Casual communication

    d) Formal verbal

3. Laura is a newly nominated project manager and has a team of 24 members and 12 other stakeholders, who all form part of her project. When she is working on her communication planning, she got confused with the number of communication lines, she will have.

    Can you help her to arrive at the number?

    a) 360

    b) 244

    c) 1260

    d) 630

4. In communication protocol, a feedback refers to

    a) a performance feedback given to a team member over any communication channel

    b) feedback from the customer on the project status and delivery accomplishment

    c) a listener reacting to a conversation

    d) the project manager sending a reminder for reply from one of the project stakeholder.

5. Which among the following BEST describes an example for formal written communication

    a) Status report

    b) Meeting Minutes

    c) Issue Log

    d) All of the above

6. Joe is a project manager working on a project that plans to produce a specially designed fuelling system for the aviation industry. He did follow all the processes and got the scope approved by all the stakeholders. The customer was very impressed with the way things have been going. One day, a senior executive of the customer organization calls Joe and asks him to include the technical expert of another department as a key stakeholder. It appears, the customer didn't recognize the impact of this project completely in the beginning. So, they overlooked the other department.

    Now, they taken a decision to include the department representative and seek their inputs on the original scope. You are now nervous about the impact of this inclusion at a later stage in the project. At this moment, you do not have idea of the quantum of impact on the project due to this decision.

    When is the BEST time, a stakeholder should be identified in a project?

    a) Planning

    b) Initiation

    c) Execution

    d) Closure

7. The primary tool used in managing stakeholders is

    a) Formal Verbal

    b) Formal Written

    c) Communication Methodologies

    d) Paralingual communication

8. You have taken over as the project manager for the telecommunication project being executed by your organization for one of the largest telecom company in Europe. The previous manager was removed from the project after too much of communication issues that seriously impacted the delivery schedule and cost related factors. Your organization has mandated you to take complete control of the project and the team of 120 members.

   During your first meeting with the stakeholders, you tried to understand their thoughts on the current status of the project and the pain points. You are told that there was no disciplined approach to the project and they do not get updates on time and are not informed of any significant happenings in the project. The list was pretty long. From your opinion, where can be the trouble in the project?

   a) Communication Plan missing

   b) Stakeholder identification

   c) Stakeholder management

   d) Scope Management Plan

9. You are presenting a status of your project to a group of stakeholders and your company's senior executives. You have plenty of interesting achievements, breakthroughs and other updates relating to the project. Each of the stakeholder has some updates for them and your senior executives are impressed by the updates and the progress being made.

   As you keep speaking to the audience, you find many of them reacting to your updates by nodding their head or approving and acknowledging verbally or by body language. Some of them ask questions over the information you are presenting.

   This is an example of....

   a) You are an efficient project manager

   b) Active Listening

   c) Stakeholder Management technique

   d) None of the above

10. What among the below list are the BEST example of an initial communication happening between stakeholders in a project environment?

    a) Project Planning

    b) Status meetings

    c) Assumptions & Constraints

    d) Kick-off meeting

11. According to a Project Management Institute (PMI) study, project managers spend most of their time in this activity...

    a) Project Planning

    b) Communication

    c) Monitoring & Control

    d) Problem Solving

12. You are working on a transportation project and your team is working on their construction activities. As the team begin making progress, you are collecting good amount of metrics and other information to consolidate and share among the project's stakeholders. You are providing frequent updates to your senior management on the performance of the project and the issues.

    Which process group are you in now?

    a) Execution

    b) Monitoring & Control

    c) Planning

    d) Closure

13. While you are monitoring the project team and their development activities, one of your senior executive approach you with a request to provide the target completion of the project along with the Estimated budget at completion details. It seems, he is more concerned about the schedule and cost overrun in the project due to some dependency factors. He plans to review the current status and the estimation to arrive at any backup plan to bring the project back on track.

    What category of communication is being requested by him?

    a) Forecast

    b) Project performance report

    c) Risk register

    d) Project Status report

14. When you are attending a meeting of all the stakeholders to discuss the progress review of your project, one of the stakeholder is asking you to schedule a daily technical review meeting with the technical team of his organization. He also want you to update your process documents to include this regular meeting and distribute among all the stakeholders.

    Which document should be updated to include this event?

    a) Project performance report

    b) Communication Management Plan

c) Project Status report

d) Risk Register

15. **When does a project manager perform most of the communication in a project?**

   a) Execution process group

   b) Planning process group

   c) Monitoring & Control process group

   d) Initiation

16. **Rebecca is a sales manager of your organization, who is along with you is in a contract negotiation with a potential customer. You prepared a very good slideshow showcasing your organization capabilities, past experience with similar projects and advantages of engaging your organization. Rebecca is supporting you with several other features to impress the customer and to influence them in taking a positive decision over the contract proposal.**

   What is the MOST important thing, you should observe during this meeting?

   a) Observe if Rebecca is conveying any irrelevant or negative information to the customer

   b) Try to find what the customer is taking note of

   c) Contents of the slide

   d) Non-verbal expressions of the customer

17. **Richard is managing a large infrastructure project for his customer and has a team of over 30 members in his team and about 15 stakeholders representing various departments of the customer. As part of his responsibility, he has started understanding the stakeholders' expectations on the project related information, frequency, mode of communication and the intended recipients of the information. This is very vital for him to have a clear understanding of the customer expectations and visibility into what goes to whom, when and how often part of the communication.**

   He is looking for a communication tool, that will help him achieve his objective. Can you help him with appropriate tool?

   a) Communication Management Plan

   b) Communication Technology

   c) Communication Requirement Analysis

   d) Stakeholder Management

18. Your team is in the middle of their execution phase and you are regularly interacting with your stakeholders and address their questions and requirements . In order to avoid scope changes, you are looking for any issues or problems in the project, that might influence its scope.

    Which process group, are you into now?

    a) Monitoring & Control

    b) Execution

    c) Closure

    d) Planning

19. Which of the following is an output of Information Distribution process

    a) Status report

    b) Organizational Process Assets

    c) Project Metrics

    d) Communication Management Plan

20. The prescribed form of communication to record meeting minutes is

    a) Formal verbal

    b) Informal Written

    c) Formal Written

    d) Informal Verbal

21. The most likely cause of a communication failure can be the absence of

    a) Communication plan

    b) Information distribution

    c) Feedback

    d) Medium

22. Legal documents are best examples of _____ Communication

    a) Informal written

    b) Casual written

    c) Formal verbal

    d) Formal written

23. The recommended output of a status meeting are
    a) Status report
    b) Meeting Minutes
    c) Updated Risk register
    d) All of the above

24. The impact of poor handling of stakeholder identification will be felt in which of the below process groups
    a) Planning
    b) Execution
    c) Monitor & Control
    d) All of the above

25. Which is NOT an example of an Active Listening
    a) A team meeting, where everyone discuss the status of their respective work packages
    b) An hiring interview conducted by an organization
    c) An unenthusiastic speech by someone
    d) A telephonic conversation between two team members.

ANSWERS

1. **Answer: B**

   Justification: When a project manager is engaged in a conversation with a customer on matters related to contract, legal or new business, it is always recommended practice to use formal communication. Representation of data and facts in the form of slides. In this situation, Mike may have a very good rapport with his customer but his approach to such an important discussion is incorrect. Such handling of discussions has the potential to erode the confidence of the customer since it conveys a negative message that the vendor is not very serious about the business proposal or contract.

2. **Answer: A**

   Justification: When talking about methods of communication, it is essential to remember that communication within the team and organization (except to senior leadership one's own organization) can be informal, both verbal and non-verbal. However, communication involving customers or senior leadership within one's own organization is recommended to be formal in both ways. The way communication takes place influences the performing organization's standing and commitments.

3. **Answer: D**

   Justification: Remembering that every team member is a stakeholder, the number of stakeholders in the project is $n = 36$

Total communication channels	=	$n (n-1) / 2$
	=	$36 \times 35 / 2$
	=	$1260 / 2$
	=	630 is the total number of communication channels in this project

4. **Answer: C**

   Justification: A feedback is something that is conveyed by the listener in a meeting or discussion or conversation. A feedback need not be a lengthy statement or reply, but a simple nodding head or short words such as "OK" would constitute a feedback. A feedback is very essential for any conversation to be meaningful. A feedback is part of an Active Listening process. A conversation without a feedback conveys the meaning that the listener need not enjoy it.

5. **Answer: D**

   Justification: A formal communication is one, which gets transmitted or circulated to several people. In this question, reports such as issue logs, status reports and meeting minutes are circulated to several participants of a meeting or project and carries information about the project, status and the issues. All of these documents are set as expectations by customers in several organization to know the status of their projects and deliverables.

6. **Answer: B**

   Justification : The earlier the stakeholders are identified in a project the less burden for the project manager in managing the project and the stakeholders expectations. However, it is to be noted that a stakeholder can be included in a project at any point of time throughout the project phases. Since the stakeholders have a direct interest on the scope of the project, it would be good if all of them are identified before the scope management planning is done. Identifying stakeholders is one important risk for a project manager.

7. **Answer: C**

   Justification : During the stakeholder identification process, one of the important responsibility of the project manager is to identify the communication requirements and preferences of all the stakeholders. These details are as important as identifying the project scope. Some of the communication requirements include status reports, meeting minutes, issue logs, risk registers. Similarly, communication preferences such as how the communication is expected to be is required to be identified and documented.

8. **Answer: A**

   Justification: One of the most important responsibility for a project manager is to have a proper communication management plan in place and approved by each of the stakeholder. A communication management plan contains the communication requirements, communication methodology and frequency of distribution of information from start to finish of the project. In this question, it appears that there was no planned communication approach in place for the project, forcing everyone to speak to every other stakeholder of the project, resulting in chaos and uncontrolled communication taking place all around.

9. **Answer: B**

   Justification : An active listening is a key requirement in a communication process. An active listening can be either verbal or non-verbal but it conveys a message to the speaker about the involvement and understanding of the listener on the subject being spoken or discussed. An active listening aids a communication process more effectively than someone sitting in a boring lecture.

10. **Answer: D**

    Justification : A kick-off meeting is conducted by the project manager involving all the identified stakeholders of a project. The meeting can also be considered a *Hand-shake meeting* between all those involved in a project environment. The purpose of such a kick-off meeting may differ between projects and organization. The timing of the kick-off meeting is left to the project manager to decide. It has to be noted that a kick-off meeting is not the exact first communication to take place in a project , but from the list of options given, it is.

11. **Answer: B**

    Justification : According to a PMI study, a project manager spends about 90% of the time in communication of one form or the other. The communication can be verbal or written both formal and informal. Some of the communication identified closely with a project manager include preparing status reports, issue logs, minutes of the meetings, metrics collection and reporting and so on.

12. **Answer: A**

    Justification : The primary responsibility of the project manager while the project team is engaged in the development or construction activity is to collect the project related data and distribute them to the stakeholders of the project. This information distribution is very essential for the stakeholders to understand the progress and to make corrections to the project components, wherever required.

13. **Answer: A**

    Justification : Anything that involves the estimation of data is considered a forecasting information. The primary input for arriving at the forecasting include the current metrics of the project. Specific tools are used to get this data processed to arrive at a required data. In this case, Estimation to Completion is the cost estimation of the project anticipated at completion is required by using the current status of the project and the project metrics.

14. **Answer: B**

    Justification : A communication management plan contains details of the communication requirements and the modes of communication. This includes any scheduled meetings of the project involving the any or all of the stakeholders. All these communication requirements and preferences are identified and included in the communication management plan, which later gets approved by all the stakeholders. Once approved, the communication plan becomes the project baseline.

15. **Answer: C**

    Justification : It is during the monitoring and Control process group, most of the communication takes place for a project manager. The communication can be in the form of providing updates, tracking risks and managing them, managing change requests, resolving issues, controlling the scope, cost and schedule to name few. Each of these activities involve a good amount of communication taking place and this makes the project manager busy during this phase more than ever.

16. **Answer: D**

    Justification : Besides responding to questions and request for clarification, the non-verbal reactions of the stakeholders become the most important reaction to be noted during any meeting that involves contract negotiation or business deals. Such expressions convey messages of their understanding or acceptance of the subject being discussed. Similarly, Paralingual communication that needs to be observed during such meetings.

17. **Answer: C**

    Justification : A communication requirement methodology is part of the communication management planning process, wherein the project manager understands and identifies the communication requirements of the stakeholders and the mode of communication and any other preferences. A communication management plan is the outcome of this tool that details the requirements of the stakeholders. This approved communication plan becomes the project's communication baseline.

18. **Answer: A**

    Justification : The primary responsibility of a project manager during the monitoring and control process group is to look for factors that might potential result in a change request being raised and an update to the scope. Any schedule deviation or cost overrun might also be influencing factors on the scope, as narrated in the triple constraint diagram.

19. **Answer: B**

    Justification : Among the listed options in the question, Organizational Process assets qualify to be the better one. Any data collected and shared with the stakeholders are primary source of metrics for a project and this metrics is required to be recorded in the project asset. Any lessons learned during the process is also recorded in the process assets.

20. **Answer: C**

    Justification : Any report or document that is prepared and exchanged with a group of stakeholders is expected to be in a formal one, since it conveys the status of the project and list of issues and risks to the recipients.

21. **Answer: C**

    Justification : To have a communication to be successful, one of the important requirement is to have a feedback from the listener. Though there is no single prescribed mode of conveying a feedback, it can either be verbal or non-verbal.

22. **Answer: D**

    Justification : A legal document and contract is legally binding and hence are expected to be formally written and signed by the stakeholders or buyer and seller in a project environment.

23. **Answer: D**

    Justification : It is always a best recommended practice to discuss the list and status of risks, open issues and any assumptions and constraints made about the project components. All of these have potential to get updates as the team makes progress with their work. A project status meeting includes the status of everything about the project.

24. **Answer: D**

    Justification : In fact, the impact of failure to identify all the stakeholders will be felt from the start of the project till finish. Since a stakeholders have direct or indirect interest in the project and the scope, their involvement becomes very critical for the success or failure of the project.

25. **Answer: C**

    Justification : In an active listening, feedback plays a very key role to keep the communication alive and interesting. In this question, an unenthusiastic lecture will not draw the interest and involvement of the participants.

This page is intentionally left blank

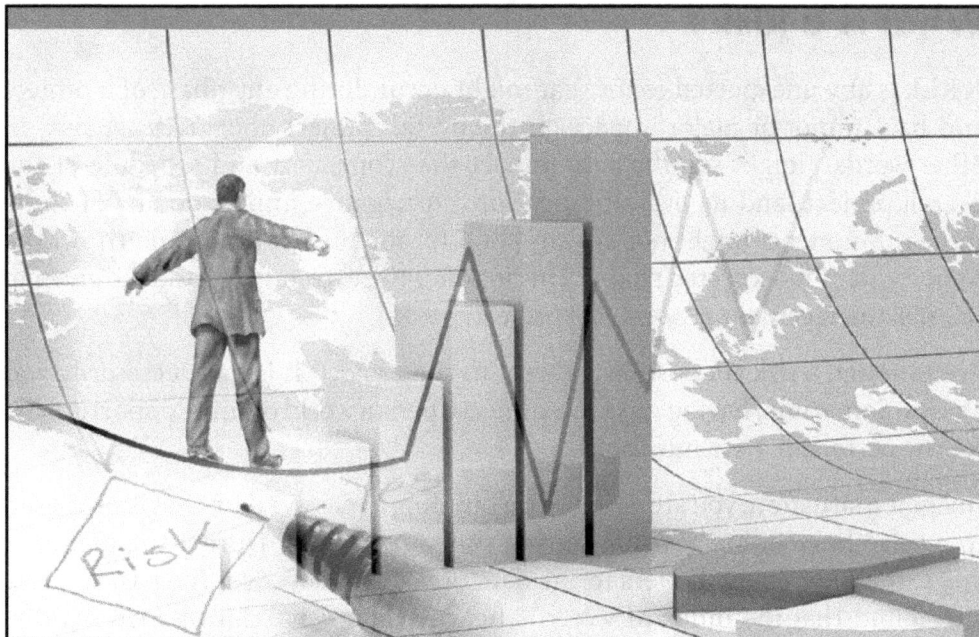

Risk Management

Objectives

At the end of Risk Management chapter, you should be able to understand:

- What is a risk in a project environment and its impact on the project objectives
- different types of risks
- components of risk planning process
- how the risk management planning is done and its contents. Understand Risk Breakdown structure
- how risks are identified using various available tools
- Risk register and its contents
- what is a qualitative and quantitative analysis. Impact and severity of the identified risks
- different methods of mitigating a risk
- the impact of change control process over risk management.

What is a Risk?

A Risk is any unexpected event that might occur during any phase of a project and have minor or major impact on the overall project objectives. A risk, in other words, might significantly impact the scope, cost and schedule of the overall project and its overall execution. A negative impact on any of these three components might not do any good for the project but would throw the project out of its expected shape. This justifies the extreme importance given to the risk management process of a project.

Even though a risk sounds like a threat to the project, it is not necessarily bad always. Sometime, having risks in a project opens a world of more opportunities for the performing organization.

Imagine a situation, you are working on building a massive dam that is proposed to receive huge influx of water during the rainy season. During the planning stage, the local council refers to the data of water inflow over the past 10 years and found that the influx of water is heavier than usual during October due to more than usual rainfall recorded in the region. After careful analysis, the sponsors of the project, the local city council, request you to analyze the risks of receiving excessive water and how to handle such inflow.

As the manager of the project, you decide to have alternate tunnels to divert the excess water to a nearby channel and thus eliminating the risk of flooding. Having a risk as narrated above has opened additional opportunities to your project and Organization, having to have new sub-projects to handle the risk. Besides bringing more money to your organization, such risks enhance your organization's management capability and level of expertise in executing projects with lesser risks.

Irrespective of the fact that a project can have positive or negative impact to the project itself and to the performing organization, it is worth given a great amount of attention. No wonder, great project managers spend significant amount of their time and attention in managing their project risks.

Significance of Risk Management

If you ever want to assess the efficiency and skills of a project manager, look nowhere but how the risks are planned and managed. For some, this statement might look exaggerated but cannot deny this basic fact of project management.

If you ever happen to take an interview for a new job, you can expect significant amount of questions on risk planning and management.

If the project planning and execution is full of pleasant surprises and only positive news, none would worry but feel happy. But, in reality, that is not possible since projects are prone to negative developments and unexpected twists in most cases. Such negative developments might suddenly surface without an invitation or a calling card. How the project manager is planning, managing and monitoring them and able to deliver the project lies a real challenge. It requires lot of skills, knowledge, confidence and influence over his team and the stakeholders.

Do you now agree about the significance of Risk Management?

Categories of Risks

In general, there can be two types of risks in any project. They are internal to the organization and external.

Internal risks are factors that are internal to the performing organization such as company strategy and resource risks. Such internal risks are something that can be influenced by the Organization and the leadership of the performing organization. Some of the internal risks can be disturbance in communication channels, resource related risks and infrastructure based risks.

External risks are more related to factors that are external to the performing Organization such as changes in the government policy. When you work on such external risks, the chances of your organization able to influence such risks are limited. A good example of external risk is a heavy rain when your organization has scheduled an event.

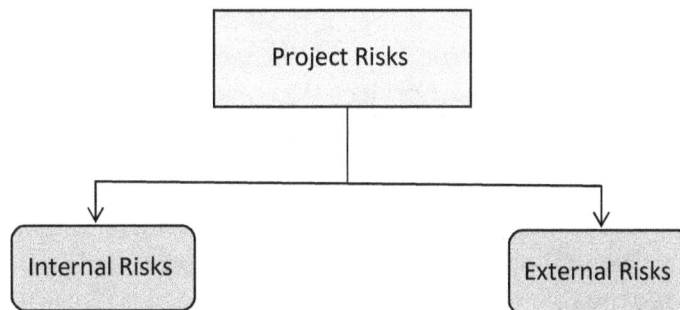

```
                        ┌──────────────────┐
                        │   Project Risks  │
                        └──────────────────┘
                                 │
                    ┌────────────┴────────────┐
                    ↓                          ↓
            ┌───────────────┐          ┌───────────────┐
            │ Internal Risks│          │ External Risks│
            └───────────────┘          └───────────────┘
```

Internal Risks

These are the risks that are very specific to your project or organization. This means, internal risks are influenced by factors that are local to your company. Further, the internal risks can be decomposed to include organizational and technical risks for easier handling. Further examples for Organizational risks include as organizational policy changes, resource related issues, management support to projects or proposals. Technical risks include availability of technical resources on time, connectivity and other technical hardware to support your project.

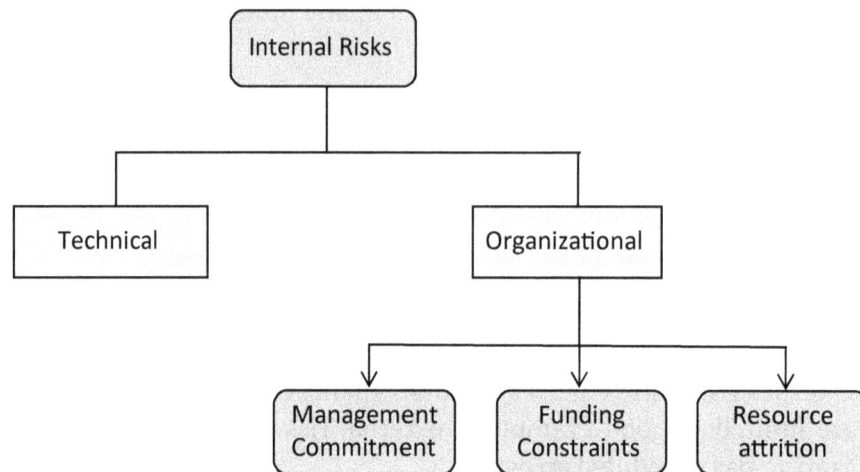

External Risks

These categories of risks may be beyond the purview of your organization but impact your organization or project. However such risks does influence and impact the execution of your project, thus making it essential to plan for handling them.

A simple example is a change in government regulations that might expect your organization to comply with certain newly introduced legislation on safety standards. As per the new legislation, you are not expected to use products that are made of certain chemicals, which are identified as harmful to the public.

Having to handle such external risks might impact your overall project scope, schedule and financial plans as well.

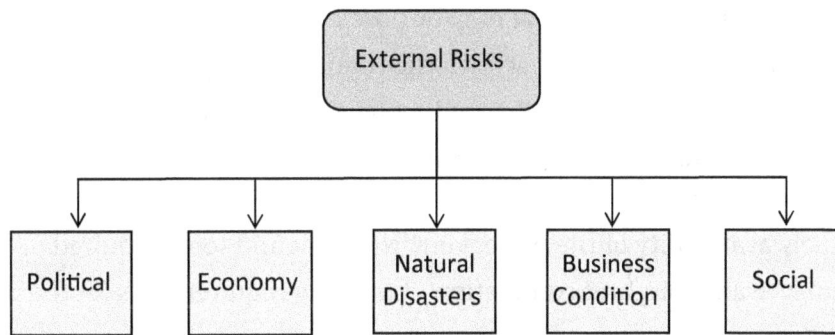

In the above diagram, Political risks are ones such as change of government, changes in policies and new regulations. When the governments change, there are more likelihood of a policy changes that impacts the overall business climate either positively or negatively.

Economical risks are resulted by lower demand, changes in market conditions, recessions. Economic related risks demand a very high level of risk management, which are to be planned much in advance for less impact on the business.

Natural disaster is one critical risk, especially in nations which are prone to such disasters. Imagine a situation, when your city is ripped by a hurricane or floods. We will be seeing more about recommended mitigation in the Risk responses section. None would forgotten the effects of the Tsunami that hit the coast of Japan few years ago, that putting the nuclear power plant at Fukushima Daiichi at a greatest amount of disaster.

Business risks involve business prospects of your customers, their policy changes which might directly or indirectly impact your project. Social risks are numerous such as any happenings in your town, social unrest at your clients' country to name few.

You should understand that the above list of internal and external risks are only sample. Since a risk can come from any direction and any moment of time, there may be much more to add to the list. A project manager is expected to be alert and stay alerted for risks of every magnitude.

So, do you like to list down some of the Internal and External risks encountered in your past projects and is worth considering.

Internal Risks	External Risks

Let me list few risks for you, that may be possible in a business environment.

- Potential troubles and issues with the vendor, if the project is outsourced
- Total number of users for the product being developed
- Customers sharing links containing confidential information that is required by project
- Timely availability of the project environment and tools required
- Timely availability and completion of training requirements for the project team
- Are the staff available for the entire duration of the project
- Familiarity of the technology to the performing organization
- Compatibility of the prototype to the real-time environment
- Potential cost and budget cut by customer before the project completion
- Management commitment and support for the project execution
- Customer involvement in verification process
- Does customer require training on the specific product or technology being used
- Availability of necessary infrastructure
- Impact of late delivery of the end product on cost
- Software licensing issues
- Resources assignments and matching project expectations
- Sharing resources between projects. Key personnel available only part time
- Visibility of the project outcome to the senior management and their level of commitment
- Potential changes in end-user requirements
- Staff motivation issues and its subsequent impact on the project
- Documentation and User guide related risks
- Realistic view of the customer's delivery expectation
- Are there any restrictions on using certain tools by the customer
- Productivity of the project team
- Unexpected low turnover of the staff during project phases
- Unexpected delay in one task and its impact on subsequent tasks
- Amount of administrative tasks required by the project team
- Contractor doesn't buy into the project and consequently does not provide the level of commitment required

Components of Risks Planning

Having understood the importance and impact of risks in a business environment, let us understand what are all involved in a risk planning process.

There are six processes involved in Risk planning in all. Each of them perform specific tasks relating to managing the risks in a project

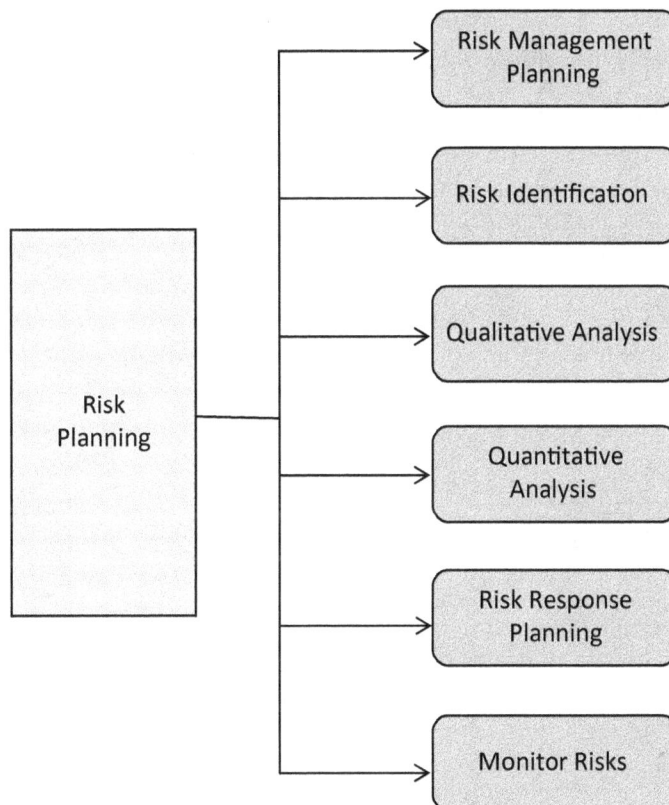

One should not get confused between the Risk Management Planning with that of the rest of the components of Risk planning processes. The Risk Management Planning is not about any particular risk or select risks. It is planning a way on how you are going to handle every risk in your project.

However, Risk identification & monitoring is dealing with specific risks that you are going to identify in your project as you make progress.

Note that all of these processes, but Risk Monitoring, are part of the planning process group. Doesn't it mean that Risk is more about planning well and in advance?

Risk Management Planning

Whenever you want to work on something, you first need to plan your work. Especially, when it is as important as Risk Planning, it needs lot of planning done in advance. A risk planning involves big amount of brainstorming, analysis, interactions and applying though process.

The below diagram explains how the Risk Management Planning is done. As every other planning process, organization process assets and Enterprise environmental factors play an important role, since every organization have their own plans, processes, forms, templates and policies.

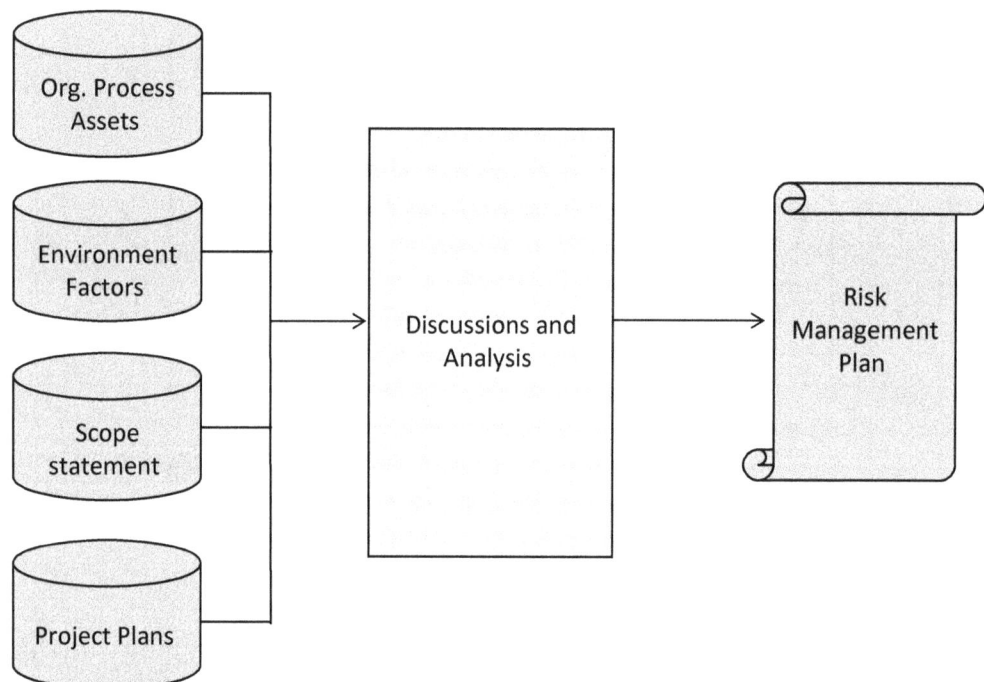

If you notice, the key input that are used as inputs in the Risk Management Planning process are Scope Statement and Project Plans. Since every project is being executed with the sole purpose of achieving certain objectives and according to customer requirements, the scope of the project is considered as a key input to understand the requirements. Remember that there is a difference between Risk Management Planning done between different projects and businesses.

Similarly, while preparing the Risk Management Planning, it is essential to understand the Cost, Schedule, Communication, Quality other subsidiary plan

---

components and analyze their objective. This will help plan for the Risks and further mitigation plans for the project.

In the above diagram, the tool that is primarily used for preparing the Risk Management Plan is *Discussions and Analysis*. This might sound very generic for many.

The best way to identify risks is by way of interactions with all the stakeholders, team, managers of projects that were executed in your organization in the past, experts to name few. Even the customers might be able to provide a list of risks that they foresee. This data might be very critical for your project. You might need to plan on how you are going to manage the risks rests with you, the Project Manager.

It is very essential for the project manager to make sure that the scheduled team meetings discussed about any potential risks in the project in the beginning through all the phases of the project. All details such as the status, severity, impact and mitigation of the risks are to be discussed extensively and update the risk register to keep it active and meaningful document.

All these above risk planning involves discussions, brainstorming and significant amount of analysis done to understand the risks and to mitigate them.

The only output of the risk management planning process is the risk management plan, which narrates how the risks are planned to be handled.

Risk Breakdown Structure

At this moment, it will help, if you could remember the Work Breakdown Structure (WBS) topic that we reviewed under the Scope Management Plan chapter. Similar to how you decomposed the entire project into multiple tasks, subtasks and group them, you can decompose the overall project risks into multiple categories of risks for easier classification. The logic behind doing is to identify as many risks as possible and to group them for easier classification.

The process of decomposing your project risks into multiple categories is defined as *Risk Breakdown Structure (RBS)*. A sample RBS is given below for your reference.

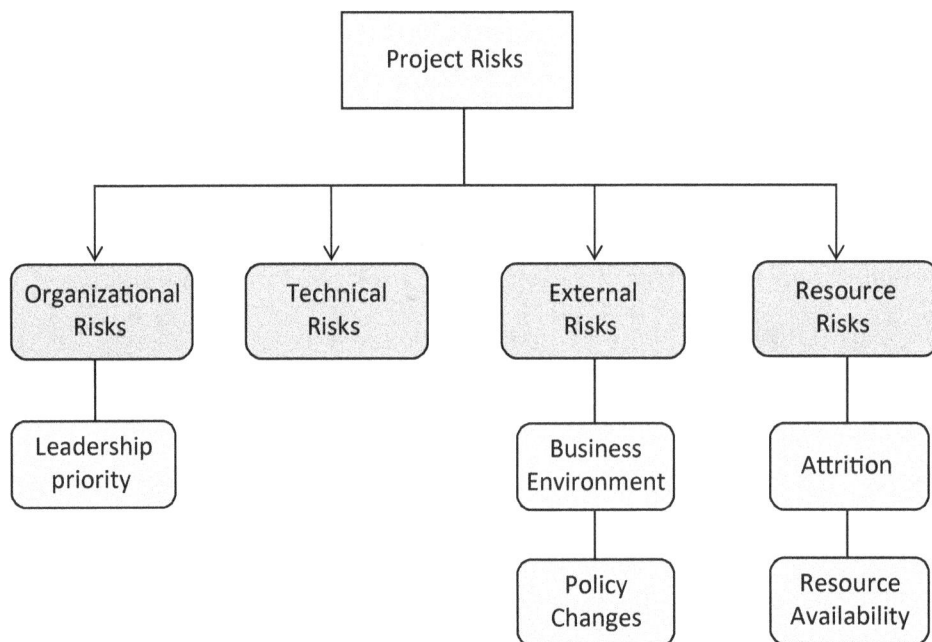

Under the Organizational Risks, what is a Leadership priority?

For every project to be successful, one of the important factor required is the buy-in and support from the senior management of the project performing organization. To have the support, the project objectives should be clearly identified and should be aligned with the organization's business objectives. The project objectives should clearly produce a result or outcome that is quantifiable and carries significant amount of material and business benefits to the organization. If the objectives are not impressive, the senior leadership might not to spend money on the project execution.

At times, the management might lose its interest in the project execution due to various reasons, which itself is a major risk for any project.

Risk Identification

As explained earlier in this chapter, the best way to execute a task is to decompose it into smaller and easily manageable subtasks. Having decomposed the project risks into easily manageable categories of tasks, now let us get into the *Risk identification* process.

To identify the risks, we will have a lot of interactions to be done with experts. This is very crucial since identifying risks doesn't depend only on your project alone, but on overall experience as well. You may be an amazing project manager but still there are potential risks hiding inside your project, which you might not have even thought about.

Since there can be any number of risks in any project, you may have to apply your mind and skills to identify as many risks as possible and makes sense to your project. The outcome of the Risk identification process is the Risk register.

Take a look into the diagram below

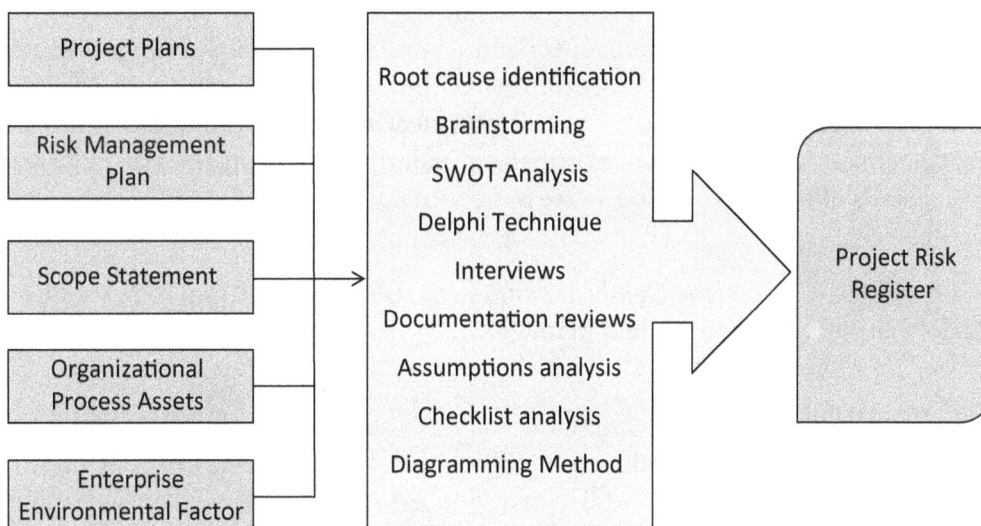

Inputs	Tools & Techniques	Output
Project Plans	Root cause identification	Project Risk Register
Risk Management Plan	Brainstorming	
Scope Statement	SWOT Analysis	
Organizational Process Assets	Delphi Technique	
Enterprise Environmental Factor	Interviews	
	Documentation reviews	
	Assumptions analysis	
	Checklist analysis	
	Diagramming Method	

Note on the inputs : One of the best and easier ways to identify risks in a project is to refer to the Organizational Process assets, which has several known risks that were encountered and analyzed in projects executed earlier by the performing organization. Similarly, referring other project management plans and scope statement will help understand any risks associated with achieving their respective objectives.

The project scope statement not only contains the details of the project's objective but has several risks hidden into it. For example, if the project's scope is to organize a launch of a movie premiere involving several distinguished guests from the movie industry, the project comes with its own risk of how many guests will be attending, how many might cancel their visit after accepting the invite. These details are essential to get their seats reserved.

Tools used in Risk identification

As stated earlier in this chapter, there is no such automated tool or process to identify the risks in a project. The best possible ways to identify risks are by way of communication and analysis. When I say communicating, it means seeking assistance from Project Management Office, Expert judgment, discussion with the stakeholders, team and referring to available resources in your organizational repository.

Prior to other mode, your skills as PM should help you identify the potential risks that exists in your project and those that are likely to come in future.

The Delphi Technique

One important way to identify risks in a project is to identify a list of experts with expertise in project management and having handled similar projects. Prepare a questionnaire asking specific questions to each of the experts about the project risks in a project environment. Once ready with the questionnaire circulate it to each of these experts. Upon hearing from them on the project risks, consolidate and brainstorm before including them in the risk register. The details of each of the experts are to be kept confidential so as to get a honest feedback.

This method is known as *Delphi Technique* of risk identification. I am sure this is not a tough task for a project manager.

SWOT Analysis

This method of analysis results in classifying the identified risks under Strength, Weakness, Opportunities and Threats. As explained earlier in this chapter, risks in a project is a mixed bag. At times, risks become major threat or turn out to be opportunities

Each of these have specific significance in the sense that threats and weakness are areas to be concerned of a potential negative threat. However, opportunities may turn out to be positive for the project, even though it is still a risk.

Checklist Analysis

Often, the organization process assets come handy when you are doing planning task for your project. The lessons learnt and other planning methodologies available in the organizational process repository are proven and accept by some customers. Though, you may not be managing the projects for the same client, you need not expect any major changes in expectations in the overall process to be adopted to your project.

When you are trying to identify risks in your project, you can utilize the available risks in your project repository. Take a look into those risks encountered in the past projects to create your own checklist of risks that you feel might suit your project needs. This checklist itself might fit good into your project risk register.

Such checklist verification helps in eliminating human error as well as helping the project manager to identify as much risks as possible in the initial phase itself.

Assumptions Analysis

It is a well-known fact that when you begin working on your project, you may not have all the required information readily available. Sometime, even critical inputs might take time to reach you. However, due to the urgency of the need you may be required to begin with the project pending those inputs.

In such situations, the common thing done is to make assumptions on unknown components or information and proceed with the project. However, these assumptions itself pose a risk to the project since such assumptions are not definite information. While a Project Manager's experience helps to take a realistic and sensible judgment prior to make such assumptions, there are more than likely that such assumptions go wrong.

Like any other risk, revisiting and reviewing the assumptions is one sensible and essential strategy while you identify the risks in your project. Sometimes, the assumptions you made might become a major risk.

Assume yourself to be managing a sizeable project that is to establish a retail supermarket in your town for a customer of yours. Some portion of the customer requirement is not very clear in the beginning. However, the customer cannot wait till the entire requirement is known. The customer wants the store to be setup and have it functional in time for the festival season.

You are making an assumption about location of certain sections of the store and begin to execute the project. If the assumption is validated and confirmed by the client in the earlier phase of the project, there may not have much impact. However, if there is lack of clarity or ambiguity till the later phase of the project, it is a major risk and a cause for serious concern.

So, doing an analysis and review of the assumptions made with the customers and stakeholder is always a good idea to identify the nature and magnitude of the risks in your project.

Diagramming Method

Also known as *Ishikawa diagram* or *Fishbone diagram*, this technique involve decomposing the entire risks into multiple categories such as technical, business, resource. Once these categories are listed, further decomposing is required to pin point specific risks relating to each of these category.

The primary logic of adapting to this methodology is to ensure ease of identifying risks without ignoring any potential threats. A sample diagram is given below for your easy understanding.

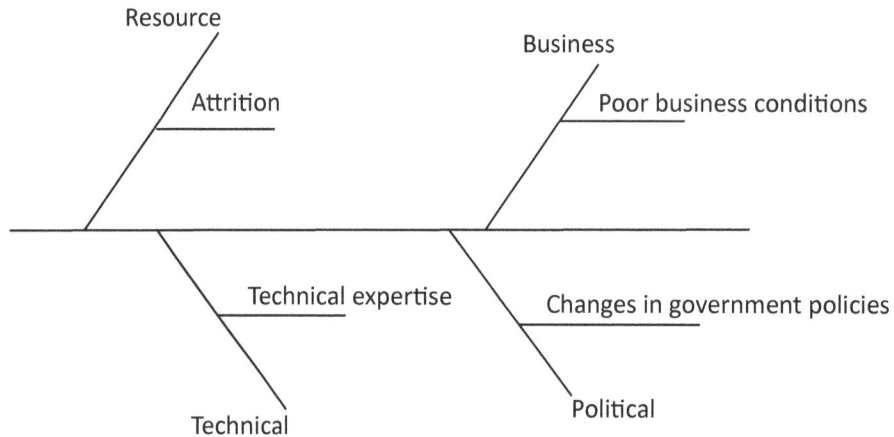

Resource

Business

Attrition

Poor business conditions

Technical expertise

Changes in government policies

Technical

Political

I am sure the above tools used to identify risks are easily understandable.

Brainstorming refers to having the entire team meet together and discuss on the potential risks in the project. This might prove to be a very efficient way to identify the risks since the construction team has more visibility of risks in their own area of operation.

Interviews is another way of seeking experts' judgment on potential risks in the project.

Documentation reviews refer to reviewing the original plan and design of the end product, which might throw more light on a potential risk for the project.

Root Cause Analysis is another critical risk identification factor. Whenever some issues or risks are identified in a project, it is always an intelligent idea to identify the root cause of the risks, rather than blindly adding them into the risk register. Doing a root cause analysis might throw more light on the risks, its impact and severity.

At times, such root cause analysis might help identify more risks as well as reduce the impact and severity of the already identified risk.

In a project environment, some of the categories of risks can be...

• Stakeholder related risks
• Transition related risks (this might include timely completion of transition and amount of inputs provided to the project team to help them carry with their work)
• Project management related risks
• Technology related risks
• Infrastructure related risks

- Management commitment risks
- Budgeting and cost related risks
- Schedule related risks
- Social events
- Scope related
- Supplier related risks
- General risks (such as logistics, policy related and so on)

Risk Register

Once you identify the list of risks that you foresee in your project, you should create a *Risk register* containing all the identified risks, their impact and probability. The impact is the extent of impact, should that risk be encountered in the project. The probability is the probability of the risks becoming a real and active.

The Organizational process repository should have a standard template for the Risk register. If not, you can create your own template for the Risk register and get it approved by the quality team prior to implementing the template in your project. A sample Risk register template looks as the one given below

I have given only one sample risk in the risk register. Why not you try to identify your own risks for your project, based on your understanding of the Risk Management process that we have covered till now. You may use the blank rows in the below table to enter yours

Risk No	Identified Risk	Planned response	Cause	Category	Priority	Probability
1.	Resource attrition will have serious impact on delivery and schedule	To have backup resource and buffer to handle unexpected attrition	Resources not happy with work or better opportunities	Resource	High	Moderate

In the above Risk register, planned response is what your plan to handle. Cause is the root cause of the risk. This root cause will be the outcome of your analysis performed on the risks identified. Criticality refers to the urgency, with which you expect the risk to be resolved to eliminate or reduce the impact.

When you create your risk register, remember to list all the risks, whether they are threats or opportunities. This Risk Register is one of the important documents that you would be using in your team in the status meetings to analyze and update.

Keeping the Risk register updated is one very important task of a Project Manager. Moreover, the content of the risk register is discussed in the regular meetings with the team and other stakeholders as part of managing the risks.

Qualitative Analysis

Your job will not be over with the risk identification and creating a risk register. A sensible way to manage your risks is to prioritize them for easier handling. Failing to prioritize your risks will end you in utter chaotic situation. Not every risk can be of equal priority. Some risks may have high visibility while some other risks may have only cosmetic requirements.

Imagine a situation where you identified 20 risks in your project. You had discussions with your stakeholders and team to identify these. There are more possibility that some of these risks are not going to cause too much of damage while few others might cause catastrophic impact on your project. So, you need to pay more attention to those risks that are high on impact while keeping an eye on the lesser impacting risks.

This classification can be achieved by way of doing an analysis called Qualitative analysis or Risk ranking. A qualitative analysis means assessing the risks based on their merit. Based on your view and knowledge of your project's current status and Risk planning, it shouldn't be difficult to rank all of these risks.

Let us now see, how the qualitative analysis of the risk is done.

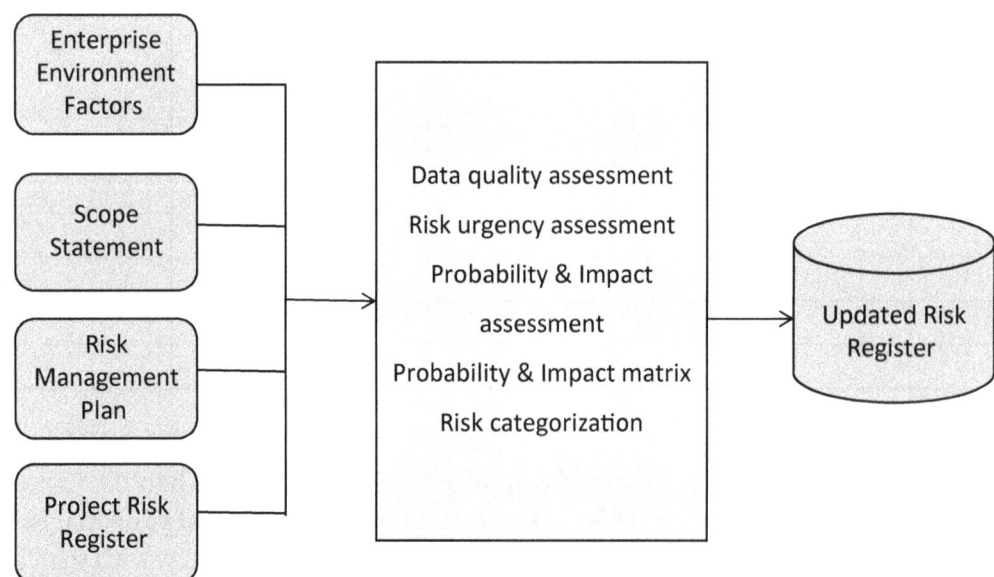

I am sure the inputs to the Qualitative analysis process is pretty much easy to understand and sensible. The use of Scope Statement means you have your project objective on hand while identifying the risks and analyzing them. This is because, project risks changes depending on the scope of the project. A building project being constructed in Chicago has different risks than constructing a skyscraper in New York City. Chicago being windy compared to New York mean you need to focus on the wind condition while planning for your project.

Similarly, the Project Risk Register is a catalog of risks identified for the current project. This list of risk is essential to make an assessment of their threat level.

Does it make sense?

Notes on the Tools used in Qualitative Risk Analysis

Coming to the tools that are used in the Risk analysis, all of them involve brainstorming and analyzing.

Not every project risk is very important. Some may be less critical, while some others may require immediate attention. This classification can be performed while analyzing the quality of the data.

Similarly, identifying the probability of certain risks from occurring and their subsequent impact might go a long way in managing them. The data that you come up with can be used in a tabular or graphical format to have the probability and impact listed against each of the risk identified in the register. This might help you to assess the risks based on the probability of their occurrence, potential impact and their quality.

This is one of the best way to manage risks thought it involves accurate analysis and computations.

Another important activity in the Risk analysis is to categorize them. As stated above, list of risks can be decomposed under internal and external. Further, they can be decomposed such as Business condition, economical and natural disaster and more.

Such *Risk Categorization* will help in assigning owners and to handle them more efficiently. Certain risks, involving political issues may not be under your scope of resolution. Such risks can be passed onto those who are taking business critical and policy decisions.

When the risk assessment is being done, it is essential to analyze the data that help in identifying a risk. At times, data might play key role in assessing the impact, probability and severity. As an example, if your project is a new business initiative of your organization, there may be possibility of risks by way of policy changes of the government. However, when this risk is being assessed, the past track record of the government, policy of the current administrators play critical role in identifying the probability.

Output of Qualitative Risk Analysis

An *updated risk register* is the sole output of the Qualitative Risk Analysis.

The very purpose of doing a qualitative analysis is to identify the impact and probability of the risks. These two factors decide the priority of the risks from the risk register. Thus, the outcome of such an analysis results in having an updated risk register.

Quantitative Risk Analysis

Now that you have identified the potential risks in your project, created a risk register too. You have ranked these risks according to their merit as well. Is it not the time to understand the impact of these risks in terms of data?

No organization would like pages of risks without quantifying data of the impact of the risks. It means nothing for the management to read pages of essay type stories. So, it is the time to quantify the impact of these risks. Quantifying may be done in terms of the cost impact or any facts that speaks with some sensible numbers.

Let us define the Quantitative Risk Analysis with the below diagram

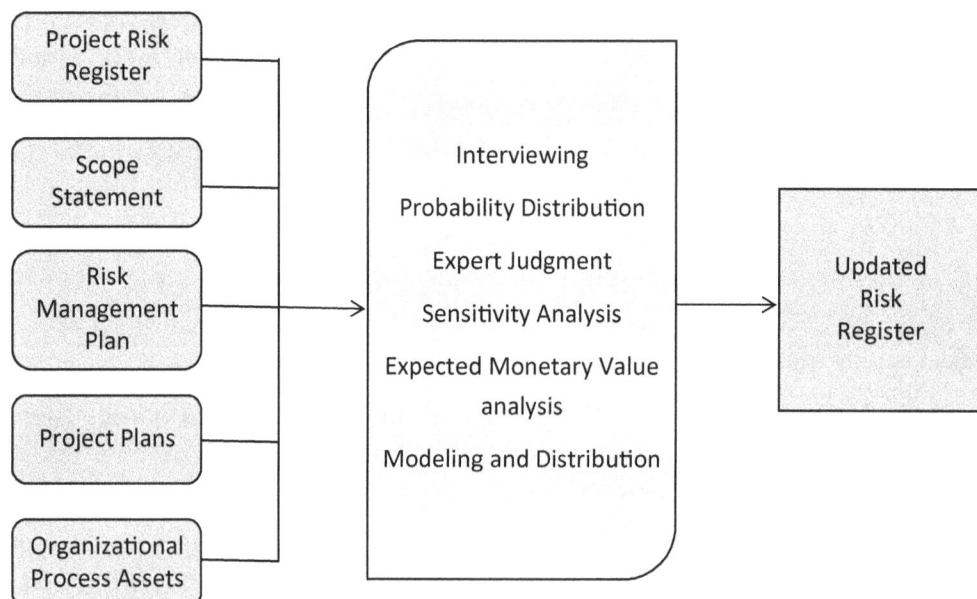

Having covered much about Risk Management Plan till now, you must be familiar with all of the inputs found in the above diagram.

Tools used in Quantitative Analysis

Interviewing

One of the best ways to analyze your risk is to interview people who have expertise and experience in handling risks in their projects. While interviewing people, your primary focus should be on obtaining the estimated cost impact of the risk, if it occurs. This would help you estimate your budget and prepare yourself with plans to manage such risks.

Probability Distribution

The best way to catch your leaders' attention is to present your report in a graphical form rather than sending pages of report. A picture conveys a lot more meaning within a shortest period of time. Do you remember the graphs that you created in your schooldays?

Creating graphs with time and cost estimates will help you obtain a graph that would prove very worth to analyze the risks and their probability.

Earned Monetary Value Technique

Earned Monetary Value Technique (EMV) is another good way to analyze your data and arrive at a decision with the help of two methods. First is to use the data to calculate the impact and the other way is to draw a decision tree with data forming part of it. These methods involves doing some calculations using the probability and potential cost impact, should the risk really occur.

Imagine a situation, you are working on a project to build a wind turbine for a customer. You are using products that are imported from overseas due to cheaper cost. The cost of this product is $600 per piece.

During your planning phase, you hear that your customer prefers locally made products over imported ones for some specific reasons. However, you haven't heard anything from them on this. You decide to include this as a risk with greater impact and moderate probability. To arrive at this, you should begin with creating a table to include the probability and impact of each risk. The impact can be in terms of the cost impact, should that risk occur. If your probability is represented in terms of per cent of occurrence, then multiplying the probability with the impacted cost would give you the solution.

Risks	Probability	Impact of risks
Equipment replacement	40%	Cost of replacement $600
Faulty machine during execution	25%	Cost to fix $280
Unavailability of motor locally	15%	Leasing cost from other source $250

Use the data in the above table to calculate the Earned Monetary Value as shown below

Equipment Replacement	50% x -$600 =	-$30
Faulty machine	25% x -$280 =	-$70
Unavailability of motor	15% x -$250 =	-$37.50

Adding the result of above will give you the Earned Monetary Value of the risks that you have.

Using Decision Tree to Analyze Your Impact of Risks

Let us assume, you are considering two different suppliers to supply the machines required for the assembly line that is setup to produce some specific components for the power utility company. You have received bids from two suppliers to supply machines required for the assembly line of your company.

You are trying to look at the risk factors of buying machines from each of the suppliers and finally decide to analyze the factors that might help you to arrive at a decision. So, you draw a decision tree as below.

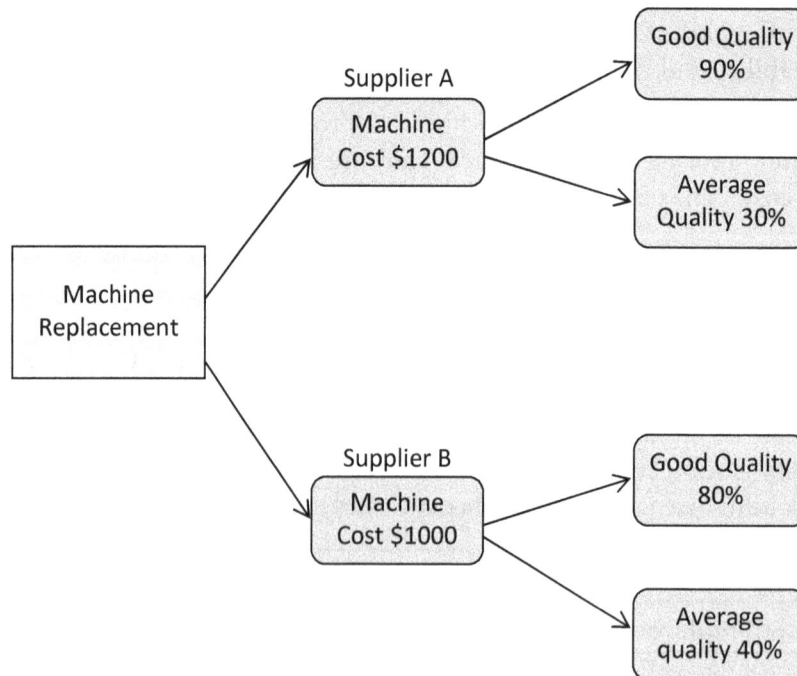

In the above diagram, both the suppliers have advantages as well as disadvantages in terms of the quality and cost. The impact and probability is analyzed using the decision tree as illustrated above and the Expected money value is derived for the risk being taken by the project performing organization.

The overall EMV involves using the machine cost and the probability of the risk as illustrated in the previous pages of this chapter.

Difference Between Qualitative and Quantitative Risk Analysis

By now, you might be wondering where the Qualitative and Quantitative risk analysis differ and what do they produce differently.

Indeed, they both are different in the context that a Qualitative risk means analyzing the quality of the risk and ranking them based on the merit. However, quantitative risk involves identifying the financial and other resource impact of the result of the risk.

Though they both perform different task, they both are interdependent on each other.

Where to Find Risks in a Project?

A Risk can be anywhere in the project.

Imagine a key stakeholder is missed out during the stakeholder identification phase of the project planning. This is a major risk for any project. If this stakeholder is identified during the middle of the project execution, it might involve a major scope change and simultaneous impact on cost, schedule and the overall execution of a project. The overall impact of this is going to be catastrophic.

Similarly, any change in leadership approach or strategy towards the project might have significant impact. Every small step performed in any project across all industries carries potential risks. This makes the Risk Management, a very critical factor in the success or failure of a project.

Can you think and identify one important Risk mitigation plan of the modern age?

If you answered Data Recovery Center or Disaster Recovery Center, hurray.... You are real good and absolutely right. Data being the most important information processed and possessed by every organization of this world, safeguarding the data becomes the most important task in every organization's business strategy.

Why Risks are Very Critical for the Success or Failure of a Project

Obviously, a Risk has the potential to derail the entire project and cause as much trouble to the team and to the performing organization, unless the risks are not managed properly.

Imagine a situation, you are a project manager wherein you are responsible for a railway project to lay a new line. During the risk planning phase, you are expected to consider every possible factor, such as internal and external risks and prepare a plan to manage the risks, if they really occur. However, you are too confident that the tracks are being laid on a hilly terrain with rocky surface. So, you haven't considered the fact that not the entire stretch may be rocky but some smaller stretches might have loose sands, which might give in, if there is heavy rain.

So, during the course of analysis, you decide to randomly inspect the surface. Fortunately for you, there was no rain during the project execution so everything went well and your railway track is laid according to everyone's satisfaction. You obtained signoff from the customer and letter of appreciation. Shortly before the inauguration of the rail line, there was a heavy downpour for several days that exposes the poor surface condition. This result in soil erosion and the track inspection group finds the railway line unfit for passenger or freight traffic. Your company seeks an explanation from you as to what went wrong and whether all processes were completed according to the guidelines.

You respond to the note saying that it was only an exceptional incident at a specific location where the laid track was weakened by the rain.

However, do you expect your client to buy that theory in? Obviously, they won't.

The client is now beginning to worry about the worthiness of the entire project, especially on the hilly terrain. Unless the completed work on the hill is proved to be satisfactory, they cannot begin operating services in a particular sector, that includes the across the hill. They decide to put the entire project on hold and not willing to allocate any additional funds to fix the problem.

This refusal is the result of losing confidence in your organization's lack of competency and your poor management skills to execute a project.

Which Risk is More Important?

This might be a question in anyone's mind, who is managing risks first time.

The answer is every risk is important. The probability and the impact of a risk appearing may be very low in your risk register. What if it does occur?

It might have some impact on your project schedule and cost, which might impact significantly. So, a low priority risk doesn't necessarily mean you need not worry about it.

Then, how would you handle these risks.

Watchlist might come handy for the Project Manager when he is managing the risks. This watchlist contains risks that are to be monitored even though they are not listed as high probable candidates causing more impact.

Let us assume, your project is producing merchandise for the local football team supporters. You have an order to make about 10,000 of such merchandise. You were more busy with designing and producing the merchandise. As the launch date is nearing, you realize that the boxes to pack the merchandises haven't arrived from the vendor yet and will take another week. The result is your launch date need to be pushed by two weeks due to non-availability of the packing material. Initially, you never thought the availability of the packing material to be a major risk, but it did become one later.

The format of the watchlist can be same that of your risk register.

When the Risk Occurs

A risk can occur any moment of time and any phase of the project, right from start to closure. Imagine a situation wherein the scope to build a massive aircraft career is finalized according to customized vessel requirement of the Navy. If the government brings in a new regulation, which prevents procuring accessories and spares from overseas, it might put the entire shipbuilding project in jeopardy. Of course, the entire project might still hold good but a lot of re-planning may be required, including a change to the already agreed scope. If this risk occurs during the early phase of the project, the impact of such risk may be limited.

Similarly, when the dates are finalized for the release of an attractive anti-virus software and you notice that the outer box of the software has incorrect name spelt or some proprietary information is missing, you might end up postponing the entire release, thus impacting your plan.

So, an intelligent project manager keeps the risks in mind always. It is strongly recommended to discuss all the risks, their status and mitigation in all the project meetings with the rest of the team. Also, the Project Manager makes sure that any mitigation plan on a risk doesn't result in the introduction of new ones. So, when you go to your next meeting with your team, remember to discuss the risks and the Risk Management Plan with the team.

When the Risks are to be Identified

Identification of risks begins along with the Project manager commencing his project planning activities.

As explained earlier, the risks can be from anywhere and every sort of risks are to be counted, no matter whether it is minor or major. One of the recommended way to assess the risks is to refer to the historical information of similar project that were executed in your organization over a period of time. These historic projects might be a good source of identifying the risks.

A great project manager captures all known risks in the risk management plan and lists the critical nature of the risks, potential impact and mitigation plans. The risk management plan is then discussed with the stakeholders, which includes the project team. During this deliberation of the risks, you might assign the owners to each of the risk and make it a complete risk management plan.

Who Owns the Risks?

While monitoring and tracking the risks is the responsibility of the Project manager. However, the PM can assign any of the risk to any of his team member or any stakeholders, depending on the category of the risk.

The risk management plan consists of the risk details, owner and the business critical nature of the risk. In any case, the Project Manager owns the overall responsibility of tracking the Risks, according to his own plan. It is very important that the communication plays a very important role in the risk management process. Any discussion on risk register or individual risks, big or small, should be transparent and involve every stakeholder or team member of the project.

What Should be Done with Risks?

The most important action to be performed after identifying the risks is to analyze them for potential impacts and the probability of the risks occurring during the execution of your project. This needs a careful analysis to be as much accurate as possible.

Now, the question of what to do with the Risks. There are four ways of handling a risk.

*   Avoid
*   Transfer
*   Mitigate
*   Accept

Also, identifying the owners for each of the risks and appropriate mitigation plan on how you are planning to handle your risks, should they occur in future.

These makes sure you are prepared for the risks with appropriate mitigation plan of action. Don't forget to add the risks discussion in your meeting agenda with all the stakeholders in every meeting. This will insure all the stakeholders are aware of the risk status and their potential impact.

Avoiding a Risk

While driving on a freeway you come across a signboard that caution the drivers of a possible congestion ahead, would you still want to take the same route and drive further?

Certainly you will not. Would you?

You will want to look for alternate and less crowded route, especially when you are heading for an important business meeting.

Similarly, in a project environment when you anticipate risks in adapting to particular strategy or plan, the first thing that should flash on mind is how to avoid the risk. You would certainly put your management skills and expertise into work and find ways to bypass the risk.

If a project is being planned to construct an oil pipeline between two corners of a country. Due to the freezing cold climate prevailing in the region for many months of the year, the construction company decide to engage some experts from Siberia due to their expertise in working in such freezing climatic condition. However, later the company realizes the communication issues of engaging the resources since none of them are able to speak English. Finally, the company decide to drop its plan.

Obviously there should be alternative plans and ideas to overcome a risky situation. Accepting the risk need not be the instant action when you begin working on the risk management plan.

Can a Risk Ownership be Transferred?

One of the best strategies to handle a risk is to consider transferring them?

Let us consider an example.

Let us take the case of leasing a cargo ship for your new startup. Your company leases a massive cargo vessel having a huge capacity. You want to protect your business interest on the huge investment you have made in your new shipping business. Of course, you obviously want everything to sail smooth in your business and with zero risks. However, there are bound to be risks and you need to accept the reality, especially if you are planning to use your cargo carrier to transport cargo across the turbulent transatlantic route. So, you look for ways to face the reality.

In this case, you decide to insure the vessel prior to taking it to the waters. Now, the risk is transferred to the insurance companies. In this, you want to protect the financial interests of your organization from unexpected event that might occur in future.

Sometimes, your organization may not have expertise in performing some specific tasks of your project. In this case, they might decide to subcontract this piece of work to another company that has expertise in the related area. Though this is also classified as a risk management strategy, this is one way to handle project execution by engaging experts.

Accepting and Mitigating a Risk

When you cannot avoid or transfer a risk, you do not have any other option except accepting the risk and begin to plan mitigate the risk.

Risk mitigation involves doing qualitative and quantitative analysis, analyze the probability and impact of the risk, if it really occurs. The outcome of such analysis is collected and use the expert judgment and your own project management expertise to list down the mitigation plan on how to handle such risks, if it really happen.

Risk Response Planning

Having the Risk register with all required inputs should help you go ahead with planning. As explained earlier, a risk can be a potential threat as well as throw opportunities. When it is a threat, you should be ready with mitigation plan and face it. If it is an opportunity, try to exploit it and convert it to your advantage for more opportunities. So, I have classified the Risk responses into two different categories for easier response planning. It is in the Risk Response Planning process, the Project Manager assigns the risks to individual owners that will help manage and track them.

Let us look into the below diagram for a detailed view of the Risk Response Planning.

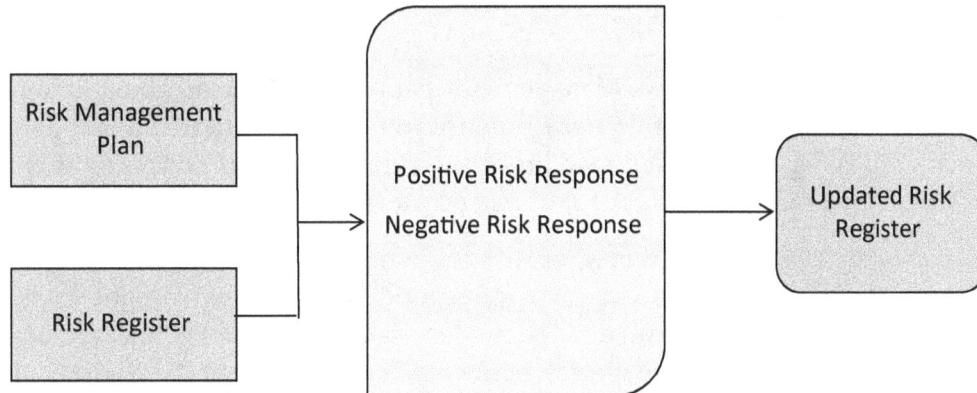

In the above diagram, Positive Risk response includes Exploit, Share, Enhance and Accept.

Positive Risk Response

Exploit

Exploiting a risk mean exploiting the opportunity to make sure you get maximum advantages, should that risk occur. Some strategies to handle this include having a special focus on such risks or having a specially skilled team member handling it. This would make sure the project gets the maximum benefit.

Share

At times, you know well that certain risks offer you great benefits or opportunity for your project. But, you may be handicapped by certain factors such as lack of expertise or resources or funding. In such cases, you can share such risks with other groups or external resources to get the maximum benefits.

Enhance

Sometime, there may be some risks that are in your register but not occurred yet. You know well that that risk offers great opportunities, should it occur. If you are sure of it, you can influence the triggers that might trigger the risk. Once triggered, you use this opportunity to gain maximum advantages for your project.

Accept

If you are not able to adopt to any of these above strategies, the best way is to accept the risk as you would do with any other risk. Once the project manager decide to accept a risk, the mitigation planning need to get started and tracked throughout the project phases

Negative Risk Response

In the beginning of this Risk Management chapter, we have read about various ways to respond to risks. I do not think, they need to be repeated again here. Just try to go back and understand how the risks are managed. At this moment, it would be good to learn a couple of more factors about risks.

A *secondary risk* is resulted by your Risk Response Planning to handle another risk. In otherwords, when you plan to respond to your risk, it might trigger further more risks. These are called Secondary risks. You are not going to handle these secondary risks in any special manner. You might want to follow the same strategy that you have been handling other risks. However, you should keep the dependency factor between these risks in mind until they are resolved.

Residual Risks are the risks that remain within your project, even after your Risk Response planning. Depending on the merit, probability and impact of the risks, you should have your response planning done to handle them.

Your project is complete and the big skyscraper is ready for its inauguration. You have planned for all the risks and finished the project. To avoid any fire accidents, you have installed fire extinguishers in every floor and corner of the building. Still, having fire extinguishers do not mean there won't be fire ever. The threat will always be there even after planning for the response.

Risk Monitoring Process

A Risk Management is an evolving process. This means, except the Risk management planning process, every other process is to be active till the end of the project. There is no definite way to identify all the risks at the beginning of the project itself. Many risks keeps evolving as the project makes progress. Some risks might surface towards the end of the project or a risk on the watch list becomes a critical risks for the project.

While you should be clear with the ways to monitor the identified risks, you should always be on the lookout for more risks that might surface

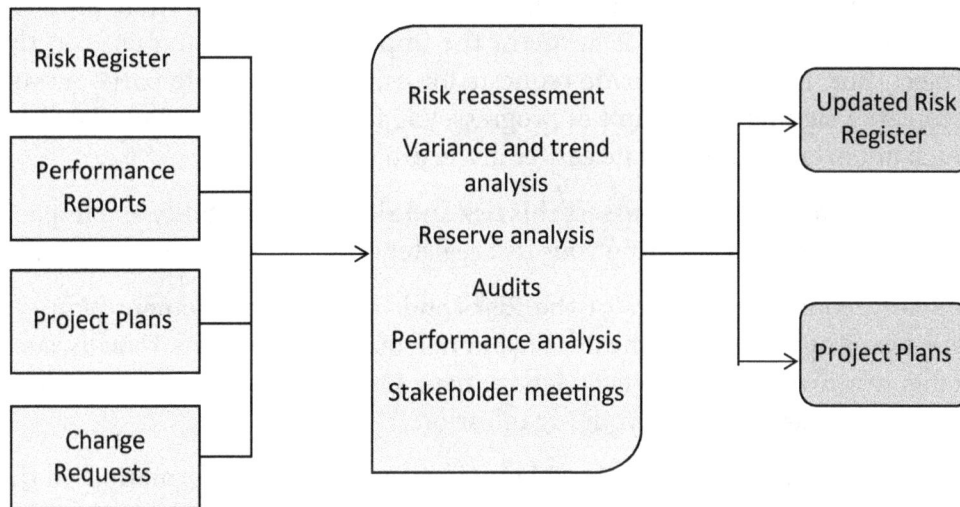

```
Risk Register ──┐
                │
Performance ────┤        ┌─────────────────────┐        ┌──────────────┐
Reports         │        │  Risk reassessment  │        │ Updated Risk │
                ├──────► │                     │ ─────► │  Register    │
                │        │ Variance and trend  │        └──────────────┘
Project Plans ──┤        │     analysis        │
                │        │  Reserve analysis   │
                │        │       Audits        │        ┌──────────────┐
Change ─────────┘        │ Performance analysis│ ─────► │ Project Plans│
Requests                 │ Stakeholder meetings│        └──────────────┘
                         └─────────────────────┘
```

Input to the Risk Monitoring Process

We understand what a *Risk Register* is. It is an updated list of risks and the relevant information about each of the risks in the list.

A *performance report* is how the project is performing as per the objective. The purpose of using the performance report in this process is to assess and understand where the project is and any potential missing deadlines or new issues and risks surfacing in the project. Only a project performance report can throw more input into this.

Tools used to Risk Monitoring Process

Analysis is one important tool that is useful in Monitoring the risks. This analysis can be in multiple forms by way of scrutinizing available data and discussions. As explained earlier in this chapter, one critical component of controlling the risks is to include the discussion on risks in the agenda of *stakeholder meetings*. Stakeholders include the project team that is executing the project.

By doing this, all the stakeholders would have updates on the status and progress of the risks management and response. In addition, such forums would help identify more risks, as the project makes further progress. As the project makes further progress, the significance of risks keeps changing. The reasons may be different for each risk.

Imagine a situation discussed earlier in this chapter, where you begin your project execution based on an assumption of using a specific tool that is imported from another country due to the cost advantage of importing. However, your customer is known to use locally made parts. Yet, you haven't heard any specific instruction from the client on using imported products from a specific country.

This was initially a major risk. However, as you make more and more progress on your project, the client is aware of the imported parts being used in the project. But, they haven't made requests for using locally made parts. As you complete a significant amount of progress, you feel this risk need not be given much importance as was done earlier in the project phase.

This means you decide to reassess this risk and alter the probability and impact. This progress of reprioritizing your risk register is called *Risk reassessment*.

Similarly, conducting *audits* of the Risks and the risk management plan is a very good way to check the health of your risk management plan. Usually, such audits can involve the Project Management Office or any experts who have handled similar projects in your organization.

The outcome of any analysis should provide you with vital information on the performance of your projects and the status and significance of the risks at that phase of the project. Such data provided by such analysis can be used to prepare a report that shows the graphical representation of the *variance and trend* in the *risk performance*.

If you notice any significance pattern or trend on the performance in your analysis, that needs more of your attention for any missing piece of action. Remember that unless there is any problems in planning things shouldn't go wrong in a systematic pattern or trend. Do you agree?

As you are aware, one of the strategies to respond to risks is to have buffer resources to handle any emergency needs. Such resources can be in the form of human resources, physical or availability of additional funding to be utilized in case of a need. As you analyze the status and progress of your risks, you may need to revisit the buffer resources and update it based on the need.

At this moment it is to be noted that whatever revision is being made to the risks and the resources, should be shared with all the shareholders of the project. This will help them to understand the current progress and to come with their inputs on the risks.

Output of the Risk Monitor Process

Since the Risk Monitoring process is similar to that of the Change management process of the scope, the Risk register gets updated as the analysis and review is done on the risks' status. Subsequently, the relevant project plans get updated.

Now, you might have a question in mind as to how other project plans might be impacted as a result of the risk Monitoring?

Whenever you working on risk planning and monitoring the primary objective of you should be to keep a very careful and close look into the status of the risks and their potential effect on the project until the risks are eliminated or bypassed. In the middle of your project, if you are suspecting an identified risk is most certain to occur, you begin planning to handle such risk.

As an example, if your project is behind schedule by a week. This is because the development phase is taking longer than planned. However, your Organization has already planned the date of launching the product. Certainly, you cannot go back to your leadership requesting them to postpone the launch.

However, being a very brilliant Project Manager, you foresaw this risk and had mitigation plan. The plan was to engage additional resources to handle any delays. You had even identified even a skilled resource to support the development or testing teams to expedite the quicker completion of the product. When you really encounter this risk in your project, you decide to engage the extra resources to plan for testing and verification.

Your responsibility is to revisit the other project plans such as Human Resource, cost and schedule to include this excess resource and the effort involved.

Does this make sense?

EXERCISES

True or False

1.   You are working on a project to build a cruise liner for a customer. Due to the project risk involved, your company has decided to utilize the facilities of the customer in building the ship. This means accepting the risk. (**True/False**)

2.   An insurance company deciding to reinsure a project can be called Transferring the risk.   (**True/False**)

3.   When there is no other option available, the best strategy is to accept the risk and plan to mitigate. (**True/False**)

4.   Whenever there is a risk in a project, the best strategy is to enhance the possibilities and utilize it as an opportunity for more opportunities. (**True/False**)

5.   All project risks are identified during the planning phase of the project. (**True/False**)

Match the Following

* Enhance   : Influence the factors of the risk and utilize the opportunity

* Exploit   : Exploiting the opportunity for maximum advantage to the project

* Share   : Sharing the expertise and opportunity for mutual benefits

* Delphi technique   : Seeking experts' opinion on risk identification

* Risk register   : List of risks identified by the Risk identification process

Fill in the Blanks

1.   Exploit is an example of _____

2.   Listing down the risks depending on their merit, impact and probability is a result of _____ Risk analysis

3.   Project risks are first identified in the _____ process group

4.   Revisiting and assessing the project assumptions made is called _____

5.   SWOT refers to _____, _____, _____ and _____ .

ANSWERS

True or False

1. False
2. True
3. True
4. False
5. False

Match the Following

- Enhance : List of risks identified by the Risk identification process

- Exploit : Sharing the expertise and opportunity for mutual benefits

- Share : Using the opportunity for maximum advantage to the project

- Delphi technique : Influence the factors of the risk and utilize the opportunity

- Risk register : Seeking experts' opinion on risk identification

Fill in the Blanks

1. Positive Risk Response
2. Qualitative
3. Planning
4. Assumptions analysis
5. Strength, Weakness, Opportunities and Threats

Test Your Knowledge

1. You are managing a project for a large automobile company, which is coming up with a massive project worth hundreds of million dollars to produce new range of autos. Your organization has won the bid to execute the project. The project is a fixed price project. The bid was approved by the customer after you created the project scope, schedule and cost baselines.

    What is the BIGGEST known risk for your organization on this project?

    a) There is no guarantee that the objectives of the project be completed due to lengthy schedule for its completion

    b) As per the contract terms, the client may terminate the contract anytime with one month notice

    c) Cost risk is on the seller in a fixed price bid

    d) Scope might undergo change, which might affect the schedule

2. Your organization has made you the project manager for its new venture and you have a team of professionals working on the execution phase of the project. One of your team member approaches you and express her intention to leave the job since she got a more attractive offer

    What type of risk this falls under?

    a) Internal Risk

    b) External Risk

    c) Customer related risk

    d) Market Risk

3. You are working as a project manager for a large engineering project, which is part of a program.

    You report to a program manager and have a 24 member team reporting to you. Your project has independent scope, schedule and cost and you track them. During one of your regular meeting with the stakeholders, you hear a stakeholder saying that there is a dependency for your project in the form of a new assembly line, which is not yet planned by the customer due to lack of resources and expertise. Unless that assembly line project gets completed, your project cannot be implemented. This has become major risk for your project.

    When you take this issue with your program manager, she decide to take a deeper look into this dependency factor. During a meeting with the customer on this dependency, she highlights the details of the dependency and the potential cost, business and schedule impact of this dependency and she offer to get this assembly line project completed since the expertise and human resources are available within your organization. She highlight the advantages and benefits to the customer if this project is executed by your organization.

What is your program manager trying to achieve here?

a) New business proposal discussion

b) Risk Management Planning

c) Risk acceptance

d) Exploiting the risk for more opportunities

4. Risk audits are part of which process group?

a) Planning

b) Execution

c) Closure

d) Monitor & Control

5. Jack is the project manager, who is done with his planning for scope, cost and schedule. As part of his Risk Process planning, he decide to refer his organization's process repository for risks managed for the similar projects of the past. He has done extensive deep dive into his project plans to locate potential risks and scheduled meetings with his project team to understand if they foresee any risks. He has also been meeting the stakeholders to understand risks from their end.

What process is he into now?

a) Risk Identification

b) Risk Management Planning

c) Planning

d) Risk register creation

6. You are driving on a freeway, when you see a warning signboard warning the motorists of a possible delay due to an accident few miles ahead. Since you are heading to work urgently to attend to a very important business meeting, you decide to exit the freeway and take alternative route.

This is the example for:

a) Risk Management

b) Avoid

c) Transfer

d) Accept

7. An updated Risk register is an output of
   a) Quantitative Risk Analysis
   b) Risk Response Planning
   c) Risk Monitoring
   d) All of the above

8. You are managing a large construction project that aims to build a massive convention center in the downtown. As part of cost strategy, material availability and since the project has a strict deadline given by the sponsor, you decide to import the components from overseas to eliminate any risk of material unavailability on time. Your customer is pleased with your assurance that material availability wouldn't be a constraint for the project and the convention center will be completed on the agreed date.

   However, when you begin planning for your risks, you find out that importing the components carry greater amount of risks such as delay in arrival, natural causes, obtaining licenses from government and clearing the shipment at the port. It is now your job to plan for these risks.

   How would you define these risks?
   a) Secondary Risks
   b) Residual Risks
   c) Risk Management Planning
   d) Risk Response Planning

9. Your project is intending to produce a gaming software for the demanding market. You are busy in planning for the project components. As part of Risk planning, you are creating a list of all potential risks in the project, big or small. After you completed all the risk analysis, you have an updated risk register that lists all the risks. As you take a relook into the list of risks, you find that some of the risks are not important and may not trigger till the later part of the project phase. You do not want to waste time tracking them daily. So, you decide to split your risk register and create a separate register for the less important and impacting ones. You handover the split list to your project leader for tracking them separately.

   How do you differentiate these two risk registers?
   a) They are both same as they both contain risks for the same projects
   b) Only the primary risk register is important due to its impact
   c) The secondary risk register should be taken up after the primary risks are managed

d) The primary risk register contains more important risks, while the secondary list is called Watchlist

10. **You are managing a week-long event management project in your town. Since the local weather office has predicted hurricane & heavy rain during the week when the event takes place. So, you decide to opt for an insurance to meet any unexpected financial loss. This is an example of**

a) Accept

b) Transfer

c) Avoid

d) Mitigate

11. **The management reducing the funding for the project before its completion is an example of**

a) Internal Risk

b) External Risk

c) Business Risk

d) None of the above

12. **You are planning for the risks for your project. The objective of your project is to conduct an analysis of the business, current trend and future prospects for one of your prestigious customer, who are market leaders in their segment of operations. You collect enormous amount of data, analyze them and have discussions with the company's leadership and several experts to arrive at a broader understanding of the market.**

As you begin foreseeing the future prospects of the company and the market in general, you predict a potential business slowdown impacted by demand-supply scenario, political issues, currency values and unrest in certain parts of the world in the near future. After a careful analysis of these, you decide to consider them as some of the influencing factor that might dictate the market trend in the next 1-2 years.

How do you classify these in your Risk planning process?

a) Internal Risks

b) Political Risks

c) Market

d) External Risks

13. Janet is the project manager for a team of 20 people. The team is busy with the construction phase. The team has a total of 52 tasks to complete, as part of their construction phase. The construction activity has been going on satisfactorily till last week. However, one of her team member approached Janet and report a delay in getting data from another interface due to some external factor. This data may be available after 3 days. Janet had expected such little troubles with the project and had included such dependency in the risk register. As the team member reported the issue, Janet has started verifying the risk and its level of impact and the forecast date of completion. She is thinking of deploying an extra resource to get this task completed on time. Her investigation will help her estimate and understand the feasibility.

    Which process group is Janet in?

    a) Execution

    b) Monitoring & Control

    c) Planning

    d) Initiation

14. Residual risks are examples of

    a) Risk Monitoring

    b) Negative Risk Response

    c) Positive Risk Response

    d) External Risk

15. David is a project manager, who is assigned to manage his first project by his supervisor. He has been assisting his boss in managing projects in the past and has shown interest in managing assignments of his team. In his new project, he has done the planning for all the components. He has created a risk register and included all the potential risks along with the level of impact, probability and mitigation plans. He identified owners for each of the risk and notified them. As he is pressed with work, he decide to handover the risk register to his project lead for tracking them to closure. He decided not to put his nose into the risk management since his leader is capable of handling.

    As the project makes further progress, David notices a whole lot of troubles in the project with unexpected issues coming up with no plan of response. This is making the project go out of shape and the impact is seen in the schedule. The customer is frustrated and decide to escalate to David's supervisor for the poor management of the project.

Where did things go wrong for David?

a) His mistake is to handover the risk managing responsibility to his leader. He shouldn't have done that but owned by himself

b) Such issues and schedule overruns are common in a project environment and cannot be avoided

c) David was over confident on his project lead

d) Risk identification should happen throughout the project phases. David identified the risks in the beginning and assigned his leader to manage them. He never thought about new risks surfacing during the later stages of the project.

16. **Reserve Analysis is part of which process group**

a) Monitoring & Control

b) Planning

c) Execution

d) Initiation

17. **Anita is the new project manager for the migration project replacing Monica, who moved to another project and location. As Anita begin to settle with her new project, she started reviewing all the processes and practices planned by Monica before she left the project. During one of the discussion with the stakeholders, Anita was informed that the stakeholders are not very happy with the way project risks were planned & managed till now since some of the risks impacted the schedule and cost. The stakeholders asked Anita to pay more attention to validating the risks and report them ,if there are any gaps found.**

What should Anita be doing next?

a) Anita should contact Monica and inform her of the stakeholders' comments on the risk management process.

b) Anita should inform her boss about this feedback of stakeholders.

c) Anita should start the risk planning from the start and track them

d) She must get someone from PMO and perform an audit on the risk planning done.

18. **As the project is in the middle of development phase, Mary find some of the risks she originally anticipated didn't get triggered and the developed components have surpassed the risk successfully without any impact. Similarly, she couldn't remember having identified any new project risks over the past 2-3 weeks. She begin getting nervous as to whether there are any risks that is hidden and waiting to impact.**

What should she do NEXT?

a) Check the Risk register and remove the irrelevant risks immediately.

b) Mary should perform a Risk Reassessment process

c) Mary need not take her instincts and fear factor seriously. There may not be any unknown risks in her project since she has performed an extensive risk identification and planning in the initial stages of her project.

d) She should PMO and seek assistance to overcome this problem

19. Two chemical companies, whose projects are located adjacent to each other joining hands to share the cost of removing the toxic materials is an example of

a) Share

b) Mitigation

c) Transfer

d) None of the above

20. What is the primary output of Risk Management process

a) Risk Register

b) Risk Management Plan

c) Updated Risk Register

d) Project Management Plan

21. What is the recommended frequency of the Risk discussion for a Project Manager?

a) Weekly

b) Fortnightly

c) Daily

d) As and when required

22. Sylvia is the project manager for a construction project. As part of identifying and understanding risks, she decide to circulate a questionnaire and seek opinion from experts on the potential risks in her project.

What is this risk identification methodology called?

a) Interviewing

b) Expert Judgment

c) Delphi Technique

d) SWOT Analysis

23. **The primary purpose of SWOT Analysis is**
    a) Identify where the project risks are
    b) Extensively analyzing the risks and looking for threat severity and opportunities
    c) Risk mitigation
    d) None of the above

24. **Which of the below can be classified as external risks**
    a) Government policies, employee attrition, funding commitment
    b) Natural disasters, social unrest, management commitment
    c) Project Infrastructure, Resource availability, stakeholder approval
    d) Government policies, council approval, natural disasters

25. **One of the major risk for a project related to stakeholders is**
    a) Managing stakeholders
    b) Managing scope changes approved by all the stakeholders
    c) Satisfying stakeholders while verifying the scope
    d) A missed stakeholders might have serious impact on the overall project objective

ANSWERS

1. **Answer: C**

   Justification: The major disadvantage for a seller in a Fixed Price bid is the cost risk. Whenever there is a cost escalation for the product or Human resources or service, it becomes the responsibility of the seller and the buyer is not legally bound to compensate for this increased cost. However, in the case of any scope changes which is outside the contract, there are possibilities for the buyer and seller to enter into a discussion in handling the change.

2. **Answer: A**

   Justification: The situation narrated in the question is resource attrition, which is internal to the project performing organization. A resource attrition is a major risk for any project, especially if the resource is a critical resource. A sufficient resource surplus is recommended for any project to backup such attrition situation. Another recommended practice for every project manager is to have a shadow resource with sufficient knowledge to backup in case of emergency requirement.

3. **Answer: D**

   Justification: One of the Risk Response Planning methodology is to exploit a risk for the benefit of the project or the performing organization. In this case, the program manager is notified of a potential schedule overrun risk, which is not the fault of the project. There is an external dependency that might potentially delay the implementation of the project. Sensing the situation, the program manager is trying to find the possibility of offering help to the customer by way of executing new project to remove the dependency factor. One might still wonder, if the dependency will be removed if the customer agrees to award the project. Certainly, it wouldn't remove the dependency. However, the project performing organization can negotiate with the customer for a revised implementation date for the completed project, keeping in mind the schedule of the planned project.

4. **Answer: D**

   Justification : If you could remember the Quality Assurance process of the Quality planning, a Risk Audit is similar in nature. As part of the Risk Monitoring process, the project manager is required to have an audit on the Risk Management Process to make sure the process is capable enough of handling the risks efficiently and deliver the desired results. Such Risk Audits are usually handled by anyone outside the project , such as the Project Management Office or any experts from another project.

5. **Answer: A**

    Justification : It is common and recommended practice to refer to the Organization's process assets to identify any risks, that might have been handled in the past projects. This includes referring to the risk register templates and consulting experts for identifying risks. All these are part of the Risk identification process.

6. **Answer: B**

    Justification : One of the Risk Response methodology is to avoid the risks, if it is possible and without impacting the project in any way. In this question, driving on a freeway will take you quick to the office. However, there is a risk ahead in the form of a road congestion, which might prevent you from reaching work on time. Taking an alternate route is one way of avoiding the risk but to reach work on time. Just the driver should make sure, the new alternate plan do not create new risks.

7. **Answer: D**

    Justification: As part of the risk planning process, the project manager create the risk register and list all the project risks in the register. However, further into the risk managing, the risks gets analyzed to identify their category, quality, impact, probability and to plan for responding to risks, if they get triggered. Similarly, any updates to the risks (which is very common and happen often in a project) will result in an updated Risk Register.

8. **Answer: A**

    Justification: A secondary risk is the result of a risk response planned to handle another risk. In this case, the feasibility of procuring components locally has some limitations and cost issues involved, so the project manager decide to procure products from overseas for cheaper price. However the response plan carries its own risk in the form of potential delay in procurement, natural calamities, government clearance and approvals.

9. **Answer: D**

    Justification: A watchlist is similar to a risk register, which contains risks of lesser importance at some point of time. However, these risks are required to be monitored for any potential impact at a later stage. A risk on the watchlist might become a critical risk impacting the overall delivery of the project. A regular risk register contains risks that needs more attention due to their potential impact and probability of occurrence.

10. **Answer: B**

    Justification: Transferring the risks is one common way of responding to risks. Insuring an event, which carries certain amount of risks helps the insurer meet the financial loss, in case the risk gets triggered. Some of the common forms of such risks include reinsurance done by large corporations, when they execute projects that carry high degree of risks. Remember that, transferring a risk do not meet the risk ownership is transferred to another person or company in such cases.

11. **Answer : A**

    Justification: Anything that is to do with project performing organization is classified as an internal risk. In this situation, the financial commitment given by the senior management of the performing organization is broken by itself. This is a major risk, that threaten to stall the project execution. In any project execution, a management commitment of funding, resources and facilities are critical factors that decide the fate of the project.

12. **Answer: D**

    Justification: Any risks that is outside the control of the project performing organization is to be regarded as an external risk. In this situation, the risk is more about the economy and business conditions, which are outside the control of the project execution. The organization has limited role to influence these factors. The best thing a project manager can do is to identify such risks and mitigate them, should they get triggered.

13. **Answer: B**

    Justification: A project manager's primary responsibility during the monitor & control phase is to look for any potential risks and factors that might influence a change request raised. In this case, Janet is being informed of a potential delay As a response plan, she decide to analyze the triggered risk and looking for impact and probability. Once the analysis is completed, she might be deploying an additional resource to bring the development back on track. These factors might very well require a change to the baselines.

14. **Answer: B**

    Justification: A positive risk response have the potential to provide more opportunities for the project. On the contrary, a negative risk response is when some risks cannot be avoided in a project but need to be carefully handled.   A residual risk is a risk, that still remains on the project even after a response plan is identified. Such residual risks need not be given a preference, but need to be handled with care.

15. **Answer: D**

    Justification: One of the key point to remember about risk identification is, a risk can surface or trigger at any point of time during the project phases. What is a watchlist now might turn into a major risk at a later point of time. In this example, David identified his risks and handed over the risk register to his project leader. The project leader's responsibility is only to manage those risks given to him. It was David's fault not to have looked for further risks in the project.

16. **Answer: A**

    Justification: As part of the monitoring & control, a project manager will be analyzing the reserves that has been identified for the project. This is to handle the cost impact of any risk, that gets triggered along the project lifecycle. Every project can have about 5-8% of the budget earmarked for handling such risks.

17. **Answer: D**

    Justification: Whenever a project manager is in doubt of the efficiency of a subsidiary plan, it is always recommended to get an audit performed on the management plan by the Project Management Office or an expert outside of the project. In this case, one of the option in front of Anita is to get the PMO involved to find the expectation mismatch.

18. **Answer: B**

    Justification: As a project manager's responsibility to discuss the project risks in every project meeting and with all stakeholders, it is essential to frequently reassess the project risk register to analyze the severity and status of each of the risks. In addition to this status analysis, the project manager might want to look for any new risks that surfaced in the project and plan to manage them.

19. **Answer: A**

    Justification: When one organization or project is having a risk and looking to share the risk with another organization or project, they both get benefits of working together and share. Besides the risk getting split between them, this results in lesser cost expended in managing the risk.

20. **Answer: B**

    Justification: A project manager uses the risk management process to plan on handling risks such as mitigation plans, communicating with stakeholders, assigning responsibilities, expectations from the stakeholders and transferring risks. The Risk plan is used as a bible to direct the entire risk process till the end of the projects.

21. **Answer: C**

    Justification: It is very essential for a project manager to keep his focus on the risks. There is no specified time a risk can get triggered. If everything goes smooth in the project, it bothers none. However, risks might carry negative impact and unless it is planned and managed well, there are more than chaos in a project. Ideally, the risk register should be included in every discussion with the team and the stakeholders. Besides this, the identified risks are to be reassessed and the register updated to keep them upto date.

22. **Answer: A**

Justification: Interviewing is one of the risk identification technique used by many project managers. Besides our own, others' experience help the project managers to identify risks, that may be hidden anywhere in the project. The information collected from the experts are kept confidential besides their details.

23. **Answer: B**

Justification: SWOT stands for Strength, Weakness, Opportunities and Threat. As explained in the earlier pages of this chapter, not all risks are a threat. At times, risks provide opportunities for the project manager to explore and utilize opportunities to get the better benefits for the project and the performing organization. An extensive analysis is required to identify strength, weakness and threats besides looking for opportunities arising out of the risks.

24. **Answer: D**

Justification: All the three options listed are external to the organization and the project manager may have little to no influence to get a resolution.

25. **Answer: D**

Justification: Nothing else can cause a catastrophic impact for a project than a missed stakeholders. It is always very essential that all the stakeholders are identified in the very early stages of a project, initiation process group. Unless all the stakeholders are completed, there cannot be any meaning scope defined for the project. Unless there is a complete scope, the project cannot start or complete. Let us assume, the project manager comes across a group, which has significantly impacted by the project but was not identified as a stakeholder. If this group head is included as a stakeholder in the middle of the execution phase, it might result in a good amount of updates to the scope, which impacts every other planned components.

This page is intentionally left blank

This page is intentionally left blank

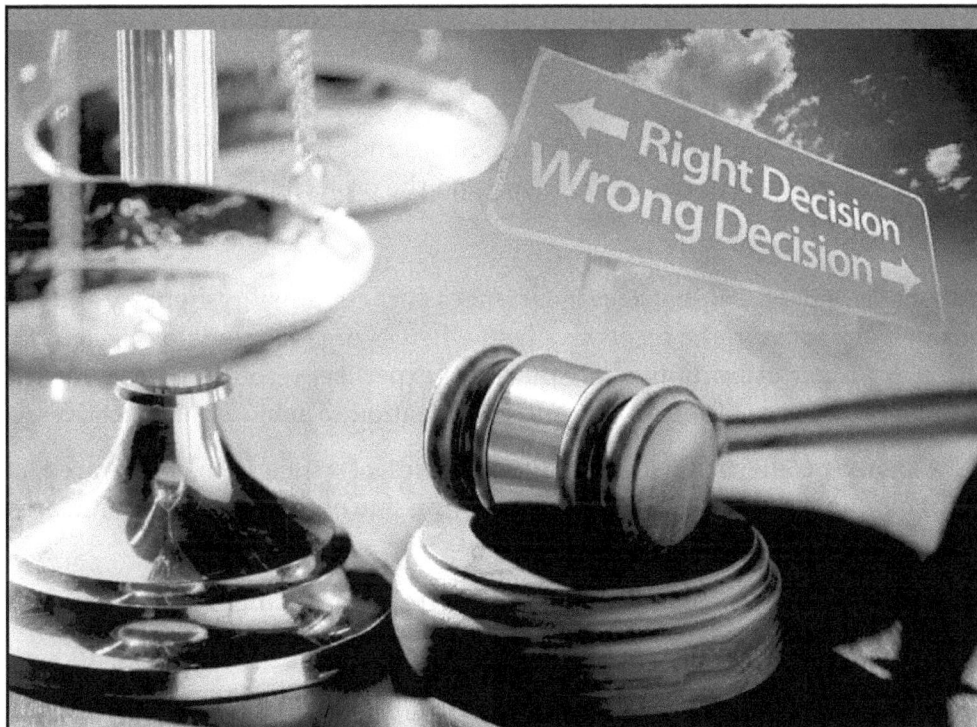

Professional Responsibility and Ethical Conduct

Objectives

At the end of this chapter, the reader must be able to learn:

- what it means to be professional and ethical at work,
- what is permitted and what is not,
- impact of doing wrong things and not doing the right things in a professional environment.
- Understand the professional responsibility in some critical cases
- Code of Professional Responsibility & Ethical Conduct

A Project cannot be executed just with good amount of knowledge and skilled team alone. On top of all, it needs ethical attitude and professional approach to be successful.

It is about respecting the law, following policies and globally accepted standards without compromising the productivity and the project objectives.

Is that all, one might wonder?

But, if you understand that a law guarantees fairness, equality, honesty and fair business practices in the respective land whereas organizational policy guides through proper utilization of organization expertise, resources, skills for the ultimate advantage of the project and organization to achieve the objectives.

How many people in this world make copies of articles, that appeared in technology magazines without a proper permission of the author and circulated those copies?

How many times someone compromised on their responsibilities at their work?

These are samples of unacceptable attitude and behaviors, that are not allowed by any law or policies.

What it Means to be Ethical?

A question might arise as to what is an ethical behavior?

The answer to this may be different from every individual's perspective. If you ask me, I would say an ethical behavior is something, when a project manager does what he is expected to do and he doesn't do what he is not supposed to do."

Project management means following the prescribed processes and the right and unbiased views to utilize the organization's resources to arrive at a predetermined objective of the performing organization. To help perform one's job, every organization has policies, objectives, vision and guidelines. It is the responsibility of the project manager to understand them and live upto that expectation.

More on Professional Responsibility

Is that all about being ethical?

I do not want to begin with a lecture on what is meant by professionalism. Take a moment to understand the below questions and give your honest responses to them.

"You are working with a supplier on certain product. The supplier is a couple of weeks behind his schedule for the supply of his components and this delay has begun impacting your project's delivery schedule. You have become increasingly nervous about this. Sensing your nervousness, someone from the client organization approaches you on a Friday afternoon and offers two complementary tickets to a soccer match scheduled for the next day. You are so excited about this match, since your favorite team is playing their crucial match of the season.

Do you accept the complementary tickets offered by the supplier, in order to build a better relationship with the seller and to get rid of the stress caused by the project delay?

Here is a second scenario.

Your customer is offering a complementary gaming voucher at the local Casino. Should you accept it, since it is for all of the team?

If your answer is Yes to both the above question, then you are heading into a deep trouble and you may need to correct yourself, should you want to stay in your job. Alternatively, if you had replied No to both the question, it means you know your professional responsibility and aware of your boundaries.

I would also define a professional Responsibility as

"Keeping the project and the performing organization's interest above individual interests and utilize the best of available resources and make the best effort to achieve the objectives of the project within the framework of the organization policies and government regulation"

I hope the above illustration is sufficient to understand professional responsibility.

The Significance of Being Professional

Professional responsibility means, doing the right thing, the right way and in accordance with the policies and laws of the land, where the performing organization operate in.

To being professional and successful, one need to be aware of the policies and laws of the land. The important reason for insisting to know the policies and regulatory systems is because policies differ between companies while different countries have different ways of regulating businesses. It is like North America and Europe having different date format and currencies.

Remember that being professional and ethical is one of the most important factor to being a successful Project Manager.

There may be instances, when many of us overlook the professional responsibility out of excitement. For example, if a letter written by someone in a popular magazine is published, everyone want to share that exciting news with others and end up taking scanned copies of the article and the letter and email to a

---

larger group of friends and workmates. Though this might be out of excitement and circulated to a smaller group of people, it is still against the copyright law.

At times, whatever one considers something to be silly might turn out to be breaching law.

Goal of Professionalism, Ethics and Values in the Business Environment

Having grown up and experienced in the business and project environment, most of us do not need someone to teach us of being professional and ethical. Do we?

However, experience has taught each of us with enormous amount of lessons on common ethical and professional issues and this needs a definite fix. Unless the issues and experiences are known to others, there are less possibilities of unethical and unprofessional business practices getting fixed.

What does the code of professionalism and ethical conduct tell us?

*   ***Responsibility for the position held*** : *People should understand their responsibility and commitment towards their position in the interest of public safety, society and environment. Accepting ownership of commitments undertaken and fixing issues when identified. When one find others of deviation from their responsibility, appropriate authorities for corrective actions. Respecting the law, policies and regulations of the organization and the land and respect for the property rights and confidential information that one work with.*

*   ***Fairness in approach and judgment*** : *Fairness refers to unbiased views or conduct when dealing with people or resources by keeping aside one's own interest and prejudice. Maintaining transparency while taking business related decisions and constantly assessing the decisions to take corrective actions as and when required. Keeping the conflict of business interest out of one's reach and refraining from decision making process, when such interest occur. Eliminating discrimination based on gender, race, region or geography is another act of fair practice.*

*   ***Honesty*** : *Taking a genuine and true approach in everything that one does, including the information exchange, making promises in good faith and facilitating expression of one's views or opinion without fear. Making false statements, half-true information or indulging in dishonest behavior for personal benefits are to be avoided.*

*   ***Understanding responsibility and living upto expectations*** : *A project manager doing wrong job or not doing his/her job according to globally accepted business practices is a serious violation of professional code and ethics.*

- *Accountability & Ownership* : *One of the most important expectation from a project manager is the acceptance of accountability and ownership with respect to the project. A project manager is expected to assume the ownership of every activity that takes place in the project. A project manager is responsible, if something goes wrong or right during any phase of the project. As I explained earlier in this book, a project manager's efficiency and skills are seen only in the health and progress of the project.*

Common Ethical Issues

Some of the most common issues to be kept in mind about ethical behavior are

Respecting others Opinion, Points, Privacy and Treating Them Equally

This is one of the most common issue in a work environment. Just because someone is successful in their task doesn't give a top score card to them. If someone's performance in a project impresses the project manager, there is a tendency to blindly accept whatever this team member says.

Is this faith justified?

Certainly not. Such blind faith limits flow of ideas and opinions of others. The best way to overcome is to treat everyone with fairness and respect everyone's opinions and thoughts.

Keep Project Interest Above Own

At times, one may not be very much impressed to work on certain project, but the organization expect the resource to work on the project since the company do not have similar expertise available internally.

It is true that not always one get to make choices. Occasionally, project and organizational interest takes more importance over personal ambition and objective. The project objective can never be compromised as a project involves a larger team and greater stake for the performing organization.

At times, making a decision might be challenging, since everyone is human. However, being professional and ethical makes the project managers stand out of the group of people, who compromise on their professional responsibilities for their own benefits.

Think and Respect the Community and Environmental Consciousness

One should realize that they are not alone but part of a community and they have responsibility for the community and its progress.

Imagine a situation, when a local chemical manufacturing unit wants to save the cost and decide to dispenses its chemical wastes into a local river without the knowledge of the local council. Being responsible and with ethical values, our responsibility doesn't end without being mute spectator of this illegal act but require us to notify the local government and prevent such offences. One need to be very vigilant and exercise a sense of care for the community and environmental, even if such illegal acts bring some benefits to the community that one belong to.

Executing a project is very important. However, respecting the environment and community is equally important.

Respecting Other Cultures

The globalized economies have not only thrown the markets wide open and with numerous opportunities but also many culture come together and coexist. Thus it is very essential to respect every culture and belief while working together for a very healthy and cordial work environment.

This may be very vital when project teams are located in several countries and continents.

Imagine a situation, you are on a business meeting with a large team from Europe How does it feel, when all others speak in their language, which is not understood by you? You tend to feel isolated with no idea of what is being discussed.

Doesn't it sound very true?

Honesty and Transparency

Treating everyone in the team with respect and managing the project with honesty and transparency might do wonders for the project manager. Decision making is the responsibility of the project manager, but accepting ownership of the decisions made and taking the team into confidence gets respect for the project manager from his team.

Unless such confidence and respect exist, the project manager cannot succeed in his role.

Learning is a Way of Life

A project is not a job but it is a learning practice. Unless someone learns in his career, he will get stuck into the same place where he started. If you notice the background of most successful persons of this world, you would notice something unique in them. None of them were doing job, but they had vision and were learning forever and always keep improving towards getting better.

The world has become increasingly competent that only those with superior knowledge tend to advance and realize their dreams. Applying the learnt knowledge in their project might get someone into quicker prominence and gets more opportunities.

Sharing the Knowledge

Learning is a continuous process and sharing the learnt knowledge is another way to enrich one's knowledge with the team or within an appropriate forum in the organization. When someone begins to share his expertise and knowledge, it leads to discussions and multiple questions on the subject. Such discussions paves way for better exchange of opinions and ideas, thus helping everyone.

Such sharing of knowledge also gets the confidence of others, which is one essential leadership quality.

Contribute to the Professional World

As a project management professional, everyone has a responsibility to share their knowledge and expertise for the betterment of this profession. The contribution can be in any form such as writing articles, participating in professional development programs, conducting trainings and getting involved in voluntary activities and the options are endless.

Not Doing the Right Thing is Unprofessional Too

Doing the right thing is fine, but how about not doing the right thing.

It is strictly unprofessional too. At times, one might be under intense pressure to complete the project according to the plan.

Imagine, if you are a project manager who is managing a complex project, which has a very strict time schedule defined by the customer. Due to some urgency, you decide to overlook the quality plan and compromise on the quality review before the end product is delivered to the customer.

What do you call this? Can this be simply branded as a case of ignorance?

NO. This is not just ignorance but unethical behavior and the impact of it would be far reaching since you may not be aware of the result of this action. Probably, you might end up delivering a faulty product, which was not agreed with the customer through the contract.

The impact of such mistakes might prove fatal for the customers, which will result in erosion of confidence in the project performing organization.

Tidbits

Handling the needs of the project team in an unbiased way is professional too.

How many times you were approached by a team member of yours, who is not pleased with his work or growth opportunities or some concerns with the performance assessment? Take a step backward and recall how did you handle them and the consequence of such issues.

Everyone has their expectations from the organization, work environment and about their future growth. Understanding their needs and help resolving genuine issues might get you wonders for the project.

Some of the Commonly found Unprofessional Practices

Now let us try to understand few of the commonly found unprofessional business practices in the professional world. At times, someone might be practicing any of these without their knowledge and at smaller scale.

Bribery

Bribing someone to get the job done is the biggest unethical business practice, no matter the amount involved and where it happens. Professional responsibilities can never be compromised for short term gains under any circumstances.

Paying or accepting any financial favors for doing or not doing one's job is against every professional practice. Sometimes, one might tend to get tempted with such goodies, keeping their forthcoming holiday travel in mind.

Imagine a Project Manager is working on a project and is ahead of schedule with the project. Going by the current trend and pace, the project is expected to be over 2 weeks ahead of schedule. This is sure to impress the customer and the performing organization.

Out of gratitude, someone from the customer office approaches the Project Manager and offers $2500 as a reward for the excellent work being done by the Project Manager and his team.

Does this constitute a bribery?

Of course, accepting cash for the work being done from anyone, except the employer, amount to bribery. The reason is simple and logical. The Project Manager and his team represent their organization on the project. Any cash reward or appreciation to the Project Manager should be from one's employer and not from the beneficiary.

Hope this makes sense.

A bribery need not be in the form of cash alone. It can be in any form of direct or indirect benefit such as complementary tickets to the ballet, games, movies, travel and shopping vouchers.

In short, any direct or indirect benefits originating from the customer is not to be accepted, even if it is directly offered by one of the stakeholders of the project.

> *In some parts of the world, corporations and individuals are expected to pay to officials or others for the benefits given.*
>
> *Is this acceptable or against the law?*
>
> *Obviously, it is against the law, professional and ethical practices, no matter whether someone force or expect the beneficiary to pay for the benefits. These amount to bribery, no matter what name is given by the other.*
>
> *One should remember that no law in any part of the world mandate the beneficiary to pay for the benefits.*

Taking Advantage of the Authority

These are other form of taking undue advantage of the authority given by one's organization.

Imagine a situation, a Project Manager is tracking the cost of the project and finds that his project has cost him $4500 lesser than estimated cost at that point of time. He is making sure that the project will end up with about $7250 at closure.

This is a good news for him since the overall estimated cost was approved by his leadership and now he has surplus cash at his disposal. So, he decide to hire a premium rental car and a hotel room in a luxury 5 star hotel, which is not permitted by his Organization's policy. The policy clearly says every employee is expected to travel by normal car and should stay in designated economy hotels, which offers 15% discount to the organization.

Is the Project Manager right in what he is doing? His efficient project management skills resulted in a cost savings for his organization and spending a couple of hundred dollars is not going to blow his project budget.

Well. He is completely wrong with his decision. He may be exceptionally talented and great Project Manager. But, every Project Manager is expected to give the best of his ability to his project and the organization. So, keeping this in mind, his exceptional performance deserves a reward granted by his organization and not by himself.

His act can never be justified.

There may be several examples given such as someone travelling by Executive Class (whereas the policy recommends only Coach class travel) and travelling by First Class air travel (while the policy restricts such First Class travel only to their top executives and the rest should only travel by economy class).

Many times, such ignorance and slippages gets the concerned people into deep trouble that might cost them their reputation and even job.

Breaking the Copyright Law

Breaking the law might not always go unnoticed. Besides getting into trouble, it amount to unprofessional and unethical behavior on the part of anyone, who indulge in such act.

How many times a licensed copy of a popular software gets downloaded beyond its licensed limit? Remember that such software companies spend millions and billions of dollars to build a vision, strategy, workforce, technical advantages, trainings, infrastructure and work hard to bring out a software to this world.

How many people photocopy a popular business management book and circulate to others without the consent of the author of the book?

How many movies are illegally copied from their original and circulated?

If a Project Manager is very impressed with an article that appeared in a technology magazine, he wants the team to go through the article and get benefited by the contents. What should he ideally do?

Certainly, he should not be making copies of the columns and circulate to his team members. Instead, he would encourage his team to buy the magazine and go through the article.

While knowing about Copyright law, one should remember that every published material is covered under the copyright law. Unauthorized copying and reproducing such protected material means breaking the law. Every website of this modern world are protected by copyright law and warnings are posted on all the sites. Not sure, how many take time to notice such warnings.

When you play your favorite movie on the DVD player, have you noticed the violation of copyright warning appearing even before the movie gets started?

Yes, the famous FBI warning of several years of prison and $250,000 penalty for any unauthorized exhibit, copying and reuse of the media content.

Violation of copyrights is fast becoming the world's greatest evil, that deprives thousands of authors, producers and businesses with losses in billions of dollars. In addition to this, such unauthorized piracy leads to loss of millions of jobs of the hardworking workforce of this world.

Speak Only the Truth

No matter what, the best and safest strategy always is to speak the truth in everything a project manager does, whether it is in a team meeting, preparing presentations or sending out status reports to the senior management on the project status.

Representing the truth helps in decision making, since the Organizations may have its own strategy and goals with respect to project objectives. A wrong decision is influenced by the wrong information provided and this becomes the responsibility of the project manager.

Take a balanced approach when handling stakeholders

This is one critical and delicate task of a project manager, having to handle the conflicting interest of the stakeholders. Assume two departments are involved in a project and are impacted by the outcome of the project, each of the department heads might want the designing be done in different ways. In such situations, it becomes a real trouble for the project manager to manage the requirement of both stakeholders and arrive at a conscience.

It is always the best practice, to keep the project and organization interest above individual interests and attitude related issues. The efficiency of the managers is seen well in handling such issues.

Avoid Conflict of Interest

Another common issue faced in many businesses and with people is the conflicting interests between the employees and businesses.

How the project and organizations are impacted?

It is pretty simple and straight. Martin is working in the design department of his ABC Enterprise for over 15 years. He is considered an expert in designing architectural design and often he mentors the other members of his department.

As he gains expertise over a period of time, he start develop his persona ambition of making additional dollars with his expertise. He begin interacting with some of ABC Enterprise's customers and offer to prepare designs for a cheaper cost. The customers of ABC Enterprises have faith in Martin's knowledge and efficiency and are attracted by the low cost offer. The ultimate impact is on ABC Enterprise's business prospects and potential loss of key customers.

Professional behavior and ethics do not accept such conflicting interests.

Tidbits

If you are on an interview panel and you happened to know a candidate as a family friend. What should you do?

Report this fact to your recruitment department and get yourself out of selection panel with someone else. This is to maintain fairness and integrity in the selection process and individual interests do not interrupt the professional responsibilities.

Right Job Vs. Wrong Job?

Doing the wrong thing is truly unprofessional. But, how about not doing the right job?

Obviously, someone ignoring their responsibility is unprofessional too. As we have seen earlier in this chapter, no excuse can be give for not doing the right job.

Let us assume, Jack is working as a Lead Tester in his Organization and working on a very critical project testing, which is planned to be moved to production upon his testing done. He is a very smart and skilled tester, who has never slipped in his schedule.

Just because Jack was running late for a drink with his girlfriend on a Friday evening, he decide to overlook five test cases while he was testing a very important program. He was very confident that his ability to do the testing without any issues and the rapport with the customer will save him from this overlooking.

What could potentially go wrong for Jack, when he gets back on Monday?

Obviously, his program might have failed in the production environment. His rapport with his customer is definitely not going to save him and his reputation of being the best tester is shattered due to his ignorance.

Why has this happened to Jack?

The reason is simple. He is always considered a very talented tester. But, he ignored his responsibilities. Moreover, he failed to realize that the program was developed by a developer, who is popular among his team for having as many bugs as possible in his code. Thus it became Jack's responsibility to have been very careful while testing. Unfortunately, Jack was rushing to join his girlfriend for a Friday evening drink. So, he completely ignored the important test cases.

Unless one is aware of his responsibilities and follows the work ethics and professional work behavior, he is sure to find himself in trouble.

Report Violations

Being professional doesn't stop being truly professional and doing the right job. There may be instances, where one might come across unprofessional behaviors, misrepresentation of facts, misusing the resources and authority and so on.

Everyone have their professional responsibility of reporting violation of professional and acceptable practices to the appropriate authorities. Unless each one contribute and participate, it is virtually impossible to see the professional environment sustain its place in this world.

Take a moment to list down about eight unprofessional tasks that you have encountered and the right professional approach against each of them.

A Test of Knowledge and Understanding

Let me ask you something now.

Assume you are working on a project and expected to invoice the customer for the work performed by your team. Your boss approaches you asking you to include the names of two resources, who have been assisting your project with informal testing activities. You know well that you haven't agreed with the customer about charging for these two resources.

What would you do? Will you accept your boss's request and include their effort in the invoice or ignore?

A professional ethics do not permit such behaviors. Whatever contract signed between the buyer and seller is binding them. Any deviation from the legally binding contract is considered a violation of law, no matter who practice it and the magnitude of the stake involved.

Most organizations in the world have something called Code of Professional Conduct clearly defined, which discourages such unprofessional behavior. So, what will you do in this case?

I would recommend you to decline the request of your boss, unless he has any written mandate of the customer that authorize charging for the resources. In addition, I would recommend you to report this unprofessional request of your boss to the team that monitors such code of conducts in your organization. The impact of losing the customer's confidence and business is very high with such unprofessional and unacceptable behaviors.

EXERCISES

Match the Following

• Doing things right	: Speaking truth
• Participating in seminars	: Report violations
• Notifying discrepancies	: Contribution to profession
• Reports with accurate data	: Individual integrity
• Discouraging unauthorized copying	: Following copyright laws

True or False

1. Accepting complementary tickets from the customer amount to unprofessional behavior   **(True/False)**

2. It is ok to bribe senior government officials, if such benefits are practiced in some countries   **(True/False)**

3. Withdrawing from a conflict involving the project team over a project related task is acceptable   **(True/False)**

4. It is acceptable, if you chose not to report some unauthorized practice being followed by your boss, since he is your supervisor   **(True/False)**

5. You decide to make photocopies of some important technical information from a magazine pending a permission granted on your request. This is an acceptable practice since you have already placed a request for permission. **(True/False)**

ANSWERS

Match the Following

• Doing things right	: Individual integrity
• Participating in seminars	: Contribution to profession
• Notifying discrepancies	: Report violations
• Reports with accurate data	: Speaking truth
• Discouraging unauthorized copying	: Following copyright laws

True or False

1. True
2. False
3. False
4. False
5. False

Test Your Knowledge

1. **Which one among the below is most accurate about being ethical?**
   a) Doing the right thing
   b) Not doing the wrong thing
   c) Doing the right thing and not doing the wrong thing
   d) Doing things better

2. **Sylvia is a project manager just got assigned by her senior management to manage a construction project. She just carried an initial analysis of the requirement and got her understanding approved by the sponsor. As she begin planning for the subsidiary components, she wants to focus more on important components such as Risk, Scope, Cost and Schedule. Since she considers the other components such as Human Resources, Communication and Quality as not much important since she can manage these components on the go. Her project do not involve any procurement process.**

   What is the potential impact of Sylvia's strategy?
   a) There won't be any impact, since triple constraint asks the project managers to focus on Scope, Cost and Schedule primarily
   b) She must realize that every subsidiary plan component is very important for a project manager. Not paying due attention is against the code of professional ethics.
   c) She may be very talented and efficient to manage the resources, communication and quality.
   d) As long as the customer is fine with her strategy, she can plan her way

3. **Your team is in the middle of execution phase. Your scope was extensively discussed with the stakeholders and approved. The cost and schedule were perfect for the customer. As you are monitoring the progress of the project, you are being approached by a stakeholder who want you to include an additional feature in the scope. Upon discussing this issue with the stakeholder, you realize that he forgot to include this when preparing the original requirement document. As per the stakeholder, unless this feature is not part of the project, his department will not gain any benefit out of the project.**

   What would you do next?
   a) You should include the requirement since the stakeholder is funding the project and customer satisfaction is more important for you
   b) You should turn down the request and tell the stakeholder that you are the project manager and have the authority to accept or reject changes

c) You should include the requirement since the project is still in execution stage

d) Ask the stakeholder to raise a formal change request since the scope was already approved and frozen

4. You are a project manager working at the customer location. As part of identifying resources, you hire a candidate, who is already working with another company. After the candidate joined your project, you come to know that the employee has developed an idea during his previous employment but the idea was not approved by the company. You are impressed by the person's innovation and understand the strategic and cost benefits in implementing it.

What would you do next?

a) Ask the employee, if he signed any NDA with his previous employer that prevent him from sharing any such innovation with other companies.

b) You should ignore his idea as it is not a recommended practice to accept such innovation, which was conceived when an employee was with another company

c) Accept the innovation and take it further towards implementing it

d) Implementing such innovation and ideas are against ethics and law

5. You are working on a construction project. Your project is already beyond schedule by two weeks due to slower than execution phase. During the annual holiday season, many of your team members are working overtime to complete the pending construction work to enable the project go live as per the schedule. As part of the work schedule, a sewage line is required to be laid from your work site to connect to the central sewage line, which is about 100 meters away. Completing this work involves earthwork to be carried, which require permission from the local council office. Unfortunately, the approving authority is on vacation for another 10 days. Since you are not able to get an approval urgently, you decide to complete the work within 3-4 days.

Is this action of yours justified?

a) No. It shows poor planning. The project manager should have planned for such approvals well in advance and should have taken the approaching holiday season into consideration and the risks of getting approvals delayed

b) It is not your fault if the approving authority at the local city council is on her annual vacation.

c) You should get the earthwork completed quickly before anyone notices it

d) You could plan the earthwork on a weekend to avoid inconvenience to the community

6. **You find that another project manager in your organization is violating many of the PMI's code of professional ethics frequently. You spoke to the person several times to help understand the right way of doing things. The person is a PMI certified professional. What should you do next?**

   a) Ignore his actions, since you do not have right to fix someone's problems

   b) Report the issue to PMI for suitable action

   c) Talk to the person's boss and explain all the unprofessional actions

   d) Talk to the person one last time

7. **You are working as a project manager for an organization, which pays well and provides security to job. However, there is one problem there. The company doesn't value your PMP certification and do not have any processes in place to manage projects. Everything is managed on ad hoc basis and according to the requirement of the situation. Your multiple attempts to explain your management of the advantage of having professional project management practices has gone in vain.**

   What should be your NEXT action?

   a) Report this issue to the PMI for suitable action

   b) Leave the company

   c) You shouldn't care the company's ignorance of professional practices since they pay well and provide job security to you

   d) You cannot change policies of an organization. You should rather follow what the company practices because they pay you.

8. **Sam is a project manager and has a team of 20 members reporting to him. He has a daily status call scheduled with his team to track the deliverables. Sam has his own assessment of every team member. Whenever he goes to a team meeting, his personal opinions about team members play a crucial role in his reaction to comments from team members. This means some of the senior members of his team gets more attention from Sam, whereas the newly joined junior members are just invited to the meeting.**

   How would such attitude positively or negatively impact the project?

   a) Sam's attitude is justified. Senior members have more expertise and knowledge than the newly joined ones and can guide them in no time.

   b) Sam's attitude is wrong. This amount to discriminating junior members

c) Sam's attitude should change and he should give more chance to junior members of the team than seniors.

d) By not focusing on junior members equally, Sam is breaking the code of ethics and may not get the best out of his project.

9. Jessica is a project manager whose project is part of a program. She is a PMI certified project manager and firm believer in professional ethics and code of conduct framed by the Project Management Institute (PMI). When she is in the middle of project management, she notice another project manager under the same program is deviating from the ethics and professional conduct very often. Some of the examples include not circulating meeting minutes, not treating all the team members equally, not following all the project management processes to name few. When Jessica speaks to the project and point his mistake, he wouldn't care much and says PMI's code of professional conduct do not apply to non-PMI members.

   Is this correct?

   a) The other Project Manager is correct. He is not a PMI member and Jessica cannot do anything

   b) The other PM is wrong. PMI code of professional conduct applies to everyone, irrespective of their PMI membership.

   c) Jessica should not worry much about the other PM but focus on her work

   d) Jessica should ask the other PM to enroll to PMI membership to know how to conduct himself.

10. You are the project manager of a project, that has team located in different geographies around the world. Which among the following present the most challenges towards Communication among the team:

    a) Language differences

    b) Misunderstanding the body language

    c) Lack of trust among team members

    d) All of the above

11. Negotiations are required to be conducted in an atmosphere of

    a) Honesty and vagueness

    b) Mutual Trust and cooperation

    c) Lack of faith and uncertainty

    d) Honesty and Caution

12. You are the project manager, who is managing a large engineering project and working at the customer location due to the requirement. Shortly before the festival holidays, one of your stakeholder approaches you and offers a festival gift as a token of appreciation. However, your organizational policy do not clearly define about accepting any gifts from customers.

    What is the BEST thing you can do next?

    a) Quote the company policy and refuse to accept the gift

    b) Accept the gift and do not forget to thank the customer for it

    c) Ask the stakeholder to wait till you verify with your supervisor or appropriate authority from your company on accepting such gifts

    d) It's ok to accept such gifts, as long as others do not know of it.

13. Simon is a project manager, who is managing a large project and 50+ members strong team and over a dozen stakeholder. As the team is making progress with their execution phase, one of Simon's team member approach him with a mistake in the approved scope. After discussing the details with the team member, Simon asks the member to ignore the scope and include the correct functionality in the program.

    This is an example of

    a) Pro-active project management strategy

    b) Wrong way of handling scope change

    c) There is nothing wrong, since Simon is asking his team member to fix an identified issue and be proactive

    d) Unethical conduct on the part of Simon. He should have taken up the issue with the stakeholders and took their concurrence before going ahead with the change

14. You are managing a team of members on a consultancy project. One day, you overhear a conversation taking place between two of your team members, where one member is inquiring about the competing consultancy business of the other. The discussion is about how good the business is and any challenges ahead.

    What should you do NEXT?

    a) Ignore the conversation since it is no way connected with you

    b) Call the team member, who own a competing business and collect details of the type of business.

    c) Make sure, the team members do not see you hearing them

    d) Report the team member to your Human Resources group

15. You are managing a large team, which is spread across many locations of the world. One of your team member approach you with a request for permission to work remotely half of the day for the next one week. This is to fulfill certain cultural responsibilities.

    How would you approach this request?

    a) Turn down the request and tell the team member that he should keep personal priorities away from professional environment.

    b) Accept the request and tell the team member that this is the last time you accept such request

    c) Talk to the team member to make sure his work priorities are taken care during this period. Once you are convinced, approve the request

    d) You cannot approve such requests as per the company policy

16. Copying an article without a written permission from the author is an example of

    a) Breaking the copyright law

    b) acceptable practice

    c) Disrespecting Intellectual property rights of the author

    d) intrusion into others' rights

17. You are writing an article in a newspaper about the best practice recommendations in managing projects. Few months ago, you came across few very nice quotes on project management from a book. You want those information to be useful to the readers of your article. So you decide to extensively reuse good amount of the contents of the book in your article.

    Is this acceptable practice?

    a) Yes. As long as the author do not notice this reuse, it is ok to do

    b) You cannot reuse the content of one book without the written permission from the author. The best you could do is to recommend the book in your article as reference material

    c) Yes. You can reuse the content as long as you don't copy the whole book

    d) You should obtain permission from the editor of the newspaper about reusing the content of the book

18. You are the new project manager, having taken over the responsibility from another person as part of a major project restructuring exercise carried on by your company. When reviewing your project planning, cost and schedule details you notice that the previous project manager has made a payment to one of the vendor, which is not yet approved.

    What is the BEST thing you could do?

a) Ignore the payment since it was not your fault

b) Bury the cost in the risk reserves

c) Contact the vendor and ask them to pay back the money

d) Speak to your supervisor about this issue

19. **One of your team member is absent from work for 3 days last week. His work was pending and this impacted the schedule. You were worried about the absence. However, you notice that his request for absence has not reached you yet. When you verify his attendance details, you notice that there was no absence recorded.**

What should you do?

a) Do nothing with this issue, since he is a key member of your team and working on important tasks

b) Call the team member and ask him to raise leave of absence for the three days

c) Call the team member to a discussion and ask how he got his attendance marked in spite of being absent from work. Seek an explanation and consider suitable action, if this is confirmed as a professional misconduct.

d) Call the team member and ask him not to repeat this again

20. **Your team is done with its construction phase of the project and your review with the stakeholders are completed. The stakeholders have approved the deliverables and you are working on the implementation plan. One of your team member is approaching you reporting of some discrepancy in the finished component, which was not noticed during the execution or verification phase. This discrepancy may have business impact once the component is delivered to the customer.**

What should you do?

a) Do nothing. The deliverables are approved by the stakeholders.

b) Report the stakeholders of the problem and ask them to verify the deliverable again

c) Ask the team member not to discuss this issue with anyone. You can get the issue fixed by him without others noticing it

d) Setup a meeting with the team member to collect more inputs on the issue, analyze and notify the stakeholders of this issue and your plan to fix it.

21. You read an article in a well known technology magazine about the advancement of aerospace industry in your country. You are very impressed by this article and wants to share the contents of the article with others in your department.

    What is the best way to share the content of the article?

    a) Copy the content of the article in an email and send to your contacts

    b) Speak to your friends to explain how much you liked about the article and recommend the magazine to your friends

    c) Print copies of the content and circulate among your friends

    d) Circulate your copy of the magazine to everyone in the office

22. You have written an article in the PMI magazine narrating the best practices that you adopted in your project and the benefits your project gained out of it.

    This is an example of

    a) Contribution to the professional world of Project Managers

    b) Volunteering

    c) Showing your superior knowledge to others

    d) Writing articles will get you a PDU

23. Your hiring department has approached you to be on an interview panel that is aiming to hire new staff members for your project. After consenting to this invite, you go through the profiles received by the hiring department to prepare yourself to frame questions for candidates. You notice that one of the profile belongs to a person, who is living next door to you and a very good friend of yours.

    What should you do NEXT?

    a) Do nothing. You know you are honest and do not favor anyone for personal gains

    b) Do nothing. Go ahead and interview the person, if his discussion is scheduled for you. Take a call about the candidate's fitment after the interview is over

    c) Call the candidate and tell him that you are on the interview panel and not to worry

    d) Call the hiring department and let them know that a known friend of yours is on the candidates' list. Ask the candidate to be scheduled with another panel

24. You are a project manager of an engineering project, which involves good amount of outsourcing done. You are working on the procurement planning and invited sellers to submit their bids. You are a great fan of football as well. The following weekend, your favorite football team is playing their rival in your own town. You tried to get tickets for the game, but it was too late since all the tickets are sold out already. During a bidder conference, one of the seller approach you with two tickets to the football game, in which your team is competing with another.

    What should you do?

    a) Lucky you. You got your tickets for the game finally.

    b) Accept it and pay for the tickets

    c) Politely decline the tickets, quoting company policy and professional conduct in business environment

    d) As long as others are not aware, it is ok to accept the offer

25. You are a project manager and your project's cost performance is much better than expected. When you do an analysis you find that you would save about $30,000 to your organization due to earlier than expected project completion. As part of your implementation plan, you are asked by your customer to visit their office in another part of the country. Your company policy limits flying by economy class, but you want to utilize the potential cost surplus to fly first class.

    Is this justified?

    a) Yes. You worked hard and smart to help reduce the cost and save $30,000. Why not reward yourself

    b) Fly first class and bury the cost in project cost or reserves

    c) If the company policy do not permit, better fly economy class irrespective of the cost performance of your project

    d) Fly first class but tell no one.

ANSWERS

1. **Answer: 3**

   Justification: When talking about ethical, it is not just about not doing wrong things but when a project manager is not doing certain things that he is expected to do. Some of the examples for this include, a project manager ignoring the planning process for project components. A project manager is expected to be fair in his approach towards people and treat everyone the same way how he/she want to be treated.

2. **Answer: B**

   Justification: The very purpose of planning for a project is to make sure every stakeholder in the project is aware of each others' responsibility and what to expect from others. A project is not all about mere planning for scope, cost and schedule. Without a human resource planning done in advance, there won't be any clarity on who is responsible for what. An ignorance by the project manager puts the whole project into a jeopardy and the responsibility of which is the Project Manager.

3. **Answer: D**

   Justification: Once the scope is frozen, it becomes the baseline and shared with every stakeholder of the project. This means, the scope baseline sets the expectation for each of the stakeholder about what to expect. In this situation, updating the scope based on one's request will create an imparity over the baseline. As a project manager, you are not declining a change request but trying to achieve the change request in a formal and legitimate way.

4. **Answer: A**

   Justification: Every employee of an organization is bound to sign an Non-disclosure Agreement (NDA) that prevent them from revealing or sharing any confidential information about their company, its inventions and business strategies. As long as the employee is not prevented by any NDA after leaving the organization, the innovations can be accepted by the their new employer without any legal or contractual restriction. However, if the innovation is already implemented in another organization, reuse of it will require a written permission from such organizations.

5. **Answer: A**

   Justification: The term 'planning' means getting oneself ready for the work to be done in future. When a project manager does planning, it is expected to include every factor and component into consideration. In this case, the project manager was having a major risk in the form of potential delays in getting approval. The approval delay is not others fault, but the project managers. 'Applying Calendar' is one of the tool used in the planning process, which takes into consideration holidays and absences. Not able to get an approval urgently do not authorize the project manager to float the law or regulations of the land.

6. **Answer: B**

   Justification: Professional responsibility of a PMI certified professional is not just to uphold the professional and ethical values of the profession, but also to stop misuse of authority by others. In this case, whenever professional and ethical protocols are floated, it is essential to keep the PMI informed of such occurrences for suitable action.

7. **Answer: B**

   Justification: A PMI certified project manager is expected to uphold the professional practices and values throughout the career. A project manager should also expect to drive the planning and deliver the outcome according to the guidelines. When such professional practices are not valued by an organization, it is better for the project manager to look for an employer who value them. The world is competitive and the fittest alone survives. Practicing proven and prescribed process is a learning exercise for the project manager.

8. **Answer: D**

   Justification: Sam's approach to his team is incorrect. It is true that senior members of a team have more exposure and experience with the project. However, they cannot represent the rest of the team for the work executed by others. Besides being a motivation factor the new faces of the project, engaging them actively offers many advantages for the project manager. A project manager is expected to treat every member of the team with fairness and equality.

9. **Answer: B**

   Justification: Project Management Institute's (PMI) code of professional conduct and ethical behavior applies to everyone equally in this world. Just not being a PMI member do not authorize or approve someone to mess up with their project or processes. PMI's professional and ethical conduct is a commitment given by the professionals around the world that they follow the best practices according to professional expectations. I wouldn't hesitate to equate this commitment with that of medical practitioners given to their profession.

10. **Answer: D**

    Justification: Greatest barrier in communication is obviously language spoken by people. This problem is more if the team is located in different geographies of the world. Besides the language barrier, not able to read the body language and gaining the confidence and trust is equally important.

If you believe that a communication is not all about only language but body language as well, then you would understand the risk of not having a team co-located. Having ground rules might help overcome other issues in a project, but need not influence the way communication takes place.

11. **Answer: B**

    Justification: When two parties are involved in a contract or negotiation, the most essential requirement is to have a cordial atmosphere and faith in professional values and business needs. Everyone has business interests and profitability expectation out of a project. Unless there is mutual trust and cooperation, there cannot be much benefit for either. Such negotiations are bound to fail as a result of mistrust. Thus every organization has policies that guarantees that both the parties stand to gain from a project or venture.

12. **Answer: C**

    Justification: If there is no clarity on accepting gifts from a customer, it is always better to check with the appropriate authority before accepting it. Same applies to accepting gifts, that are above the permitted value. In some organizations, clients' token of appreciation is routed through the respective managements. Offering gifts is sometimes considered as bribing, if there are any benefit expectations attached to it. Respecting one's organizational policies gains the confidence respect of the customers as well.

13. **Answer: D**

    Justification: This is a classic example of not following change management process. Whether a scope update is small or large, it has to undergo a formal change management process to get analyzed and verified for impact on other components of the triple constraint diagram. To put it easy and simple, the scope has defined what to expect from the project. If there is any feature is added, it becomes a surprise for the customers. In a business environment, there cannot be such surprises since the clients' expectation is already defined by way of scope.

14. **Answer: B**

    Justification: Conflict of business interest is one serious problem in this world. One's focus is expected in their organization's goals and vision. Every staff of an organization is expected to align their focus towards the same. Having a competing business is a major factor that prevent such alignments from happening. In such a situation, the project manager should collect the details of the competing interest and check with the appropriate authority on the issue. Once the competing interest is proven, then it is upto the organization to take further actions on this.

15. Answer C

Justification: Respecting others' culture and belief is very essential in a collaborative environment, no matter which part of the world the team member is from. However, it is an essential responsibility of a project to make sure the personal commitments and belief do not come in the way of fulfilling professional responsibility. So, a project manager has to balance between these two factors while handling such issues.

16. Answer: A

Justification: It is a very common practice seen in the world today, where people do not care about one's ownership rights. A copyright is a ownership of certain articles, information or a newspaper column written by someone. Such copyright violations are handled with severe penalties by countries around the world.

17. Answer: B

Justification: This situation is another example of respecting copyright laws. At times, you might come across very interesting articles in a magazine or book. Waiting for a permission may be prolonging. In such eventuality, you can recommend the book in your article, if you think the book would be of great use to several others. Such recommendation is not prevented by the law.

18. Answer: D

Justification: Handling such unauthorized transaction is pretty sensitive, since it involves money. The transaction was made by another manager, but it is your responsibility to set things straight since the transaction has cost implications on your project. In this situation, the better option is to discuss the issue with your supervisor and find out whether any request is pending with him or how to address this issue and settle it once for all.

19. Answer: C

Justification: Simply because someone is an important member of a team do not authorize them to take advantage of the authority or liberty given. The very basic expectation in a business environment is a professional conduct, which is a commitment given by every staff of an organization. A project manager cannot overlook such issues, since it might amount to acceptance of such practices. A very healthy and professional environment is essential if the project or organization has to achieve its objectives.

20. Answer: D

Justification: One of the key success factor of a project is the professional and ethical conduct of the team. In this situation, once an issue is identified at any point of time, it becomes the ultimate responsibility of the project manager to stop the issue from escalating and impacting the intended objective of the project. Such proactive approach gains the confidence of the customers. Remember, a professional practice is all about doing the right thing, the right way.

21. **Answer: B**

    Justification: Circulating a copy of the book or taking photocopies with the written consent of the author is a clear violation of the copyright law. The most recommended way of handling such issues is to explain the key features of such books or articles to the known ones and encourage them to purchase the book or magazine, if they are interested to get more information on the subject.

22. **Answer: A**

    Justification: There are several ways, one can contribute back to the professional world of the project managers. Joining a PM community or chapter of the professionals to assemble, exchanging ideas and sharing knowledge, writing articles, conducting trainings, seminars and encouraging best practices in their organizations and creating awareness of those who are new to the profession are some of the ways to keep the profession from getting stronger and powerful.

23. **Answer: D**

    Justification: Similar to conflict of business interest, keeping the organizational interest above personal preference is another essential quality expected out of a professional. It is not a recommended practice to have someone interviewing a known candidate. The best choice is to keep the hiring department informed of this factor and allow them to take a call on this issue.

24. **Answer: C**

    Justification: The action of the potential seller amount to bribery in this case. Above everything else, it is strongly against every professional and ethical conduct to accept such favors from someone, who has business interest with your organization. Though the seller may not attach any benefit expectation at this moment, there are more possibilities for it in future and it becomes a delicate situation for the project manager due to the favor received from the seller.

25. **Answer: C**

    Justification: A company's policy is defined only for the staff to follow. Just because a project is going to get better cost advantage doesn't approve using the cost benefit for personal gains, which is a conflict of professional conduct. This type of misconduct erodes the confidence in the staff, who is involved in such acts.

This page is intentionally left blank

This page is intentionally left blank

Glossary

Activity Definition

Defining each of the activity to be performed in a project

Ballpark estimate

An approximate cost, which is estimated in the initial stages of project planning

Benchmarking

Setting up minimum performance level of the project components

Budget at Completion (BAC)

The total budget of the project till its completion

Change Management

Managing change requests from stakeholders

Corrective Actions

Fixing problems and issues, after they were identified

Cost

Planned expenses incurred in executing a project

Cost Performance Index (CPI)

The difference between the actual cost performance against the planned performance at any given point of time

Cost Variance

The variance between the actual cost mapped against the planned cost at any given point of time

Critical Path

Establishing a relationship between the longest path with a sequence of activities

Deliverables

Final end product or any delivery commitment given to the customer

Design of Experiments

Designing sample experiments to test the quality of the planned deliverables

Earned Value (EV)

The value of the project at any given point of time

Enterprise Environmental Factors

Details of company policies, strategies and recommendations with respect to business.

Estimate at Completion (EAC)

The expected cost of the project, when it is complete. This expected cost is calculated based on the current cost performance.

Estimate to Completion (ETC)

The cost, that is expected to complete the remaining portion of the project

Expert Judgment

Consulting with experts and other project managers

Fixed Price

Planned cost which is fixed against each of the project components such as cost on human resources, administrative, materials and services .

Formal Communication

A business formal communication, usually carried with customers and senior executives of one organization. In several cases, such communication are legally binding both the parties involved.

Gold Plating

Providing 'extras' than what was asked for

HALO effect

In order to motivate best performers, some organizations tend to engage them into roles, which are not familiar to them

Informal Communication

A casual talks, calls or meeting in order to get some clarification or provide updates to each other

Integration

Performing various activities or processes, that are interrelated to each other and essential in executing a project.

Knowledge Area

A collection of specific group of planning components.

Lifecycle Cost

The total project cost involved in planning, executing and maintenance of a project and its deliverable

Murder Board

One of the project selection criteria

Operational Work

A group of tasks that are executed on a regular basis or depending on the need, which has no target start or end dates.

Opportunity Cost

The amount of money that is at stake, when the performing organization had to choose between two projects

Organization Charts

This documents illustrates the pictorial representation of the organization setup, in terms of staff and their position in the organization

Organization Process Assets

A collection of templates, historic data, forms, templates and any organizational and process related information of the performing organization.

Planned Value (PV)

The expected value of the project at any given point of time

Planning Components

Defining dummy activities in place of unknown components of a project.

Portfolio

A group of programs and projects, that need not share the same objective but resources.

Preliminary Scope Statement

High level project scope

Preventive Actions

Pro-actively working to eliminate problems

Process Groups

A collection of process, that are interrelated.

Procurement Documents

Any document that is prepared and legally valid. Such documents are mutual agreed by buyers and sellers

Product Scope

Objective of the end product

Program

A collection of projects, that has a shared objective and interrelated activities.

Project

A group of activity executed within a limited and predetermined time limit, that produce an unique result

Project Charter

A document that assigns a project manager to a project and also provides high level objectives

Project Management

A systematic and disciplined approach to execute a project, which involves processes and tasks.

Project Management Office

A group of experts, who are part of a team and responsible to support the project managers and projects with expertise, forms, templates and guidance in executing projects.

RACI Chart

A document that defines Roles & Responsibilities of each of the stakeholders of a project. RACI stands for Responsible, Accountable, Consult & Inform.

Reserve

A small portion of money, planned for every project, to meet contingency expense requirements

Resource Leveling

Analyzing the critical path to identify resource dependencies

Risk Breakdown Structure

A formal decomposition of all identified risks, that are categorized into different components

Risk Register

A list of identified risks along with the mitigation plans and owner details

Risks

An unexpected event that might potentially occur in a project and can cause positive or negative impact on the project execution

Rolling Wave Methodology

Similar to Planning components, but unknown activities are ignore and known components are estimated and worked upon.

Schedule Compression

One of the strategy to compress the schedule to meet the committed schedules.

Schedule Performance Index (SPI)

The actual performance of the project at any given point of time compared against the planned performance.

Schedule Variance

The schedule deviation from the planned schedule performance of the project

Scope baseline

Scope statement, that is approved by the stakeholders.

Scope Statement

Detailed project scope collected from the stakeholders

Sponsor

The funding authority for a project.

Stakeholders

A group of people, who are positively or negatively impacted by the execution of a project.

Statement of Work (SOW)

A document that narrates the details of the work to be executed

Triple Constraint Diagram

The dependencies between Scope, Cost, Schedule and Quality. Expanded version of Triple Constraint diagram include Risks, Human Resources & Customer Satisfaction.

Variable Cost

A planned cost components, which is not fixed but likely to change according to human resources and material requirements and availability

Variance at Completion

The expected cost variance, when the project is complete. The variance is calculated based on the current cost performance against the forecast data

Virtual Team

Team that is located in different offices or geographies but communicate using available communication channels

WBS Dictionary

Provides details of WBS tasks

Work Breakdown Structure (WBS)

List of decomposed work packages into smaller and manageable tasks

This page is intentionally left blank

Index

A

Acceptance Criteria 79, 129, 136, 173
Acquire Team 364, 365, 392
Acquisition 9, 222, 365
Activity Attributes 219, 221, 226, 228, 230,
 234, 239, 241, 245, 249, 355
Activity Definition 214–221, 228, 251, 252
Activity Duration Estimation 41, 231–234
Activity List 218
Activity Resource Estimation 41, 211, 227–232
Activity Sequencing 221–223, 226, 227
Actual Cost 283, 287, 288, 289
Administrative Closure 48, 49, 91, 93, 94,
 202, 206
Advertising 183
Alternative Identification 154, 160
Analogous Estimation 233
Analytical Systems 184
Analytical Techniques 179
Applying Calendars 240
Approved Changes 83, 188
Arrow Diagram 222, 223, 226, 236
Assumptions 3, 49, 53, 75–76, 79, 91, 127, 136,
 145, 157, 169, 172, 173, 218, 236, 281,
 292, 411, 424–425, 439, 461
Audits 8, 189, 190, 311, 330, 331, 478

B

Bad Changes 143
Balanced Matrix 21
Ballpark Estimation 270
Benchmarking 317, 318, 322
Beneficiaries 16, 405
Benefit Cost ratio 272
Benefit Measurement Analysis 74
Bidder Conference 181
Bottom-up Approach 217, 278
Brainstorming 52, 74, 425, 432, 456, 457,
 462 465
Bribery 504
Budget At Completion 285, 286, 288, 289
Business Need 44

C

Cause and Effect Diagram 323
Change Control Board 84, 88, 89, 119, 120,
 137, 139, 186, 247, 249
Change Log 419

Change Management 3, 8, 16, 38, 47, 48, 71,
 83–86, 88, 90, 123, 124, 127, 128, 138,
 143, 144, 185, 186, 246, 250, 271, 285,
 293, 330, 366, 420, 478
Channel 402
Checklist Analysis 460
Claims Administration 190
Close Procurement 165
Close Project 48
Co-location 369
Collect Requirement 117, 121
Communication Channel 16, 320, 400, 402,
 421, 451
Communication Management 41, 81,397
Compromise 376, 498, 501, 503, 504
Conduct Procurement 41, 165, 178
Conflict of Business Interests 193
Conflict of Interest 507
Conflict Management 351, 375
Confrontational 375
Constraints 12, 75, 76, 79, 127, 172, 173, 236,
 424, 425
Context Diagrams 121
Continuous Improvements 328
Contract 176
Contract Change Control 188
Contract Closure 163, 190–193
Contract SOW 173
Control Charts 322
Control Procurement 165, 186
Corrective Actions 84, 85, 247, 249, 291, 330
 249, 331, 327, 377, 500
Cost Aggregation 279
Cost Baseline 50, 267, 270, 271, 278, 280, 283,
 284, 291, 292
Cost Benefit Ratio 276
Cost Budgeting 38, 40, 271, 277–279
Cost Control 267, 271, 282, 283, 285, 290,
 291
Cost Estimation 6, 41, 49, 79, 231, 271–274,
 276, 277, 279, 284, 425
Cost Management 41, 81, 267
Cost of Quality 275, 311 , 318
Cost Performance Index 287–289
Cost Reimbursement 177, 178
Cost Risk 291, 292
Cost Variance 288, 289
Crashing 242, 243
Create WBS 41, 133, 136
Critical Chain Methodology 240
Critical Path Analysis 237

D

Decision Tree 467, 468
Decoding 403
Defect Repairs 327, 330
Deliverables 54, 79, 81, 83, 85, 127, 134–136,
        141, 143, 213, 215, 245, 275, 276, 292,
        312, 318, 321, 322, 327, 332, 416, 420
Delphi Technique 460
Depreciation Cost 276
Design of Experiments 317
Develop Project Team 367, 368
Diagramming Method 222, 223, 226, 236,
        262, 461
Documentation Reviews 462

E

Early Finish 239
Early Start 239
Earned Monetary Value 467, 468
Earned Value 285-291, 322
Encoding 403
Enterprise Environmental Factors 8, 35, 50,
        77, 118, 169, 215, 228, 229 279, 316, 356,
        363, 405, 407, 410, 456
Estimate At Completion 288, 289
Estimate To Completion 288, 289
Estimation Techniques 233, 272
Ethical Conduct 497, 498
Ethics 500, 507-509
Evaluation Criteria 174, 175, 180, 185, 191
Execution 352-354, 360-362, 367, 377, 378,
        400, 401, 404, 406, 408, 410, 414, 415,
        419, 420, 422, 424, 450, 452, 454, 458,
        467, 469, 470, 473, 474, 477
Expectancy Theory 372
Expert Judgment 73, 119, 126, 171, 182, 217,
        229, 232, 233, 357, 406, 460, 474
Expert Power 370, 371
External Risks 451-453, 470

F

Fairness 184, 498, 500, 501, 508
Fast Tracking 243
Feedback 181, 191, 377, 397, 403, 413
Financial Closure 38, 48, 49, 90, 192
Fishbone Diagram 323, 324, 461
Fitness to Use 313
Fixed Price 145, 176, 177, 269, 291, 292, 358,
        405
Float 238
Flowcharts 321
Focus Group 121
Forecast Data 416

Forecasting 288, 290, 291
Formal Communication 401, 402, 422
Formal Verbal 411, 412
Formal Written 411
Functional 17, 18, 19

G

Gold Plating 144
Good Changes 143
Ground Rules 368, 369

H

Halo Effect 363
Herzberg's Theory 372
Histograms 325
Historical Information 49, 51, 53, 407, 472
Human Resource Cost 169, 268–270, 272,
        280
Human Resources 351-358

I

Independent Estimates 172, 182
Informal Communication 397, 401, 402, 412
Informal Verbal 412
Informal Written 412
Information Distribution 397, 403, 410, 414,
        416, 417
Information Technology 54, 177, 182, 364
Initiation 37, 38, 41-46, 60, 70, 71, 93, 272
Integration Management 41, 45, 67, 81
Internal Risks 451-453
Interviews 122, 413, 462
Ishikawa Diagram 323, 324, 461
Issue Logs 417, 377, 425-427

J

Just In Time 187

K

Kickoff Meetings 46, 76
Knowledge Areas 35, 36, 40, 41, 45, 46, 51, 70,
        80, 81, 164, 167, 186, 216, 217, 285, 416

L

Lags 225, 239, 241
Late Finish 239
Late Start 239, 240
Leads 225
Legitimate Power 369
Lifecycle Cost 276
List of Activities 115, 218, 221, 226, 228, 230,
        233, 237, 239-241, 248, 249

M

Make or Buy Analysis 170
Management Team 91, 329, 353
Manage Project Team 373, 374
Manage Stakeholders 418, 352
Maslow's Hierarchy 372
Material Cost 176, 268, 269, 273, 279, 280, 292
Mathematical Model 74
Matrix Organization 17, 19–22
McGregor's Theory 372
Mcleiland's Theory 373
Meeting Minutes 190, 411, 417, 420, 430, 432
Milestones 75, 79, 136, 212, 219, 236, 240, 244, 249
Mitigate 172, 356, 457, 473, 474
Monitor and Control 245
Murder Board 74

N

Negative Risk Response 476
Negotiations 183, 364
Net Present Value 276
Network Diagram 224, 226, 236–239, 241
Networking 357
Non-Disclosure Agreement 193
Noise 403
Non-Verbal Communication 397, 413

O

Operational Work 4
Opportunity Cost 276
Organizational Process Assets 35, 119, 124, 169, 181, 215, 228, 236, 249, 279, 316, 322, 327, 330 407, 410, 459
Organizational Theory 357
Organization Chart 356

P

Paralingual Communication 413
Parametric Analysis 280
Pareto Chart 325
Payment Systems 189
Performance Appraisals 377
Performance Assessment 378
Performance Reports 188
Performance Measurement 247, 249, 285, 287, 330
Planned % Complete 286, 289
Planned Value 285–290, 322
Planning 37, 41, 45, 52, 54, 354, 355, 356, 358, 361, 366, 406, 409, 414, 415
Planning Component 217, 218
Plan Procurement 92, 165, 166

PMBoK 73
PMIS 51, 73
Portfolio 10
Pre-assignment 362
Precedence Diagram 222, 223, 226, 236
Preliminary Scope 77, 79, 116, 118
Preventive Actions 89, 327, 330
Probability 463, 465, 466, 467, 468, 469, 471, 473, 474, 476, 478
Process Analysis 331
Process Groups 37, 40, 41, 71
Procurement Audit 190, 192
Procurement Decision 168, 170, 173, 176, 180, 184
Procurement Documents 163, 173, 174
Procurement Management 41, 81, 163
Procurement Management Plan 81, 172, 186, 191, 269
Product Analysis 125
Product Scope 93, 111, 125, 142
Professional Responsibility 497, 498
Professionalism 498, 500
Program 9, 10
Project Charter 42, 43, 71–73, 75, 93, 118, 212, 401
Project Closure 6, 8, 41, 48, 90
Project Contract 72, 76
Project Cost Management 267
Projectized Organization 17, 18, 19, 70
Project Management Methodology 23, 73
Project Management Office 1, 7, 8, 28, 49, 54, 91, 119, 126, 317, 332, 460, 478
Project Objective 42, 79, 127
Project Planning 45, 75, 80, 212
Project Schedule 246
Project Scope 13, 16, 43, 111, 142
Project SOW 173
Project Statement of Work 72, 76, 173
Project Team 41, 53, 360, 362, 365, 367, 368, 373, 409
Proposal Evaluation Technique 181
Punishment Power 371
Purchase Order 173, 176

Q

Qualitative Analysis 184, 464–466
Quality Assurance 244, 311, 315, 317, 328–331
Quality Audits 8, 32, 311, 330, 331
Quality Baseline 181, 319, 320, 322, 328
Quality Checklists 318, 319
Quality Control 41, 315, 53, 320, 321, 322, 325, 327, 328, 329, 330, 333, 401
Quality Management 41, 81,311
Quality Metrics 319, 320, 330
Quantitative Analysis 449, 467, 474

R

RACI Chart 186
Rate of Return 276
Receiver 399, 402, 403
Records Management 190, 192
Referent Power 371
Replanning 139
Request For Bid 173, 178
Request For Proposals 174, 178
Requirement Analysis 407
Requirement Gathering 122
Reserve Analysis 234, 279
Resource Availability 124, 185, 228, 230, 231,
    365, 365, 366
Resource Breakdown 230
Resource Calendar 231, 240, 245
Resource Cost 169, 178, 268–270, 272, 274,
    280, 292, 293
Resource Levelling 235, 240
Resource Planning 166, 213, 320, 351, 354,
    355, 357, 358, 369
Resource Risks 451
Responsibility 122, 124, 143, 145, 164, 166,
    170, 178, 180, 189, 192, 193
Revised Requirement 139
Reward Power 370
Risk 477
Risk Breakdown Structure 449, 458
Risk Categorization 465
Risk Identification 455, 459, 460, 462, 464
Risk Management 41, 81,449
Risk Monitoring 456, 476, 477, 478
Risk Performance 478
Risk Register 168, 285, 406, 420, 449, 457,
    459–466, 471–472, 474, 478
Risk Response 41, 453, 474–476
Roles & Responsibilities 120, 361, 362
Rolling Wave 218
Root Cause Analysis 327, 332, 462
Run Charts 326
Rule of Seven 322

S

Scatter Charts 326
Schedule Baseline 3, 83, 87, 88, 107, 245,
    246, 248, 284
Schedule Compression 211, 242
Schedule Control 245–249, 282
Schedule Development 211, 235, 236, 242,
    245
Schedule Model 241, 249
Schedule Network 224, 239, 240
Schedule Performance Index 248, 287–289
Schedule Variance 247, 248, 287–289, 322

Scope Baseline 48, 111, 122, 123, 128, 136, 137,
    138, 139, 141, 168
Scope Control 136, 137, 141
Scope Creep 143
Scope Definition 111, 116, 117, 120–124, 126,
    139
Scope Management 41, 81,111
Scope Management Plan 53, 77, 81, 111, 113,
    115–121, 123, 128, 129, 133, 134, 136, 138,
    140, 145, 166, 230, 270, 363, 458
Scope Planning 78, 113, 117–119, 128, 129, 133,
    137, 216, 217, 219, 273
Scope Statement 111, 112, 113, 116, 117, 118, 121,
    122–124, 126–129, 133, 136, 138, 140, 142,
    143, 145, 168, 172, 216, 236, 273, 279,
    316, 456, 459, 465
Scope Verification 48, 120, 321
Screening Systems 184
SDLC 36
Selected Sellers 185
Selection Criteria 74, 180
Seller Evaluation Criteria 180
Seller Proposals 180
Seller Rating 184
Seller Response 182
Sender 399, 402, 403
Smoothing 376
Sponsor 14, 71, 79, 89, 90, 112, 113, 139, 212,
    235, 242, 245, 249, 272, 278, 280, 281,
    282, 286, 292, 293, 315, 400, 422, 423
Staffing Plan 351, 354, 355, 356, 359, 360, 361,
    362, 365, 366
Stakeholder Analysis 124
Stakeholder Meeting 477
Stakeholder Requirement 116
Stakeholders 4, 5, 7, 8, 13–16, 23, 41, 47, 48,
    52, 54, 400, 401, 403–411, 413–426,
    430, 451, 457, 460, 464, 472, 473, 477,
    505, 507
Standard Forms 174
Statement of Work 72, 76, 77, 123, 172, 173,
    176, 178
Status Reports 411, 417, 420, 429, 432, 507
Status Review Meetings 417
Strong Matrix 22
SWOT Analysis 460

T

Technical Risks 452
Templates 332
Terms and Conditions 194
Testing Strategy 328
Test Plans 411, 332
Three Point Estimation 233
Time and Material 176, 177, 178

Time Management   41, 81, 211
Top-Down Approach 53, 217
Traceability Matrix   121, 122, 137, 140, 141
Training requirements   359, 454
Triple Constraint Diagram 1, 11–13, 88, 293
        312, 320

U

Unprofessional Practice   504
Utilization of Resources   228, 356
Unique   2, 4, 5

V

Variable Price 269, 358
Variance Analysis 248, 290
Variance At Completion   288, 289

Vendor Bid Analysis 274, 275
Virtual Teams   351, 364, 369

W

War Room   369
Watchlist 471
WBS   111, 120, 129, 130–133, 135, 136, 140, 169,
        172, 213, 214, 216, 217, 219, 270, 273,
        277, 279, 284, 351
WBS Dictionary 213, 216, 219, 273, 277, 279
Weak Matrix   20
Weighing Systems   184
What-if Scenario   241
Withdrawal 376, 377
Work Performance Data 188, 322
Work Product Review 137, 141, 327, 328, 332,
        428, 429

This page is intentionally left blank

www.ingramcontent.com/pod-product-compliance
Lightning Source LLC
Chambersburg PA
CBHW080809280326
41926CB00091B/4116

* 9 7 8 9 3 5 1 9 6 9 6 1 7 *